# Community Activism and Feminist Politics

## *Organizing Across Race, Class, and Gender*

Edited by

# Nancy A. Naples

Routledge
New York and London

Published in 1998 by
Routledge
29 West 35th Street
New York, NY 10001

Published in Great Britain by
Routledge
11 New Fetter Lane
London EC4P 4EE

Library of Congress Cataloging-in-Publication Data

Community activism and feminist politics : organizing across race,
class, and gender / edited by Nancy A. Naples
p.   cm.
Includes bibliographical references and index.

ISBN 0-415-91629-1 (hardcover) — ISBN 0-415-91630-5 (pbk.)

1. Women in community organization—United States.
2. Women social reformers—United States.
3. Minority women—United States.
4. Feminism—United States.
5. Social action—United States.
6. Action research—United States.
I. Naples, Nancy A.
HQ1421.C65   1998
305.42'0973—dc21          98-26531
                                    CIP

*This book is dedicated to*

SARAH RACHEL STERN

*November 12, 1970 – February 17, 1997*

*who, at an early age and in her own special way, lived the promise of transcending boundaries of race, class, and gender. May her gentle and tenacious feminist and activist spirit continue to inspire other young people who are striving toward freedom, working to protect and preserve the environment, and remaining steadfast in their commitment to social justice.*

# Contents

# Acknowledgments

The idea for this collection first took hold in conversations with Terry Haywoode, Celene Krauss, and Susan Stern during our graduate-student days at the Graduate Center of the City University of New York, and was cemented in discussions with Susan Stall, who I met when I joined the faculty of Iowa State University in 1989. All five of us are white, college-educated women who were involved in local struggles and had worked in multiracial coalitions on behalf of low-income and working-class communities before returning to graduate school. We hoped that our graduate training would give us tools of analysis and research that we could bring back into these struggles for social and economic justice. Over the years, we recognized that few models of writing activist scholarship existed, particularly ones that explicated the ways in which women of different class, racial, ethnic, and regional backgrounds have fought on behalf of their communities.

We came to our studies as committed feminists who were concerned that many of the women who fought alongside us did not define themselves as such. In fact, we identified closely with many other women who felt distance from the Women's Movement. To those of us from working-class backgrounds, the Women's Movement did not speak as loudly as it did to women from white, middle-class families. Therefore, a major subtext of our work includes the desire to reconcile our community-activist and feminist identities. It was through analyses of low-income women's political activism that I came to a broader understanding of feminism, which has in turn enhanced my own political engagement. Further, I recognized how the history of the U.S. Women's Movement of the 1970s was written in a way that rendered invisible the women-centered activism of many women of color as well as working-class and poor women of all racial-ethnic backgrounds.

I have been blessed with the support of many who share my commitment to creating scholarship that both documents and promotes progressive social-change efforts. Marilyn Gittell provided me with important research-training opportunities in the early 1980s and helped inspire my work on women's community activism. Gaye Tuchman, Bill Kornblum, Judith Lorber, George Fischer, Michael Brown, and the late Joseph Bensman also provided valuable research experiences and intellectual challenges.

I wish to thank all the authors for their willingness to contribute to this collection. The authors represent widely diverse professional and academic backgrounds; they include independent scholars and community-based activists as well as university-based researchers from anthropology, architecture, environmental design, education, history, political science, sociology, and urban planning. Space limitations led to the exclusion of several excellent papers. To these authors I express my sincere appreciation for their interest in contributing to this collection and offer my regrets that their important work could not be featured here.

In my effort to generate an accessible, coherent, and interdisciplinary collection, I have gained profound respect for the editorial process. My persistence with this project is explained by the excitement expressed by contributors and other activist scholars with whom I have discussed the book. It is furthered by the demands of many students I have worked with over the past decade who are in search of models for activist scholarship. The enthusiasm expressed by graduate students Lionel Cantú, Adrienne Hurley, Karen Kendrick, Julia Ann McClendon, Elizabeth Ribet, Chelsea Starr, Charlene Tung, Clare Weber, and Bekkah Willman has been especially encouraging. Over the years, the Society for the Study of Social Problems (SSSP) has also been an important site for my ongoing conversations with activists and activist scholars; I first heard about the work of several of this book's authors through the numerous sessions on community activism which I organized at the annual SSSP meetings.

Without the help of colleagues and friends, this collection might never have seen the light of day. Myra Marx Ferree offered crucial advice and support from the initial development to the completion of this project. Sherna Berger Gluck graciously read numerous drafts and generously offered her wise counsel over the course of many conversations about the collection. Sheila Radford-Hill, Karen Brodkin, Theresa Montini, Sandra Morgen, and Carolyn Sachs read portions of the manuscript and offered valuable suggestions that contributed greatly to the book's clarity. Francesca Cancian, Terry Haywoode, Judith Lorber, and Judith Wittner also played key roles in reviewing chapters and discussing possible directions for the collection. Conversations with Susan Stern, Celene Krauss, Susan Stall, and Cynthia Truelove have been extremely valuable as well. Papusa Molina read the entire manuscript in record time. Her insights, as well as suggestions offered by Sherna Berger Gluck and Sandra Morgen, were particularly helpful in the final stages of editorial decision-making.

I am greatly indebted to Cherry Anaba, who, as an undergraduate research assistant, worked tirelessly to systematize references, input chapters into the computer, and help keep files in order during a stressful move from one office to another. Anita Famili took up where Cherry left off and provided eager and skillful assistance. Cheryl Larsson expertly scanned the reprinted articles.

Ellen Broidy, Laura Hyun Yi Kang, John Smith, Judy Stephan-Norris, Chelsea Starr, Clare Weber, and Robyn Weigman carefully reviewed chapters, often on very short notice. My thanks to them and to the many other faculty and staff at the University of California, Irvine, who have supported this project. I am also grateful for the 1995 and 1996 Faculty Career Development Awards from the University of California, Irvine, that provided me course release to complete the book.

*— Nancy A. Naples*

# Women's Community Activism and Feminist Activist Research

## Nancy A. Naples

This collection represents years of activism, exploration, and debate among activist scholars committed to research on behalf of progressive social change. Writing simultaneously as activists and scholars remains one of the most difficult forms of communication. The authors whose work is featured in this collection have negotiated many personal and political dilemmas in their efforts to contribute to it.

More significant, however, is the persistence of the community activists whose struggles are chronicled here. These women wage campaigns for social justice and economic security, and against abuse, in diverse settings and often under extremely adverse conditions. Along the way, they challenge deeply rooted patriarchal and heterosexist traditions, confront the limits of democracy in the United States, and, in some instances, experience sharp disapproval from other members of their communities. They fight against the abuse of women, against corporate poisoning of their neighborhoods, against homophobia and racism, and for people-centered economic development, immigrants' rights, educational equity, and adequate wages. Many have been engaged in such struggles for most of their lives and continue despite the decline in the wider society's support for a progressive social agenda. While not every struggle analyzed here has been successful, the volume as a whole illustrates the creativity and power as well as the diversity of women's collective action.

In presenting an array of women's community activism from the 1960s to the 1990s, we hope to provide a useful resource for others engaged in progressive social-change efforts as well as to encourage such participation. By shifting our attention to the perspectives of women who are usually left out of our historical record, we can discover new analyses and political strategies to help us reinvent progressive movements in more inclusive and relevant ways. Lesbians, American Indian women, Asian American women, Latinas, African American women, and white, working-class women work, as grassroots activists, through the intimate connections of their everyday lives to strengthen the grounds for community action and social change, and through these rich encounters create new political analyses. In many cases, women activists also ensure continuity of community activism by educating others in their communities about successful fights for social and economic justice.

While generational differences in political contexts and political analyses are salient in some of these accounts, gendered experiences consistently shape the grounds upon which women organize their political responses (albeit with significant racial, ethnic, and class distinctions as well). Probably one of the most persistent problems that community activists face is how to organize across race and class. *Community Activism and Feminist Politics* offers lessons from successful cross-race and cross-class coalition building, as well as cautions from failures to negotiate across differences.

### Feminist Scholarship on Women's Community Activism

This book builds upon the efforts of feminist scholars and activists who have chronicled the long history of, and important lessons derived from, women's community-based political struggles,[1] and who helped break down the false analytic separation between community and labor organizing.[2] It also takes to heart feminist calls to contextualize race, class, and gender relations rather than privilege one dimension or produce an additive formulation.[3] Space prohibits a comprehensive survey of this rich literature. Here I offer a brief overview of some of this book's key themes, with special emphasis on scholarship that has contributed to the conceptual framework for the collection.

In the very influential book on women's activism, *Women and the Politics of Empowerment*, edited by Ann Bookman and Sandra Morgen, the authors effectively argue for a redefinition of politics to include women's grassroots organizing, underscore the significance of women's social networks for their political lives, highlight gendered differences in organizing styles, and explore "the ways race, ethnicity, and class intersect with gender in shaping political action and consciousness."[4]

Contributors to *Women and the Politics of Empowerment* also explore the challenges of organizing across race, class, and gender. For example, examining cross-race and cross-class alliances in a struggle to reopen health clinics in a small New England city, Sandra Morgen (1988, 110) found that, "[a]lthough race and ethnicity were not so primary as class and gender in the political vocabulary," they contoured class-based experiences. Racial and ethnic identities concretely influenced "who were allies in the campaign and which groups had access to power."

Strong evidence exists documenting the tradition of cross-class activism by middle-class African American women.[5] For example, Cheryl Townsend Gilkes (1988, 54) reports that middle-class African American women she interviewed in the 1970s built "'Black-oriented' institutions" in their diverse workplaces and retained a firm commitment to labor on behalf of the Black community. Gilkes (1983) describes the creative ways these women organized their lives to "go up for the oppressed." They constructed their careers to benefit the Black community and maintained their commitment through ongoing grassroots activism. Gilkes also points out the importance of early childhood socialization in constructing their motivation for community work on behalf of "the Race."[6] Their efforts to combine their professional careers with service to their racial-ethnic communities was not without conflict; however, these tensions frequently enhanced their politicization and political commitment.[7]

Research on women's community-based activism has also contributed significantly to the reconceptualization of sociological categories—especially "politics," "work," and "family"—typically used to analyze social life, as Gilkes's study illustrates. I have explored the ways in which African American women and Latinas living and working in poor, urban neighborhoods understand the politics of their community work (Naples 1991a, 1991b, 1992), and found that traditional conceptualizations of "politics" did not fit the ways in which the community workers viewed their community-based political activities.[8] In addition, the traditional definition of "mothering," as nurturing work with children who are biologically or legally related and cared for within the confines of a bounded family unit, failed to capture the community workers' radical political activities and self-perceptions of their motherwork.[9] Furthermore, women who did not have children also described their activism on behalf of their communities as a form of community caretaking (also see Collins 1990). As employees of state-funded community agencies, the community workers harnessed their paid work to support their community activism as well as their motherwork, thus blurring the boundaries between employment, politics, and mothering. The term "activist mothering" (Naples 1992) was generated from analysis of the community workers' oral narratives. It draws attention to the myriad ways these women challenged the false separation of productive work, socially reproductive work, and politics under changing historical contexts.

Another contribution of the scholarship on women's community activism involves challenging limited constructions of feminism that derive solely from white, middle-class women's experiences. In her conceptualization of "working-class feminism," Terry Haywoode (1991, 152–153) argues that "in many urban neighborhoods a new and important form of political organization emerged in the 1970s and early 1980s . . . grounded in the informal networks of association which had already been established by the working-class women who were residents of these neighborhoods." Working-class feminists in these communities drew on their traditional gender roles as well as religious and cultural traditions.[10] This form of organizing was also influenced by ideas generated by the Women's Movement and other social movements of the 1960s and early 1970s, and featured the mobilization of women's "preexisting networks of communication and organization" for political campaigns to improve the quality of life and protect the integrity of their communities (also see Ackelsberg 1988). While the working-class women Haywoode interviewed disagreed with the Women's Movement's critiques of family and the broadened understanding of sexualities, they "heartily embraced the concept of an increased public and employment role for women" (p. 184).

Central to all research on women's community activism has been the recognition of the significance of women's social networks and their constructions of community for their political work. For example, Karen Brodkin Sacks (1988b) describes working-class women's social network-based approach to organizing in her analysis of their key role as "centerwomen" (as distinguished from "spokesmen") in community and labor struggles. Haywoode emphasizes that the key to urban, working-class women's effectiveness as organizers was the way they understood the social organization of community, for "[w]omen know a great deal about community life because it is the stuff of their every day experience."[11] Furthermore, women's issues were articulated as "community issues" in the working-class women's organizations she studied. The working-class women tied their concerns as women directly to their communities. They could not be separated—either practically or analytically.

Calls to join theory with practice for the development of feminist praxis form a consistent theme within feminist texts from the early 1970s to the present, and constitute a central feature of scholarship on women's community activism.[12] Jacqui Alexander and Chandra Mohanty (1997, xx) stress the vitality of analyses that remain integrated with "feminist communities in struggles." By shifting the standpoint to Third World feminist explorations of women's resistance, Alexander and Mohanty (1997, xx) contest "the still firmly embedded notion of the originary status of Western feminism" since they do "not summon Third World feminism in the service of (white) Western feminism's intellectual and political projects." They argue that this conceptual and practical shift "provides a position from which to argue for a comparative, relational feminist praxis that is transnational in its response to and engagement with global processes of colonization." While *Community Activism and Feminist Politics* focuses on U.S.-based struggles, the authors remain sensitive to how broader political and economic contexts influence women's local political action. Women are drawn into global processes of economic and social restructuring in specific ways that intersect with their race and class, as well as with colonial histories. Mohanty demonstrates how daily strategies and ideologies of global capitalism make visible "the common interests of Third-World women workers" that can serve as the basis for organizing across racial and ethnic differences and national boundaries.[13]

Yet, as Bernice Johnson Reagon (1983) cautions, organizing across differences poses a number of significant challenges that often inhibit coalition-building even when actors appear to share common material interests.[14] Understanding how different women come to see their interests in common and struggle across their differences is at the heart of *Community Activism and Feminist Politics*. In addressing this issue, Cherríe Moraga (1981, xviii), in the preface to *This Bridge Called My Back*, passionately ties the political consciousness of women of color to the material reality of their lives. This "politics of the flesh" does not privilege one dimension and artificially set it apart from the context in which it is lived, experienced, felt, and resisted. In fact, Paula Moya (1997, 150) argues that Moraga's "theory in the flesh" provides a powerful "nonessentialist way to ground . . . identities" for the purposes of resistance to domination.

Scholars of women's community activism also emphasize the fluidity of racial categorizations and the diversity within socially constructed groups such as Latinas, Asian Americans, and African Americans.[15]

Whiteness is racialized as well.[16] Jewish women, regardless of class, cannot avoid the experience of "otherness" in a society that privileges Christianity.[17] Furthermore, as lesbian feminists of color powerfully demonstrate, dynamics of sexuality fracture race, class, and gender relations, generating complex personal and political "identities." For example, Gloria Anzaldúa (1987) analyzed her experiences growing up as a lesbian within multiple "cultures" as "mestiza consciousness." Struggles over identities from within the gay and lesbian movement have also given rise to what Joshua Gamson (1995, 390) describes as "destabilized identities," categorized by some under the rubric of "queer" (also see Duggan 1992; Stein 1992). Many who examine these "destabilized identities" highlight the contradictions in such impulses. As Gamson (1995, 390) notes: "Fixed identity categories are both the basis for oppression and the basis for political power." Shane Phelan (1993, 782) recognizes this dilemma as well, but argues that one can draw on constructed identity categories in strategic ways in order to enhance political mobilization.

*Community Activism and Feminist Politics* further elaborates the construction of political identities and social networks; the relationship between women's differing communities and feminist praxis; the connections between local struggles and broader social processes; the interplay of mothering, political action, and labor; and the challenge of organizing across race, gender, ethnicity, and class. Authors also examine the role of feminist activist research in reframing scholarship on political participation, labor organizing, and community studies.[18] Feminist researchers have long debated what constitutes activist scholarship and how researchers within the academy can contribute to social-change efforts outside the university walls. The authors in this collection are committed to this enterprise and have negotiated the challenges of producing politically useful analyses while, in many cases, also participating in the struggles they chronicle.[19]

### Defining, Implementing, and Writing Activist Research

Every author in this collection who reported on community actions in which she participated experienced some apprehension when constructing her chapter. As with all ethnographic work,[20] the author's goal was to produce a narrative that retained the integrity of the specific events, actors, and context while revealing the broader processes at work, which may not have been visible to the individual participants, or even to the researcher, at the time they were engaged in the struggle.

For some, the personal frustrations of roads not taken or individuals whose need for control undermined community-building and successful community action made the process of analysis more difficult. For others, the desire to include other participants in the writing process also required an extensive series of negotiations and rewrites (also see Naples with Clark 1996). Roberta Feldman, Susan Stall, and Patricia Wright (chapter 11), coming from different disciplinary and professional frameworks, faced a further challenge as they worked to create a jointly authored narrative.

Another demand placed on the authors was to find a balance between the passion they felt for the community action or activists they were working with and the detachment needed to present their analyses. For the most part, researchers are trained in dispassionate forms of presentation and find it difficult to put themselves into the account or to use a more personalized voice. When one's personal vantage point is incorporated into the frame, it may be harder to retain the analytic stance required for sociological exposition. However, by highlighting the gendered processes of racialization and class dynamics, each author successfully found that balance. In fact, by centering this intersectional framework and consistently focusing on the complex ways race, class, and gender shaped political experiences and political strategies, each author was able to construct an analytic narrative of specific community actions. By writing themselves in, they also present a more honest account of the community action or activist organization in which they participated. Further, as these authors demonstrate, analysis of the community action or the process of politicization can be deepened by making visible one's own activist experiences and standpoint.

While most of the authors in this collection draw upon qualitative methodologies, such strategies do not themselves define activist research. In fact, the questions we ask and the purpose to which we put the analysis are much greater indicators of what constitutes activist research than our specific methodologies. Roberta Spalter-Roth and Heidi Hartmann (1996), working out of the Institute for Women's Policy Research in Washington, D.C. (one of the few feminist research institutes and think tanks), used a national longitudinal sample of single mothers to demonstrate how women "income package," that is, combine welfare and paid employment. They developed their research in response to the conservative attacks on women receiving Aid to Families with Dependent Children (AFDC), which framed reliance on public assistance as dependency. Their statistical analysis accents the multiple strategies low-income women utilize for their economic survival (Spalter-Roth, Hartmann, and Andrews 1992).

Presenting scholarship that supports an activist campaign or a progressive organization and that chronicles the lessons of organizing against oppression in its many guises constitutes the central purpose for progressive activist research.[21] A wide array of research strategies, data analyses, and cultural products can serve this goal. Yet such analyses and cultural products can be of more or less immediate use for specific activist agendas. For example, activist research includes chronicling the history of activists, activist art, diverse community actions, and social movements.[22] Such analyses are often conducted after the completion of a specific struggle or examine a wide range of different campaigns and activist organizations. Sherna Berger Gluck in collaboration with Maylei Blackwell, Sharon Cotrell, and Karen harper (chapter 1) gathered oral histories from American Indian, Asian American, and Latina activists usually left out of the historical record. In light of their life stories, as Gluck points out, we are forced to reconceptualize the history of women's movements in the United States. Verta Taylor and Leila Rupp (chapter 2), drawing upon in-depth interviews and archival materials as well as their own extensive participation as lesbian activists in Columbus, Ohio, are also participating in this revisioning of feminist activism.

This form of research on activism is extremely important for feminists working toward a broadened political vision of women's activism, and can help generate new strategies for coalition-building. However, these studies may not answer specific questions activists have about the value of certain strategies for their particular political struggles. Yet these broad-based feminist historical and sociological analyses do shed new light on processes of politicization, diversity, and continuity in political struggles over time.

On the one hand, many activists could be critical of these apparently more "academic" constructions of community activism, especially since the need for specific knowledges to support activist agendas frequently goes unmet. The texts in which such analyses appear are often not widely available and further create a division between feminists located within the academy and community-based activists. On the other hand, many activist scholars have developed linkages with activists and policy arenas in such a way as to effectively bridge the so-called activist/scholar divide. Ronnie Steinberg (1996) brought her sociological research skills to campaigns for comparable worth and pay equity.[23] She reports on the moderate success of the movement for comparable worth and the significance of careful statistical analyses for supporting changes in pay and job classifications. As one highlight, she relates that systematic standards for assessing job equity developed with her associate Lois Haignere "were incorporated into specific guidelines on gender neutrality issued by the Ontario Pay Equity Tribunal" in 1991 (p. 231).

Roberta Spalter-Roth and Heidi Hartmann (1996) testified before Congress and produced policy briefs as well as more detailed academic articles to disseminate their findings about low-income women's economic survival strategies. Throughout the process of research and dissemination, they confronted the challenge of constructing "the dual vision of feminist policy research . . . to create research that meets both the standards of positivist social science and feminist goals of doing research 'for' rather than 'on' women" (pp. 206-207). Like Steinberg, they negotiated the difficulties that result when opponents attempt to discredit researchers for their explicitly activist stance. Measures of a rigid positivism are often used to undermine feminists' credibility in legal and legislative settings. Even more problematic is the fact that research generated for specific activist goals may be misappropriated by those who do not share feminist political perspectives to support antifeminist aims. For example, Katherine Edin (1996) describes how her research on welfare recipients' strategies to "make ends meet" could be used to stigmatize low-income women who are forced by their economic circumstances to gain additional funds through illegal means or who do not report income earned in the informal (or unofficial) labor market. Proponents of "workfare" programs for women on public assistance could also use Spalter-Roth and Hartmann's analysis of welfare recipients' income packaging strategies to justify coercive "welfare to work" measures.

Some activist scholars working directly in local community actions have also brought their academic skills to bear on specific community problems, or have trained community members to conduct activist research. Rina Benmayor (1991, 159) describes the action-research model used by the El Barrio Popular Education Program established by the Center for Puerto Rican Studies at Hunter College, City University of New York, to empower Spanish-speaking adults "through native-language literacy training and education." She explained how oral testimonies generated in a group context "become more than empirical data and transcend their static destiny as archival documents" (pp. 159-160). The group process empowered participants to speak about their experiences and promoted collective analysis. Terry Haywoode

(1991) worked as an educator and community organizer alongside women in her Brooklyn community and helped establish National Congress of Neighborhood Women's (NCNW) college program, a unique community-based program in which local residents can earn a two-year associates degree in Neighborhood Studies. By promoting women's educational growth and development within an activist community organization, NCNW's college program helped enhance working-class women's political efficacy in struggles to improve their neighborhoods.

## Beginnings

Activist researchers enter "the field" in a variety of ways. Each point of entry influences the researcher's relationship to the defined community, the strategies that are used, and the context for the participation of community members. Some activist researchers search for a community-based site from which they might assist in the political agendas defined by community members (see Maguire 1987; Whyte 1991). For example, Pierrette Hondagneu-Sotelo (chapter 8) drew upon methods of participant observation to develop an understanding of the experiences of immigrant Latinas employed as domestic workers. The findings of her research were incorporated into *fotonovelas* and used as a framework for community organizing.

A second opportunity for activist research arises when a group, community, or organization seeks outside assistance with research needs they specify themselves (also see Light and Kleiber 1988). As an ethnographer who observed and interviewed women inside and outside domestic-violence court, Judith Wittner (chapter 3) was able to help feminist advocates understand the complex ways women used the courts for their own purposes. Roberta Feldman, Susan Stall, and Patricia Wright (chapter 11) were brought into the struggle against the White Sox baseball stadium and for community-centered economic development by the African American women of Wentworth Gardens, a low-income housing development in Chicago, who had grown to trust them as allies. Their ongoing commitment to the women in Wentworth Gardens can be traced back more than a decade through many different struggles.

Another path to activist research opens when we enter the field as participants personally affected by the issue that is the focus of our work. Since most personal and community-based problems are politically constituted, feminist activists, in the course of struggles against institutionalized power relations, inevitably discover the value of activist research to support social-change efforts. Many of the authors in this collection who chose to use their personal and community-based struggles as sites for activist research did not begin the work with a research agenda in mind, but rather redefined their engagement as activist research projects during the process. For example, because of her prior experience developing an activist research strategy with Puerto Rican prisoners, Stern (chapter 4) quickly decided to pursue a similar strategy with the parents in her daughter's school. In contrast, Howe (chapter 10) did not redefine her relationship to the tax-override campaign until the campaign was over.

When a participant chooses to analyze a past community action or activist engagement by drawing on notes and other source material that were not generated with research in mind, numerous difficulties ensue. Activists turned activist researchers must confront dilemmas relating to authorship, "interpretive authority,"[24] confidentiality, and audience as they reconstruct and analyze the political narrative. But these limitations can be overcome, to a certain extent, by including the perspectives of key actors within the struggle, as well as systematically reviewing agendas, meeting notes, and other materials (see Weber forthcoming). Here we can see the value of sociological and ethnographic training in providing the framework within which to reconstruct and systematically analyze often fragmented evidence and diverse perspectives. On the one hand, the sooner such reconstruction can occur, the easier it is to locate participants and gain access to relevant materials. On the other hand, following a difficult and bitter struggle, community members may not welcome a close examination of their experiences. With distance, participants may come to a richer understanding of the meaning their involvement had for them and their community.

### Gaining and Retaining Trust

Regardless of how an activist scholar joins a community action or initiates an activist research project, she must gain the trust of other participants. Since trust is earned over time, longer commitment to the local struggles is more likely to bring greater access to, and deeper understanding of, other community members' political engagement. As a long-term unpaid worker at the Korean Women's Hotline, Lisa Sun-Hee Park (chapter 7) had "insider" knowledge of the organization. However, when she redefined her role as researcher, she also altered the way in which she was viewed by the other activists. Howe faced this same dilemma. Both these authors were forced to deal with questions of "confidentiality" as they began to situate their findings for this collection. Both authors chose to disguise the names of their organizations and gave pseudonyms to those they interviewed; however, this does not guarantee that someone knowledgeable about the community would not recognize it.

Given the lack of anonymity that many of the accounts require, authors also had to assess how they represented tensions within organizations or among participants. At times, careful analysis of a specific community action or activist organization reveals the limits of the actions taken by certain identifiable leaders, or highlights internal conflicts among key activists, and such honest assessment inevitably increases tensions between activist researchers and other participants. Fear that taking a critical stance would be read as betrayal, especially for those researchers who wish to continue their activist engagement, constrains what can be reported in a written account. In some cases, activist researchers who are central participants themselves are forced to take public positions that might prove to be at odds with the positions of key members or community residents. Not surprisingly, such positioning does compromise trust and access to different perspectives within the organization or community. Given the pressures against airing "dirty laundry" and the threat of losing friendships and allies in the process, it is not surprising that there are so few accounts of local community struggles. While we often blame the scarcity of such accounts by citing the time constraints on the activists themselves, we must also recognize the many moral and practical difficulties faced in producing such analyses.

### Emancipatory Participatory Research

In an effort to democratize the research process, many activist researchers argue for adopting participatory strategies that involve community residents or other participants in the design, implementation, and analysis of the research.[25] Collaborative writing also broadens the perspectives represented in the final product. Participatory research has been promoted in a variety of arenas by university-based researchers as well as those working in the applied fields of agriculture, education, and economic development.[26] One of the most frequently cited approaches is known as participatory action research, which, like many other types of participatory research, presumes a separation between the "researcher" and the "activist" that may not, in fact, exist (see, e.g., Whyte 1991). For example, some activist scholars like Clare Weber (forthcoming) have entered the academy after years of participation in diverse political struggles. As one reviewer of this chapter asked: "Where is the theory or methodology for the 'organic intellectual' or for an activist whose academic identity remains secondary to her activism?"[27] As she pointed out, "some people never 'enter the field,' instead they enter academia."

Some arenas of struggle, such as environmental justice and economic development, require access to expertise that few participants can claim.[28] On the one hand, as Feldman, Stall, and Wright demonstrate in chapter 11, local groups with a strong activist history can make demands on technical assistants to serve community needs rather than their own professional agendas, and create participatory workshops that can enhance resident input into the technical process. Activists who gain new knowledge about economic development or toxic waste and corporate strategies become even more effective spokeswomen for their cause, as Celene Krauss documents in chapter 5. On the other hand, as Karen Kendrick points out in her chapter on activists in battered women's shelters, institutional pressures from funding sources, governmental officials, and professionals in law and social welfare might displace community members as central players.

Several authors highlight the value of community activism for bringing social science perspectives into dialogue with the knowledges generated by participants in local struggles. From her vantage point as a sociologist and participant in a fight against institutionalized racism within her daughter's school, Susan Stern (chapter 4) demonstrates the value of social science theories of racism and social science methodologies for community activism. By incorporating these perspectives into a reflexive dialogic process with other parents, she was able to increase the participatory features of the research process and to deepen the analysis.

### Consciousness-Raising and Activist Research

Many of the authors in this collection highlight the value of dialogue and conversation for developing grassroots analyses of personally experienced but politically constituted problems. In Stern's construction of this approach, she points out the significance of friendship for providing the grounds for conversation-based activist research. She describes how "[c]onversation-based research builds on ordinary friendship conversations in which exploration of the personal realm grows to include investigation of shared social conditions."[29] In this sense, conversational research is an integral part of daily life. In small groups or as conversation partners, participants in the conversational research project can assess findings and refocus research questions.[30] Stern's analysis also demonstrates the challenge of entering a specific community-based "conversation." In fact, she found it necessary to initiate a dialogue among parents who had not related to one another in this way before.

The consciousness-raising approach that served as a model for many of the authors' activist research was premised on "insiders" sharing common as well as contrasting perspectives. However, many activist researchers experience themselves in a shifting insider/outsider relationship to the community (see Naples with Clark 1996). Sharon Bays, who was born in the central California town that was the site of her study, did not, however, share the racial-ethnic or class background of the women with whom she organized. The dialogic approach illustrated by Bays (chapter 13) and other authors in this collection (e.g., Howe, Park, Stern) challenges the "insider" (or community member) and "outsider" (or researcher) dichotomy that characterizes much of the literature on participatory action research (see, e.g., Freire 1970).

### Organization of the Book

The chapters in this collection model ways in which women's "standpoints" (variously defined) remain central sites from which to explore how and in what ways gender, race, ethnicity, sexuality, class, and region shape women's political consciousness and political practice. Sensitivity to regional diversity in women's activism is rare in feminist political analyses to date.[31] Analyses that center immigrant women as political actors are even more uncommon. Such diverse vantage points provide ways of seeing the possibilities for organizing across our differences on behalf of movements for progressive social change. The authors share the premise that any progressive movement must take into account the multiplicity of women's community activism if it is to succeed. By analyzing the diversity of women's community activism and providing rich case studies of disparate struggles in urban, rural, and suburban communities, we also hope to build a bridge from the broad-based concerns of social movement theorists to the practical struggles for social justice and economic security that are being waged on a daily basis by women across the United States.

The book is divided into four major sections that highlight: (1) how feminist activist research challenges academic categories and frameworks of analysis; (2) the processes by which women of differing racial-ethnic and class backgrounds develop oppositional political consciousness and how their activism contests traditional and some feminist political practices; (3) how women draw on, and develop, their social networks as political resources; and (4) the means by which women create the communities that sustain and nurture their political activities.

## Challenging Categories and Frameworks

Throughout the collection, the authors demonstrate how feminism and political analyses must be redefined in light of women's diverse community-based activism. While the qualitative methodologies utilized by the authors in this book differ, for the most part they are inherently activist in spirit, participatory in design, and dialogic in analysis. In chapter 1, Sherna Berger Gluck and her collaborators document the multifaceted women-centered organizing of women activists in the western region of the United States—a region often neglected in accounts of the Women's Movement.[32] In particular, they examine the political work of women on welfare in Watts, Asian American women in Los Angeles, Chicanas organizing in Long Beach, and Native American women activists. In each case, Gluck and her collaborators demonstrate the diversity of women-powered organizing efforts that occurred in the time frame usually identified with the U.S. Women's Movement. Yet neither these women nor the organizations they created became part of the historical record of the Women's Movement. It is for this reason that Gluck argues for the need to construct histories of the multiple women's movements in the United States. Although she would hesitate to apply the label "Third World feminists" to the women whose lives she chronicles (since she believes it "promotes the same kind of oversimplified unitary view of feminism that the conventional three- or four-fold typology of the white women's movement does"), her chapter addresses Chela Sandoval's (1991) call to center the lives of Third World, non-white, and non-U.S.-born women.[33]

Revisioning women's movements to include the diversity of women's political analyses and strategies also requires us to rethink the labels used to categorize feminisms more generally. Gluck begins by challenging analyses of the Women's Movement that rely on descriptions of separate branches: liberal or reform feminism; socialist and Marxist feminisms; radical feminism (which sometimes includes lesbian feminism); and lesbian feminism (if not included within radical feminism).[34] In chapter 2, Verta Taylor and Leila Rupp contest the theoretical and practical distinctions made between so-called cultural feminism, radical feminism, and lesbian feminism by offering an analysis of the lesbian community in Columbus, Ohio. These chapters serve to blur the categories of feminism usually treated as separable analytic frames.[35]

A related question of concern to the authors in this section is how feminist and oppositional political analyses are developed and sustained over time. Taylor and Rupp discuss the ways in which women's movement activists reproduce political identities through their everyday lives and, by extension, help sustain social movement goals and analyses during periods of political "abeyance" (Taylor 1989). As we consider the ways in which activists contribute to the continuity of feminist women's movements, we must also address the questions posed by Gluck and her collaborators, namely, "Whose Feminism, Whose History?" are being reproduced here.

In chapter 3, Judith Wittner illustrates the power of analyses that situate sociological investigations in dialogue with various community members who are experiencing specific social and economic problems. Wittner describes how feminist advocates, funded partially by state grants, were able to work on behalf of battered women who sought help through the state-sponsored domestic violence court. In the course of their work, they introduced the battered women to feminist analyses of violence against women, thus continuing the feminist activism that gave rise and substance to the domestic violence courts. By analyzing the multiple ways low-income and working-class battered women in Chicago utilized the courts to gain control over their domestic lives, Wittner also helped broaden advocates' understanding of battered women's agency in relation to the courts.

### Transforming Politics

The chapters in this section explore the process of politicization and demonstrate how women's community-based activism can also transform politics. Susan Stern's chapter offers an explicit methodology for accomplishing the goals of activist scholarship by embedding social scientific analyses in ongoing discussions with participants in specific struggles for social justice. Stern demonstrates how the process of conversational research can serve as a methodological tool for deepening participants' analyses of the social-structural dynamics shaping their world, while producing knowledges that can transform more distanced, academic understandings. In fact, she argues, a critical social science designed for emancipatory social change cannot proceed without a dialogic process that is deeply embedded in local struggles.[36]

Many of the authors in this collection explore how women translate the consciousness they develop through daily interactions with the state and other oppressive institutional arrangements into political action, as well as how women's activism challenges traditional and feminist political practices. In chapter 5, Celene Krauss describes how white, working-class women growing up in a privileged position within the racialized United States were unprepared for the callousness of government officials and businessmen who ignored or denied the extent to which toxic wastes were poisoning their communities. Their process of politicization required a painful recalculation of their taken-for-granted beliefs about democracy and social justice. Krauss' analysis reveals how white women's experiences of politicization differ from those of women of color who have had to fight against inequality and discrimination most of their lives. White women's blindness to the ways racism and xenophobia construct the daily lives of people of color and immigrants in this country appears in these accounts initially as a major obstacle to cross-race coalition building. The "privilege" of whiteness also blinds white women to the oppressive structures that circumscribe their own everyday worlds. In the case of toxic waste, this blind faith in the fairness of government and industry can be deadly.

Whiteness and other constructed structures of privilege contour how we experience and interpret our social worlds. Ironically, constructions of "feminism," as well as of other categories that derive from politically progressive struggles, can become rigid systems of classification that operate to exclude diverse experiences and perspectives. In chapter 6, Karen Kendrick describes how her constructed identity as a feminist impeded activism on her own behalf. She discovered that her definition of what it meant to be a "good feminist" interfered with her ability to claim the label "battered woman" and to get the help she needed. When Kendrick initiated her research on the politics of battered women's shelters, she expected to find a very vocal radical feminist perspective among the shelter staff, one that contrasted sharply with the perspective of the police and lawyers, for example. Her research led her to a much richer analysis of the politics of race, class, sexuality, gender, and institution-building as they intersected in constructing "battered woman" as the target of shelter work (also see Loseke 1992).

In chapter 7, Lisa Sun-Hee Park also highlights the limits of feminist perspectives on domestic violence in her analysis of the Korean Women's Hotline (KWH) (also see Huisman 1996; Dasgupta and Warrier 1996). She documents the ways in which anti-immigrant legislation and public discourse opened spaces for KWH among more mainstream Korean American community organizations. As KWH activists took advantage of these openings to gain greater visibility within their racial-ethnic community by relocating their office to a building that included other Korean American social service agencies, they were challenged by anti-domestic violence activists in the wider community for establishing an "open" presence in the community and possibility compromising confidentiality. KWH activists were aware of this potential danger and made arrangements to meet women who called at "safe" spaces in other locations. However, as Park reports, some members of the anti-domestic violence community, "including some of KWH's funders, were openly skeptical about the Hotline's unconventional move." Park's analysis reveals the contrasting perspectives held by feminist activists whose class and racial-ethnic identities position them differently within broad-based struggles combatting violence against women and anti-immigration policies.

### Networking for Change

Activist networks established in and through local struggles for social and economic justice provide one of the primary means by which activists sustain and promote progressive analyses and alternative political strategies during times of political quiescence and backlash. Women's social networks, in particular, are powerful resources for promoting resistance strategies, especially for those most marginalized in contemporary society. In chapter 8, Pierrette Hondagneu-Sotelo explores how domestic workers, who have rarely been the focus of any formal organizing efforts, created and drew upon their dispersed networks to share information about employment opportunities and about their rights on the job. Hondagneu-Sotelo brings to light how undocumented immigrant domestic workers in San Francisco used their social contacts at church, parties, and other community events to define the boundaries of housecleaning work and create a community referral system. The "domestics' networks" demonstrate a blurring among communities based on "kinship, friendship, ethnicity, place of origin, and current residential locale" in this urban context.

In chapter 9, Virginia Seitz's study of the Daughters of Mother Jones illustrates how rural women activists play a central leadership role in their communities during periods of economic and social crisis. The Daughters of Mother Jones was organized in 1989 by members of the Family Auxiliary of District 28 of the United Mineworkers of America to support the eleven-month strike against the Pittston Coal Company. At a time when most observers decried the death of union organizing in this country, these working-class women in Appalachia helped wage an intense and successful battle against a powerful mining company. The Daughters of Mother Jones mobilized across fourteen union locals to create a web of resistance that challenged the Pittston Coal Company, as well as the sexist assumptions of the male union leadership. Seitz's study further reveals the blurring between labor and community organizing. In fact, her work demonstrates that effective labor organizing requires building strong ties with other community residents, and that women play a key role in creating and sustaining these linkages.

In exploring the limits and possibilities of organizing across race, class, and gender, Carolyn Howe (chapter 10) describes the short-term gains and long-term losses involved in a local struggle to override Proposition 2 $\frac{1}{2}$, Massachusetts's tax limitation law, for public school funding. Howe details the different political strategies developed by two groups, one favoring a traditional electoral approach and the other hoping to generate a strong network of parents who would work together beyond the election "to impact the local state by changing the way education decisions are made in the city." The former group, composed of businessmen and local politicians, effectively imposed their approach on the broader campaign and sabotaged the efforts of the predominantly female parents who were working to establish a broader political network. Consequently, while the override campaign was successful, Howe reports, "the grassroots organizing campaign had little lasting impact." Howe also explores the limits of multirace and cross-class organizing of the parent-led group and demonstrates how Latino, African American and Asian American parents were left out of the traditional electoral approach due in part to "racially coded 'common-sense' ways of doing" politics in this city.

**Constructing Community**

Women's community activism can only be understood in terms of varying definitions and experiences of community. Since the social construction of community in American society involves distinctions between genders, sexualities, classes, races, and ethnic groups, community activism frequently reaffirms these divisions and may inhibit the continuity of this work between generations, from one issue to the next, or across neighborhood boundaries. However, once we recognize the continued importance of community for political consciousness and political practice and explore the different ways people define and experience community, it is possible to identify the similarities that exist as well as to work through the differences—or at least to recognize early who are our allies in different struggles (a lesson that Carolyn Howe and the parents she helped organize for the tax-override education campaign learned all too late).

In chapter 11, Roberta Feldman, Susan Stall, and Patricia Wright describe how the process of politicization and community-building led the women of Wentworth Gardens, the low-income housing project in Chicago that formed the site of their activism and research, to develop greater cohesiveness and political efficacy. Yet, as Stern's study demonstrates, such social cohesiveness is not a necessary outcome of participation in collective action. Differences in social cohesion among activists in these two different African American communities could be explained by variations in class, in housing patterns (which are themselves patterned by class), or by the nature of the conflict. For example, housing conflicts and economic development require long-term activist engagement. Residents maintain a legitimate position within the struggle as long as they reside in the community. In contrast, parents fighting for justice in the schools may lose both their motivation and their legitimate role within the struggle as soon as their children graduate. Furthermore, they may find themselves embroiled in struggles on behalf of their children at the next level of education. Finally, sharing racial-ethnic identities does not ensure that we see our interests in common or define our community in similar ways—as the Wentworth Gardens' activists discovered when they attempted to organize with nearby homeowners to prevent the White Sox from building a baseball stadium in their community.

In chapter 12, Mary Pardo uses life histories of Mexican American women to demonstrate how their community-building efforts linked "family concerns to a wider network of resources." She describes the variety of ways women community workers of East Los Angeles used their ongoing contacts with residents to identify needs and attempt to mobilize and expand existing resources. While Pardo is sensitive to the fact that "[w]omen's community activism can either change the traditional domestic division of labor or reinforce 'traditional' gender expectations," her analysis also reveals the creative ways women marshall their domestic skills to promote the sense of community vital to effective community action. In other words, the gendered division of labor creates the grounds for resistance, as well as the reproduction of inequality.

In chapter 13, Sharon Bays chronicles a successful multiethnic and multiracial community action in which Hmong, Lao, Mien, and Lahu women organized across their differences and with non-Laotians to challenge the male-led Laotian community and the male-defined welfare system in Visalia, a town located in the San Joaquin Valley of California. The main organizer, Pajhoua Her, herself a Hmong refugee who lived and worked in Visalia, came to her leadership role with previous community work experiences with other ethnic Laotians and non-Laotians in Denver. Pajhoua's "multiethnic perspective [on] community politics" was not well received by the male Hmong leadership. However, she gained the trust of other women in the town and was effective in organizing the multi-ethnic Asian American Women's Advancement Coalition.

The final chapter offers a conceptual framework for analyzing how women activists develop an awareness of the processes of domination that structure their daily lives. I argue that a multidimensional standpoint analysis provides the conceptual framework through which to explore the diversity of women's activism. Drawing upon studies of urban and rural women of different racial-ethnic and class backgrounds, I describe how the processes of racialization and the constructions of community contribute to women's politicization and oppositional consciousness. Since the state is often implicated in women's activism either as a target for action or as a site that fosters women's political work, I also highlight the state's contradictory role.[37] I illustrate this process through the experiences of women activists hired by the Community Action Agencies funded through the War on Poverty. I conclude by calling attention to the larger political-economic processes that contribute to inequality and injustice in local communities throughout the U.S., and emphasize the challenge faced by community activists in their efforts to link local struggles with broader movements for social change.

This collection represents only a very modest sample of the rich scholarship on women's community activism in the U.S. Furthermore, it offers but a small window onto the diverse and ever-changing world of women's community-based political action. Of course, community-based social-change efforts are limited with respect to the structures of inequality that shape the wider political and economic environment. Global processes of economic restructuring are undermining unioniza-tion, job security, and the welfare state, as well as the viability of many rural communities and former industrial cities. Yet, as these case studies and analyses illustrate, community actions on behalf of progressive agendas remain salient features of local encounters with the state, with corporations, with employers, and with racist, sexist, and homophobic forces pervading many spheres of social life. We offer this collection as a resource for specific knowledges about these encounters, as a broad-based analysis of community activism and feminist politics, and as a col-lection of models for activist scholarship.

### Notes

1. See, e.g., McCourt 1977; Gilkes 1980, 1988; Kaplan 1982, 1997; Giddings 1984; Jones 1985; McCarthy 1990; West and Blumberg 1990; Haywoode 1991; Omolade 1994; Stout 1996.
2. See, e.g., Tax 1980; Milkman 1985; Maggard 1986; Ackelsberg 1988; Book-man and Morgen 1988; Sacks 1988. Also see Katznelson 1981; Brecher and Costello 1990; Aguilar-San Juan 1994.
3. See Davis 1981; hooks 1984; Morgen 1988; Sacks 1989; Albrecht and Brewer 1990; DuBois and Ruiz 1990; Mohanty, Russo, Torres 1991; Frankenberg 1993; Lorber 1994; Chow, Wilkinson, and Zinn 1996.
4. Bookman and Morgen 1988a, 7. In *Women and the Politics of Empowerment*, Martha Ackelsberg highlights the implications of women's community activism for a democratic polity; Bonnie Thornton Dill draws upon life his-tories of African American domestic workers to show their unique strate-gies of workplace resistance; Wendy Luttrell analyzes the political transfor-mation of white, working-class women engaged in a struggle to establish a new high school in their community; Ida Susser (1988, 257) demonstrates the relationship between women's community activism and "the growing instability of the household economy" in a working-class neighborhood in Brooklyn; and Patricia Zavella explores the race and gender politics in organizing Chicana cannery workers.
5. See, e.g., Davis 1981; Giddings 1984; Jones 1985; Collins 1990.
6. My research on community workers in the mid 1980s, and follow-up inter-

views in 1995, confirm the continuity of this work among another cohort of urban professional African American women (Naples forthcoming a; also see Omolade 1994).

7. See Barbara Omolade (1994) and Kisho Scott (1991) for discussions of some of the psychological and social costs paid by professional African American women community workers who struggle on behalf of others in their communities.

8. Women's community work has often been framed as "maternalism" or "social housekeeping"—a political claims-making strategy that served as a justification for white middle- and upper-income social reformers to transcend the ideological barrier between women's "proper place" in the home and the so-called public sphere. Seth Koven and Sonya Michel (1993, 4) define maternalism as "ideologies and discourses that exalted women's capacity to mother and applied to society as a whole the values they attached to the role: care, nurturance, and morality." While many women draw on their gender identities to describe their activism, they do not adhere to a traditional gendered division of labor ideology, nor do they believe that all women could unite on the basis of their "mothering" status. Race and class form powerful dimensions of mothering, as do political analyses. Through the lens of maternalist politics, the specificity of low-income, working-class, and non-white women's activism is rendered invisible.

9. Also see Glenn, Chang, and Forcey 1994; Collins 1991; Gordon 1991a; S. James 1993; Pardo 1990b; Roberts 1995.

10. These processes are also profoundly shaped by race and ethnicity. See Rayna Green's (1980) analysis of Native American women's leadership styles, and Mary Pardo's (1990b) discussion of Mexican American women's community organizing.

11. Haywoode 1991, 183. Clearly such strategies can also be utilized to promote racial, gender, and class inequality. See, e.g. McCourt 1977; Ginsburg 1988; Klatch 1992; Blee 1996.

12. See for example Stanley and Wise 1979; Mitchell 1971; Hartsock 1981; Russell 1981; Mies 1983; Cook and Fonow 1990; Lather 1991; Gottfried 1996; Hartmann et al. 1996; Alexander and Mohanty 1997.

13. Mohanty 1997, 13. Another important collection that explores "women's multicultural alliances" was launched at the 1988 National Women's Studies Association conference in the Twin Cities, Minnesota. In *Bridges of Power*, editors Lisa Albrecht and Rose Brewer (1990a, 10) highlight the significance of three factors for broadening our understanding of women's movements: "(1) autonomous movements of women of color . . . ; (2) the intellectual critique of white feminism by feminists of color . . . ; and (3) the impact of the global political economy on women internationally."

14. Also see Charlotte Bunch's (1990) powerful analysis of the limits and possibilities of coalition-building among diverse women, and Gloria Anzaldúa's

(1990a) discussion of how lesbians of color negotiate the demands of coalition-building with white women.

15. See, e.g., Moraga and Anzaldúa 1981; Anzaldúa 1987, 1990; Zavella 1993; Zinn and Dill 1996.

16. See, e.g., Roediger 1991; Ignatiev 1995.

17. Anti-Semitism remains a powerful oppressive force that shapes Jewish women's lives. For discussions of the Jewish women's experience of femaleness and race see Kaye/Kantrowitz 1992; Frankenberg 1993; Sacks 1994; Thompson 1994.

18. Also see Thorne 1979; Quest Staff 1981; Susser 1982; West and Blumberg 1990; Omolade 1994; Gottfried 1996.

19. I am grateful to the many students and colleagues who have shared their experiences of conducting and writing activist work. This chapter has been shaped in large measure by my ongoing conversations with Terry Haywoode, Susan Stern, Karen Brodkin, Clare Weber, and Lionel Cantú. Special thanks to Sherna Berger Gluck, Myra Marx Ferree, Francesca Cancian, Gilbert Gonzalez, Louis Mirón, Hector Delgado, Chelsea Starr, and Clare Weber for comments on earlier drafts of this chapter.

20. See, e.g., Fine and Weis 1996; Hale 1996; Wolf 1996.

21. Francesca Cancian (1996, 187–188) defines activist research as: "empowering the powerless, exposing the inequities of the status quo, and promoting social changes that equalize the distribution of resources." She argues "that researchers will be more effective in challenging inequality insofar as they emphasize major changes in equalizing power, as opposed to improving services for the disadvantaged within the existing power structure, and they incorporate collective action into their research instead of restricting themselves solely to academic analysis, i.e., they include 'practice' as well as 'theory.'"

22. See, e.g., Bookman and Morgen 1988; Cameron 1990; Delgado 1996; Simonds 1996.

23. Campaigns for comparable worth concern "correcting for the underpayment of wages to those performing such historically female jobs as registered nurse, legal secretary, clerk, food-service worker, and housekeeper because that work has been and continues to be performed primarily by women" (Steinberg 1996, 225).

24. Katherine Borland (1991, 64) explains the dilemma of "interpretive authority" for feminists as follows: "On the one hand, we seek to empower the women we work with by revaluing their perspectives, their lives, and their art in a world that has systematically ignored or trivialized women's culture. On the other, we hold an explicitly political vision of the structural conditions that lead to particular social behaviors, a vision that our field collaborators, many of whom do not consider themselves feminists, may not recognize as valid."

25. Writing from a feminist perspective, Patricia Maguire (1987, 35) outlines three features of participatory research. It is:

> a method of social *investigation* of problems, involving participation of oppressed and ordinary people in problem posing and solving. It is an *educational* process for the researcher and participants, who analyze the structural causes of named problems through collective discussion and interaction. Finally, it is a way for researchers and oppressed people to join in solidarity to take collective *action*, both short and long term, for radical social change. Locally determined and controlled action is a planned consequence of inquiry. (emphasis in original.)

Maguire points out the logical relationship between feminist critiques of the dominant approaches to knowledge creation and those of participatory research. Also see Light and Kleiber 1988; Lather 1991; Stanley 1990; Fonow and Cook 1991; Reinharz 1992; Fine 1992; Mies 1983; Cancian 1996.

26. Participatory research strategies that highlight the significance of including "indigenous" peoples in the design, implementation, and analysis stages of investigation have been promoted by researchers in a number of diverse areas: agricultural development projects in Third World countries, most notably those interested in identifying and diffusing indigenous knowledge; educational and economic development projects that draw upon Paulo Freire's dialogic approach to knowledge development and learning; and social-science methods such as action science and participatory action research that derive from the "proposition that causal inferences about the behavior of human beings are more likely to be valid and enactable when the human beings in question participate in building and testing them" (Arygris and Schön 1991, 86). In many ways, feminist standpoint epistemologies that stem from Marxist historical materialism provide the grounds for a similar argument (see Hartsock 1983; Harding 1986, 1991).

27. This question was raised by Chelsea Starr. She refers here to Antonio Gramsci's (1971) conceptualization of those indigenous leaders who help articulate a "philosophy of praxis" that develops in the course of political struggle. According to Gramsci, this "philosophy of praxis" has the potential to supersede "the existing mode of thinking and existing concrete thought (the existing cultural world)" (p. 330)—i.e., to challenge the dominant order. In this way, the grassroots activists play a crucial role as "organic intellectuals" who provide informed leadership to their communities.

28. Recognizing this, some activists choose to enter academia to gain the technical knowledge and professional credentials that will enhance their political effectiveness.

29. Stern differentiates her framework from Freire's dialogic approach. Most who follow Freire's lead understand the process as one enhancing understanding between "insiders" and "outsiders." For example, Elden and Levin (1991, 134) describe how participatory research can empower participants through the process of "cogenerative dialogue." They point out that for Freire a dialogical relationship "is characterized by '*subjects* who meet to name the work in order to transform it'" (quoted in Elden and Levin 1991, 134; emphasis added); however, they focus on the dialogue between insiders and outsiders. Also see Code 1991; Hale 1996.

30. Maria Mies (1991, 71) describes this process as "reciprocal research." Although she shared neither culture, nor class, nor ethnic background with her "conversation partners" (to use Stern's term), Mies found this process enriched her work with Indian women.

31. Recent work by feminist social geographers and sociologists offer new ways to conceptualize the relationship between gender and place. See, e.g., Momson and Townsend 1987; Rocheleau, Thomas-Slayter, and Wangari 1996; Sachs 1996.

32. In chapter two, Verta Taylor and Leila Rupp argue that the experiences of lesbians from smaller cities like Columbus, Ohio, have similarly been left out of analyses of the Gay and Lesbian Movement.

33. Chela Sandoval (1991) resists reducing Third World feminism to one political strategy. Instead, she explains:

> This study identifies five principal categories by which "oppositional consciousness" is organized, and which are politically effective means for changing the dominant order of power. I characterize them as "equal rights," "revolutionary," "separatist," and "differential" ideological forms. All these forms of consciousness are kaleidoscoped into view when the fifth form is utilized as a theoretical model which retroactively clarifies and gives new meaning to the others. (2–3)

In order to demonstrate the relationship between material oppressive conditions and the development of oppositional politics, Sandoval outlines how "differential" consciousness "enables movement 'between and among' [Anzaldúa 1981] the other equal rights, revolutionary, supremacist, and separatist modes of oppositional consciousness considered as variables, in order to disclose the distinctions among them" (p. 14).

34. Various other categories of feminism appear in Women's Studies texts, including historical categorizations such as "first wave" (up to 1950) and "second wave" (1950–early 1980s) feminisms (Humm 1992); labels that refer to more specific theoretical frameworks such as psychoanalytic feminism (Tong 1989; Humm 1992); and designations connected to the racial-ethnic identities or social locations of the authors and/or designations that center race, postcolonial analyses, or gendered processes of global capitalism, such as multicultural feminism, U.S. Third World feminism,

and global feminism (Sandoval 1991; Jaggar and Rothenberg 1993). Terry Haywoode (1991) has outlined dimensions of "working-class feminism." Maxine Baca Zinn and Bonnie Thornton Dill (1996, 323–324) use the term "multiracial feminism" to describe approaches that locate both men and women "in multiple systems of domination." African American women and Latinas have created terminology that self-consciously eschews the feminist label, with words such as "xicanista" and "womanist" (Walker 1983; Castillo 1994; also see Johnson-Odim 1991; Mohanty 1991b). Some lesbian, gay, and bisexual activists have adopted the term "queer" to refer to a broad array of "identities" and "sexualities" that go beyond the bipolar gay/straight or homosexual/heterosexual designation (see Stein 1992; Gamson 1995). This term has been taken up to form a new body of literature that, while influenced by feminism, is not exclusively, or even predominantly feminist (see, for example, Sedgwick 1990).

35. In a recent effort "to contribute to the creation of multi-centered, women-affirming, and transformative politics," Angela Miles (1996, x-xi) demonstrates how "types of feminism usually perceived as absolutely different, even opposing, share important integrative principles." Her articulation of "integrative feminisms" further challenges rigid distinctions between liberal, radical, and socialist feminisms.

36. To a certain extent, Stern's analysis distinguishes between traditional or "inherent" knowledges and structured or "derived" knowledges (to paraphrase George Rudé's [1980] distinction between commonsense "popular" beliefs and a systematic analysis of social and economic conditions that are "'derived' or borrowed from others, often taking the form of a more structured system of ideas") (Fisher and Kling 1990, 73). Like Stern, Rudé argued that "resistance has transformative potential only when an inherent ideology has become strongly suffused with a derived one" (p. 73). However, Stern is not only referring to certain knowledges but to a methodology with which to create the "conversation" between different forms of knowledges.

37. The contradictory role of the state as both a catalyst for and a site of women's community activism forms another significant theme in other chapters as well. Feldman, Stall, and Wright detail how public housing provided a site for organizing against the state-run housing authority. Residents of Wentworth Gardens organized their community with the assistance of tenant-relations representatives from the Chicago Housing Authority (CHA). They subsequently used this organizational base to press CHA for better services and additional resources.

# Part I

# Challenging Categories and Frameworks

# Chapter 1

# Whose Feminism, Whose History?

*Reflections on Excavating the History of (the)
U.S. Women's Movement(s)*

**Sherna Berger Gluck** in collaboration with Maylei Blackwell,
Sharon Cotrell, and Karen S. harper

## Whose History? Old Perspectives, New Dilemmas

The parentheses in the title of this chapter are less a sign of my infatuation with postmodernist gimmickry than of my own continuing ambivalence about how to "do" the history of feminist activism in the U.S.—what is still conventionally referred to as "the second wave." Initially annoyed by bell hooks's refusal to use the article—as in "the" women's movement—in one of her earliest works, I now realize that it actually captures my own dilemma (hooks 1984, 26). Referring to women's movements in the plural, on the other hand, reflects a deepening awareness of how the multitudinous forms of women's activism throughout the world all work to challenge patriarchal hierarchies.

Yet, even as we now recognize multiple "feminismS" in contemporary discourse, with few exceptions the histories of their recent manifestations in the U.S. are still largely based on the old hegemonic model.[1] Trapped in a time warp, and constrained by our particular historical trajectories and relationships, most U.S. historians of contemporary feminism still resort to the old litany, describing "the women's movement" as having three (sometimes four) branches variously described as: liberal/reform feminism; socialist/Marxist feminism (a category that at times also includes anarchist-feminism); and radical feminism, which sometimes also encompasses lesbian feminism and sometimes classifies it as a separate branch. Because this model provides such a convenient pedagogical tool, and one that is more manageable than the real complexity of feminist activism based on the intersections of race, class, gender, sexuality, it is reproduced continuously.

Women of color whose feminist activism cannot readily be placed within this paradigm are consequently left out of the histories of the early days of "the women's movement." Moreover, as Katie King (1994) points out in her far-reaching analysis of some of this literature, even when women of color—particularly African American women—were central players in radical feminist groups, they remain largely unmentioned. To counter the restrictiveness of the three-fold typology and the invisibility it confers upon women of color, at least one Feminist Studies class at Stanford has added a fourth category: "feminism and women of color" (Lee 1995). And while this might be an effective heuristic tactic, it does little to address the basic historiographic problem.

For the most part, the early history of feminist activism among women of color and/or working-class and poor women remains, at best, particular and separate, and does not challenge the accepted paradigm of "second wave" feminism.[2] It is only when autonomous groups like the National Black Feminist Organization (1973) and the Combahee River Collective (1977) come out with statements that explicitly ally them with "the women's movement," that at least some women of color become incorporated into the master narrative.

This veil of silence, particularly with respect to working-class and poor women activists who remained anchored in their local communities, was lifted only after these women became more visible to the larger movement at and following the 1977 National Women's Conference at Houston.[3] By 1982, on the heels of difficult political struggles waged by activist scholars of color, groundbreaking essays and anthologies by and about women of color opened a new chapter in U.S. feminism (see especially Moraga and Anzaldúa 1981). The future of the women's movement in the U.S. was reshaped irrevocably by the introduction of the expansive notion of "feminismS." Nevertheless, this new perspective has not been seriously applied retroactively to re-vision the earlier history.

One of the difficulties in revising the historical narrative and embracing the concept of "feminismS" is the historian's genuine concern about presentism, i.e. projecting contemporary meanings onto the past. Even more problematic is the issue of "ownership," the deep investment on the part of the participants in the early days of the women's liberation movement in preserving the primacy of our particular experience and analysis (also see King 1994). Not directly faced with race-ethnic or class oppression, the mainly white, middle-class activists—

regardless of their analysis of the causes of women's oppression—foregrounded gender. As a result, they assumed both that feminists of color would form autonomous groups and that they would *openly* criticize the men in their communities. This expectation only widened the chasm and caused many working-class women, poor women, and women of color to distance themselves from "the women's movement," although they were often pursuing similar goals in the context of their own communities or movement groups.

Because so many of the white, middle-class activists themselves—or their admirers—initially charted the course of feminist history, it is no surprise that their own pasts have shaped how that history has been written. In contrast, women of color and U.S. Third World feminists like Chela Sandoval have challenged the hegemony of "white feminism" and forwarded more plural and differentiated "feminismS" (Sandoval 1982). However, what is often counterposed is a model that implies a unified movement among feminists of color—the result, perhaps, of a homogenization assumed by white feminists (Sandoval 1982; Alarcon 1990). Furthermore, because this vision evolved and was elaborated by members of a cultural and literary elite, the implications of class have not been well integrated into this emergent discourse. In contrast, the hallmark of so much of the activism of working-class and poor women has not been their *articulated* gender or race or class analyses, but rather their activities growing out of immediate needs. These have been referred to by some as practical gender interests, and in the Latin American context their expression has been dubbed "popular feminism" (Molyneux 1985; Jaquette 1994).

By and large, this kind of neighborhood-based organizing of women in the U.S. has been ignored by feminist historians, except for the discussions of housewives organizing in the Depression years, largely under the aegis of the Community party organizers (Orleck 1993). On the other hand, there is a growing body of feminist sociological studies that document this kind of activism.[4] However, this work is usually focused on individual case studies, and is often produced within the framework of social movement theory. The broader implications for a re-visioning of U.S. women's feminist activism have not been fully explored.

The issues raised by the community activism of women place in sharp focus one of the major dilemmas facing any historian who wishes to rewrite the history of contemporary feminism. Focusing on groups whose activities are based on an analysis of women's subordination— what has been referred to by Molyneux as strategic gender interests—

seems merely to reinforce the old hegemonic model and discourse. Alternatively, widening our lens to include the kind of community organizing that is the hallmark of working-class and poor women's activism can reduce the idea of feminism to mean simply the empowerment of women.

In an attempt not to focus only on groups driven by a gender analysis or, alternatively, merely to equate feminism with any activity that empowers women, regardless of its intent, the California State University, Long Beach, Feminist Oral History Collective (a.k.a. "De-Centerers") developed the following working definition of feminist activism:[5]

> Women's groups (including formal and informal committees, subcommittees and caucuses) organized for change whose agendas AND/OR actions challenge women's subordinate [or disadvantaged] status in the society at large (external) and in their own community (internal).

The definitional process was not itself uncomplicated and the oral histories we were conducting with a range of activists were used to evaluate its usefulness and to guard against it being either too broad or too narrow. The question of *intended* and *unintended* effects remains somewhat ambiguous, but a distinction can be drawn. For example, a group dedicated to promoting women's education as a way to empower them would fall within this net. But a group whose members are *individually* empowered by virtue of organizing, e.g. to close down a neighborhood toxic-waste dump, might not—unless they were also challenging the gendered basis of the decision-making process or began to confront the gendered hierarchy within their community as they organized.

As complicated as the question of intent is when the focus is on working-class community activism, it is even more confusing when it comes to deciding how and where lesbian activism fits. Like most women's liberation groups, lesbian feminists were part of a constructed social community, not a spatial or ethnic community. They are usually considered in the master historical narrative of "the" women's movement to the extent that these groups often spun off from radical feminist groups. But where does a group like the Daughters of Bilitis (DOB), founded in 1955, belong? Although many of its early members depict the group as serving mainly a social function (Gittings 1976), was their gender-bending nevertheless a challenge to women's subordinate status? If so, the conventional periodization of "second wave" feminism is further undermined, and a new twist is added to the dual question, whose feminism, whose history?

## New Perspectives, New Dilemmas

In 1963, at the same time that women professionals were convening the President's Commission on the Status of Women in Washington, DC, a handful of Black women in Watts (Los Angeles) met to found the first grassroots welfare-mothers organization, ANC Mothers Anonymous (named for the Aid to Needy Children program under which they received assistance). In 1968, radical feminists from New York tossed their bras into the trash bins outside the convention hall of the Miss America pageant—a piece of guerilla theater that became mythologized as bra-burning. At the same time, a group of women students in Long Beach, California, were laying the foundation for one of the first modern-day Chicana *femenista* groups and newspapers, *Hijas de Cuauhtemoc*. In 1970, to celebrate the fiftieth anniversary of woman's suffrage, one hundred thousand women marched in New York. That same year, American Indian women (who did not win suffrage until 1924) met to form the North American Indian Women's Association. And, in 1972, when *Ms.* magazine was launched, Asian American feminists in Los Angeles were already working on the second special women's issue of the radical Asian American community magazine, *Guidra*.

While the actions of the mainly white women's groups have become major historical markers, the actions of these women of color and poor women in the American west have been little more than footnotes. The study, and particularly the oral histories, of women from the ANC Mothers Anonymous, *Hijas de Cuauhtemoc*, and Asian Sisters, and of those involved in American Indian women's organizing, adds not just the dimension of race and class, but also a sorely needed western regional perspective.[6] As Ellen DuBois and Vicki Ruiz (1990, xii) so eloquently point out, looking to the west provides an important corrective:

> For the possibilities of a richer palette for painting women's history, we turn to the "west" . . . if only because grappling with race at all requires a framework that has more than two positions. Nor is white history always center stage. Even the term "the west" only reflects one of several historical perspectives: the Anglo "west" is also the Mexican "north," and the Native American "homeland," and the Asian "east."

Moreover, Asian American and Chicano activism had their origins in the west in the 1960s. The feminist activism of women in these groups actually predated that of east-coast groups, which are the ones usually cited (see, e.g., Chow 1987; F. Davis 1991). Indeed, the birth of the west-coast Chicana and Asian American women's groups was contemporaneous with the east-coast white women's liberation groups that are at the center of the master historical narrative. Like them, the groups that poor women, Chicanas, and Asians formed in the west were significant beyond their initial, small numbers.

Some of these groups embraced the feminist label, while others elaborated their own versions; and some of the activists openly challenged the sexism of the men in their communities, while others were more oblique in their approach. Regardless of these differences, all drew on their daily life experiences and their political organizing, and were oftentimes attracted to feminist ideas by the contradiction between the liberation discourse of their movements and their practices. They pursued agendas that were designed to mobilize the women in their own communities (national/ethnic, if not necessarily local) and to redress the ways in which sexism, racism, and class domination disadvantaged them in the larger society. Most sought the sources of their strength in their own histories and heroines.

An exploration of the similarities and differences among these groups challenges the conventional history of feminist activism, even as it also reveals some similarities with the experiences of the white feminists. It also challenges what is sometimes presented as a unitary notion of "Third World feminism." Such an exploration is not unproblematic, furthermore, because it must rely so heavily on oral histories, and thus poses serious intellectual and ethical dilemmas revolving around the issue of interpretive authority. For example, to what extent can the consciousness and experience of individual key activists be used to construct the meaning of a group's agenda, particularly when written documentary sources are either missing or minimal? Even more critically, what are the implications of incorporating into a re-visioned history of the women's movement individuals and groups who eschewed the feminist label because of its implications of skin and class privilege? In other words, does an attempt to be inclusive by imposing our 1990s historical sensibility in fact subvert their politics?

These are some of the questions to which I will return after reviewing the history and work of poor women in Watts who became involved in the ANC Mothers Anonymous, the Asian American women activists who formed a host of women's groups within the context of the Asian American movement in Los Angeles, the Chicanas who began to formulate their own gender politics in groups like the Long Beach-based *Hijas de Cuauhtemoc*, and the American Indian women who came together in the west to forge a common bond of sisterhood and address their issues as native women.

This chapter, strictly speaking, is not a collective product. It is, however, the product of a collective process and represents an ongoing dialogue among us that began in a women's oral history seminar, Spring 1991. The following section draws on my own research as well as that of the three named collaborators, including their oral history projects. Maylei Blackwell conducted interviews with members of *Hijas de Cuauhtemoc*; Karen harper with activists in the L.A. Asian American Women's Movement; Sharon Cotrell with American Indian activists.[7] The material on the various groups discussed here also draws heavily on the research that we each did and the papers we separately produced and/or presented. And while the discussion of each of these groups is drawn from our individual research projects, the framework for the discussion is a result of our earlier collective process and our ongoing conversation.

### Origins, Roots, and Traditions

The Black civil rights movement of the 1960s, so often cited as one of the major sources for the emergence of the women's liberation movement in the later part of the decade, also had a profound impact on students and youth in the Asian and Mexican communities. In contrast, the poor women's movement that took hold in local communities in many cities in the early 1960s had little connection to the civil rights movement. Groups like the ANC Mothers Anonymous of Watts (whose anonymity could not be maintained after they appeared on Alan Lomax's radio program in Los Angeles) predated the formal organizing by the male founders of the National Welfare Rights Organization (NWRO). These groups developed out of the immediate survival needs of welfare mothers. As Johnnie Tillmon (1991), one of the founders, made eminently clear, the group was organized on behalf of class interests. Rubbing her thumb and forefinger together, she commented: "It wasn't a Black thing, it was a green thing."

Tillmon, who later led the NWRO, was typical of the women who founded many of these early grassroots groups. After taking ill in 1963, she decided not to return to her factory job, but rather to follow the advice of her neighbors that she stay home to supervise her youngest daughter. A hard worker all her life, going on welfare was new to her, and she did not take kindly to a slight she overheard about welfare mothers from a middle-class African American woman in her neighborhood. Through rather ingenious and somewhat devious means, she managed to pull together a meeting of other women in the public housing project where she lived. From this meeting, a core group of eight women formed the ANC Mothers Anonymous. This spontaneously organized community-based group was one of the first links in the chain of a poor women's movement that was eventually joined together in the National Welfare Rights Organization.

The main issue for these women was survival. For many, their jobs did not pay enough to support their children. For others, like Tillmon, their children were beginning to get into trouble and needed more supervision. The women of ANC Mothers demanded attention, respect, and the full share of benefits to which they were entitled under various federal programs.

In contrast to the poor single mothers who founded groups like the ANC Mothers, the younger women who constituted some of the earliest women's groups in the Asian American and Chicano movements emerged within the context of these movements, particularly as they were beginning to flower on college campuses in California. Both the Black Panthers and the largely militant Mexican and Filipino United Farm Workers (UFW) provided the model and often the training ground for these ethnic-based and/or nationalist movements. And while the women who joined the Chicana *femenista* group, *Hijas de Cuauhtemoc*, and those who worked in the array of Asian American women's groups in L.A. followed similar courses, each drew on their own cultural roots.

By 1967, student groups like UMAS (United Mexican American Students) were developing a broader political agenda. They also provided a safe haven for the Chicanos/as, who represented a very small minority on the college campuses.[8] Anna Nieto-Gomez, who was to become a major Chicana figure, quickly moved into a leadership position in the organization after she enrolled at California State University, Long Beach (CSULB) in 1968. The male leadership charged her with the task of educating the women, and keeping them in line (Nieto-Gomez 1991, Tape IVA3). Like the leaders of the Chicano student movement, generally, the CSULB men believed that women had less political knowledge and consciousness and that it was the responsibility of the women in the organization to politicize and raise the consciousness of new women (Blackwell 1991, 22).

Ironically, and predictably, the women's discussion group that formed for this purpose evolved into a feminist consciousness-raising group,[9] a place where the women explored the contradictions between the civil rights values espoused by the men and the way they treated women in the organization. It gave the women a voice, as Nieto-Gomez explains:

> [What the women] wanted, in essence, was some accountability from the men . . . that they be consistent with their ideology, because the women weren't treated with respect. (Nieto-Gomez 1991, Tape IVA2)

Researching their own history as Chicanas/Mexicanas, the members of the discussion group unearthed information about a Mexican woman's organization that had published an underground newspaper during the 1910 Revolution: *Hijas de Cuauhtemoc*.[10] The discovery was momentous, as Nieto-Gomez indicates:

> . . . it was like I had been in a cave and someone has just lit the candle. I [suddenly] realized how important it was to read about your own kind, the women of your own culture, or your own historical heritage, doing the things that you were doing. [It] reaffirmed and validated that you're not a strange, alien person, that what you're doing is not only normal but a part of your history. . . . So then they became our models, our heroes. And to carry on the tradition, we used their name in the newspaper. (1991, Tape IVA5)

Discovering the history of the Mexicana feminist group did more than provide a name for the group and the newspaper they began publishing in January 1971. It also provided legitimacy in the face of increasingly hostile responses from the men in the Chicano movement (which will be discussed later). Many of the original members of *Hijas* eventually became leading figures in the emergent Chicana movement, and were also involved in launching the first major national Chicana studies journal, *Encuentro Feminil*.[11]

The Asian American movement, much like its Chicano/a counterpart, was fueled by the growing consciousness among the largely first-generation college students. And like many activists in the Chicano movement, students organized both on the campuses and in their communities. The Vietnam war, in particular, radicalized many Asian American students. In Los Angeles, a group of these radicalized activists broke off from the more conservative "Oriental Concern" organizational structure (which initially grew out of a 1966 youth conference) and instead formed a grassroots organization, Asian American Political Alliance (AAPA).

The focus and constituency of AAPA was broad and included groups as diverse as "Asian Hardcore," a group of gang members and ex-convicts, and "Asian Sisters," which focused on drug-abuse intervention for young women. Committed to meeting the needs of the community, the young people established a Service Center in Little Tokyo and ran a variety of programs, particularly focused on health needs (harper 1992). While engaged in reformist activities, they were also busy developing their own revolutionary consciousness. Several activist women, like Miya Iwataki, joined the Community Workers Collective, and started an experiment in communal living. Members of the collective worked in the community by day and discussed politics at night, even as they were ready to rush out to deal with emergency drug overdoses. Their activities in these various contexts set the stage for the evolving feminist consciousness and agenda of the women, as Iwataki recounts:

> When you work with ex-gang people and elderly men—they are the most chauvinistic. If you have a mind of your own and there are things you want to accomplish, there is no way you cannot fight for women's liberation, too. It was an evolutionary thing. To be told by people, "We're going out to do field work, you stay here and answer the phones"—so much work to be done in those days. We had to stand up for ourselves. (Iwataki 1991, Tape IB6–7)

In meetings among the different groups of women, they discussed their own situations. Not surprisingly, it was not only their relationships with the men in the movement that they explored, but also the particular ways in which they experienced and internalized racialized sexism:

> In the first informal groups, women began talking about years of scotch-taping eyelids to create a double eyelid fold and then carefully painting in over with Maybelline eyeliner. Women began to break through years of checking out each other as competition for

Asian men; of fearing being found out that one was not a virgin; or having to be anything but a "natural woman." (Iwataki 1983, 36)

Although these activists later read and discussed white feminist works like *Sisterhood is Powerful* (1972), they mainly sought their feminist inspiration from the women involved in the revolutionary struggles in China and Vietnam, and even adopted some of the language of the Chinese, e.g. dubbing patriarchal practices and beliefs "feudal."

American Indian women also looked to their own cultural roots for the source of their strength, but their feminist trajectories appear to be different than those of the Chicanas and Asian American women. Despite the long history of separate Indian women's organizations dating back to the 1920s, the members of the newer generation who were active in the American Indian movement community of the late 1960s and early 1970s did not form their own women-centered groups until considerably later. They did engage in informal networking, like the potlucks held by the women connected with AIM and the Alcatraz occupation, and later the meetings and conferences held by women professionals involved in education and social services (Cotrell 1991b).

These women's gatherings apparently aroused the same kind of suspicion among American Indian men as they did among Chicanos, and the same critique about their divisiveness was forwarded by the men.[12] However, while the men's suspicion served early on to spur some Chicana *femenistas* to form autonomous groups like *Hijas*—even as the *Hijas* women continued to work with the men in the larger movement groups—the outcome was different for American Indian women. For one thing, given the history of Indian peoples in the United States, the slogan calling for Indian sovereignty played a major role in the strategy for Indian self-determination. And while it might have served to unify diverse tribes, it might also have served as a deterrent to criticizing tribal policies, and by extension, the male leadership of the American Indian movement community. As Rayna Green pointed out, the "Native American" women activists themselves did not know how to react to the 1980 Supreme Court decision that tribal sovereignty took precedence over women's equality:

We debate whether such [tribal] rules are traditional with Indian cultures or whether "imported" from European "patriarchal" traditions. And we debate whether we should attack Native tradition the way majority feminists have attacked their own. . . . If we tamper with things, some of us think we'll be worse off then ever. . . . The double bind of race and sex is too real. Two powerful words—tradition and equality—do battle with one another in Indian country. But whose versions of tradition and whose version of equality should we fight for? (Green 1982, 172)

Even when a women's group like Women of All Red Nations (WARN) was eventually formed in 1978 as an "arm" of AIM, or when women held their historic Ohoyo Conference in 1979, the criticism of Indian men and of sexism, as Sharon Cotrell points out, remained oblique (Cotrell 1995). At the same time, the matrilineality that characterized so many Indian people's past provided the women a form of indigenous feminism which they quickly grasped. This seemed to serve both to empower the women and to silence the men's criticisms—especially in light of the way that "traditional" Indian culture was being valorized in the process of decolonization. Nothing illustrates this better than the 1977 retort by a Mohawk woman to the lament of a middle-aged man about the passing of the old days and the increasing number of women running for tribal council:

I'm certainly for a return to the old ways. In the old days the women in my tribe ran things, and in some tribes they still do. So bring back the old days. (Green 1982, 172)

Recounting the incident, Rayna Green, a leading Indian feminist writer, comments:

My friend and I are delighted. Her speech isn't exactly the opening shot of the revolution, but it puts Indian women where I don't always believe we are—squarely in the feminist consciousness. (Green 1982, 172)

In many ways, 1977 marks a turning point in Indian women's activism, as native women delegates from around the country gathered at the National Women's Conference in Houston. Despite tremendous enthusiasm about the opportunities this gathering offered, leading activists like Green expressed grave concerns about the problems of pulling together an assembly of all Indian women in attendance at the conference:

Tribal differences and the press of other life—and death—issues may rob us of what majority feminists call "sisterhood," we worry. "Perhaps," I say, "but Indian women will be seen and heard in the context of the Women's Movement." Bring on the new days. Bring on the new days. (Green 1982, 172–173)

The Indian women did pull together, issued a Manifesto to the conference (later published in *Ms.*), and began to lay plans to form a new national women's organization. Two years later, Ohoyo (the Choctaw word for woman) was formally founded and established a resource center in Tahlequah, Oklahoma, with a grant from the Women's Education Equity Act program. By the time Ohoyo, together with the North American Indian Women's Association, sponsored a national conference in 1981, "Indian Women at the Crossroads," Indian women had planted themselves firmly in the women's movement. The flowering of an Indian feminism was evident not only in the proliferation of autonomous women's groups in the late 1970s and early 1980s, but also in the burst of publications on, about, and by Indian women.

### Challenging Women's Subordination

All of the groups discussed above drew on their daily life experiences, including race and class oppression, and focused largely on their survival needs. In their own ways each was also engaged in challenging women's subordination, although this may not have been articulated as their primary goal. For the ANC Mothers, the focus was on the ruling establishment, and went to the heart of the definition of gender roles. Others, as a result of their activities in raising women's issues, found themselves confronting not only white, male, patriarchal values, but also the men in their own communities and movements. While the Chicana and Asian American activists were often embroiled in rather combative relationships, the American Indian women usually trod more lightly.

The women in the ANC Mothers were solidly rooted in their own community, but in contrast to the American Indian, Chicana and Asian American women activists, they were not allied with the civil rights or nationalist movements of their community. Indeed, as the grassroots movement grew and was incorporated into the structure of the emergent National Welfare Rights Organization, these groups increasingly cut across the various movements and communities. The welfare mothers, from the beginning, were focused on getting respect and what was due them, and this brought them into direct confrontation with the welfare bureaucracy. At the local welfare office in Watts, for instance, Tillmon and her band of welfare mothers in ANC Mothers were viewed as a cantankerous watch-dog force that was acknowledged, respected, and even feared.

It is difficult to determine how many of the grassroots leaders of the earliest welfare-rights groups had a vision that extended beyond their immediate goals, but it is clear that from the start Johnnie Tillmon did. She believed that welfare mothers should be trained and receive an education in order to get decent jobs, if they wanted; and that publicly funded child care was absolutely vital. She came up with a child care model which, as she later discovered, closely resembled the original kib-butz design; a place where the children would be kept during the week, especially for the mothers who were working as live-in domestics. The demand for control over their lives appears in later statements of the NWRO, and is a recurring theme in the Tillmon oral history, focusing on the right to stay home and be full-time mothers, with a guaranteed income for their social-reproductive roles (prefiguring the later argu-ment of Wages for Housework); or the right to be trained and gain employment, and have the necessary services available.

Like other poor women and most women of color, Tillmon felt that "the" women's liberation movement did not address the bread-and-but-ter issues so critical to welfare recipients. At the same time, she began to build alliances with it, particularly by 1972, when she wrote her now famous, "Welfare Is a Woman's Issue" for *Ms.* magazine. Playing on the stereotypes of the women's liberation movement, she nevertheless makes clear in her oral history that what was at stake was survival, not privilege:

> Most of the women in women's liberation groups were white women. Most of the welfare recipients were also white women. . . . The women's liberation part, they don't want to wear no bras, they don't want to wear no girdles, they was concerned about men opening the door, that kind of stuff. That isn't where our heads were. Our heads were—do we have a door; do we have money to buy a bra to put on, or panties. . . . Our thing was survival. (Till-mon 1991, Tape VE6–7)

Their movement, which was largely run by and for women, did also include men. In fact, the founder of the national organization was a man, George Wiley, and so were many of the original staff. However, even as many of the male staff members continued in the organization, the women soon became the dominant force. By all accounts, they held their own.[13] And while they might have engaged in some confrontations with the men on gender issues, or on class issues with national leaders like Martin Luther King, these seem to have been largely asides.

For the American Indian women, too, the skirmishes with the men seemed to be treated like minor annoyances, and they generally tried to smooth the waters by legitimizing their gender interests with historical precedents. Group unity was critical in the face of the continued racism and genocidal practices of the U.S. government, like the sterilization of an estimated one-fourth of Indian women. As a result, even as the women began to form their own groups and develop an agenda focused on their gender interests, they framed most issues in terms of group survival and tribal rights (WARN 1980; Ohoyo 1981).

The June 1979 WARN International Year of the Child Conference, which was viewed an "an attempt, from a traditional Native perspective, to identify the many problems—the very threat to survival—currently facing the future generations," included a workshop on sterilization abuse, midwifery and natural healing, and herbal medicine (WARN 1980, 1). A thread running through this conference and continuing through subsequent Indian women's gatherings was a dual focus on education and spirituality. Oftentimes, these were integrated, for instance in "The Women's Dance: A Women's Health Course for Native American Women," which focused on traditional concepts of womanhood as well as practical steps to educate women on gynecological complaints, sexuality, and herbal medicine.

The need for unity in the face of continuing assaults on Indians made it particularly difficult for women to deal with issues such as sexual assault perpetrated by Indian men. In 1979, rape was reported to be the number one crime on the Navaho reservation (Allen 1986). And although the ultimate blame was placed squarely on the effects of colonization, Indian women did begin to mobilize around the issue of spousal and child abuse, forming groups like the White Buffalo Calf Society as early as 1977. By 1983, even WARN, a group that had skirted conflicts with male leaders, showed a greater willingness to focus on gender and to promote women's leadership. When Gail Sullivan, a longtime AIM supporter, expressed surprise at this unexpected turn, WARN leader Madonna Thunderhawk retorted, "after all, we are feminists" (Sullivan 1983, 79–80).

While the change in organizing and in agendas was evolving towards a more feminist orientation among reservation-based and/or -focused Indian women, a similar turn was occurring among the more highly educated, urban, professional women, particularly those involved with education and social services, in which Indian women played central, leadership roles. Following their successful caucusing at the 1977 Houston conference, and the establishment of the Ohoyo Center, and particularly with the assistance of Women's Equity Action grants, these women began to produce educational materials and to host conferences. And while the handful of highly published women like Rayna Green and Paula Gunn Allen came to represent Indian feminism for many white women, the conferences gave voice to many more. Kate Shanley, for example, wrote, it "was a returning home . . . taking my place beside other Indian women . . ." (Shanley 1995, 416).

Survival remained a basic theme for Indian women, and running through all the literature and through the interviews of several activists is the theme of both physical and cultural survival. This dual struggle also meant fighting multiple oppressors, as so eloquently elaborated by Paula Gunn Allen:

> To survive culturally, American Indian women must often fight the United State government, the tribal governments, women and men or their tribe or their urban community who are virulently misogynist and who are threatened by attempts to change the images foisted on us over the centuries by whites. (Allen 1986, 93)

Fighting the misogyny of the men in their own communities and movements, as well as the racialized sexism of white society, was a task in which Chicana and Asian American women activists also engaged—even as they, too, worked on basic survival issues in their communities. And while their agendas seem to have had many parallels, their experiences with and responses to their male activist counterparts differed.

Even if the fears about divisiveness expressed mostly by male leaders were legitimate, it is important to note that in the Chicano movement potential differences based on class or regionalism were largely ignored, while battle lines were drawn when it came to gender issues. Women like Anna Nieto-Gomez and her *femenista* cohorts were labelled *vendidas* (sell-outs), and worse (Garcia 1989; Nieto-Gomez 1974). For instance, when Nieto-Gomez ran for the presidency of *MEChA* at CSULB in 1969, she was hung in effigy and a tombstone was erected bearing her name and the names of several other outspoken women.

Arguments raged in the Chicano movement between those who were embraced as *loyalistas* (i.e., women in the forefront of the Chicano movement who by their actions were feminists, but who toed the party line that women should wait until the Chicano won *his* liberation) and the *femenistas* who were excoriated for being "Anglicized."[14] Faced with this charge, the *femenistas* legitimized their ideas by turning to their Mexicana history. Their allusion to groups like the original *Hijas de Cuauhtemoc* was a particularly powerful defense in light of how extensively the Chicano movement as a whole drew its imagery from Mexican history. As Nieto-Gomez explains:

> It made it more like a national issue as opposed to an individual issue—which made us feel less selfish. Because it took us a while to feel comfortable in talking about ourselves as women and women's problems because they were always being minimized and diminished; they were always being viewed as something that was petty. . . . (Nieto-Gomez 1991, Tape IVA6)

The young women who founded *Hijas* were concerned about the problems that this first generation of Chicana college students faced, including racialized sexism, reproductive issues and the paucity of sex education, and the sexual politics of the student movement, coupled with financial and social/family pressures. Seeking to understand the causes of drug use, on the one hand, and a high drop-out rate, on the other, the activist women uncovered a high incidence of pregnancy and of self-performed abortions among these students. In response, they became involved in providing social support and services to other Chicanas, and some participated in the late 1960s underground abortion movement at one of the local churches. At the same time, they were trying to secure a better future for other Chicana college students by recruitment and retention programs and by introducing a Chicano/a curriculum. While their focus began on their own campus, their activities were broadened through regional Chicana feminist organizing. Eventually, members of *Hijas* were drawn into playing a leading role in the national dialogue among Chicanas.

At the same time that they were organizing among students, the early activists in *Hijas* remained rooted in their community, working with welfare mothers in East L.A, in the community in nearby Hawaiian Gardens, and with the Long Beach La Raza Center. They maintained and expanded their ties to community-based groups, such as the East L.A. Welfare Rights Group, Catolicos for La Raza, Comision Feminil and, after they left the college campus in the early 1970s, with various *Teatro* groups. In addition to their persistence in raising women's issues in the larger Chicano movement, members of *Hijas* initiated the publication of the first Chicana feminist journal, *Encuentro Feminil,* in 1974; they introduced courses on women in the newly developed Chicano Studies programs; and they began to develop the new Chicana scholarship.

The Asian American women activists shared the dual focus of the Chicanas, working both on the college campuses to develop courses on women, and in the community to address women's immediate needs. As one of the activists explained, everyone was busy doing community organizing as well as women's theory (Quon 1984). The range of activities in which the Asian women activists were involved and the number of different groups they formed in the late 1960s is staggering.[15] And so was their broad constituency. Asian Sisters, for instance, attempted to combat drug addiction and prostitution among young women by working to raise their self-esteem through feminist consciousness. The Asian Women's Center was designed to reach out to Asian women of all ages in the community, while the Little Friends Playgroup established a day-care center in collaboration with Chinese immigrant women in China-town. A media group developed a traveling multimedia program on Asian American women's history and oppression, including skits on abusive date situations.

While many of the educational programs developed by the new generation of activists in other movements were frequently addressed to their own peers or to a white Anglo audience, the Asian American women's theatrical group also attempted to address their parents' generation, even going to service organizations such as the Japanese American and Chinese American Rotary club meetings. The highly energetic group of women wrote regularly for the Asian activist newspaper *Guidra* and produced two special issues in 1971 and 1972.

Like the Chicana *femenistas,* the Asian American feminists in Los Angeles remained firmly anchored in the larger movement. But in contrast to the Chicanas, their focus on women was not perceived as a parallel, women's movement. Rather, they incorporated their fight against misogyny into all aspects of their work in the Asian American movement. For instance, the decision of three women activists to move into the Community Workers Collective reflected the women's determination to force activist men to confront their sexism twenty-four hours a day.

The women were incredibly daring and undaunted in their confrontations with men. They directly intervened to extricate women from gang activity and/or life on the streets and when men were abusive toward women. For instance, if a parent or friend called Asian Sisters about a young woman in a motel somewhere, two women would jump into a car, go to the room and take the woman out of the situation. Afterwards, they would arrange counseling and try to get her involved in community work instead of drug use/dealing and prostitution (Iwataki 1991).

Perhaps taking their cues from the Chinese, whenever any of their male cohorts behaved inappropriately, the women "jammed up" a man, i.e. three or four of the women pinned him against a wall as they criticized his behavior. Miya Iwataki, one of the activist women leaders, recounts a rather dramatic incident in which a young woman came to one of the communes seeking comfort and protection from a boyfriend who had beat her up again. The women's study group happened to be meeting and in a spontaneous burst they decided to go as a group to confront the man, a young thug who had a reputation as a dangerous gang member. Frightened, but nevertheless determined, the women first explained to him why his behavior was wrong and why he had to change. According to Iwataki, "even the most meek and quiet ones" then set upon him, each striking a blow or kicking him as a statement of solidarity and to emphasize the seriousness of the issue. Much to their relief, he took the blows without defending himself. After that, word went out on the street: "Don't mess with the women anymore" (Iwataki 1991).

The men might have been more responsive to the women's critiques because of their shared admiration of the Vietnamese and Chinese Communist revolutionaries. In any event, by the late 1960s, all mixed-gender organizations in the Asian American activist community in Los Angeles reportedly had a strong women's presence in the leadership (Nishio 1993).

### Whose Feminism?

The thumbnail sketches of the activism and consciousness of the women and groups highlighted here are by no means definitive, nor are they meant to supplant the very sorely needed histories of these groups by the participants. Rather, they are a way to concretize some of the problems we face as historians trying to replace the old, hegemonic model. We have no doubt that the conventional narrative history of contemporary women's movements does not work. But what happens if we use our formulation to try to write a new one? In different voices, Anna Nieto-Gomez, Miya Iwataki, Johnnie Tillmon, and the other women interviewed all expressed their alienation from the white women's movement. They felt that it did not deal with survival issues and was not relevant to them.

Today there is a new language used by many women of color that emphasizes a feminism rooted in their own experiences and positionality. And while some Black women like bell hooks claim the feminist label, others feel more comfortable adopting Alice Walker's "womanist" identification (Walker 1983, xi–xiii; hooks 1984). And while some Chicanas have consistently used the *femenista* label which, from the beginning, set them apart from the white women's movement, many are now adopting the more differentiated feminist consciousness implied in Ana Castillo's "xicanista" (Castillo 1995).

This language might provide important tools for writing a much more expansive and inclusive chapter of current feminist activism/consciousnesses, but it does not necessarily provide a solution to the dilemmas faced in writing the past history. We must still ask if we are distorting the experiences and histories of the groups we have been discussing here by incorporating them into a narrative that includes the various white women's movement groups? Does it make sense, for instance, as Maylei Blackwell has asked, to include groups like "Redstockings" (a radical feminist group that repudiated the family as the site of women's oppression), alongside Chicana *femenistas* who organized with their families as a base? Though Chicanas may have struggled within the family over its patriarchal character, this did not detract from their commitment to it and their belief that it was basic to their cultural and racial/ethnic survival.

When we asked our narrators how they fit into a more broadly conceived history of the women's movement, most were still ambivalent. The memory of their alienation, and particularly their disdain for what they viewed as more frivolous issues, still weighed heavily. Living the intersection of race, gender, and class, many resented what they perceived as "the" women's movement's single-minded focus on gender, and the gender separatism that often resulted from this analysis. For, regardless of the differences they had with the men in their movements, activist women of color remained aligned with them. And although not all of the activists were from poor backgrounds, their ties to their communities made class issues paramount.

For many Chicana and Asian American activists, the earlier repudiation of the feminist label was a political statement. Instead, like the women in *Hijas*, many refashioned feminism in their own image. And although they took much of their inspiration from their own historical roots and were busy creating their own literature, they also read and discussed the literature of "the women's movement," particularly the essays in *Sisterhood is Powerful*. Indeed, some of their activities and groups in the late 1960s look like those of the women involved in the white women's-liberation movement. However, what most clearly differentiates them from the white feminist activists is that they remained anchored in their own communities/movements, where they worked together with the men—even as they repudiated their misogyny—on issues of cultural, racial/ethnic and economic survival.

Anna Nieto-Gomez's expansive description might most appropriately capture the way in which both the *femenistas* and the Asian American women activists straddled their own ethnic/national movements and the women's movement:

Yea, yeah, there was a Chicana women's movement. It was part of the larger women's movement that was going on in the United States. It was part of the Chicano Movement and it was part of the Civil Rights Movement that was going on and a part of the institutional changes that were going on at the time. . . . (Nieto-Gomez 1991, Tape IVF6)

And, we might add, the birth of both these movements fits into the same historical time frame of the 1960s.

By comparison, Johnnie Tillmon and her welfare-mothers' group preceded them, and the American Indian women's groups seemed to evolve a women's agenda considerably later. These two groups, in very different ways, and in contrast to the Chicanas and Asian American activists of the late 1960s and early 1970s, might best be characterized as representing "hidden gender insurgencies." For the ANC Mothers, their demand amounted to a call for self-determination, i.e. for the conditions that would enable them to choose whether they would stay home or become wage earners. As noted earlier, Tillmon also repudiated the white women's movement, but by 1972 her "Welfare is a Woman's Issue" was a clarion call to the women's movement to include poor women's issues. Although her response was terse when I asked if the welfare mothers should be considered part of the women's movement, it clearly demonstrates her own criteria—the very same criteria espoused initially in defining feminist research: "Well, welfare rights, the organization itself was started by women, of women and for women" (1984, Tape IA, 1). There is documentary evidence to support the feminist visions of the Chicana and Asian American activists, but none remains for the earliest activities of the ANC mothers. This makes it difficult to assess if the consciousness revealed both in Tillmon's oral history and in her 1972 article also characterized the early ideas of the group.

The American Indian women, despite the much later emergence of a clear women's agenda, from the start used their own indigenous imagery—particularly of the "strong woman"—to articulate what might also have been a "hidden gender insurgency." Like the Chicana and Asian American activists, their gender interests could not be separated from their ethnic/national identities; and because of the unique situation of the indigenous people in the United States, the women had to tread more softly, and slowly. The later emergence of a clearer agenda and espousal of Indian feminism might be suggestive of earlier activities that were largely hidden from view—activities that might be uncovered only through many more interviews.

The oral histories of women involved in these movements, and particularly our dialogue with them about the meaning of their activism, might help to avoid violating the historical integrity of their activism. But we must still ask if we can safely use the individual experience to represent the group. The question is not necessarily resolved by turning to written documentary sources. All too often, the literature that was published was penned by the very same women whose stories we have been collecting. We must also keep in mind that during this time period government funding heavily influenced how groups publicly articulated their goals. Obviously, interviewing as many former participants as possible is important, though still not a solution, since those who can be located are usually the ones who remained more visible and, hence, more traceable.

The inclusion of action in our definitional framework takes some of the edge off our discomfort, to the extent that it captures not only the articulated analysis of leaders, but the practice of followers, too. The invasion of welfare offices by groups like ANC Mothers, demanding their right to choose their future, and the willingness of the Asian American activists to take direct action in confronting sexism in their community, testify to the agendas of both groups to challenge women's subordinate status and to empower women. Even if all the members of her local group might not have conceived of their confrontations with establishment bureaucracy in Johnnie Tillmon's language of self-determination, the very nature of their acts asserted it, as did those of the Asian American activists. So, too, the underground abortion network in which members of *Hijas* participated, and the workshops that gave American Indian women the tools to control their own fertility, including how to resist involuntary sterilization.

Once we concede the plurality of "feminismS"—and the differences among them, captured so well in some of the new language used by Afra-Americans and Chicanas—and abandon the investment in the conventional one-sided history of "the women's movement," there remains the difficult task of figuring out how to "do" a new kind of history. How can we avoid compartmentalizing each group, on the one hand; or blending them to such an extent, on the other hand, that very real differences both between them and with the white women's movement are submerged.

Indeed, forwarding a construct of feminism of women of color (Lee 1995), or of Third World feminism (Sandoval 1991), promotes the same kind of oversimplified unitary view of feminism that the conventional three- or four-fold typology of the white women's movement does. And while it might be appropriate in reconceptualizing and writing feminist theory, it might actually distort the lived activism of community-based groups. In fact, the kind of "differential" mode of consciousness that Sandoval claims as the mode "enacted by Third World feminists over the past thirty years" (1991, 12) has marked the organizations and activities both of *different* women of color and of white women. This "differential" mode of consciousness—the non-exclusive embrace of different forms of consciousness identified by Sandoval as equal-rights, revolutionary, supremacist, and separatist—seems to represent little more than the kind of fluid strategies adopted, sometimes simultaneously, by activists on the ground. For while individuals and groups might have had a defined ideological stance—which has become the basis for the tripartite distinction, also captured in Sandoval's taxonomy—their *actions* and programs were responsive to the immediate needs of women and were not as distinct as their ideologies. For example, the socialist, anarchist, and radical feminists who staffed both the Crenshaw and Venice

Women's Centers in Los Angeles in the early 1970s were extensively involved in social services for women, i.e. reformist activities. These ranged from rape counseling to abortion counseling to workshops on "doing your own divorce." Similarly, the Asian American women's groups discussed here might best be characterized as espousing a socialist ideology. Yet they, too, engaged in providing services to women in the community, ranging from health screening to drug intervention.

Furthermore, when we start to redo the history and look at organizing strategies, we find evidence of coalition work across racial-ethnic and class lines taking place in the community well before the 1977 Houston conference. Chicanas, Asian Americans, American Indians and Anglo-Europeans often came together to act in concert around very specific issues. In Los Angeles, in the early 1970s, these included demonstrations against the forced sterilization of Chicanas at Los Angeles Country General Hospital; fund-raising for the defense of Joanne Little, the African American woman who stabbed her jailor to death when he attempted to rape her, and for Yvonne Wanrow, the native woman who was being tried for killing the man who tried to abuse her children; and demonstrating support at the trial of Esther Lau, a Chinese woman who was assaulted by a police officer when she was stopped on a Los Angeles freeway.

Indeed, when we listen carefully to the activists who were challenging women's subordination in a host of ways, what we hear are multiple voices that sometimes sound like a cacophony, and other times are in harmony. At times each one may be saying something jarringly different; other times it might sound more like variations on the same theme; and occasionally the voices may come together, perhaps even using the same notes. I can conceive of how to do this as performance, but to write it is more daunting. Perhaps that is another reason that the first generation to write the history of both nineteenth- and twentieth-century feminism has settled into complacency and not tackled the problems inherent in producing a more complicated, multilayered history. The task might best be left to the new generation of feminist scholars who are developing a language and style that might better communicate this more nuanced understanding—a generation whose understanding of historical processes is not tied up with their own direct experience and the sense of "ownership" that this seems to have engendered.

## Notes

1. See Sandoval 1991; King 1994; Wolfe and Tucker 1995.
2. See Siefer 1973; West 1981; Giddings 1984; Chow 1987; Garcia 1989.
3. This conference was convened by the National Commission on the Observance of International Women's Year (appointed by President Ford in 1975 in response to the IWY conference in Mexico City). Regional conferences were held in all fifty states, where delegates were elected to attend the national meetings.
4. Siefer 1976; Bookman and Morgen 1988b; Naples 1991a; West 1990; West and Blumberg 1990.
5. This definition was developed over the course of four years and in concert with others who participated in the Women's Oral History seminars from 1991–1995 as cited below (see note 7).
6. At the historical juncture being discussed here, the Asian Pacific Islander, or Asian Pacific American identifications were not yet current. And, among Indian activists, American Indian has been the preferred designation, Native American being viewed as a construction created by white liberals and academicians.
7. Each of the collaborators gave me feedback on early drafts of this paper, but they cannot be held responsible for the particular articulation of the ideas presented here, including the ways in which I used the materials. I have tried to weave their reactions and comments into the text, and have added some additional comments in the endnotes regarding points they wished to emphasize. In addition to the direct contributions of the three named collaborators, other students have greatly influenced my thinking, particularly Julie Bartolotto, Vivian Deno, Rubi Fregoso-U, Ken Garnet, Cris Hernandez, April Johnson, Karen Jackson, and Chanzo Nettles.
8. UMAS, founded in 1967, was supplanted by MEChA (*Movimiento Estudantil Chicano de Aztlan*) in 1969, following a national conference in Santa Barbara. El Plan de Santa Barbara, issued out of this conference, eschewed a hyphenated identity and embraced Aztlan and Chicano identity, leading to the change of name.
9. The sources vary in regard to the group's original name. It was either *Las Chicanas, Las Hermanas, Mujeres de Longo,* or *Las Chicanas de Aztlan.*
10. The historically correct spelling of the name is Cuauhtemoc, but it is often spelled Cuahtemoc.
11. Although it was the first journal edited by the new *femenistas* (Ana Nieto-Gomez and Adelaida del Castillo were the co-editors), there was at least one precedent; a feminist paper, *Mujer Moderna,* published in the early part of the twentieth century in Texas by Andrea and Teresa Villarreal (Cotera 1976, 68).
12. These same tensions over women's discussion groups undoubtedly also surfaced in the Asian American movement, but they are not foregrounded

in any of the interviews, either with the several women activists or with one of the men. This might be a result of the way these particular Asian American activists looked to both Vietnam and China in defining their politics.

13. West 1981. This was also confirmed in a personal conversation with Tim Sampson, one of the key staff people in the NWRO.

14. This scenario was played out dramatically at the first national Chicana conference (*La Conferencia de Mujeres por la Raza*) in Houston, Texas, in May 1971. The *loyalista/feminista* categories were devised by Nieto-Gomez, who believed that the only difference between the two groups of women was in how the men targeted them (Nieto-Gomez 1974).

15. Karen harper adds: "At least three informal study/discussion groups with non-hierarchical leadership and fluid membership worked hard on consciousness-raising, theory, and development of actions. Formal groups then formed to carry out needed actions. In other words, both formal and informal groups operated simultaneously and influenced each other."

Chapter 2

# Women's Culture and Lesbian Feminist Activism*

## *A Reconsideration of Cultural Feminism*

## Verta Taylor and Leila J. Rupp

The rise of cultural feminism within the U.S. women's movement, according to the current feminist orthodoxy, spelled the death of radical feminism. Because cultural feminism is based on an essentialist view of the differences between women and men and advocates separatism and institution building, it has, say its critics, led feminists to retreat from politics to "lifestyle." Alice Echols, the most prominent critic of cultural feminism, credits Redstockings member Brooke Williams with introducing the term *cultural feminism* in 1975 to describe the depoliticization of radical feminism. "Cultural feminism is the belief that women will be freed via an alternate women's culture. It . . . has developed at the expense of feminism, even though it calls itself 'radical feminist.'"[1] Since 1975, denunciations of cultural feminism have become commonplace. From all sides—from socialist feminists, Black feminists, postmodern feminists, and especially from radical feminists who reject cultural feminism as a betrayal of their early ideas—come charges that cultural feminism represents the deradicalization and demobilization of the women's movement.[2] In Echols's (1989, 6) words, "radical feminism was a political movement dedicated to eliminating the sex-class system, whereas cultural feminism was a countercultural movement aimed at reversing the cultural valuation of the male and the devaluation of the female."

Implicit in most discussions of cultural feminism is the centrality of

*Originally published in Signs, vol. 19, no. 1., 1993, pp. 32–61. Reprinted by permission of the authors and the University of Chicago Press.

lesbianism to the process of depoliticization. The critique of cultural feminism sometimes is a disguised—and within the women's movement more acceptable—attack on lesbian feminism. By *lesbian feminism*, we mean a variety of beliefs and practices based on the core assumption that a connection exists between an erotic and/or emotional commitment to women and political resistance to patriarchal domination. Cultural feminism's three greatest "sins"—essentialism, separatism, and an emphasis on building an alternative culture—are strongly associated with the lesbian feminist communities that grew up in U.S. cities and towns in the 1970s and 1980s. Brooke Williams, herself lesbian, identified the development of cultural feminism with the growth of lesbianism; later critics have strengthened this association. Echols (1989, 44) sees cultural feminism as growing out of lesbian feminism but modifying it, "so that male values rather than men were vilified and female bonding rather than lesbianism was valorized." In the context of the 1980s "sex wars"—the struggle over sexual expressiveness and regulation between, on one side, feminists who emphasized the dangers of sexuality and the need to fight pornography as a form of violence against women, and, on the other side, those who stressed its pleasures—cultural feminism came to stand for an "antisex" variety of lesbian feminism.[3] Although lesbian voices are among those raised in condemnation of cultural feminism, the boundary in common usage between cultural feminism and lesbian feminism is highly permeable, if it exists at all.

Our goal here is to reposition what has been called "cultural feminism" as one tendency within dynamic and contested contemporary U.S. lesbian feminist communities. By shifting our focus from the ideology of cultural feminism to concrete social movement communities, we make explicit the central role of lesbians in what is often euphemistically called the "women's community," and we emphasize that a movement's culture is more than a formal ideological position.[4] To understand the culture of any group requires attention to the contexts in which it is produced, so we turn our gaze to the communities that give birth to "women's culture."

Lesbian feminist communities in the United States are made up of women with diverse views and experiences. They encompass "cultural feminists"—significantly, this is not a label that any women, as far as we know, apply to themselves—and their critics, as well as "antisex" and "pro-sex" feminists and separatists and antiseparatists. In contrast to critics who view lesbian feminist communities as embodying the evils of cultural feminism, we see the debate over essentialism, separatism, sexuality, and so on taking place within these communities. As Jan Clausen (1992, 9) has pointed out, even critics of the racism and Eurocentrism of "the women's community" remain identified with it.

Our intent is not to defend the ideological position that has been described as "cultural feminism," but to change the terms of the debate by focusing on the consequences for feminist activism of lesbian feminist culture and communities. We identify four elements of lesbian feminist culture that promote survival of the women's movement during periods of waning activity: female values, separatism, the primacy of women's relationships, and feminist ritual. The culture of lesbian feminist communities both serves as a base of mobilization for women involved in a wide range of protest activities aimed at political and institutional change, and provides continuity from earlier stages of the women's movement to the future flowering of feminism. Rather than depoliticizing the radical feminist attack on the multiple roots of women's oppression, lesbian feminist communities preserve that impulse.

Our argument is shaped by historical analyses of women's culture and by theories of social movement continuity. From a historical perspective, Echols's and others' indictment of cultural feminism is curious, given that women's culture and intimate bonds between women have generally played a benevolent role in the development of the women's movement.[5] As Estelle Freedman (1979) explains in her classic article "Separatism as Strategy," the decline of the U.S. women's movement in the 1920s can be partly attributed to the devaluation of women's culture and the decline of separate women's institutions. And Blanche Cook (1977) argues persuasively that female networks of love and support were vital to women's political activism in the early twentieth century. Although no monolithic women's culture has developed across lines of race, class, and ethnicity, women involved in a wide array of collective action—from food riots in immigrant neighborhoods, to labor strikes, to protests against the lynching of African American men, to suffrage demonstrations—have shaped oppositional cultures that sustained their struggles.[6] These women were motivated by what Nancy Cott (1989) has distinguished as three forms of consciousness: feminist consciousness, female consciousness, and communal consciousness.[7] The lesbian feminist culture we explore here is such an oppositional culture.

Recent work on social movements by sociologists also points to a positive relationship between the culture of lesbian feminist communities and the persistence of feminist activism. Focusing on the 1960s, scholars have documented the role that preexisting organizations and activist networks from earlier rounds of protest played in the emergence of all of the so-called new social movements, such as the civil rights, student, and gay rights movements. These studies illuminate the importance of researching movements in differing stages of mobilization and in various organizational forms. To conceptualize periods of the U.S. women's movement that previously have been overlooked, we draw on the concept of "abeyance stages" in social movements (Taylor 1989). The term *abeyance* depicts a holding process by which activists sustain protest in a hostile political climate and provide continuity from one stage of mobilization to another. Abeyance functions through organizations that allow members to build their lives around political activity. Such groups ensure the survival of a visionary core of the movement, develop a strategy or project for realizing the movement's vision, and allow activists to claim an identity that opposes the dominant order. We see lesbian feminist communities as fulfilling this function for the radical branch of the women's movement in the 1980s and early 1990s.

The argument we develop here is based on preliminary research for a larger study of lesbian feminist communities and on our own extensive participation in the Columbus, Ohio, lesbian feminist community. Although we use published movement writings, formal and informal interviews with members of various communities, and participant observation in Columbus and at national events, we see this article as less an empirical study than a conceptual piece.[8] Our perspective is, of course, shaped by our identities as white, middle-class, academic lesbians immersed in the issues we discuss. But we try to use our experience to reproduce for nonparticipants the flavor of involvement in a lesbian feminist community. Much of what we report will be familiar to other participants, even those from quite different communities. Columbus is a noncoastal but urban community where developments in New York, Washington, D.C., Boston, San Francisco, and Los Angeles are played out later and on a smaller scale. In that sense, Columbus both reflects national trends and typifies smaller communities that have been less studied by feminist scholars.[9]

### Lesbian Feminist Communities: A Movement in Abeyance

The late 1960s and early 1970s brought the full flowering of both the liberal and radical branches of the women's movement. Radical feminism—which is what concerns us here—emerged as women within the civil rights movement and the New Left (the antiwar and student movements) began to apply a leftist analysis to their own situation as women. In contrast to "politicos" who thought that a socialist revolution would automatically liberate women, radical feminists blamed both capitalism and male supremacy for women's oppression and conceptualized women as a "sex class." With its use of consciousness-raising and dramatic "zap actions" designed to expose sexist practices, radical feminism had a profound effect on both leftist politicos and liberal feminists. But increasingly the concept of a sex class foundered on differences of race, class, and sexuality among women (Spelman 1988; Gordon 1991b).

No issue proved more volatile than sexuality. The surfacing of the "lesbian question" in both the liberal and radical branches of the women's movement resulted in part from the gay/lesbian liberation movement emerging in the late 1960s, and paved the way for the emergence of lesbian feminist groups such as Radicalesbians in 1970 and The Furies in 1971. As more women came out as lesbians within the radical branch of the women's movement, radical feminism and lesbian feminism became conflated. Small groups that were motivated by the radical feminist vision and composed primarily of lesbians sprang up in a variety of locations, including, by the 1980s, smaller communities, especially those with major colleges and universities.

Since the 1970s, feminists who view fundamental change as necessary to the eradication of male domination have faced an increasingly unfriendly social milieu. The civil rights movement and New Left, which gave birth to the radical branch of the women's movement, began to ebb in the 1970s, while the gay liberation movement was, like the other '60s movements, more congenial for men than for women. As liberal feminism became more institutionalized, explicit antifeminism emerged in the late 1970s as a major foundation of the ultraconservative New Right; the election of President Ronald Reagan reflected the influence of that countermovement. The early 1980s saw the failure of the Equal Rights Amendment to the U.S. Constitution and increasing challenges to reproductive freedom. That, and complacency among some young women who saw no further need for feminism, prompted the media gleefully to proclaim the death of feminism.[10] The heyday of the contemporary women's movement gave way, by the early 1980s, to a period of abeyance. Most recently, the media-fanned attack by conservatives on "political correctness" and multiculturalism has targeted radical feminism. Given all this, what critics of cultural feminism have portrayed as deradicalization can be viewed instead as survival in a climate of backlash and declining opportunities.

Since 1980, the women's rights branch of the women's movement, forming policy networks at the national and local levels, has gained influence in such traditional arenas as electoral politics, academic institutions, and the professions (Boles 1991). At the same time, the alternative institutions founded by early radical feminists—including rape-crisis centers, battered women's shelters, bookstores, newspapers, publishing and recording companies, recovery groups, support groups concerned with health and identity issues, spirituality groups, restaurants and coffeehouses, and other women-owned businesses—have increasingly come to be driven by the commitment of lesbians and women in the process of coming out. Women find in this world a social context supportive of lesbian relationships and identity that was unavailable in early feminist organizations or in the predominantly male gay liberation movement. This is not to say that feminist counterinstitutions are solely the preserve of lesbians. The commonly used term *women's community* emphasizes access for all women even if feminist institutions fail to include women of every race, class, and sexual identity. Nevertheless, the base of mobilization of the "women's community" stems primarily from interpersonal networks and organizational ties in the lesbian world.[11]

The history of the Columbus community illustrates developments at the national level and provides a model of the kinds of institutions, organizations, and events that undergird the lesbian feminist community.[12] The radical branch of the women's movement in Columbus emerged in 1970 out of Women's Liberation at Ohio State University, made up of women from the civil rights and New Left movements. This group fought for changes on campus, including the establishment of a Women's Studies program. In 1971, it sponsored a consciousness-raising group that gave birth to the Women's Action Collective, an off-campus umbrella organization that became the heart of the women's community. The collective sheltered a variety of groups, including Women Against Rape, the Women's Co-op Garage, Lesbian Peer Support, Single Mothers' Support Group, *Womansong* newspaper, and Fan the Flames Feminist Book Collective. A large proportion of early Women's Action Collective members were lesbian; more members came out throughout the 1970s until the collective was almost entirely lesbian. Outside the Women's Action Collective, women in Columbus formed Central Ohio Lesbians; the Women's Music Union, which produced feminist concerts; and Feminists in Self-Defense Training, which grew in part out of the self-defense workshops sponsored by Women Against Rape. Heterosexual women found the local chapter of the National Organization for Women (NOW) a haven for radical feminist activity; in what became a local cause célèbre, five NOW members were arrested in 1979 for spray-painting antirape slogans on a freeway sound barrier covered with misogynist graffiti.

By the late 1970s, Women Against Rape had come to dominate the Women's Action Collective, largely as a result of a major grant from the National Institute for Mental Health for a community rape-prevention project. This grant, which paid indirect costs to the collective, funded a paid staff and the rental of a house in the university area for offices, meeting rooms, and a bookstore. As Women Against Rape expanded its operations and grew in size, a number of other original collective groups dissolved. At the same time, the late 1970s and early 1980s witnessed the start of a variety of short-lived feminist organizations and two enduring ones, the Child Assault Prevention project (spawned by Women Against Rape) and Women's Outreach to Women, a twelve-step recovery group. But in the increasingly antifeminist climate of the early 1980s, both members and funds began to disappear. The end of the grant that had catapulted Women Against Rape to local (and national) prominence had dire effects on the entire community. When the Women's Action Collective found itself devoting more time to maintaining the house than to engaging in political activity, its remaining members moved to a smaller space in 1983, and a year later disbanded the collective.

But these changes meant abeyance and not death for the lesbian feminist community. Women Against Rape and Fan the Flames Feminist Book Collective (which moved from the Ohio State campus area to a downtown location and, in early 1993, to a neighborhood with a relatively high lesbian population) survived the death of their parent organization and continue to thrive, as has Women's Outreach to Women, which sponsors groups for incest survivors as well as for women recovering from substance abuse. The Child Assault Prevention project developed into the National Assault Prevention Center, based in Columbus, and the Women's Music Union continued to produce feminist concerts until 1990. In 1990, a revived Take Back the Night march to protest violence against women (an annual event in the late 1970s) led to the establishment of an ongoing Take Back the Night organization. A lesbian support group, Sisters of Lavender, continues; a Lesbian Business

Association publishes a local lesbian newsletter entitled *The Word Is Out!;* lesbian mothers and lesbians hoping to bear children have formed a group called Momazons that has launched a national newsletter; and members of the lesbian feminist community have moved into pro-choice and lesbian/gay community organizations. For example, Stonewall Union, central Ohio's gay/lesbian advocacy group, has had lesbian feminists as president, executive director, and head of its antiviolence project in the 1990s.

What this history suggests is that the lesbian feminist community is characterized by a shifting core. In Columbus, the nucleus of the community moved from the university women's liberation group, to the university-area Women's Action Collective, to the more focused Women Against Rape and Women's Outreach to Women; perhaps Take Back the Night is in the process of becoming a new core. The organizations and the personnel have changed, but the basic character of lesbian feminist culture has remained. Thus the demise of a radical feminist organization may represent less the "death" of radical feminism than a movement of members and resources to a new local movement core.

In a climate of increasing political opposition, decreasing funding, and lower levels of mobilization, the Columbus community never lost sight of its political goals. Rape-prevention workshops, which might have become a depoliticized community service, continued to interpret rape as a "pillar of patriarchy" and to advocate strategies to prevent rape as a means of knocking out one support of the system (Community Action Strategies to Stop Rape 1978). Even the growth of the recovery movement and a turn to feminist spirituality, associated by critics of cultural feminism with a sacrifice of politics for lifestyle, did not depoliticize the community. Lesbian feminists devoted to recovery from incest or substance abuse, for example, argued the political ramifications of their work (Direen 1991). And when the Women's Action Collective newsletter appeared in the fall of 1982 with a new title, *Womoon Rising,* whose explanation was suffused with references to matriarchy and spirituality, the change met with resistance from collective members who insisted that a "Womoon . . . certainly doesn't sound like a political activist" (*Womoon Rising* 1982). The newsletter ceased publication soon after its change of title; feminist spirituality may have sparked heated debates, but it never replaced politics in the Columbus community.

## The Culture of Lesbian Feminist Communities

Lesbian feminist communities do show signs of the essentialism, separatism, and "lifestyle politics" that cultural feminism's critics view as anathema to radical feminism. But a closer examination of the ideas, separatist strategies, primary relationships, and symbolic practices of community members reveals that these elements of lesbian feminist culture are what sustain and nourish feminist activism.

### Female Values

The question of whether women are fundamentally different from men is central throughout the women's movement. Although a variety of individuals and groups assert the existence of "female values," this position is closely associated with contemporary lesbian feminists, who are more forthright than earlier feminists in proclaiming the superiority of women's values over men's. This is also the aspect of cultural feminism that is most disputed, in part because the notion of universal female values sits uneasily with the recognition of differences among women.

Critics of cultural feminism denounce belief in female values as essentialist, that is, based on biological determinism. According to Linda Alcoff (1988, 408), "cultural feminism is the ideology of a female nature or female essence reappropriated by feminists in an effort to revalidate undervalued female attributes." Some lesbian feminists do see female values as linked to women's biological capacity to reproduce, but others take a social-constructionist position and attribute differences between female and male values to differences in women's and men's socialization and prescribed roles. Explanations aside, belief in fundamental differences between female and male values permeates lesbian feminist communities. Indeed, this emphasis on difference serves to justify the existence of a "women's community."

Lesbian feminists find support for the belief in female values in a large body of scholarly and popular writing that valorizes egalitarianism, collectivism, an ethic of care, respect for knowledge derived from experience, pacifism, and cooperation as female traits. In contrast, an emphasis on hierarchy, oppressive individualism, an ethic of individual rights, abstraction, violence, and competition are denounced as male. Not all such works are written by lesbian women or by women who would identify with the lesbian feminist community, but they nevertheless set forth positions embraced by lesbian feminists.[13]

Exposed to these intellectual debates through books, periodicals, and Women's Studies classes, lesbian feminists often find support for their belief in superior female values. Even women who intellectually reject the notion of male and female difference are apt to use *male* as a term of derision. It is common in the Columbus community to hear everything from controlling and aggressive behavior to impersonal relationships and hierarchical organizational structures characterized in casual conversation as "male." Our point here is that while most lesbian feminists do not embrace biological explanations of sex differences, such a drawing of boundaries between male and female values promotes the kind of oppositional consciousness necessary for organizing one's life around feminism.

### Separatism

Lesbian feminist communities advocate both separatism as strategy and separatism as goal (see Frye 1983; Hoagland and Penelope 1988), but it is total separation from men as an end in itself that has proven most controversial and that has given the impression that radical feminism has evolved into a politics of identity. Some groups have attempted to withdraw from all aspects of male control by forming self-sufficient rural communes, but these are the exceptions. Critics of such total separatism point to the race and class bias inherent in the assumption that women want to and can separate from men in this way (Jagger 1983; hooks 1984).

In general, however, the lesbian feminist community endorses temporally and spatially limited separatism. The Columbus Women's Action Collective statement of philosophy asserted plainly that "the work of the women's movement must be done by women. Our own growth can only be fostered by solving our problems among women."[14] Often men, and even male children over a very young age, are explicitly excluded from participation in groups and events. Some early lesbian feminist communes included male children but barred them from decision making and social events on the grounds that "male energy" violates women's space. This tradition continues at the annual Michigan Womyn's Music Festival in Hart, Michigan, where male children over the age of three are not permitted in the festival area but must stay at a separate camp. Men were not permitted to attend any sessions at the National Lesbian Conference in Atlanta in 1991 (Stevens 1991). In Columbus, the annual Take Back the Night march welcomes men at the kickoff rally but permits only women to march—a source of ongoing controversy. Supporters of this policy maintain that women gain a liberating sense of power specifically from separating from men for the march, reclaiming the right to walk the streets at night with no vestiges of male "protection."

The importance of such limited separatism is asserted even by critics of total separation from men and boys. Lesbian women of color, working-class lesbian women, and Jewish lesbian women with an interest in working politically within their own racial, class, and ethnic communities argue for separate space to organize and express solidarity apart both from men and from lesbian women who are white or middle-class or Christian.[15] The very structure of the National Women's Studies Association embodies separatism as strategy: caucuses for women of color, lesbian women, Jewish women, and working-class and poor women reflect women's different and competing interests. The need for this kind of organizing within the lesbian feminist community was illustrated at the National Lesbian Conference in Atlanta, at which women of color caucused separately in an attempt to make the conference deal more directly with issues of racism (Sharon, Elliott, and Latham 1991). Separatism in the lesbian feminist community has thus come to mean organizing around one's identity.

Many participants in lesbian communities consider the women's movement their primary allegiance but work actively in movements for gay and lesbian rights, AIDS education and advocacy, Latin American solidarity, environmental causes, peace, animal rights, reproductive freedom, and labor unions, and movements against racism, apartheid, and nuclear weapons. Nevertheless, separatist events and caucuses remain important for women who are disenchanted with the politics of the mainstream; separatism is a means of both drawing sustenance and maintaining feminist identity.

### The Primacy of Women's Relationships

Lesbian feminist communities view heterosexuality as an institution of patriarchal control and lesbian relationships as a means of subverting male domination. Relationships between women are considered not only personal affairs but also political acts, as captured in the often repeated slogan, "Feminism is the theory and lesbianism is the practice."[16] The statement of philosophy of the Columbus Women's Action Collective, for example, defined lesbianism as a challenge to male domination.[17] It was no accident that the coming out of a large number of radical feminists in Columbus coincided with the founding of the Women's Action Collective and Women Against Rape. That lesbian women were central in the antirape movement undoubtedly shaped the feminist analysis of rape as an act representing one end of the continuum of what Susan Cavin (1985) calls "heterosex."

For some community members, lesbianism is defined by overriding identification with women and by resistance to patriarchy rather than by sexual attraction to or involvement with women. Rich's (1980) classic article "Compulsory Heterosexuality and Lesbian Existence" introduced the notion of the "lesbian continuum," which embraces women who resist male control but are not sexual with women. Earlier writers had also accepted what were originally known in the movement as "political lesbians." Ti-Grace Atkinson (1973, 12), for example, denounced married women who engaged in sexual relations with women as "collaborators" and praised women who had never had sex with women but who lived a total commitment to the women's movement as "lesbians in the political sense." More recently, Marilyn Frye (1990), in an address to the 1990 National Women's Studies Association conference entitled "Do You Have to Be a Lesbian to Be a Feminist?" equated lesbianism with rebellion against patriarchal institutions.

Lesbian feminist communities indeed include some women who are oriented toward women emotionally and politically but not sexually; they are sometimes referred to as "political dykes" or "heterodykes."[18] Some are women in the process of coming out, and some are "going in," or moving from lesbian to heterosexual relationships. For example, singer and political activist Holly Near (1990) explains in her autobiography that she continues to call herself lesbian even though she is sometimes heterosexually active because of the importance of lesbian feminism as a political identity. In the same vein, a feminist support group sprang up in 1989 at Ohio State University for "Lesbians Who Just Happen to Be in Relationships with Politically Correct Men." What is significant is that lesbian identity is so salient to involvement in the women's community that even women who are not, or no longer, involved sexually with women claim such an identity.

Most lesbians are, of course, erotically attracted to other women, and a strong current within the community criticizes those who downplay sexuality. The popularity of lesbian sex expert JoAnn Loulan, who spoke to a large and enthusiastic audience in Columbus in 1991, signals that the erotic aspects of lesbian relationships have not been completely submerged (Loulan 1990). The "sex wars" of the early 1980s have spawned an assertively sexual style on the part of some members of the lesbian feminist community (Stein 1989; Echols 1991). Advocates of sexual expressiveness, including champions of "butch-femme" roles and sado-masochism (S/M), challenge the less sexual style of what S/M practitioners call "vanilla lesbians" and denounce any notion of "politically correct" sex (see, e.g., Califia 1981; Dimen 1984). The lines are explicitly drawn by the very titles of the periodicals associated with each camp: *off our backs*, the classic radical feminist newspaper, now confronts the magazine *On Our Backs*, with its sexual "bad girl" style. But the role of politics in structuring relationships is undisputed, even for those who emphasize sexual pleasure over the use of (hetero)sexuality as a means of social control of women.

In other words, the lesbian feminist community includes both women who emphasize relationships between women as a form of political resistance and women who stress the sexual pleasures of lesbianism. The sex wars are fought within the community over who best deserves the label "feminist." Although advocates of lesbian S/M and associated sexual practices experience exclusion from some community events, the nature of lesbian sexuality is contested openly at community conferences and in movement publications (Califia 1981). Even smaller communities have been affected by the national debate. In Columbus, when a gay bar placed ads featuring S/M imagery in a local gay/lesbian publication, lesbian members of Columbus's women's S/M group, Briar Rose, came to blows, metaphorically, with antipornography lesbian feminists offended by the depiction of what they perceived as violence.

Lesbian feminist communities make explicit—and sexual—the ties that bind women. The contemporary antifeminist charge that one "has to be a lesbian to be a feminist" is in an odd way an acknowledgment of the central role that lesbians play in the contemporary women's movement and that women with primary bonds to other women played in earlier stages of feminism. Women's relationships are especially crucial to the maintenance of the women's movement when mass support for feminism ebbs; such bonds tie together groups of women who are unlikely to find acceptance for their relationships outside the movement. Furthermore, lesbian feminist communities provide fertile ground for recruiting young lesbian women into feminism. Thus, the relationship between activism and woman-bonding (lesbian or otherwise) is a symbiotic one: women with primary commitments to other women find support within the women's movement and, in turn, pour their energies into it.

### Feminist Ritual

Among lesbian feminists, both public and private rituals are important vehicles for constructing feminist models of community and expressing new conceptions of gender. Public rituals are local or national cultural events such as concerts, films, poetry readings, exhibitions, plays, and conferences. Most prominent nationally is the annual Michigan Womyn's Music Festival, a five-day celebration that attracts several thousand women for musical performances, workshops, support groups, political strategy sessions, "healing circles," and the sale of woman-made crafts, clothing, and other goods. The National Women's Studies Association (NWSA) conference is another annual cultural event; it goes far beyond the usual parameters of an academic conference by providing a forum for feminist performances and by featuring open and often highly charged debate over issues central to the women's movement.[19] Dozens of specialized national and regional conferences and festivals take place each year. Other local events, such as antiviolence marches and pro-choice rallies, occur in much the same way in different communities. Publicity in national publications and participation in national demonstrations foster a common culture of protest across the country; chants and songs, for example, spread from one community to another. Lesbian feminist events in Columbus mirror those in both larger and smaller communities. The Women's Action Collective for many years sponsored an annual Famous Feminist Day to raise money and educate the community about feminist foremothers; Stonewall Union or Women's Outreach to Women bring nationally known performers to town (as the Women's Music Union did until 1990); the Lesbian Business Association puts on an annual Ohio Lesbian Festival; and Take Back the Night continues to sponsor an annual march and rally.

What is known among contemporary feminists as "women's culture"—women's music, literature, and art—plays a central role in recruiting women and raising their feminist consciousness. Musicians such as Meg Christian, Holly Near, and Sweet Honey in the Rock, as well as dozens of other feminist performers, have introduced issues as well as songs to communities across the country. For example, in Columbus as in other areas, Near introduced the lesbian feminist community to sign language interpretation of concerts. Now no feminist—or even mainstream—event is without such interpretation for the hearing-impaired. Likewise, Christian brought discussion of alcoholism and the recovery movement to the Columbus community by performing such songs as "Turning It Over" and talking of the Alcoholism Center for Women in Los Angeles. And Sweet Honey in the Rock exposed Columbus audiences composed primarily of white women to an Afrocentric perspective and African American history and culture. Women in local communities read many of the same lesbian novels and poetry and listen to the same music. At the 1979 gay/lesbian march in Washington, women at the rally joined in to sing and sign when lesbian performers came on stage, while gay men in the crowd, lacking such unifying rituals, seemed to wonder how all of the women knew the words.

Private ritual or the politicization of everyday life is, in many respects, the hallmark of the lesbian feminist community and the most damning aspect of cultural feminism in the eyes of its critics. Through the tenet that "the personal is political," every aspect of life—where one lives, what one eats, how one dresses—can become an expression of politics (Hanisch 1978). The sale at feminist bookstores, conferences, concerts, and festivals of feminist T-shirts, jewelry (especially labryses), books, music, and bumper stickers means that women can adorn and surround themselves with their politics.

The most significant displays challenge conventional standards of gender behavior that subordinate women. In the early years of lesbian feminism, comfortable, practical, less "feminine" styles of dress, unshaved legs and armpits, and extremely short hair were de rigueur. Although flannel shirts, jeans, and boots are no longer a uniform, the dominant mode of presentation is still unisex or what Holly Devor (1989) has termed a deliberate "gender blending." In the Columbus community, attire at cultural events has changed markedly over the past fifteen years. What was once a fairly monolithic crowd has become more diverse. Although most women remain "gender blended," some appear in leather and mohawks and some in skirts, lipstick, and long hair. At one feminist event, billed as "Girls Just Want to Have Fun," members of the community participated in a fashion show, albeit one that included political commentary on style. The use of the term *girls* (previously anathema), the emphasis on fun rather than serious politics, the reference to a mainstream popular song (Cyndi Lauper's "Girls Just Want to Have Fun") rather than women's music, and attention to clothing, including traditional women's attire, all marked this event as a new departure for the community.

Such changes in self-presentation are in part a consequence of the sex wars and in part an expression of the preferences of working-class women, women of color, and young women. "Antifeminine" styles associated with the downplaying of sexuality are under attack from advocates of sexual expressiveness who sometimes adopt fashions associated with the sex trade (Stein 1989). "Pro-sex" lesbian feminists sport high-heeled shoes, short skirts, low-cut tops, and other items of clothing denounced by "antisex" lesbian feminists as the paraphernalia of oppression. In addition, some working-class women and women of color criticize the "politically correct" styles of the dominant faction as an imperialist imposition of white, middle-class standards. And young lesbian feminist women have brought their own ideas on fashion and self-presentation, including the grunge and punk styles, to the community.

The intensity of the debate over cultural expression is an indication of the significance of ritual for distinguishing who is and is not a feminist—just as lesbian women historically have developed cultural codes to identify one another while remaining "hidden" to the mainstream culture that stigmatized them (see, e.g., Faderman 1991). Feminist ritual reaffirms commitment to the community and openly embraces resistance to the dominant society. Thus, what Echols and other critics of cultural feminism have denounced as a "profoundly individualistic" retreat to lifestyle does indeed have political consequences (Echols 1989, 251).

### Conclusion: The Political Functions of Lesbian Feminism

Our reconsideration of cultural feminism in the context of lesbian feminist communities suggests a number of interpretations that run counter to the standard view. First, cultural feminism, as it has been defined by its critics, represents just one ideological position within lesbian feminist communities. Second, these communities have forged a rich and complex resistance culture and style of politics that nourishes rather than betrays the radical feminist vision. Third, the dynamics of lesbian feminist communities are shaped at least in part by the politics of the Right that dominated the period of abeyance or maintenance in which the women's movement found itself in the 1980s. And, finally, the lesbian feminist community intersects with many contemporary struggles for political and institutional change and carries a feminist legacy that will shape the future of the women's movement itself.

In our earlier collaborative work on the U.S. women's rights movement in the period from 1945 to the 1960s, we argued that a small group of white, well-educated, economically privileged old women, primarily recruited to the women's movement during the suffrage struggle, greatly influenced the resurgent liberal branch of the women's movement. We showed that the women's rights movement that hung on in the doldrum years provided activist networks, the ultimately unifying goal of the Equal Rights Amendment, and a feminist identity that maintained a focus on women's subordination. Yet this group of committed feminists sustained their vision in a homogeneous community that did not and could not attract women of color, working-class women, or young women. Although the women's movement that blossomed in the 1960s differed in fundamental ways from the more limited women's rights movement that preceded it, the legacy, both positive and negative, of that early activism lingered (Rupp and Taylor 1987).

In the same way, lesbian feminist communities both sustain the women involved in them now and also have consequences for the next round of mass feminist activism. Perhaps a new wave of the women's movement is already taking shape; witness the ground swell of outrage at Anita Hill's treatment in the U.S. Senate confirmation hearings for Supreme Court Justice Clarence Thomas in October 1991, and the huge turnout for the pro-choice march on Washington, D.C., in April 1992. Since the presidential election of 1992 and the passage of antigay/lesbian legislation in Colorado, the National Organization for Women has decided to make lesbian and gay rights a priority in the 1990s.[20]

Our discussion of the culture of lesbian feminist communities has emphasized how belief in female difference, the practice of limited or total separatism, belief in the primacy of women's relationships, and the practice of feminist ritual create a world apart from the mainstream in which women can claim feminism as a political identity. At the same time, of course, the ideas and practices of lesbian feminist communities can exclude potential participants. Most heterosexual feminists may not find the lesbian world congenial. The association of feminism and lesbianism, as several scholars have found, alienates some young heterosexual women from feminist identification.[21] Our experience suggests that there is, even among older women, a widespread sense of the "lesbianization" of the women's movement. The revelation by Patricia Ireland, president of the National Organization for Women, that she lives with a "female companion" undoubtedly reinforced that perception (Minkowitz 1992). One feminist quoted in the Washington Post commented on the public view of NOW as "a gay front group" (*off our backs* 1992a). Participants at the 1992 NOW conference report that it had the feel of a lesbian conference. The 1992 Bloomington (Indiana) Women's Music

Festival offered a workshop on "Networking for Straight Women in a Lesbian World."[22] At the local level, one lesbian-affirming heterosexual Columbus woman went to a local NOW meeting with a profeminist male friend involved in a men-against-rape group and reported feeling completely unwelcome because of her association with a man. Equally important, the dominance of white, middle-class, Christian women creates barriers to the achievement of a truly multicultural lesbian feminist community despite the ongoing community dialogue about race, class, ethnic, and other differences. As Judit Moschkovich, a Jewish Latina, put it, the assumption that she should reject her Latin culture means accepting "the American culture of French Fries and Hamburgers (or soyburgers), American music on the radio (even if it's American women's music on a feminist radio show), not kissing and hugging every time you greet someone" (Moschkovich 1981).

Our point is not that the lesbian feminist community is a pure expression of radical feminism. Rather, we want to highlight its political and transformative functions. A wide variety of struggles have been influenced by the involvement of lesbian feminists or by ideas and practices characteristic of the community (Whittier 1991, esp. chap. 7). Direct action movements concerned with peace and other issues have adopted from the lesbian feminist community a view of revolution as an ongoing process of personal and social transformation, an emphasis on egalitarianism and consensus decision making, an orientation toward spirituality, and a commitment to shaping present action according to the values desired in an ideal future world (Epstein 1991; *off our backs* 1992b). Similarly, the ongoing dialogue in the lesbian feminist community about diversity has carried over into the gay/lesbian movement, and the radical feminist analysis of rape shapes the struggle against anti-gay/lesbian violence (Vaid 1991). Further, the AIDS movement has been driven by the radical feminist definition of control of one's body and access to health care as political issues (Hamilton 1991). Lesbians also have played a leading role in the development of the recovery movement for survivors of incest (Galst 1991). In short, lesbian feminist cultures of resistance have had political impact not only by sheltering battle-weary feminists, but also by influencing the course of other social movements.

Finally, lesbian feminist communities affect a younger generation of women who hold the future of the women's movement in their hands. In our research on women's rights activists of the 1940s and 1950s, we found these women longing for "young blood" but unwilling to accept the new ideas and new strategies that young women brought with them (Rupp and Taylor 1987). An aging generation of activists may always long for fresh recruits who will be drawn to their cause but will not change anything about their movement; such an inclination, in part, lies behind the cultural clash between Meg Christian fans and Madonna devotees within the lesbian feminist community.[23] The next round of the women's movement is likely to take a different course, but it will not be untouched by the collective processes, consciousness, and practices of lesbian feminism. One of the major mechanisms of transmittal is Women's Studies, which mobilizes young women who identify as feminists.[24]

Some young activists identify themselves as a "third wave" of feminism, thus making a connection to the first two waves and at the same time claiming responsibility for a new resurgence. "I am not a postfeminism feminist. I am the Third Wave," writes Rebecca Walker (1992, 41), a student at Yale University and a contributing editor to *Ms.*[25] Already we can see elements of change and continuity in the activities of a new generation. Young lesbians attracted to the gay/lesbian protest group Queer Nation, for example, reject the tradition of nonviolence and female pacifism when they adopt the "Queers bash back" response to violence against lesbians and gay men. At the same time, the formation of women's caucuses in Queer Nation and the AIDS activism group ACT-UP echoes the struggles of earlier generations of women within male-dominated organizations.[26] Lesbians engaging in direct action tactics are transforming the face of activism. In Columbus, female Queer Nation members, in a protest reminiscent of the early radical feminist zap actions, have engaged in kiss-ins at local shopping centers and the city zoo as a means of challenging heterosexual privilege. The Lesbian Avengers, founded in New York City in 1992, engage in "creative activism: loud, bold, sexy, silly, fierce, tasty and dramatic" ("Dyke Manifesto" 1993). In their first action, they marched into a Queens, N.Y., school board meeting to the tune of "When the Dykes Come Marching In" and handed out lavender balloons inscribed "Ask about Lesbian Lives" to first graders to protest the board's refusal to allow a multicultural curriculum that included discussion of lesbians and gay men ("Dyke Manifesto" 1993; Jule and Marin 1993).

In the climate of the 1980s and early 1990s, then, the culture of lesbian feminist communities has not just served to comfort, protect, and console activists in retreat. It also has nourished women involved in myriad protests, both within and outside the women's movement, whose vision of feminist transformation goes beyond political and economic structures to a broad redefinition of social values. Rather than squelching mobilization, we see lesbian feminist communities as sustaining the radical feminist tradition and bequeathing a legacy, however imperfect, to feminists of the future.

**Authors Note:** We are full coauthors and have listed our names in reverse alphabetical order. We would like to thank Phyllis Gorman and Kelly McCormick for helpful discussions of current developments in the Columbus lesbian community; Nancy Whittier, whose contributions to this article are legion; Myra Marx Ferree, Mary Margaret Fonow, Roberta Ash Garner, Susan M. Hartmann, Joan Huber, Carol Mueller, Laurel Richardson, Barbara Ryan, and Beth Schneider, whose comments on earlier drafts were extremely helpful; the participants in the conference "New Theoretical Directions in the Study of the Women's Movement," Aarhus, Denmark, October 28–November 1, 1990, for fruitful discussions of this research; the anonymous reviewers for *Signs*, whose comments helped us immeasurably in the long process of revision; and Kate Tyler for her perceptive editorial work.

### Notes

1. Williams 1978, 79 cited in Echols 1989, 301. Restockings was a radical feminist action group founded in New York City in 1969. On cultural feminism versus radical feminism, see also Echols 1983a, 1983b, 1984.
2. For a critique of total separatism from a socialist feminist perspective, see Jaggar 1983; for a black feminist critique of the race and class bias of cultural feminism, see hooks 1984; for postmodern critiques, see Alcoff 1988—juxtaposing the cultural feminist and poststructuralist answers to the problem of defining the category of women—and Young 1990—rejecting the ideal of "community" as unable to encompass difference. For attacks on cultural feminism as a betrayal of radical feminism, from a radical feminist perspective, see Willis 1984; and Ringelheim 1985.
3. The "sex wars" became a national issue after the 1982 "Scholar and the Feminist IX" conference at Barnard College, New York City. The conference, which focused on women's sexual autonomy, choice, and pleasure, included speakers who advocated sadomasochism, sexual role-playing, and pornography, provoking an attack by Women against Pornography, Women against Violence against Women, and New York Radical Feminists.

See the discussion and bibliography in Vance (1984, 441–53); and see Segal and McIntosh 1993. The two major feminist anthologies associated with the "pro-sex" position (Snitow, Stansell, and Thompson 1983; Vance 1984) both included essays by Alice Echols in which she looked critically at the development of cultural feminism; see Echols 1983b, 1984. See also Echols 1991.

4. Our thinking on movement culture is influenced by Rick Fantasia's (1988) study of emergent cultures of resistance within the labor movement.

5. The basic positions on the nature of women's culture and its relationship to feminism are clearly stated in an exchange between Ellen DuBois and Carroll Smith-Rosenberg (DuBois et al. 1980). DuBois defines women's culture as "the broad-based commonality of values, institutions, relationships, and methods of communication, focused on domesticity and morality and particular to late-eighteenth- and nineteenth-century women" (29). For her, women's culture and feminism stand in a dialectical relationship. In contrast, Smith-Rosenberg questions the use of the term women's culture to describe the acceptance of mainstream cultural values and insists that a culture must have "its own autonomous values, identities, symbolic systems, and modes of communication" (58). Eschewing the word *culture*, she argues that feminism cannot develop outside a "female world" in which women create rituals and networks, form primary ties with other women, and develop their own worldview (61).

6. Scholars of African American and working-class women, in particular, have rejected the notion of a universal women's culture. But their evidence suggests that various groups of women—enslaved African American women, mill workers, and working-class housewives—did create "women's cultures," albeit multiple ones that often supported men of their groups. See Hewitt 1985. See Pascoe 1990 for a recent work that attacks the idea that there is a women's culture based on women's values.

7. Feminist consciousness involves a critique of male supremacy, the will to change it, and the belief that change is possible. (Cott 1989 draws on Gordon 1986, 29, in defining feminist consciousness). Female consciousness, which Cott bases on Kaplan's (1982) exploration of working-class food protests and strikes, is rooted in women's acceptance of the division of labor by sex. Communal consciousness is based on solidarity with men of the same group. Feminist consciousness is necessarily oppositional, while female and communal consciousness can support the status quo or can lead women to engage in a variety of kinds of protest.

8. Written sources include books, periodicals, and narratives by community members, and newsletters, position papers, and other documents from lesbian feminist organizations. We also have made use of twenty-one indepth, open-ended interviews with informants—from Provincetown, Boston, and the rural Berkshire region of western Massachusetts; Portland, Maine; Washington, D.C.; New York City; St. Petersburg, Florida; Colum-

bus, Yellow Springs, Cleveland, and Cincinnati, Ohio; Minneapolis; Chicago; Denver; and Atlanta—conducted between 1987 and 1989, mostly by Nancy E. Whittier (1988) but also by Verta Taylor (Taylor and Whittier 1992). In addition, we have both been a part of the lesbian feminist community in Columbus since the late 1970s, have attended national events such as conferences, cultural events, and marches in Washington, D.C., and have over the past fifteen years informally interviewed lesbian feminists in a variety of communities across the country. All of these interviews were conducted with the understanding that quotations would not be attributed to named individuals.

9. Columbus is the largest city in Ohio, the state capital, and the home of the largest university campus in the country, Ohio State University. The lesbian feminist community is overwhelmingly, although not exclusively, white and middle-class, with a large proportion of students and professionals. Most scholarship on the women's movement focuses on developments in large cities. See, e.g., Cassell 1977; Echols 1989; Staggenborg 1991; Ryan 1992. A notable exception is Krieger 1983.

10. See, e.g., Bolotin 1982; Friedan 1985; S. Davis 1989; Ebeling 1990.

11. The concept of "social movement community" comes from Buechler 1990.

12. This discussion is heavily indebted to Whittier 1991. In addition, we draw on other unpublished research on Columbus, including Haller 1984; Matteson 1989; Dill 1991; Wilkey 1991; Gorman 1992; McCormick 1992. Finally, our account is shaped by our own involvement, since both of us were peripheral members of the Women's Action Collective and have attended meetings, marches, demonstrations, concerts, and community conferences for the past fifteen years.

13. See, e.g., Rich 1976; Walker 1983; Cavin 1985; MacKinnon 1987.

14. Women's Action Collective "Statement of Philosophy," adopted by consensus May 21, 1974, in the personal papers of Teri Wehausen, Columbus, Ohio.

15. See, for a variety of perspectives, Beck 1980; Moraga and Anzaldúa 1981; Hull, Scott, and Smith 1982; Smith 1983; Bulkin, Pratt, and Smith 1984; Lorde 1984a, 1984b; Anzaldúa 1990b; Trujillo 1991.

16. This statement is attributed to Ti-Grace Atkinson in Koedt 1973. Echols points out that Sidney Abbott and Barbara Love record the original version of this remark quite differently: in 1970, Atkinson addressed the lesbian group Daughters of Bilitis in New York and commented that "Feminism is a theory; but Lesbianism is a practice" (Abbott and Love 1972, 117; Echols 1989, 238). In any case, the phrase has been widely quoted within lesbian feminist communities.

17. Women's Action Collective "Statement of Philosophy."

18. Clausen 1990; Smeller 1992; Bart 1993.

19. The issue of racism within the organization blew apart the twelfth annual

NWSA conference, "Feminist Education: Calling the Question," held in Akron, Ohio, June 20–24, 1990. See Ruby, Elliott, and Douglas 1990.

20. Communication from Jo Reger, Columbus, Ohio, 1992.
21. See Schneider 1986, 1988; Dill 1989; Kamen 1991.
22. Communication from Suzanne Staggenborg, Bloomington, Ind., 1992.
23. Echols 1991; Yollin 1991; Starr 1992; Stein 1993.
24. Dill 1991; Houppert 1991; Kamen 1991.
25. At the American Sociological Association meetings in Cincinnati, August 23–27, 1991, a group of women issued a call for an ad hoc discussion of "third-wave feminism." See also Kamen 1991.
26. Faderman 1991; Hamilton 1991; Yollin 1991.

# Chapter 3

# Reconceptualizing Agency in Domestic Violence Court

## Judith Wittner

The movement to end violence against women has scored impressive victories over the past two decades. Had it not been for women's activism, there would be no recognition of violence against women as a social problem, no domestic violence legislation, no police assistance, few judges and lawyers willing to hear women's complaints or to offer even token remedies. Had it not been for this activism, there would be no made-for-TV movies about male violence against women, no reports on the nightly news about men who batter, no recognition that private violence is anything other than a personal problem. Alberto Melucci (1989, 79), writing on social movements, suggested that successful movements wrest policy-making from the exclusive control of professionals and the state. If the ability to enter into and affect debates on policy is a measure of movement success, then the battered women's movement is one of the most successful movements of our time (see Schechter 1982; Dobash and Dobash 1992).

In Chicago, the battered women's movement has pressured local and state authorities to redraft the laws on domestic violence, train police in domestic violence intervention, support shelters for battered women, and pursue the criminal prosecution of batterers. The media, the police, service providers, and women's own personal networks have helped to disseminate knowledge about new programs. Watching television, talking with case workers and counselors, and hearing reports from friends and family, women of working-class and poor communities gain access to new resources for challenging power relations: conceptual resources, such as the ability to call men's assaults "abuse" or to envision freedom from fear as a "women's right"; and institutional resources, such as hot lines, shelters, and legal services, which offer material support and technical assistance to women pressing for change (see Mansbridge 1993).

An important resource for Chicago women is a centralized domestic violence court that has jurisdiction over all cases of domestic assault and abuse that occur within the city limits. Between twenty- and thirty-thousand cases have come to this centralized court every year since 1984, when the court was established at the urging of feminist social workers, lawyers, and community activists, whose work often brought them face-to-face with battered and abused women. One of their central concerns was that police, lawyers, and judges failed to take seriously women's complaints of domestic violence. They knew from personal experience that women who called the police or went to court to press charges against husbands and boyfriends were usually denied relief. Police did not often take a woman's side when called to a violent dispute; lawyers and judges rarely counted men's actions as criminal. The activists discovered through trial and error that if women were accompanied to the police station or to court by someone who knew the law, officials were more likely to listen to their complaints. On the basis of this experience, they successfully lobbied for domestic violence cases to be brought to a central location staffed by lawyers and judges familiar with the law, and for a permanent place within the court as independent watchdogs and advocates for women. In January, 1984, the centralized domestic violence court opened for business and six feminist advocates, funded independently of the court, were allowed to set up an office on the premises.

The activists' proposal to create a centralized domestic violence court grew from their daily experiences on the job and in their communities. Their success in convincing members of the judiciary and the State's Attorney's office to implement the plan was the result of the emergence of violence against women as a political issue on a national scale, the activists' persistent pressure on the courts to treat domestic violence as a criminal offense, and possibly because a brewing scandal involving local judges who were accused of taking bribes made this proposal seem an attractive move toward reform. However, once it was established, the court did not automatically begin to function as an arm of the battered women's movement. Far from it. Many warrant officers, clerks, attorneys, and judges assigned to the court continued to view domestic violence as a welfare issue or a family problem and shared the popular notion that women were partly to blame for their own victimization (see

Ewing and Aubrey 1987; Ptacek 1988). Nor did the court offer women greater control over their cases. Under the criminal law, women with complaints became witnesses for the prosecution, not principals in their own cases. Additionally, the laws of evidence and the adversarial proceedings limited what women were permitted to say in court and suppressed what many complainants thought were crucial components of their stories. As women submitted to the round of interviews necessary to bring cases to trial, first with police, then with court clerks and lawyers, the experts expunged from the complaints whatever they believed to be irrelevant, out of bounds legally, or likely to displease the judge. In effect, women's accounts became the raw data which legal experts interpreted and fashioned into cases before the court.[1]

The marginalization of women in court was not simply the consequence of procedures that elevated legal professionals to center stage in processing complaints, but reflected power inequalities of race, class, and gender. Because women, as well as working-class, poor, and less educated groups, regularly use the lower courts to settle problems and resolve conflicts over personal relationships, gender, class, and cultural differences between these groups and court workers are not uncommon (see Merry 1990). This was certainly true in domestic violence court, where attorneys and their aides believed that many of the complaints they heard grew from family disputes and personal troubles that did not belong in a courtroom, that violence was a way of life for many of the people who used the court, and that they were being asked to do "social work," a waste of their time and professional training.[2]

But that is not the whole story. If domestic violence court and the criminal justice system silenced women, ignored and trivialized their complaints, and subjected them to its control, the court also became a resource which women used to their own advantage, an ally in their quest to establish control in relationships in which they had been relatively powerless. Once women discovered the court, many embraced the idea that private conflicts were public crimes and came to believe that they were entitled to the services the law provided. Despite the hegemony of legal discourse and professional authority in the courtroom, many wanted the right to tell their stories in public, authority to participate in the determination of punishments, and freedom to fashion courses of legal action suited to themselves rather than to the seemingly arbitrary demands of the judicial system. As a result, domestic violence court became an arena in which women and their advocates contested court workers' judgments about the seriousness of their cases and the correct courses of action as they pursued cases against the men who dominated and abused them.

This chapter describes the ways in which women used domestic violence court to help them restructure relations with men who threatened and beat them. The court's very existence, the expanded options it offered women, its public character, and its place as an arm of the state brought women together in a politically charged arena, one wrested by feminist activists from the criminal justice system. With or without an advocate to guide her through the system, each complainant in that courtroom had at her disposal a range of perspectives and tools, collectively constructed in a movement built on women's experience, which once did not exist for women opposing sexual violence. Some women had the additional assistance of advocates employed through the Network's project, whose job was to help them use the law to advance their safety and their interests, to plead their cause in the court, to hearten and encourage them along the way, and to help them establish lives outside of court that were free from violence and threat.

Here I describe how women made their way through the court alone and with advocates, and how their passage drew upon and contributed to the battered women's movement and to feminist politics. I undertook this study at the request of the advocates, who wanted to understand better why large numbers of women dropped cases. Court staff complained with a single voice about the problems caused by women who did not follow cases through to their conclusion, and advocates had little cause to question the lawyers' assumption that dropped cases were disastrous for women and for the criminal justice system. Many advocates worried that the high rate of dropped cases showed that domestic violence court was being undermined by the very population it was supposed to serve. This worry colored their work. They felt defensive and believed they had to account for the behavior of battered women. According to Peggy Luft,[3] now Director of the Uptown Center Hull House and midwife to the advocates' project, advocates felt "driven" to say, "'Please Mrs. Jones, please don't drop this case,' because in the back of their minds they're thinking, 'Oh God, another drop.'"

For eight months in 1993, I followed twenty women and two men as their cases proceeded through the court. I sat in on their interviews with police officers, advocates, and attorneys, returned to court with them for every hearing and, when possible, interviewed them about the final disposition of their cases. Occasionally, a defendant was willing to speak to me about his completed case. I also observed court proceedings in scores of other cases and spoke with court staff—clerks, sheriffs, judges, states' attorneys, victim-witness advocates, public defenders, interpreters, and social workers—about specific cases and about their views of the impact of the court and legal process on domestic violence. Peggy Luft and her colleagues in the court advocacy project had invited me to do this study, and my connections to the advocates were clear to everyone in the court. Attorneys and judges sometimes questioned me about a complainant or exhorted me to intervene to persuade a woman to continue with her case, as they might do with any advocate. The women I accompanied around the courthouse usually treated me as if I were an advocate, expecting to receive information, guidance, and emotional support from me. But in my ignorance of court practices I was for a time like the women who used the court, and for several months I spent my days in court with complainants so that I could see and experience the site as they did, and not as professionals, or even advocates, might.

## Women in Court

Domestic violence court is de facto a women's court. Although men bring charges against women and other men there, the vast majority of complainants are women, and most of their complaints concern abusive and violent men. Although the majority of the attorneys and judges present in court every day are men, there is a larger concentration of female prosecutors here compared even to other misdemeanor courts. Women also staff the court as sheriffs, police officers, interpreters, and social workers.

The physical presence of women in the court does not assure that women's perspectives on violence and the law will dominate the proceedings. Nor is it simple to discern just what a "woman's perspective" might be. Certainly, not all women in the courthouse shared a point of view. Many women who were state's attorneys, public defenders, clerks, and sheriffs viewed the court from the standpoint of the legal system and interpreted women's claims from the point of view of the law. The authority of this law and these representatives carried much weight among women who brought their cases to court. Some felt intimidated, overpowered, and uncertain in their interviews with court staff, much as they had felt in the violent situations that brought them to court in the first place. Their ideas about right and justice were tentative, insufficiently tested in discussions with friends and family, and easily reshaped by the unequal encounters between themselves and the experts (see S. Fisher 1993).

Other women came to court more confident their claims were legitimate and their expectations of justice and restitution reasonable and appropriate. They argued and debated with court staff about the scope of chargeable offenses. They wanted the lawyers to permit them to recount the history of the violent relationship instead of forcing them to decontextualize a violent event. They wanted the judge to order their attackers to drug or alcohol or violence counseling. They wanted the state to force men to pay for their injuries or the damage to their property. They wanted the court to make violent men own up to their crimes. But women were constantly admonished to stick to the "facts"—to give accounts that they believed did not allow them to explain their cases. Such women were at a disadvantage, for it was difficult to argue with the attorneys and the judge without an expert's knowledge of the law and an insider's knowledge of how the court actually worked.

Court staff had their own ideas about what acts did or did not fall under the provisions of the domestic violence law, and about what women could and should do in each case. Their concerns were those of attorneys; their knowledge derived from experience with the law, not with violent men. The advocates provided an alternative standpoint from which to view the court and the law, one grounded simultaneously in the lives of the individual women complainants they counseled every day and in their feminist political history as activists in the battered women's movement. Their ongoing connections to battered women kept them abreast of the everyday struggles of many women and apprised them of women's self-defined needs and desires. Their connections with the women's movement meant that they participated in a dialogue among women and women's advocates about their political work, a dialogue that helped to underscore the work's wider significance, its place in a comprehensive set of strategies built on the combined experience and practices of the movement.

The advocates' aim was to educate women about the possibilities and limits of the law, to guide them through the system, and to help them improve their situation by identifying new resources for their emotional, material, and interpersonal support in the future. Because of the advocates' labor-intensive practice, listening to women's full stories, counseling and sometimes cajoling them to take particular steps in and out of court, and accompanying them to hearings and court appearances, they were able to work only with a tiny fraction of all the women in the courthouse. However, as major architects of the court and a continuing, daily presence there, the advocates made their mark on the consciousness of the legal staff and on courtroom procedures. In nine years time, staff's overtly hostile and antagonistic stance toward the advocates had abated. More positively, some of the court's routine practices bore the stamp of the advocates. For example, prosecutors allowed women more latitude in telling their stories, and their assistants, the victim-witness advocates, kept in touch with them by phone and provided them with lists of resources. Peggy Luft believed changes such as these showed that the court staff had "absorbed some of our influence." Directly and indirectly, then, advocates provided resources for women within the court, including an expert's knowledge of the legal system delivered from a sympathetic point of view, a commitment to helping women end domestic violence, and a political standpoint, partially institutionalized in the court's practices, derived from long years of activism directed at the state.

### Who Uses the Court?

Many of the women I met in domestic violence court were low-wage service and clerical workers, housewives, or welfare recipients who had no choice but to depend on public agencies rather than hire attorneys or use other private resources to escape violent men. Many of the men charged with assault and battery were factory and construction workers, truck drivers, stock clerks or messengers, often out of work or erratically employed, or men with no discernable means of support. A high proportion of people at court were people of color, primarily African American and Latino/a, but there were also women and men from Chicago's white working-class and immigrant/ethnic communities.

When women came to court to press charges, they entered an unfamiliar world, a world whose values they did not necessarily share and about whose practices they knew little. The courthouse is replete with markers of class and professional status, markers that marginalize lay persons who take part in the proceedings only with the consent and direction of court workers. The appearance of the suited lawyers, women and men, contrasts sharply with the everyday and sometimes shabby dress of the witnesses and defendants. The armed sheriffs who bark commands to be quiet, order people out of the courtroom, and stand guard over the courthouse can be intimidating. As a work group that comes together daily to process complaints, people who work in domestic violence court—judges, state's attorneys, and public defenders, who are experts in the written law and its interpretation; the support staff of warrant officers, clerks, and victim-witness advocates; and the sheriffs who maintain order and control—share commitments to legal traditions and everyday practices in which battered women have had little or no voice, and the easy familiarity of people who have worked together for a long time. It is a consequence of the social distance between workers and clients at the court that although it was established to penalize and restrain abusive men, most women who made use of it were guarded and wary, almost as if they, not their attackers, were on trial.

### "Some Women Don't Know Any Better": Dropping or Continuing Cases

In fact, the women were outsiders in the courtroom and the multitude of class and cultural differences between the complainants and the court workers who served them created a divide that was not easily bridged (see Yngvesson 1993). Court workers witnessed a daily parade of violent men and battered women that must have shaken any confidence they had in the promise of families to shelter their members and unsettled any faith they held in the lasting devotion of lovers or friends. Domestic violence court highlighted the menacing side of private life and the dangers of intimate relationships. Consequently it is not difficult to understand the appeal to court workers of accounts about the causes of violence that fixed the blame for domestic violence on problems of character and culture, explanations that separated the men and women who came to court from "normal" men and women in untroubled families, and rationales that focused on isolated, individual acts and cultural deficiencies rather than on systemic gendered power struggles crossing racial and class boundaries. Ed Burton, a seasoned public defender, believed that most domestic cases were the product of ignorance and bad example. He said,

> These are people who have not been exposed . . . or educated. They haven't developed alternatives to deal with their frustrations, their aggression, dealing with poverty. They just come from this environment and this is what they've seen all their lives and this is how they deal with it.

This viewpoint helped court workers to explain what they saw as the court's central problem and its most baffling contradiction. On the one hand, they saw many women in court with genuine and serious complaints, women with solid cases who needed what the court had been established to provide. Nonetheless, court workers had real trouble persuading such women not to drop their cases. Anne Fager, a state's attorney, said, "They'll come down, they'll get an emergency order of protection, and then we never see them again." On the other hand, there were women with the most minor complaints and injuries—"the simple push or the verbal threats or maybe an offensive touching"—who, as another state's attorney, Marion Seldes explained, were "the most adamant about prosecuting, want to see the abuser punished, and follow this through to the end if it means coming back to court nine times."

Court workers rarely questioned the assumptions behind their condemnation of women's behavior. They did not wonder if there were sound reasons for dropping good cases or if a plausible argument could be made for persisting with weak ones. Immersed in the logic of legal discourse and in professional concerns with winnable cases, admissible evidence, and compliant witnesses, lawyers and court workers rarely contemplated the drawbacks involved in using the law as they prescribed. So convinced were they that adherence to court procedures offered the only route to safety and protection, they seldom entertained the notion that certain complainants had other, more fruitful agendas involving the law. So committed were they to a legal timetable, that they viewed a woman's repeated use of the court as proof that her failure to follow through to the end of a case doomed her to continued victimization. From within the discourse of the law, women were guilty for the failures of the court, either because they did not follow through on good cases, or because they wasted court workers' time and energy by using the law to settle non-criminal family disputes. Such judgments rested on widely held beliefs that the poor and racial minorities who used the court were immersed in a culture of violence. Assistant state's attorney Seldes suggested that women who dropped cases tolerated abuse because they "just don't know any better. They were raised in an abusive environment and they just feel that this is normal." Janice Williams, a victim-witness advocate in the state's attorney's office concurred. "They don't have any self-worth. [They think] this is the way it's supposed to be." As for the women who bothered the court workers with trivial complaints or pursued hopeless cases, they seemed often to be misguided or vindictive women who abused the law for personal gain: to get even with a straying husband; to fight a custody dispute; to force a man from his home.

Court workers gleaned their understanding of women's motives from their actual daily work, but it was experience refracted through the lens of professional, legal discourse and practice, experience that provided only a partial view of the events in the courtroom. The same actions, viewed from the vantage point of the women who came to court with complaints and situated in the context of their lives, took on different meanings.

First, court workers rarely learned of the ramifications of a court appearance on the everyday lives of women and their assailants. Caroline Adams lived in one of the poorest African American neighborhoods on Chicago's West Side. Caroline's husband was out of work; Caroline was a domestic in hotels and private homes. Caroline found she had "a little more authority" with her husband after she went to court, even though she did not return: "I got him to move out of the house and now he's gonna stay out of the house." Jessica Easton lived in Roseland, another poor African American neighborhood on Chicago's far South Side. Jessica shared a house with six other women and their children, all of whom relied on welfare. James Johnson, the man who attacked her and her former long-term boyfriend, was unemployed. One day, after her court appearance, Jessica ran into James in a neighborhood grocery store. He said loudly to no one in particular, "Better watch out for her. She calls the police."

Second, women often calculated the costs to themselves and their families of continuing a case as they became aware that the law would provide dubious protection from abusive men and might make things worse (see Bumiller 1987). Caroline knew many women who were afraid to use the courts.

> They're afraid of what might happen if they bring the courts or policemen in. They're afraid that person's gonna be more rebellish toward them and do more bodily harm.

Rose Perez, a beautician, was in the process of divorcing her husband, Joe, an out-of-work truck driver, although they still saw each other regularly. Occasionally Joe turned violent. Rose's friend Alice Connolly was afraid of what Joe would do when he saw Alice's name on the complaint.

> I'm afraid of repercussions. He may feel I provoked her to do this. He drinks a real lot. He got in the mail yesterday some papers

from the lawyer, so he knows things are gonna be final soon. He's been acting goofy all day. Also I signed the complaint too, and he'll see my name on it.

Third, women often had to consider the attitudes of other family members as they decided whether or not to press charges. Frances Martin and her husband, Bill, were retired factory workers who owned a home in a middle-class, African American neighborhood, around the corner from the judge who presided over their case. Bill Martin drank a lot and had become abusive since his retirement, and this time he had threatened Frances with a gun. Frances's daughter didn't want her to come to court at all. Frances dropped, then reinstated charges only after her eighteen-year-old grandson threatened to move out of her house unless she did so, but then failed to appear again, paralyzed by the pushes and pulls of her divided family. By then, however, the situation had become less urgent, as her husband was now living in their daughter's house.

Helen Callas, a middle-aged woman who came to Chicago from Greece in the 1950s, worked in a bakery. Her husband, Peter, was an independent contractor, in recent years only sporadically employed. After Peter threatened and shoved her in front of their children, Helen came to court. Unlike Frances's divided family, Helen's children were so unanimous in their opposition to their mother's action that they lied to the judge about their father's conduct on the night in question. Although Helen persisted with her case, she regretted her decision when her husband was acquitted of the charges. When last we spoke, she was estranged from three of her four children.

Fourth, it takes tremendous energy and resolve to persevere in the court. Margarita Bustamente, who was receiving public aid, came to court with her friend, Karen, two of her children, and a little boy she cared for during the day. Margarita spoke almost no English, but Karen was there to help her. Margarita's boyfriend, Juan, had been harassing her and Margarita's oldest daughter was threatening to move out if her mother refused to do something about it. Margarita had been to the court twice before on other charges against Juan and said she believed it was important to show up for each scheduled hearing. But she had to bring three small children along with her each time she came to the courthouse. Karen, her friend and interpreter, explained that one appearance was sufficient for Margarita's purposes anyway. "[She was] waiting too long. Waiting too long. 'Cause the kids drive you crazy. . . . She was saying that she doesn't want [the order of protection]. She just wants to scare the guy."

Fifth, there were a variety of personal reasons why women didn't show up in court. Jessica Easton was depressed and lethargic when I visited her in her home after she had failed to appear for her third court date. Her sister was moving to Michigan, and she had no job, no boyfriend, and no idea what she was going to do with her life. Her former boyfriend had stayed away after her seven housemates and their children attacked him when he punched her in their presence. When I asked why she hadn't come back for her court date she said, "I didn't have the carfare." Emily Smith was a young Black woman, the mother of three, who was living with a Polish factory worker when he attacked her. Emily had taken off with her abusive boyfriend's car. Her mother hadn't heard from her since she was last in court and thought she had run away to Indiana, where she had many friends.

Erica Chase, a secretary, had come to court because her ex-husband, Patrick, had shouted threats at her in family court the day before. Erica had gone to family court to force Patrick to pay their son's Catholic-school tuition. A white woman, Erica felt out of place in the courtroom dominated by people of color. She said, "[Family court] is different. This place is a dump. I don't like being here. I don't like being around these people, but I don't want my husband to get away with what he did." Most of the court workers who heard Erica's story told her they didn't think the judge would issue her an order of protection. These discouraging assessments reinforced her discomfort with the court. When court recessed for lunch hour before her case was called, she walked out, not wanting to miss another full day of work for nothing.

It is clear that there was no one reason why women dropped cases nor, for that matter, why they persisted despite the obstacles the law and the court put in their way. Nor is that the important matter here. Instead, it is necessary to place these decisions within an extended history of the power relations that led to them and that emanate from them. These more lengthy sequences of events help to show how a woman's appearance at court can reshape her personal relations, lead to greater appreciation among family and friends of her right to peace and bodily integrity, and insert her more centrally into the daily workings of the court and the system of criminal justice. In the next section, I present three cases situated in this wider context.

## The Proceedings from Women's Vantage Point

Cheryl Edwards spoke with Denita Woods, an advocate, who explained to Cheryl what she could expect when she returned in two weeks for the hearing before the judge. Cheryl returned for the second court date, but by the end of the day she dropped her case over the strenuous objections of the prosecutor. Caroline Adams, who spoke briefly with an advocate, never bothered to come back to court a second time. Bonnie Jordan was the ex-wife of a suburban police officer who had threatened her with a gun. Unlike Cheryl and Caroline, Bonnie insisted on continuing her case, despite the vehement opposition of the prosecutor. Court staff believed that reasonable women would bow to their greater knowledge, but these women rejected expert opinion. In doing so, they actively negotiated with members of the court to win support for their own claims and strategies. In these skirmishes advocates played important, but not always visible, roles.

### "I Thought I Was Gonna Be in Charge": Setting an Agenda

Cheryl Edwards was sitting in the waiting room early one morning when I approached her and asked if she would be willing to have me tag along as she pressed charges in court. The left side of her face was swollen and her left eye was bloody red. She said that her boyfriend, Asa Moore, had punched her on Saturday, sending her to the hospital. The police, whom she called after discussing the incident with her mother and uncle, told her to go to domestic violence court and press charges against Asa. Cheryl hoped to be able to use the court to force Asa to pay her medical bills and to frighten him enough "so he won't touch nobody else."

Cheryl didn't think what Asa did should land him in jail, "because there are people out there who did worse than that who can go to jail." However, she did want him restrained and rehabilitated, which is why she called the police and went to court. She knew that Asa was genuinely frightened of going to jail—as a teenager he had spent a night in a notorious youth-detention facility in Chicago. She believed he needed the kind of help the state provided: drug, alcohol, and violence counseling, remedies which seemed even more sensible as she observed the judge use them while she waited in the courtroom for her case to be called. Cheryl had a specific agenda when she pressed charges. She intended to show her violent ex-boyfriend she "meant business," she wanted reparations for the damage he did, and she "wanted to let him know . . . that it wasn't never gonna happen again, that I wasn't a fool."

With bruises, cuts, and four stitches under her eye—all duly attested to in the hospital records—Cheryl had a good case against her boyfriend. There were witnesses as well: his aunt and his friend, who were there when he hit her. Corroborating witnesses are rare in these cases and the state's attorneys did their best to persuade Cheryl to keep on with what they assessed as a "winnable" case. Cheryl came back for her next court date, but before the day was done, she dropped the case. From the state's perspective this was another example of women's failure to follow through with charges and their ultimate responsibility for the failures of the court.

When Cheryl and Asa turned up in court for the hearing, Cheryl was already having second thoughts about the case. The first court appearance had frightened Asa. Asa's mother had apologized and offered to pay Cheryl's hospital bills and Asa had stayed away. Waiting in the courtroom, with Asa and his mother clearly visible across the room, Cheryl observed that many people, women and men alike, were not showing up for their court date. She whispered to me, "If I wouldn't have come the case would've been thrown out." Cheryl was unsure what she wanted to do. She now saw it was really her choice, whether to charge Asa with a crime or to let it go. She was ambivalent about whether Asa should receive more punishment. "I don't know if I should say yes or no." As we waited outside the courtroom for a recess to end she said, "If I didn't come here it wouldn't have happened at all."

Cheryl's debate with herself over whether to continue her case against Asa was cut short, however, when the clerk at last called her and Asa up to the bench. The judge looked over the papers, and said to Asa,

> Oh, wait a minute. The attorney will come and speak to you about the case, but right now there's a warrant for your arrest for $3,000. So right now the sheriff will take you and make arrangements for your bond.

Watching the sheriff lead Asa away to the lock-up, Cheryl and I were totally surprised. We were certain (and my field notes later confirmed) that there had been no arrest warrant issued after Cheryl's first court appearance, but only a summons notifying him to be in court on this date. Cheryl was upset. "How do they put a warrant out and I don't have no say-so?"

Cheryl claimed ownership of the case. It was her pain and her decision to hold Asa responsible for his actions that brought the case to court in the first place, and yet she believed that the judge and the attorneys were ignoring her purposes.

> They put a warrant out and I don't have [a] say-so. It's not fair for me or for him. It makes me feel like I don't have [a] say-so over it. . . . They're wrong, cause I didn't put a warrant out. I don't want [any]body to go to jail. It ain't that serious.

This moment was a turning point for Cheryl. Now she was unwilling to put up with some of the inconveniences and obstacles in the way of women seeking redress in the courts. At 12:15 she whispered to me that it was "taking too long." At the bench, the judge and a case worker were discussing a hearing on a violation-of-supervision case. She said, "Can I do that? I want him to go to counseling. I already have my bills paid. Can't I just go up there and tell him that before they go to lunch?" By the time court recessed, she had made her decision. When she told the state's attorney working on her case that she would not proceed, the young woman was surprised. "Did you talk to her?" the lawyer asked me, treating me as an advocate whose job it was to persuade complainants to go on with the case.

Cheryl received a one-year order of protection barring Asa from contacting her. If Asa were to violate the order while it was in effect, it would be a criminal act, punishable by a fine and possibly a jail sentence. Court workers routinely refer to orders of protection as "just pieces of paper" that don't carry the weight of a conviction. But Cheryl believed otherwise. When the lawyer said she could have an order of protection despite dropping the charges, Cheryl agreed to wait, even though she was concerned about missing another day of school. She said, "That's fine because he didn't violate the first one."

### "The Police are My Manpower": Using State Resources

On a cold Monday in February, Caroline Adams, a housekeeper at a downtown hotel, came to domestic violence court to press charges against her husband of three months. Caroline had called the police on several occasions and had been in court before. Court workers might have sympathized with Caroline's problems, but they likely would have seen her as a typical "abuser" of the law, one without the strength or the wisdom to follow through on her case.

In court this time, Caroline told the story of an assault by her new husband, Ezra Jones, an unemployed former hotel worker. She had spent the previous Saturday shopping downtown, leaving her husband locked out of their apartment for several hours. When she returned, Ezra accused her of spending the time with her ex-husband, who lived down the street with his new wife. During the intake interview at court, she told the warrant officer, "He was throwing me on the bed, cursing, ripping my shirt. I was trying to get out of the room 'cause I was yelling, but the kids were next door." The next day, she said, he "swung the phone at me, but I ducked. He was coming up on me like he was gonna hit me." The judge granted Caroline an emergency order of protection prohibiting Ezra from coming to the house. The order would be in effect until the next court date. The judge issued Ezra a summons and told Caroline to return in two weeks. Caroline did not return.

Despite what must have appeared to members of the court as Caroline's lack of interest in pursuing her case, the truth was that Caroline dropped the case against Ezra at the end of a period of intense activity on her part, during which time she used the police and the law strategically to free herself from her husband. Caroline called the police "my manpower" and believed she had every right to ask them for protection.

> My husband told me, "Yeah, you call the police on me, so what?" [I said:] "That's what I pay my tax dollars for, to get you where I want you to go. If you wanna move, that's what I pay my tax dollars for. To get you out of my way.". . . Because they charge me ninety-five cents a month for that 911 number. I might as well use it. . . . So when I told him, "Yeah, I use my manpower, 'cause that's my manpower, the police."

Just as Caroline used the police to give her protection on the spot, she used the courts for a more long-term shield. She was well aware of how low the problems of a woman like herself—Black, poor, and living in a high-crime district—were likely to rank with police. An order of protection might not keep an angry husband away forever, but if she had to call the police for help again, an order of protection might authenticate her complaint and speed the police to her door.

The emergency order of protection that the judge gave Caroline after her first court appearance did the trick this time. Ezra was required to stay away from the house until the next court hearing, but once he was gone, Caroline saw to it that he would not come back.

I told him, "I don't want you at home and I don't want to be both-ered with you." I feel better. I don't have to argue with nobody, fuss or fight. . . . And he asks me, he always asks me: "Can I come back home?" "No you can't come back home," I said. I'm comfortable here now. I enjoy this.

When the return court date arrived, Caroline opted to go to a job inter-view rather than to court, a mere formality now that her husband had moved out of the house. To Caroline this move was the result of her long-term strategy.

You just make up your mind that you don't want to do it no more, the fussing and arguments. You try to work it out with that person. If you can't work it out with that person, you got to . . . keep going, getting your order of protection and keep them out.

When I asked her why she didn't show up for her last court date, she responded: "Because I got him to move out the house now and he's gonna stay out the house."

### "I Want it on the Record": Pursuing a Hopeless Case

In the ladies room opposite the courtroom, I found advocate Gloria Ramirez having a cigarette with a client, Bonnie Jordan. Bonnie was the former wife of Don Jordan, a suburban police officer. She had come to court to charge Don with a violation of an order of protection. Twice before, despite an order of protection already in force, her husband had threatened her, slashed her tires, and once, in front of two police offi-cers, he had pushed Bonnie in the chest as she was coming out of the courtroom.

Each of these times Bonnie had brought and then dropped charges. Now she was here again because Don had threatened her with a gun. This time there were no witnesses and Tom Klein, the assistant state's attorney assigned to her case, wanted Bonnie to drop the charges. Bon-nie reported, "He said it's hard because [my husband's] a police officer. [Tom] said: 'Why the hell don't you just drop the damn case because it's not gonna go nowhere.' . . . [I said:] 'I know I won't win and they'll lose the order of protection and then there's nothing I can do about it.'" But Bonnie decided to pursue the case.

Don had arrived at Bonnie's house very late the night before to pick up their four children. According to an agreement negotiated in divorce court, he was supposed to have met them earlier that evening at the police station. When Bonnie and he got into an argument, he pointed his service revolver at her. Bonnie called the police, but it was more than an hour before they arrived, claiming that they had just received her call. Because there were no witnesses and Don was no longer there, the police report made no mention of the gun.

Even though it was Bonnie's word against Don's, almost certainly insufficient evidence for a conviction, Bonnie was determined to press charges. After many clashes with Don, she had learned the law well enough to redefine his ongoing behavior as "harassment," "stalking," and "battery," all legally cognizable offenses.

> Like the police told me, "even if he just touches you, it's still a battery case because he's not supposed to be around." It didn't do no good. That's what I told them. He harassed me for a week. He's stalking me. I can't walk the streets with him following behind me. He's trying to talk to me. I tried to be nice last week. I talked to him, socialized with him. It didn't do no good because he can't keep his hands off me. So I told him I'm not dropping the charges this time. I was the fool for dropping charges before. No more!

Gloria was supportive. "She has no violation of an order of protection, I don't care what nobody says."

Tom threatened to withdraw from the case if Bonnie did not follow his advice. He maintained that as the legal expert, he alone was competent to decide what to do. When Bonnie said she wanted to consult with Gloria before she made up her mind, he responded:

> She doesn't know what she's talking about. I'm the best damn lawyer you got around here. She doesn't know. Believe me she doesn't know. There's nothing she can do about it. You need to see me.

Tom had little respect for the women whose cases he prosecuted and no patience with those who disregarded his advice. He resented the advocates as interfering amateurs who goaded women to act against what he believed were their best interests.

Gloria had impressed on Bonnie the value of getting the charge on the record, even though it was unlikely that the judge would find Don guilty. Despite Tom's opposition, but encouraged by Gloria, Bonnie decided to go ahead. In the ladies room she told us, "I'm not gonna sit back here with this man and put another revolver to my damn head because he has a badge to say it's okay. No!"

Later in the day Gail Johnson, the young attorney who supervised the feminist advocates concurred, saying:

> Well, she knows that she could lose. But I think she did the right thing. I mean if this guy used a gun, you never know what's gonna happen. I would want that on the record.

Later that day, Tom stormed into Gail's office to reproach her and Gloria for encouraging Bonnie to persist in bringing the charge of aggravated assault against Don. He was furious that the advocates took the ideas of women "from the ghetto with no education" more seriously than the advice of lawyers like himself. He predicted that Bonnie would lose the case and her order of protection. He told Gail that he thought Don was a "time bomb" and that he "would rather get an order of protection and win on the assault than to lose with the gun." He argued that Bonnie "should choose what I told her to and you are supposed to back me up." He compared himself to a doctor advising a patient with cancer. "If the doctor tells her A is the best treatment for her and she chooses B, then what are we gonna do?" Gail answered, "If she chooses something that we disagree with, that's her right." The feminist perspective of Gail and the other advocates allowed them to value and support Bonnie's choice over Tom's professional opinion. The advocates' approach—informing women of their rights, educating them about the scope and limits of the law, and supporting them in their choices—helped to give women like Bonnie a voice in the courtroom.

### Transforming Relations and Identities

Domestic violence court, the law, and the advocates furnished resources that enabled individual women to confront and reshape their relationships with abusive men. In addition, the court was a setting in which collective definitions of justice and right could emerge. In domestic violence court, women made public and visible, to themselves and to each other, their everyday forms of resistance to men's violence. Here, women came face-to-face with the social dimensions of their situation as they enlisted state powers on their own behalf. They received useful information, which they often passed along to friends and relatives, learned alternative definitions of their situation, legitimated their desire to hold men responsible for violence, and altered their sense of themselves.

Thanks to the activists in the Battered Women's Network, Chicago police now routinely refer women to the court, and many of the women I met in court learned of its existence from the police. Several of these women had called police to their homes many times before they placed the call that finally brought them to the court. Until recently it had been common knowledge that if police showed up (which did not always happen) they offered women little assistance, often sympathizing with the men or taking them out of the house, only to release them within hours to do more harm.

During the thirteen years she lived with James Johnson in the South, Jessica Easton called the police many times, but received little satisfaction. Usually they took James' side and treated her as the person needing restraint. Her last call to the Chicago police had a different outcome. She reported that this time the police were sympathetic and willing to advise her about how to cope with James's violence. They listened to her, took her seriously, and gave her advice. She explained her surprise.

> . . . I always hated the Chicago police. I used to always hear their sirens at night. They would side with the man whether it's right or wrong. I didn't know nothing about the domestic thing. It was like undercover.

When I asked her what she meant when she said the police would "side with the man," she responded:

> If a man's arguing with them the man will jump to their side and tell you to shut up because you [are] gonna go to jail or something [is] gonna happen to me. . . . [JW: And they would say to you to be quiet?] Yeah. "You can't talk" or "let him talk" or they'll take me to jail. Why the hell they don't take him to jail? I'm the one that called the police.

Women also learned about domestic violence court in other ways. If a case made the local TV news, as some occasionally did, the court was swamped with new cases on the days following. Sometimes a social worker, visiting a woman for another reason, noticed bruises, and suggested that a woman go to court. As women learned about the court and used it, they told others to do the same. Jessica told her sister-in-law about the court.

> I said if I had known [about domestic violence court] years ago when I lived here I would have used it. I said that goes to show you. If people don't know they can't tell you. I tell my sister-in-law about it too. My brother is very abusive.

Caroline also let her friends know about the court and tried to persuade them to use it. The husband of Caroline's friend, Jacqueline, had broken Jacqueline's finger, and Caroline pressed her to pursue the complaint.

> So I'm just going along with what she tells me. Because I had told her once before, don't drop the charges. If you drop the charges, he gonna be a nigger about it and he is gonna do something else wrong.

Passed along through personal networks, reports of visits to the court became the occasion for women to talk to each other about past responses to men's violence. Cheryl's court encounter dislodged opinions about resistance from her mother and aunt and their friends, based on experiences they had never before discussed with each other. Cheryl's aunt told her that she was sorry she had not pursued the case against her own boyfriend some years before.

> My Auntie, she told me about her experiences with her boyfriend. He cut her hair with a knife and knocked her teeth out. The police came but she never followed through with it. She was telling me her experiences, her mistakes. She told me her mistake was she never followed through, because he came back and she didn't have protection. That was six or seven years ago.

Whatever else the outcome, a court encounter acquainted the women with some unfamiliar ideas and helped them evolve some new ideas of their own. At the end of her first day in court, Cheryl was briefed by advocate Denita Woods about what to expect two weeks hence when Cheryl's boyfriend was to appear in court to answer her charges. Denita encouraged Cheryl to pursue the case. She said,

If he hit you once he's gonna try again. I know you don't want to be no one's punching bag. You're too young. Even if you're not young you don't want that. No one deserves that.

At the end of their session, Denita said, "Now you know something about the court. Spread the word." Cheryl absorbed the message, reinterpreting an earlier incident in light of Denita's words. The following month, she explained to me why she came to court when she did.

Well, you see, the first time, maybe I didn't see the light then. Maybe it took a harder blow for me to see the light because the first time it hurt inside, but not really physically. I wasn't really that much upset about it. So I got over that. But the second time it was totally different. I know it's a saying that "once they do it they'll do it again."

Broadening what counts as violence and developing a firmer recognition of grievances, rights, and injustices was often the outcome of a woman's court experience. Caroline redefined violence with Denita's help. Denita asked Caroline if her husband had been abusive before. "No. He didn't hit me with his fists," Caroline answered. Denita said, "Any time someone puts his hands on you, it's abuse. There's mental abuse too, that's the worst kind. He doesn't have to put marks on your face to be abusing you."

Taking action to change their relationships with abusive men also stimulated women to rethink their image of themselves. Jessica said she came to court "get back on the track," to take control of the chaotic life she lived with a brutal man. In the shelter for battered women to which she fled after many years of fear and abuse at the hands of James, Jessica "had a lot of counseling therapy. . . . It was mandatory [in the shelter]. You learn a lot about yourself."

Some women reassessed the implicit contracts they had with the men they were now confronting, calling into question the roles and relationships that had governed their everyday lives together. Thinking over their lives together, Jessica came to believe that James had not lived up to his part of the marriage bargain. "I used to clean and cook for him. I spent my money on the house. He had money but he didn't give it to me." Along the same lines, Caroline considered, then rejected, the idea that she leave the house for her own protection.

I'm gonna take care of me and my kids. I'm gonna be staying here. I'm the survivor. I'm the one who takes care. This may encourage him to take care in his own way.

In these often mundane ways—broadcasting the news about court, discussing the problem of violence among friends and relatives, redefining the meaning and scope of unacceptable violence, rethinking their relationships with abusive men, reconceptualizing their rights and obligations, and reflecting on themselves—women moved to change existing power relations in their own households, changes that reverberated in their personal networks and communities. At the same time, they demanded that the system of criminal justice make space for them in the official proceedings and respond to their self-defined needs.

## Conclusion

I have argued here for a perspective that gives credit to the ways poor and working-class women have taken up feminist ideals and resources to reshape their personal relationships. I do not mean to say that the laws and the courts always or even most often serve the interests of such complainants, nor do I wish to minimize the complexities and contradictions of relying on state institutions to apportion justice among members of poor, exploited, and oppressed communities (see, e.g., Merry 1990). However, the feminist critique of the criminal justice system has emphasized its failures and the ways it victimizes poor and working-class women.[4] In this chapter I highlight the creativity and successes of ordinary women who use the court and of their feminist allies.

For the women described here, the court is a public site of negotiation and struggle over power relations, a new locale for the pursuit of both protection and justice. As the direct product of feminist political action, the court legitimizes women's struggles against male violence and offers them alternative courses of action to oppose it. Feminist activists have set the stage for such action and have made it possible for the masses of women who use the court every year to exert pressure that constantly challenges the court and the criminal law to accommodate to them. The changes advocates have helped to institutionalize in the criminal justice system, as well as their continuing presence at the court, help to focus and politicize women's complaints about power relations in their personal lives. Feminist activists have also provided battered women with a standpoint from which to criticize the hegemony of normal law and to claim legitimacy for their alternative versions of justice. In this context women have been learning to identify their interests and speak up to those in power in court as well as at home. Such activity is an important, if unacknowledged, part of the women's movement, activity that community activists and feminist researchers should recognize and celebrate.

**Author's Note:** I thank Caryn Aviv, Arlene Kaplan Daniels, Anne Figert, Heidi Kon, Helena Lopata, Jane Mansbridge, Nancy Naples, and Mary Jo Neitz for helpful comments and suggestions.

### Notes

1. Alcoff and Gray (1993, 264) discuss the power relations governing talk between experts and women speaking about sexual violence: "In any given discursive event there will be a normative arrangement in which some participants are designated speakers and others are designated hearers. In many speaking situations some participants are accorded the authoritative status of interpreters and others are constructed as 'naive transmitters of raw experience.'"
2. These attitudes may be common among lawyers working in the lower courts. See Yngvesson 1993, 121.
3. Peggy Luft is the real name of a real person. All other names have been changed.
4. Gordon (1990) makes this point with respect to social-welfare agencies.

# Part II

# Transforming Politics

# Chapter 4

# Conversation, Research, and Struggle over Schooling in an African American Community

## Susan Parkison Stern

The following account relates my experiences working with a small group of African American parents who were trying to preserve for their children the gains they had achieved as a result of the Civil Rights Movement. Specific policies and practices of the local school system in our suburban Washington, D.C., community were operating to perpetuate lower academic expectations for students attending predominantly African American schools. To address the resulting problem of racial educational inequality, I facilitated an ongoing, conversation-based, community research project that formed an integral part of the parents' struggle for equality.

The term "conversation-based research" describes a form of emancipatory and participatory research of which I first became aware during the 1970s, while working with a Latino prisoner group for whom research and struggle were closely integrated (described at length in Stern 1994). In this model, the research process itself constitutes a form of struggle, as most of the knowledge produced is generated through "mutual interview" conversations among people in the community affected by the problem at hand. With this "bottom-up" method, structurally disadvantaged groups can go far to produce their own critical knowledge; but the prisoners' model did not take advantage of, nor critique, potentially useful academic critical theory, methods, and knowledge.

The model described here goes further, as I recount both the African American parents' struggle and my attempt to implement and further elaborate the prisoners' conversation-based research method by bringing social science into the community conversation. Conversation-based research contributes to a bottom-up methodology for developing a critical social science (Fay 1987) that is grounded in the perspective of those carrying the burden of the struggle. It also contributes to a grassroots approach to struggle that is informed by several sources of critical knowledge. I begin with the narrative description of my entry into the community struggle and conversation.

With our move to a middle-class, predominantly African American, suburban area in metropolitan Washington, D.C., in 1981, my daughter, husband, and I were plunged into a predicament and puzzle about our daughter's school. The neighborhood, with its well-kept residences and school, resembled many mostly white suburban parts of the metropolitan area, and census data showed that its population was solidly middle class, as indicated by levels of income, education, and occupation (Stern 1986). However, the schooling behind the closed doors of this more than ninety percent Black elementary school was far from our expectations based on the neighborhood's appearance and socioeconomic level.[1]

Both the curriculum and teachers' attitudes reflected the low expectations typical of schools in lower-income Black areas. The kinds of problems we observed corresponded to sociological research and theory about the ways large-scale social and economic forces (Bowles and Gintis 1976) and school-based mechanisms produce academic failure among lower-class children and reproduce their lower-class position: through tracking (Persell 1977; Oakes 1985), unequal distribution of resources (Guthrie, et al. 1971), the "hidden curriculum" (e.g. Apple 1982), teaching practices such as too little time on task, and teachers' verbal and nonverbal communication of "low expectations" (Wilcox 1982). Such studies, however, have previously focused on "ghetto" schools in lower-income, often African American areas. Large residential concentrations of middle-income African Americans are still unusual, so there has been little previous study of the role of race and class forces in schooling in these communities—communities like mine.

In my daughter's school, non-teaching was manifested by teachers who often left their classes altogether unattended, spending much of what should have been teaching time completely outside the classroom, talking with other teachers in the hall. On returning to their loud and chaotic classes, teachers would take up further time meting out valueless punishments (e.g., requiring the whole class to write hundreds of repetitions of sentences such as, "I will never talk out of turn again"). Assigned homework and classwork were often not even collected by the teachers, or collected but not returned. Educationally substantive assignments were rare and took little critical or creative thought; instead, for English or history, answers were often to be copied verbatim from the book, and there were no word problems in math. Corrections emphasized form rather than substance, so that, for example, the lack of a comma in the date in the heading could result in an "F," while few or no corrections might appear in the body of the assignment.

Forms of mis-teaching included mistakes in spelling and grammar both being taught and going uncorrected in written assignments, while the math teacher taught incorrect algorithms. The school also made education a punitive experience by devoting a significant amount of time to individual and group punishments rather than educational content, and by combining punishment with the educational tasks themselves. For example, assignments that might have been intellectually challenging, such as book reports, were given by some teachers only as punishments.

The teachers projected very low educational expectations of the children both by the way they presented the curriculum and by what they said directly to the children. In my daughter's English class, there were three groups. The lowest group was "Lost at Sea." The highest level to which the students in that class could aspire was called "The Survivors," which my daughter said left her feeling she was barely hanging on by her fingernails, almost ready to drown. Throughout the school, there were no above-grade-level groups in reading or math. One of the teachers said, "My dog could have done this better than you." Another stamped a picture of an owl on an almost perfect paper and wrote, "You think you're so wise, don't you."

Before we moved to our suburban neighborhood, the realtor told us it was "heavily mixed" (a euphemism for mostly Black). We had been favorably impressed by the appearance of the nearby housing developments and by the neighborhood's other desirable characteristics, especially our home's proximity to public transportation and its quasi-rural setting, and we moved there without much regard for the racial composition of the area. Previously, our daughter had found it a positive experience to have been in a racially mixed school in another metropolitan area, and my husband and I had looked forward to living in another racially mixed area.

My husband and I saw our daughter's schooling experiences as a crisis and responded in the ways to which we had been socialized as white, middle-class persons, such as calling or writing the teachers and principal, and making appointments to discuss our concerns. Our individual efforts, however, were unwelcome and mostly ineffective, and we hoped to find other parents with whom we might join. We began to ask ourselves three broad, interrelated questions: How could race and class dynamics explain the appalling school conditions in this solidly middle-class African American community? Why had the parents as a group not effectively addressed the crisis of their children's schooling? And why were we as parents receiving disrespectful treatment at the hands of the teachers and principal? These questions represented both practical (activist) and theoretical (sociological) interests.

## Conversation-Based Participatory Research

Conversation-based participatory research shares many goals, concerns, and characteristics with a broad array of academy-based activist and critical research models in feminist, sociological, anthropological, and educational traditions.[2] These models have a common interest in various aspects of the relationship between knowledge and struggle, especially the politics of knowledge production. A brief catalogue of shared concerns includes the problematic role of the activist social scientist vis-à-vis disadvantaged grassroots groups; myriad issues about objectivity, perspective, and epistemological standpoint; critical consciousness; and the development of critical communities.

Conversation-based research builds on ordinary friendship conversations in which exploration of the personal realm grows to include investigation of shared social conditions. In this sense, conversational research is an integral part of life. Though not all conversation-based research projects have emancipatory intent, emancipation-oriented conversation-based research projects like ours involve building on the conversations within disadvantaged groups to understand the oppressive social conditions affecting them, and finding ways to resist them at three levels. At the individual level, the struggle is to uncover the ways racism becomes unintentionally internalized (see Fanon 1966; Freire 1970); at the interpersonal level, the struggle is to identify commonalities and differences between participants and to overcome barriers to forging solidarity; and at the institutional level, the struggle is to understand oppressive structures and discover possibilities for creating meaningful changes in them. The conversations raise questions for discussion and bring out data, usually in the form of personal experiences, for mutual or collective reflection and analysis. In an ongoing process, the group tests its conclusions and redefines its research topics through a continuing spiral of praxis-in-struggle and dialogue.

Conversation-based activist research begins with locating existing conversations among local community participants, then aims to gradually widen the base of participants sharing the same social concerns, so that private conversations about shared problems take on a more public character, thereby increasing not only knowledge but also solidarity and the capacity for creating social change. By starting with existing conversations, the process builds on local participants' ways of talking about the problem at hand—their definitions of the problem, their perspective on it, and the very language they use to discuss it. This strategy facilitates a participatory community conversation among ordinary citizens (not just community leaders, politicians, or academic experts), and preserves the community's approaches to the problem so that "ordinary" citizens' perspectives are legitimized, valued, and can be set into productive critical dialogue with other relevant perspectives and discourses, especially those of social science.

In conversation-based research, several kinds of conversations contribute to the growth of knowledge and to the community's struggle. Many conversations take place between pairs or among small groups of individuals affected by the community conditions. Sometimes, however, a research conversation can be facilitated in the context of a fairly large meeting. At times, conversations between individuals in the affected community and someone outside the affected community help move the research process forward. Such conversations can be with outsiders who have either cooperative or adversarial relationships with the group.

Our conversation-based community research project took considerable time to develop, for I found that it was a slow and difficult process to find and enter conversations about the school conditions. I began from my own position as parent of a child in the school, and gradually facilitated the development of a small group of women numbering about half a dozen in its first two years, and growing to about forty or fifty people comprising a less cohesive but more broad-based network over the next five or six years.

It can be difficult for a social scientist to find and enter the conversations of a community about a community problem if they are mostly held in private spaces like individual homes and have not yet assumed a public character. Even longtime residents of the area had difficulty finding and entering such conversations outside their homes. In a suburb like mine, most people live in single-family homes, drive cars to and from their front doors, and know few of their neighbors well enough even to say "hello." They also attend church and go to work out of the neighborhood. There are few public spaces for casual meeting and socializing. My situation was further complicated by my outsider status: my husband and I were not only new to the community, but we were also not African American. Fortunately, the PTA provided a context that allowed me to enter the community's conversation about the school conditions.

## Beginning a Community Research Conversation

I had hoped to find a group of activist parents already organized to improve the school conditions, so my first step was to attend a Parent-Teachers Association (PTA) meeting. My entry into the PTA was not particularly auspicious. The meeting was poorly attended, and when I brought up issues such as the amount of time the children were spending in group punishments, very little attention was paid. The only comments by other parents came from one or two who spoke on behalf of the staff, for "all the hard work our teachers and principal are doing." The principal brushed off my concern, and the PTA president went on to other business. The small nucleus of what later emerged as an activist group of parents was invisible to me at the meeting, but I later learned that two or three people had taken note of my expressed concerns. They had wondered "where I was coming from" at first, especially because I was not African American and was criticizing "their" school. They later told me that it was important for me to have spoken in the meeting, because despite their wariness, they had formed some favorable impressions and learned that I had a child in the school.

My second step was to conduct two informal interviews with my daughter's teacher and principal. After several attempts, I finally arranged a meeting with my daughter's homeroom teacher, and my first interview produced some very illuminating information. The teacher, an African American woman in her fifties, gave what I found to be a very surprising response to my concerns about the lack of challenging assignments being given, the class time spent in group punishments, etc. She told me that Black children could simply not be expected to perform at the same level as white ones! She rather sarcastically asked me if my daughter had been in a "similar" school before (i.e. a predominantly Black one), as if to remonstrate me for expecting the same of this school as the former, which she had assumed was mostly white or

Anglo. I pointed out that in fact my daughter had just moved from a very racially mixed inner-city school in another city, but the teacher insisted that that school was not "like" this one. I told her that I saw no reason why an almost entirely African American group of students could not be expected to achieve at the same academic level as a more equally mixed group—as in our daughter's former school—or an all-white group, and that I felt it was a disservice to all the children for her not to assign more book reports, more critical-thinking assignments, more science projects, and the like.

My daughter's teacher replied that on the contrary, giving the students such work would "stress them out." The theme of the supposed dangers of "stressing" African American students by setting high standards for their academic performance would be articulated again and again by both African American and Anglo teachers and administrators. The "stress" theme arose promptly again in my next conversation, which was with the school principal. The principal, also an African American woman, had no hesitation in defending the school's low academic standards. She referred to the supposedly disorganized nature of the homes of the children attending the school, in which "the radios are always blaring" and the families are "always on the move." Over time, it would become clear that because our school had an almost entirely African American student body, it had been stereotyped as a "lower class" school by its own staff and the district administration; its racial composition determined its status in the hierarchy of schools in the district. It would become clearer why many African American teachers and administrators accepted these stereotypes, and how certain formal and informal institutional policies reinforced and reproduced the inferior treatment of African Americans.

In my interview with the principal, she revealed one of the most profound institutional mechanisms that reinforced stereotypes about the students' abilities to achieve, namely, the district's testing policy, which used average scores from a standardized Cognitive Abilities Test to predict "expected" scores on standardized achievement tests. The principal was reluctant to let me see the school's results, and I later learned that the other parents had not even been notified about the school's extremely low test scores; parents had only been notified about their own individual children's scores. I was shocked to learn that our school's scores were not only below grade level, but in the bottom fifth of all the elementary schools in the district. The scores had been below grade level for years, a fact the principal used to further justify why no higher academic performance should be expected from this group of children. She also showed me the scores from the other predominantly African American schools in our area, which were also in the bottom fifth for the district. It was clear that the principal believed the Cognitive Abilities Test was an intelligence test. Her belief was that because the children had been scientifically proven by the Cognitive Abilities Test to be of "low ability" as a group, they should not be "stressed" by being held accountable to perform at higher levels.

## Conversations with Other Parents

After I spoke out at my first PTA meeting, the PTA president called me to ask if I would like to join the PTA education subcommittee. The PTA president became my first community research conversation partner, and one of the very few men connected with the group. Two features of our first conversations were typical of my early conversations with my other community research partners, and both demonstrated the importance of making race an explicit ongoing conversational topic.

First, much of this two- or three-hour conversation was devoted to his interview of me, mostly about my attitudes and experiences around race and racism. The other parents would later ask similar questions: what my past experiences had been with Black people and African American communities; why I had moved to this predominantly Black area; what I would do if white people in the area started to burn crosses on my lawn because a Black person had "shown up on the doorstep"; whether I was concerned that my daughter might be labelled a "nigger lover"; and whether I was a religious Christian. I tried to answer these questions as candidly as possible, even when it was uncomfortable for me to do so. One of the women who became a friend and frequent conversation partner explained early on, "We have to be suspicious, you know, so we're going to be asking you a lot of questions."

Second, much of the conversation consisted of my partners' descriptions and revelations about their own experiences of racism. The PTA president, for example, told me a very long story about the many unpleasant adventures he and his family had experienced trying to buy their home. Although it took time for me to realize it, my conversation partners' reactions to their painful experiences helped explain why they had not done more to investigate the ways racism was operating to depress the children's achievement at the school. They cast their experiences in terms of strong feelings and beliefs that "racism is everywhere," "racism is here to stay," "racism is bigger than all of us," and the like. So if the problem at the school was racism, it seemed impossible to change it. One of the women on the education committee said, "I used to lie in bed at night (during the Civil Rights Movement) wondering whether I would live or die . . . race is a big issue . . . I haven't had the energy to go back into it for a long time . . . sometimes people don't like to think about it (the school conditions) that way" (as evidence of a racist school system). Conversations among a small group of parents would eventually identify two other factors accounting for the parents' reluctance to cast the school's problems in terms of racism: a self-imposed "blindness" derived from their fervent desire to have left racism behind when they left the inner city and came to the suburbs, and their conception of racism in terms of white people's personal prejudice, which made it difficult to see Black educators as the carriers of racism.

Race was so prominent in our discussions for obvious reasons. At the personal level, our different racial backgrounds threatened to maintain a barrier between us. At the social level, racial differences and race-based policies and procedures were at the core of the problem at hand—our children's school.

## Using Conversation-Based Research to Begin Organizing the PTA

At the time I entered, the PTA was not functioning well. It had poor attendance, few meetings, no actively functioning subcommittees, and no organized group of parents attending to quality-of-education issues. When the PTA president asked, I expressed my interest in serving on the education subcommittee. After he shared that he, too, was concerned about the low quality of education, I suggested that perhaps the education subcommittee might work on this problem. He gave me the names and telephone numbers of the other five or six women on the non-functioning subcommittee, and I began calling them.

### Conversations Within a PTA Subgroup

Our conversations began over the telephone in the spring and summer of 1981 with exchanges of personal information, such as where we were from, when we had moved to the area, etc.; discussion of the problems our children and we were having at the school; and free-ranging discussions about race and racism. I learned that all the mothers were worried about their children's lack of academic progress, had gone to the school time and again with complaints, and had had many unpleasant and unproductive encounters with the teachers and principal. However, their conversations about the school had remained almost entirely within the privacy of their own homes with their spouses. I was surprised to learn that the women on the subcommittee did not even know each other, much less talk to each other about the school, even though they lived in the same housing development and their children went to the same school. I found myself working to build some trust between neighbors who didn't know each other, helping them learn about each other.

Information from my conversations with the teacher and principal provided some interesting talking points in these early conversations. The teacher's and principal's low expectations for Black students, since they came from African Americans, helped define our children's predicament as a real puzzle to solve. The fact that the teacher and principal had said these things to me, a white person, made it all the more interesting and complex.

Even though I felt sure at this point that our school's very poor academic program was the result of race-based factors, my conversation partners seemed reluctant to embrace this suggestion. Our conversations were full of contradictions: we discussed race and racism incessantly, yet the other parents avoided concluding that our school was the victim of a racist school system. Instead, in the early stages of our group's formation, the most dominant formulation of the problem of our children's schooling was one of "personalities": the poor personality characteristics of some of the worst teachers, especially their sour and punitive attitudes toward the children; the poor personality "fit" between the principal and some of the teachers; the "personality problems" many of the parents had with both the teachers and the principal; and the inability of the teachers to deal with some of the children's difficult personalities.

The time I spent one-to-one on the telephone during these early months accomplished several steps in terms of developing the conversation-based community research project. First, by "researching" each other's children's experiences at the school, we developed an informational base about the nature of the detrimental school practices directly affecting our children, and raised the level of awareness among ourselves about the severity of the school situation. Second, we began to see that the district's testing policy was implicated in setting low standards for our school and other predominantly African American schools. These steps helped the struggle because we began to see the problem as lying in school-based practices rather than in individual personalities: there was a collective problem that required collective solution. Third, the concept of "low expectations" began to appear as a conversational research topic. Fourth, we began to talk about the negative treatment we had received at the hands of the school staff when we had attempted to intervene on behalf of our children, and to see this treatment as a pattern of discouragement. For example, we discussed how we felt when teachers avoided speaking to us when we entered the building, or when the principal called us by our first names while insisting on being called by her title, and how this disrespectful treatment detracted from our ability to act. Fifth, we were developing a small nucleus of peer participants with enough mutual understanding and solidarity to engage fruitfully in a conversation-based research project.

Exploring our race-based differences was particularly valuable for increasing personal trust and friendship and for developing insights about conditions at the school. My perspective on the school situation, coming from my experience of white privilege, differed from the perspectives of the African American parents, and we often talked in quite personal ways about how race affected our understandings. For example, I first saw the school conditions as a crisis we could address with pragmatic measures such as meeting with the responsible people in charge to discuss needed changes, partly because I was not surrounded by other similarly critical oppressive social conditions, and partly because I had grown up with the experience of having people in authority be at least somewhat responsive to me. My conversation partners had less energy to deal with yet another crisis, and their past experiences gave them reason to be much less optimistic about their ability to make changes.

The content of much of our dialogue centered on discussions about our very different perspectives on the same situation, reflecting our different positionalities. Such conversations slowly led into discussions about my conversation partners' reluctance to look beneath the surface appearance of the school being a self-imposed blindness to preserve the illusion of middle-class success. Later, we could identify the ways this blindness was being actively reinforced by the school district's policies. Such conversations led to our discovery that schools reproduce racial inequality partly through differential and inferior treatment of Black parents, creating "Black parent push-out" (Stern 1987a, 1987b)—a phenomenon not developed in the academic literature.

### Engaging the PTA Body in our Research Conversation

I obtained some testing reports from our school district and compiled data from them, preparing some charts showing that the higher the proportion of African American students in a school, the lower were both the average Cognitive Abilities Test scores and the achievement test scores. This was the first kind of sociological data I introduced into our group conversation. The data, clearly showing a pattern of racial inequality across the schools in the district, helped demonstrate that our school's problem was part of a larger problem, worthy of organizing our own PTA to address. We decided, with the support of the PTA president, to reformulate our group as the PTA Program Committee, and we continued our discussions in the context of planning PTA programs for the next year.

In the Fall of 1981, we began meeting as the Program Committee. The PTA president had appointed me as the chair, and we finally began having face-to-face meetings as a group, though I also continued having long telephone conversations with all of the group members. (This membership was somewhat fluid: there were four people who remained solidly at the nucleus, and four or five others who came intermittently to our meetings.) We developed a plan to present programs for the PTA at large that would address some of our concerns about the educational quality at the school. The group felt it would be best to organize the programs around the subject of testing—especially the Cognitive Abilities Test. This would avoid a program series framed outrightly about racism and schooling, which my conversation partners felt would be "touchy," given the "sensitivity" of the issue and the racial composition of the school staff.

For the year's first PTA meeting, we invited the testing administrator for the school district. His presentation caused a stir because, appealing to science and the statistical meaning of "expected," he clearly stated that our children could not be "expected" to perform as well as others. He implied that the children's low average performance on standardized achievement tests was due at least in some part to a lack of native "ability." He also explained that the district used the Cognitive Abilities Test to predict average "expected" achievement test scores, and defended this use of the Cognitive Abilities Test over the parents' objections. In addition, echoing the principal's earlier remark to me, the testing administrator referred ominously to the dangers of "stress" if we were to push the children to achieve beyond their "abilities." The administrator also suggested that the children were suffering from a combination of cultural deficits, especially disorganized homes not conducive to study.

The administrators' remarks caused considerable consternation. Many of the parents angrily spoke out, saying that they were educators themselves, or had college educations, that their homes were certainly not disorganized, that they supervised their children's homework, that their radios and TVs were not "blaring," and that they did not accept his explanations for the low achievement scores. Additional questions posed by the parents to the administrator unveiled the way the district's use of the Cognitive Abilities Test helped perpetuate racial inequality in the school district. The administrator revealed that the test was used in the system of school accountability: schools whose average achievement levels fell below expectations based on the scores on the Cognitive Abilities Test were "flagged" and given special attention and resources. This policy served to benefit those schools with high "ability" scores—mainly the predominantly white ones—because it provided resources to prevent them from "underachieving." But in schools like ours, where "ability" scores were low, low achievement was "expected" and did not lead to the provision of additional resources. As our small group would learn shortly through one of our conversations with a parent from another school who worked as a district-level administrator—"resources" included the allocation of teachers, and schools which were "flagged" benefitted from the district policy to allocate the best and most experienced teachers to those schools. Accordingly, by default, our school had a preponderance of comparatively inexperienced and less qualified staff.

The data I had gathered from school district reports served an important role in helping the parents gain a critical perspective on the district's testing policy and to begin to identify specific mechanisms perpetuating inequality. The revelation about how the district used the Cognitive Abilities Test to justify the systematic allocation of more resources to the mostly white schools caught the parents' rapt attention in the PTA meeting. Other ramifications of the district's testing policy also came to light afterwards as a result of the PTA meeting: the policy also released the staff at the predominantly Black schools from both parental and school organizational pressure to raise low achievement scores.

With this meeting, we had taken a big step forward. We had identified some of the mechanisms at the district level that negatively affected the quality of education at our school by lowering expectations not only for student performance, but also for that of the principal and teachers. The group interview of the testing administrator had also engaged other parents from the PTA, broadening our base of support. It was becoming clearer that the problem was not primarily one of personal racial prejudice, and the African American teachers' and principal's roles in perpetuating low academic expectations could be somewhat understood (though not forgiven) as having been set in motion by district policies.

To the next PTA meeting, the program committee invited two African American professors of education from a local university, one of whom was a woman, to talk about research on testing. Our committee wrote an invitation letter describing the school conditions and the testing policy, which summarized some of our conversation-based research results and served as an informal "working paper" or reference document.

The professors presented research data discrediting the use of the Cognitive Abilities Test as a measure of intelligence. Their position was that the test measured past academic achievement as well as basic ability. They answered many questions, and when asked about the problem of "overstressing" the children, they simply replied that these children were like any other children, and should respond well to academic challenges. They said that in their roles both as African American parents and African American educators, they felt strongly about the need for all African American children to have equal educational opportunity, and concluded by urging the parents to be concerned about our school's low test scores and to expect their children to achieve at the same average levels as white children.

The group interview process at this PTA meeting was a high point in the development of the community-research conversation, drawing many additional parents into the PTA and into the discussion. The two professors had lent their professional expertise, brought relevant social-scientific research to bear, inspired the parents to work on behalf of the group, delegitimized the "stress" argument, legitimized the activist parents' efforts, and supported the Program Committee's efforts to apply pressure to change school conditions on behalf of the school population as a whole.

The PTA meetings were so successful that we went on to plan additional similar programs, some based on the group interview format, and others in which we made presentations about our research to date and broke the meeting into several small discussion groups, which we led. Parents from other PTAs in our area began attending our meetings, and the frequency of telephone calls I received increased greatly. I made many new telephone friends during this period and put many parents who did not know each other—both from our school and from other schools—in touch with each other. Our small group had clearly begun to develop into a larger network with a sense of shared problems and purpose.

From the outset, sociological knowledge influenced my telephone conversations with other parents, informed my interviews with the teachers and principal, and helped me structure PTA meeting programs.[3] Soon after I began talking with the education subcommittee members, I started systematically collecting sociological and anthropological articles pertaining to racial inequality and schooling because it was clear that I could make a more valuable contribution to the group if I had more expertise in that area. As I began to read the articles, I shared some of the concepts and findings with the other parents and occasionally gave someone a copy of an article in which she was particularly interested.

### From Conversation to Action

Our successes increased the acrimony among parents and between parents and teachers at the PTA meetings. Those who opposed us began to mobilize counter-resistance against us both as individuals and as a group. At one meeting, two or three white district administrators, an African American administrator, our principal and teachers, and some parents all joined in accusing the Program Committee and activist parents of "negativity" and putting the children in danger of being "overstressed." The teachers raised the stakes with retributions on the activists' children and even in some cases on whole classes of children. Some of our children soon went for days without being called on, or were singled out and embarrassed for small mistakes, or were not allowed to go to the bathroom. Retribution on the children was one of the teachers' most effective ways of fragmenting parental opposition, deterring parents from "making waves."

As the relations between the activist parents and school staff worsened and veered toward crisis, several parents (some from the Program Committee) requested a meeting with the principal to discuss the educational quality at our school. Simply deciding to request the meeting as a group represented a major step forward in the development of group solidarity in the face of efforts to discourage our opposition. The principal refused outright; she said she would meet with us individually about our own individual children, but not with a group of us about school-wide issues, and she appealed to the authority of district administrators who supported her position. Although we did finally succeed in meeting with her, we could not win her agreement about the need to address the low quality of education or the punitive environment at the school. (We met as a group with one of the teachers about the issue of group punishments, but she was equally unresponsive.) The principal insisted that "positive" parent involvement was needed at the school. Our role was to make money for the PTA, volunteer at the school, and be concerned only about our own individual children, not groups of children or our school as a whole. It was clear that so long as she was principal, improving the school conditions would be impossible.

After this meeting, we began to talk more about how the school treated us as parents. We gathered data by talking to each other about what had happened to us individually when we attempted to talk with the teachers or principal, and about our different perceptions about these events. We had all had telephone calls and notes to the teachers and principal go unanswered and efforts to schedule meetings ignored. But most troubling of all was the retribution the teachers took on our children for our having "made waves." Although I found this kind of treatment shocking, the African American mothers, though equally outraged, were not surprised at all. I learned that they were routinely disrespected, ignored, patronized, and intimidated by the teachers and principal, and that they had learned to expect that their interventions would result in retribution on their children. It was by sharing our different reactions that we began to explore the racial and class implications of our different expectations about our treatment by the school staff and administrators. From these conversations, the hypothesis emerged that part of the reason the academic standards were so low at the Black schools was that those schools' parents were systematically discouraged from pressuring the schools to perform better. We later investigated this idea more closely with some on-site visits to other schools and interviews with other parents.

Eventually, we formulated our hypothesis as "Black parent push-out": the idea that parents receive poorer treatment and are discouraged from participation if their children attend predominantly Black schools (Stern 1987a). This process increases racial inequality by making it more difficult for African American parents to intervene, even as their children experience other forms of race-based disadvantage in the predominantly Black schools.[4] These forms of counter-resistance embedded in school-based mechanisms created strong barriers to parental intervention at predominantly African American schools, and suppressed the parents' expectations that it was possible to make needed changes. In sum, our school needed such intervention more desperately than the white schools where academic standards were set higher, but we as parents in African American schools found it much more difficult to intervene.

At the end of the second year of programs, when elections were held for the next year's PTA president, the parents elected one of the activist parents by a narrow margin over the principal's chosen candidate. With this evidence of support, the activist parents decided to apply pressure on the Superintendent to replace the principal. The parents had little hope of soon affecting a change in the district-wide testing policy, but felt they could make immediate changes in the concrete conditions of their children's education by replacing our principal with one "with a proven track record."

Demanding to remove the principal was a step only a very few parents wanted to take, no matter how dissatisfied they were. The risks of retribution loomed large. However, six parents—my husband and I, the PTA president and his wife, and one other couple—did eventually meet with the Superintendent to demand that the principal and one teacher be replaced. Our efforts were successful, to most parents' surprise.

The new principal, also an African American woman, was much more effective. She surprised us, the teachers, and perhaps most of all the district administration, by using the PTA organization to help her put pressure on district officials to obtain badly needed resources for the school. Instead of seeing the PTA parents as an adversarial body, she developed a very positive working relationship with the PTA, and thus created a very different role for it than the one advocated by the previous principal. Under the new principal, the school treated parents cooperatively and with respect, more like the predominantly white schools treated white parents. The new principal also put pressure on the teachers to demand more from the students. However, these activities put her in an adversarial position with the district administration. As she told me some years later, she was grateful to have entered the situation with a relatively well organized group of parents to whom she could turn for support when she went to the district to demand additional resources for the school.

## Theorizing and Acting Against Inequality

Although many of our children had graduated from the school by this time, the parents who had met through the program committee continued talking, mostly on the telephone, both among ourselves and with many other parents, and our community conversation grew. The parents-in-conversation began, somewhat self-consciously, to work on developing a theory about the mechanisms responsible for reproducing inequality in our schools. In doing so, they relied on the central concept of "expectations," which helped account for the power relations embedded in those mechanisms, moving both their theory and their struggle forward. The parents began with the district's low expectations for the children's academic performance as measured by standardized achievement tests, but also took note of the teachers' and principals' low expectations of them as parents, and went on to incorporate their growing observations that their own expectations of the teachers and principals were lower than they should be. Once the parents started thinking about the reciprocity of expectations, they noticed other sets of mutually low expectations, such as between our school's principal and the teachers, and between the district administrators and the local principal. This last relationship was especially instructive when the new principal arrived and the whole arrangement of expectations was disrupted. (The school district officials themselves had to adjust to the expectation that the principal and many parents would come en masse to demand more resources.)

The insight about the interrelationship of mechanisms perpetuating "low expectations" provided an interesting theoretical handle for the parents to continue to develop their community conversation in a direction that would enhance their struggle for educational equality. Their insight also suggested that the parents had at least some power to interrupt the cycle of negative expectations. If the parents expected the district administrators to be concerned about our school, they might in turn put more pressure on the principal; if the parents expected more respect from the teachers, the teachers might expect more academic output from the children, and so on.

A parent group that evolved from the original parent network had some lasting success interrupting the chain of low expectations. The groups were connected through a mother in a nearby neighborhood whom I had gotten to know over a period of about two years. Through our conversations, she made use of the insights that had emerged from the parents' network and sociological articles I gave her about tracking. She did an investigation and learned that in her son's middle school, the students who came from predominantly Black schools had been "levelled" at their elementary schools of origin to enter a curricular track from which it was almost impossible to get the prerequisites for a college-preparation high-school course. Pupils from predominantly white schools were enrolled in higher tracks.

She communicated her findings to a friend of hers, a PTA president at the local high school. When the school superintendent presented a plan to turn that high school into a "professional" high school, the PTA president was skeptical. Given the tracking of the Black middle-school students, he doubted that they would be prepared for an academic high school with a college-preparatory curriculum. He insisted on seeing the proposed curriculum for the "professional" high school, and confirmed his suspicions: "professional" was a euphemism for what is usually called a vocational curriculum. He then organized several PTAs in his area to protest the curriculum, and the school district upgraded it to include more college-track courses.

### Conclusions

A community research conversation might be thought of as an ongoing, open-ended process involving interlocking, overlapping conversations between individuals, within small groups, and between groups in a broader network. Such conversations can incorporate the direct observations and reflections of participants, together with relevant concepts from the social-scientific literature; they can also include individual social scientists who add perspectives and thus help to define the problem and seek solutions. Such community research conversations can link "epistemological communities" (Nelson 1993) and democratize both the production and distribution of knowledge. By combining a "people's research" approach, in which ordinary people do research as a part of life through conversation, with approaches from academic social science, the parents' process illustrates a democratic, emancipatory, and critical form of social science that produces knowledge in the community's interests, from its perspective, and in the service of its needs.[5]

Building a conversation-based participatory research project in disadvantaged communities can increase their ability to create knowledge-based community struggles against oppressive conditions. The African American parents' research project shows, among other things, that conversation-based research improved the group's understanding of how institutionally based mechanisms reproduced racial inequality in the school system, and helped the group identify specific forms of internalized oppression that interacted with institutionally based mechanisms to deter them from resisting the school district's imposition of low academic expectations. As the conversation-based research process grew to include more people, solidarity increased and the knowledge-production process was infused with more sources of "data."

Though the parents' conversation-based research project was grounded first in our own conversations and our own local struggle, social-scientific theory and research entered the process at several points and in several ways: I introduced some tentative, sociologically informed hypotheses about the school conditions in my conversations with other parents; interviewed school staff using sociological knowledge; gathered sociologically informed background data about the schools; suggested that social scientists be invited to make presentations to the group; wrote working drafts summarizing our research to date; and gathered sociological, anthropological, and educational research articles and books pertinent to our situation, giving them out to parents at opportune times. Sociological theories about how race and class forces reflect and reproduce social-structural conditions provided theoretical guidance throughout. In return, the parents' process contributed to a positive critique of existing social-science research on race and schooling: the group discovered that schools' differential treatment of Black parents negatively affected the quality of education, and developed the concept of "Black parent push-out"—ideas similar to those developed in the academic literature with regard to Black children.

Finally, the parents' experience shows the usefulness of building different perspectives into an integrated process of research and struggle. One advantage lies in gaining knowledge from both academic social science and from the participation and perspectives of people who see a social problem "from below" (Huizer and Mannheim 1979), who may observe phenomena that elude researchers otherwise socially situated. Another lies in creating a dialectical process that incorporates a cross-critique of perspectives within the community conversation, thereby increasing the quality of the knowledge that informs the group's efforts. Finally, the parents' process shows the variety of ways in which an activist social scientist can contribute to the efforts of a marginalized community to understand and change its circumstances.

## Notes

1. At the time the parent group was meeting, the general population in the school district was nearly fifty percent African American and the proportion of African American school pupils was heading upward through sixty percent. Of nine elected school board members, only one was African American. There were very few middle-level African American school district administrators but many principals and teachers, most of whom were assigned to predominantly African American schools like ours. Our school was staffed by a female African American principal and an almost entirely African American teaching staff. Racial inequality was a major issue in the school system, which was responding to a series of court desegregation orders by busing Black students to predominantly white schools. There was no public discussion at the time of addressing educational inequality by directly altering educational policies or practices. A few years later, however, a magnet school was instituted to attract white students to predominantly Black schools.

2. See, e.g., Freire 1970; Huizer and Mannheim 1979; Schensul 1980; Shor 1980, 1993; Schensul et al. 1982; Fay 1987; Collins 1990; Lather 1991.

3. The many ways this knowledge entered the conversations and influenced the parents' and my own thinking would require discussion beyond the possibilities for this paper. A brief and incomplete list of theory and research that surely penetrated the network's discussion gives a general idea of the range of theory and research that might be useful in such a situation: the literature on theories of political participation and democracy (e.g. Dewey 1966; Pateman 1970); theories of power and empowerment (especially Hartsock 1983); Bowles and Gintis's (1976) theory of the relationship between the economy and schooling; research on parent participation in schooling (e.g., Pousada 1984); and the literature on the relationship between expectations and school performance (e.g. Rosenthal and Jacobson 1968).

4. I describe racial differences in parents' power to bring about change through the "everyday politics of schooling" in more detail in Stern (1987b).

5. See Stern (1994) for elaboration. Elements of the parents' research approach can also be seen in writings on emancipatory-participatory research and pedagogy (e.g., Shor 1980, 1993; Lather 1986, 1991; Maguire 1987); critical social science (Fay 1987); feminist praxis, research, and theory, including consciousness-raising (Mies 1983); the theory of second-person knowledge (Code 1991); women's standpoints on everyday experiences (Smith 1987a), and story telling in Black women's epistemology (Collins 1991).

# Chapter 5

# Challenging Power

## Toxic Waste Protests and the Politicization of White, Working-Class Women

Celene Krauss

Over the past two decades, toxic waste disposal has been a central focus of women's grassroots environmental activism.[1] Women of diverse racial, ethnic, and class backgrounds have assumed the leadership of community environmental struggles around toxic waste issues (Krauss 1993). Out of their experience of protest, these women have constructed ideologies of environmental justice that reveal broader issues of inequality underlying environmental hazards (Bullard 1990, 1994). Environmental justice does not exist as an abstract concept prior to these women's activism. It grows out of the concrete, immediate, everyday experience of struggles around issues of survival. As women become involved in toxic waste issues, they go through a politicizing process which is mediated by their experiences of class, race, and ethnicity (Krauss 1993).

Among the earliest community activists in toxic waste protests were white, working-class women. This chapter examines the process by which these women became politicized through grassroots protest activities in the 1980s, which led to their analyses of environmental justice, and in many instances to their leadership in regional and national toxic waste coalitions. These women would seem unlikely candidates for becoming involved in political protest. They came out of a culture that shares a strong belief in the existing political system, and in which traditional women's roles center around the private arena of family.

Although financial necessity may have led them into the workplace, the primary roles from which they derived meaning, identity, and satisfaction are those of mothering and taking care of family.[2] Yet, as we shall see, the threat that toxic wastes posed to family health and community survival disrupted the taken-for-granted fabric of their daily lives, politicizing women who had never viewed themselves as activists.

Progressive social analysts have often dismissed the community protests of white, working-class women as parochial or particularistic, viewing with suspicion their emphasis on localism, community, and tradition (see Boyte 1980; Kling and Posner 1990). In contrast to these views, this chapter shows how white, working-class women's involvement in toxic waste issues has wider implications for social change. It is true that these women became involved around particular single-issue protests: they fought to close down toxic waste dump sites, to prevent the siting of hazardous waste incinerators, to oppose companies' waste-disposal policies, to push for recycling projects, and so on. Their voices show us, however, that their single-issue community protests led them through a process of politicization and the broader analysis of inequities of class and gender in the public arena and in the family. Propelled into the public arena in defense of their children, they ultimately challenged government, corporations, experts, husbands, and their own insecurities as working-class women. Their analysis of environmental justice and inequality led them to form coalitions with labor and people of color around environmental issues. These women's traditional beliefs about motherhood, family, and democracy served a crucial function in this politicizing process. While they framed their analyses in terms of traditional constructions of gender and the state, they actively reinterpreted these constructions into an oppositional ideology, which became a resource of resistance and a source of power in the public arena.

### Subjective Dimensions of Grassroots Activism

In most sociological analysis of social movements, the subjective dimension of protest has often been ignored or viewed as private and individualistic. Feminist theory, however, has helped us to see its importance. Feminists show us how experience is not merely a personal, individualistic concept: it is social. People's experiences reflect where they fit into the social hierarchy. Feminist standpoint methodologies inquire into how different groups construct truth or knowledge out of their experiences, influenced by their social location and the conditions of their lives. The notion that subjective experience and knowledge are central to our understanding of women and other oppressed groups rests on the assumption that oppressed groups have subjugated knowledge and perspectives, which are not reflected in the conceptual schemes of dominant groups.[3] Thus, white, working-class women interpret their experience of toxic waste problems within the context of their particular cultural history, arriving at a critique that reflects broader issues of class and gender.

Recent feminist research in social movement theory has focused on the subjective processes that underlie collective action, examining the important role of subjective beliefs, grievances, and identity in social change.[4] Politicization is a term used to describe the ways in which individuals develop a framework of meanings and beliefs that challenge dominant ideologies and empower political action. Central for these writers is the analysis of how individuals move from their everyday experiences to develop an oppositional consciousness. These theorists argue that oppositional consciousness cannot be taken for granted because oppressive experiences are interpreted and internalized through the distorting lens of dominant ideologies, which mask the systemic causes of oppression and lead people to view their personal troubles as individual or idiosyncratic, and constrain their political action. The construction of new interpretative frameworks is a subjective process through which people attribute their discontent to structural, cultural, or systemic causes, rather than to personal failings or individual deviance (Taylor and Whittier 1992, 114).

Following feminist perspectives, this article focuses on the subjective process by which white, working-class women involved in toxic waste protests construct an oppositional consciousness out of their everyday lives, experiences, and identities. As these women became involved in the public arena, they confronted a world of power normally hidden from them. This forced them to re-examine their assumptions about private and public power and to develop a broad reconceptualization of gender, family, and government.

The experience of protest is central to this process and can reshape traditional beliefs and values (see Thompson 1963). My analysis reveals the contradictory ways in which traditional culture mediates white, working-class women's subjective experience and interpretation of structural inequality. Their protests are framed in terms of dominant ideologies of motherhood, family, and a deep faith in the democratic system. Their experience also reveals how dominant ideologies are appropriated and reconstructed as an instrument of their politicization and a legitimating ideology used to justify resistance. For example, as the political economy of growth displaces environmental problems into their communities, threatening the survival of children and family and creating everyday crises, government toxic waste policies are seen to violate their traditional belief that a democratic government will protect their families. Ideologies of motherhood and democracy become political resources which these women use to initiate and justify their resistance, their increasing politicization, and their fight for a genuine democracy.

## Methodological Considerations

My analysis is based on the oral and written voices of white, working-class women involved in toxic waste protests. Sources include individual interviews, as well as conference presentations, pamphlets, books, and other written materials that have emerged from this movement. Interviews were conducted with a snowball sample of twenty white, working-class women who were leaders in grassroots protest activities against toxic waste landfills and incinerators during the 1980s. These women ranged in age from twenty-five to forty; all but one had young children at the time of their protest. They were drawn from a cross section of the country, representing urban, suburban, and rural areas. None of them had been politically active before the protest; many of them, however, have continued to be active in subsequent community movements, often becoming leaders in state-wide and national coalitions around environmental and social justice issues. I established contact with these women through networking at activist conferences. Open-ended interviews were conducted between May 1989, and December, 1991, and lasted from two to four hours. The interview was designed to generate a history of these women's activist experiences, information about changes in political beliefs, and insights into their perceptions of their roles as women, mothers, and wives.

Interviews were also conducted with Lois Gibbs and four other organizers for the Citizens Clearinghouse for Hazardous Wastes (CCHW). CCHW is a nation-wide organization created by Gibbs, who is best known for her successful campaign to relocate families in Love Canal, New York. Over the past two decades, this organization has functioned as a key resource for community groups fighting around toxic waste issues in the United States. Its leadership and staff are composed primarily of women, and the organization played a key role in shaping the ideology of working-class women's environmental activism in the 1980s.

My scholarly interest in working-class women's community activism grew out of my own involvement as a community activist and organizer in the 1970s. This decade marked the period of my own politicization as a white, middle-class woman working with women from many different racial-ethnic backgrounds as they challenged corporate and governmental policies that were destroying urban, working-class neighborhoods. My subsequent academic research has focused on the community protests of working-class women, who are often forgotten in our understanding of movements for social change. My experiences within the environmental movement helped guide my research and deepen my analysis. Through the issue of toxic waste protests, I have examined different facets of working-class women's community activism, most recently the ways in which consciousness and agency are mediated by different experiences of race and ethnicity (Krauss 1993).

### The Process of Politicization

Women identify the toxic waste movement as a women's movement, composed primarily of mothers. As one woman who fought against an incinerator in Arizona and subsequently worked on other anti-incinerator campaigns throughout the state stressed: "Women are the backbone of the grassroots groups, they are the ones who stick with it, the ones who won't back off." Because mothers are traditionally responsible for the health of their children, they are more likely than others within their communities to begin to make the link between toxic waste and their children's ill health. And in communities around the United States, it was women who began to uncover numerous toxin-related health problems: multiple miscarriages, birth defects, cancer, neurological symptoms, and so on. Given the placement of toxic waste facilities in working-class and low-income communities and communities of color,[5] it is not surprising that women from these groups have played a particularly important role in fighting against environmental hazards.

White, working-class women's involvement in toxic waste issues is complicated by the political reality that they, like most people, are excluded from the policy-making process. For the most part, corporate and governmental disposal policies with far-reaching social and political consequences are made without the knowledge of community residents.

People may unknowingly live near (or even on top of) a toxic waste dump, or they may assume that the facility is well regulated by the government. Consequently, residents are often faced with a number of problems of seemingly indeterminate origin, and the information withheld from them may make them unwitting contributors to the ill health of their children.

The discovery of a toxic waste problem and the threat it poses to family sets in motion a process of critical questioning about the relationship between women's private work as mothers and the public arena of politics. The narratives of the women involved in toxic waste protests focus on political transformation, on the process of "becoming" an activist. Prior to their discovery of the link between their family's health and toxic waste, few of these women had been politically active. They saw their primary work in terms of the "private" sphere of motherhood and family. But the realization that toxic waste issues threatened their families thrust them into the public arena in defense of this private sphere. According to Penny Newman:

> We woke up one day to discover that our families were being damaged by toxic contamination, a situation in which we had little, if any, input. It wasn't a situation in which we chose to become involved, rather we did it because we had to . . . it was a matter of our survival. (Newman 1991, 8)

Lois Gibbs offered a similar account of her involvement in Love Canal:

> When my mother asked me what I wanted to do when I grew up, I said I wanted to have six children and be a homemaker. . . . I moved into Love Canal and I bought the American Dream: a house, two children, a husband, and HBO. And then something happened to me and that was Love Canal. I got involved because my son Michael had epilepsy . . . and my daughter Melissa developed a rare blood disease and almost died because of something someone else did. . . . I never thought of myself as an activist or an organizer. I was a housewife, a mother, but all of a sudden it was my family, my children, and my neighbors. . .

It was through their role as mothers that many of these women began to suspect a connection between the invisible hazard posed by toxic wastes and their children's ill health, and this was their first step toward political activism. At Love Canal, for example, Lois Gibbs's fight to expose toxic waste hazards was triggered by the link she made between her son's seizures and the toxic waste dump site. After reading about toxic hazards in a local newspaper, she thought about her son and then surveyed her neighbors to find that they had similar health problems. In Woburn, Massachusetts, Ann Anderson found that other neighborhood children were, like her son, being treated for leukemia, and she began to wonder if this was an unusually high incidence of the disease. In Denver, mothers comparing stories at Tupperware parties were led to question the unusually large number of sick and dying children in their community. These women's practical activity as mothers and their extended networks of family and community led them to make the connection between toxic waste and sick children—a discovery process rooted in what Sara Ruddick (1989) has called the everyday practice of mothering, in which, through their informal networks, mothers compare notes and experiences, developing a shared body of personal, empirical knowledge.

Upon making the link between their family's ill health and toxic wastes, the women's first response was to go to the government, a response that reflects a deeply held faith in democracy embedded in their working-class culture. They assumed that the government would protect the health and welfare of their children. Gibbs (1982, 12) reports:

> I grew up in a blue-collar community, it was very patriotic, into democracy . . . I believed in government. . . . I believed that if you had a complaint, you went to the right person in government. If there was a way to solve the problem, they would be glad to do it.

An Alabama activist who fought to prevent the siting of an incinerator describes a similar response:

> We just started educating ourselves and gathering information about the problems of incineration. We didn't think our elected officials knew. Surely if they knew that there was already a toxic waste dump in our county, they would stop it.

In case after case, however, these women described facing a government that was indifferent, if not antagonistic, to their concerns. At Love Canal, local officials claimed that the toxic waste pollution was insignificant, the equivalent of smoking just three cigarettes a day. In South Brunswick, New Jersey, governmental officials argued that living with pollution was the price of a better way of life. In Jacksonville, Arkansas, women were told that the dangers associated with dioxin emitted from a hazardous waste incinerator were exaggerated, no worse than "eating two or three tablespoons of peanut butter over a thirty-year period." Also in Arkansas, a woman who linked her ill health to a fire at a military site that produced agent orange was told by doctors that she was going through a "change of life." In Stringfellow, California, eight hundred thousand gallons of toxic chemical waste pumped into the community flowed directly behind the elementary school and into the playground. Children played in contaminated puddles yet officials withheld information from their parents because "they didn't want to panic the public."

Government's dismissal of their concerns about the health of their families and communities challenged these white, working-class women's democratic assumptions and opened a window on a world of power whose working they had not before questioned. Government explanations starkly contradicted the personal, empirical evidence which the women discovered as mothers, the everyday knowledge that their children and their neighbors' children were ill. Indeed, a recurring theme in the narratives of these women is the transformation of their beliefs about government. Their politicization is rooted in a deep sense of violation, hurt, and betrayal from finding out their government will not protect their families. Echoes of this disillusionment are heard from women throughout the country. In the CCHW publication *Empowering Women* (1989, 31) one activist noted:

> All our lives we are taught to believe certain things about ourselves as women, about democracy and justice, and about people in positions of authority. Once we become involved with toxic waste problems, we need to confront some of our old beliefs and change the way we view things.

Lois Gibbs summed up this feeling when she stated:

> There is something about discovering that democracy isn't democracy as we know it. When you lose faith in your government, it's like finding out your mother was fooling around on your father. I was very upset. It almost broke my heart because I really believed

in the system. I still believe in the system, only now I believe that democracy is of the people and by the people, that people have to move it, it ain't gonna move by itself.

These women's loss of faith in "democracy" as they had understood it led them to develop a more autonomous and critical stance. Their investigation shifted to a political critique of the undemocratic nature of government itself, making the link between government inaction and corporate power, and discovering that government places corporate interests and profit ahead of the health needs of families and communities. At Love Canal, residents found that local government's refusal to acknowledge the scope of the toxic waste danger was related to plans of Hooker Chemical, the polluting industry, for a multi-million dollar downtown development project. In Woburn, Massachusetts, government officials feared that awareness of the health hazard posed by a dump would limit their plans for real-estate development. In communities throughout the United States, women came to see that government policies supported waste companies' preference of incineration over recycling because incineration was more profitable.

Ultimately, their involvement in toxic waste protests led these women to develop a perspective on environmental justice rooted in issues of class and a critique of the corporate state. They argued that government's claims—to be democratic, to act on behalf of the public interest, to hold the family sacrosanct—are false. One woman who fought an incinerator in Arizona recalled:

I believed in government. When I heard EPA, I thought, "Ooh, that was so big." Now I wouldn't believe them if they said it was sunny outside. I have a list of the revolving door of the EPA. Most of them come from Browning Ferris or Waste Management, the companies that plan landfills and incinerators.

As one activist in Alabama related:

I was politically naive. I was real surprised because I live in an area that's like the Bible belt of the South. Now I think the God of the United States is really economic development, and that has got to change.

Another activist emphasized:

We take on government and polluters. . . . We are up against the largest corporations in the United States. They have lots of money to lobby, pay off, bribe, cajole, and influence. They threaten us. Yet we challenge them with the only things we have—people and the truth. We learn that our government is not out to protect our rights. To protect our families we are now forced to picket, protest and shout. (Zeff et al. 1989, 31)

In the process of protest, these women were also forced to examine their assumptions about the family as a private haven, separate from the public arena, which would however be protected by the policies and actions of government should the need arise. The issue of toxic waste shows the many ways in which government allows this haven to be invaded by polluted water, hazardous chemicals, and other conditions that threaten the everyday life of the family. Ultimately, these women arrived at a concept of environmental injustice rooted in the inequities of power that displace the costs of toxic waste unequally onto their communities. The result was a critical political stance that contributed to the militancy of their activism. Highly traditional values of democracy and motherhood remained central to their lives: they justified their resistance as mothers protecting their children and working to make the promise of democracy real. Women's politicization around toxic waste protests led them to transform their traditional beliefs into resources of opposition which enabled them to enter the public arena and challenge its legitimacy, breaking down the public/private distinction.

### Appropriating Power in the Public Arena

Toxic waste issues and their threat to family and community prompted white, working-class women to redefine their roles as mothers. Their work of mothering came to extend beyond taking care of the children, husband, and housework; they saw the necessity of preserving the family by entering the public arena. In so doing, they discovered and overcame a more subtle process of intimidation, which limited their participation in the public sphere.

As these women became involved in toxic waste issues, they came into conflict with a public world where policy makers are traditionally white, male, and middle class. The Citizen's Clearinghouse for Hazardous Waste, in the summary of its 1989 conference on women and organizing, noted:

Seventy to eighty percent of local leaders are women. They are women leaders in a community run by men. Because of this, many of the obstacles that these women face as leaders stem from the conflicts between their traditional female role in the community and their new role as leader: conflicts with male officials and authorities who have not yet adjusted to these persistent, vocal, head-strong women challenging the system. . . . Women are frequently ignored by male politicians, male government officials and male corporate spokesmen.

Entering the public arena meant overcoming internal and external barriers to participation, shaped by gender and class. White, working-class women's reconstructed definition of motherhood became a resource for this process, and their narratives reveal several aspects of this transformation.

For these women, entering the public arena around toxic waste issues was often extremely stressful. Many of them were initially shy and intimidated, as simple actions such as speaking at a meeting opened up wider issues about authority, and experiences of gender and class combined to heighten their sense of inadequacy. Many of these women describe, for example, that their high-school education left them feeling ill-equipped to challenge "experts," whose legitimacy, in which they had traditionally believed, was based on advanced degrees and specialized knowledge.

One woman who fought to stop the siting of an incinerator in her community in Arizona recalled: "I used to cry if I had to speak at a PTA meeting. I was so frightened." An activist in Alabama described her experience in fighting the siting of an incinerator in her community:

> I was a woman . . . an assistant Sunday School teacher. . . . In the South, women are taught not to be aggressive, we're supposed to be hospitable and charitable and friendly. We don't protest, we don't challenge authority. So it was kind of difficult for me to get involved. I was afraid to speak. And all of a sudden everything became controversial. . . . I think a lot of it had to do with not knowing what I was . . . The more I began to know, the better I was . . . the more empowered.

Male officials further exacerbated this intimidation by ignoring the women, by criticizing them for being overemotional, and by delegitimizing their authority by labelling them "hysterical housewives"—a label used widely, regardless of the professional status of the woman. In so doing, they revealed an antipathy to emotionality, a quality valued in the private sphere of family and motherhood but scorned in the public arena as irrational and inappropriate to "objective" discourse.

On several levels, the debate around toxic waste issues was framed by policy makers in such a way as to exclude women's participation, values, and expression. Women's concerns about their children were trivialized by being placed against a claim that the wider community benefits from growth and progress. Information was withheld from them. Discourse was framed as rational, technical, and scientific, using the testimony of "experts" to discredit the everyday empirical knowledge of the women. Even such details as seating arrangements reflected traditional power relations and reinforced the women's internalization of those relations.

These objective and subjective barriers to participation derived from a traditional definition of women's roles based on the separation of the public and private arenas. Yet it is out of these women's political redefinition of the traditional role of mother that they found the resources to overcome these constraints, ultimately becoming self-confident and assertive. They used the resources of their own experience to alter the power relations they had discovered in the public arena.

The traditional role of mother, of protector of the family and community, served to empower these activists on a number of levels. From the beginning, their view of this role provided the motivation for women to take risks in defense of their families and overcome their fears of participating in the public sphere. A woman who fought the siting of an incinerator in Arkansas described this power:

> I was afraid to hurt anyone's feelings or step on anyone's toes. But I'm protective and aggressive, especially where my children are concerned. That's what brought it out of me. A mother protecting my kids. It appalled me that money could be more important than the health of my children.

A mother in New Jersey described overcoming her fear in dealing with male governmental officials at public hearings, "When I look at a male government official, I remember that he was once a little boy, born of a woman like me, and then I feel more powerful." In talking about Love Canal, Lois Gibbs showed the power of motherhood to carry women into activities alien to their experience:

When it came to Love Canal, we never thought about ourselves as protestors. We carried signs, we barricaded, we blocked the gates, we were arrested. We thought of it as parents protecting our children. In retrospect, of course, we were protesting. I think if it had occurred to us we wouldn't have done it.

In these ways, they appropriated the power they felt in the private arena as a source of empowerment in the public sphere. "We're insecure challenging the authority of trained experts," notes Gibbs, "but we also have a title of authority, 'mother.'"

Working-class women's experiences as organizers of family life served as a further source of empowerment. Lois Gibbs noted that women organized at Love Canal by constantly analyzing how they would handle a situation in the family, and then translating that analysis into political action. For example, Gibbs explained:

If our child wanted a pair of jeans, who would they go to? Well they would go to their father since their father had the money—that meant that we should go to Governor Carey.

Gibbs drew on her own experience to develop organizing conferences that helped working-class women learn to translate their skills as family organizers into the political arena.

I decided as a housewife and mother much of what I learned to keep the household running smoothly were skills that translated very well into this new thing called organizing. I also decided that this training in running a home was one of the key reasons why so many of the best leaders in the toxic movement—in fact, the overwhelming majority—are women, and specifically women who are housewives and mothers. (Zeff 1989, 177)

Of her work with the CCHW, Gibbs stated:

In our own organization we're drawing out these experiences for women. So we say, what do you mean you're not an organizer? Are you a homemaker—then God damn it you can organize and you don't know it. So, for example, when we say you need to plan long-term and short-term goals, women may say, I don't know how to do that. . . . We say, what do you mean you don't know how to do that?

> Let's talk about something in the household—you plan meals for five, seven, fourteen days—you think about what you want for today and what you're going to eat on Sunday—that is short-term and long-term goals.

Movement language like "plug up the toilet," the expression for waste reduction, helped women to reinterpret toxic waste issues in the framework of their everyday experience. "If one does not produce the mess in the first place, one will not have to clean it up later," may sound like a maternal warning, but the expression's use in the toxic waste context implies a radical economic critique, calling for a change in the production processes of industry itself.

As women came to understand that government is not an objective, neutral mediator for the public good, they discovered that "logic" and "objectivity" are tools used by the government to obscure its bias in favor of industry, and motherhood became a strategy to counter public power by reframing the terms of the debate. The labels of "hysterical housewives" or "emotional women," used by policy makers to delegitimize the women's authority, became a language of critique and empowerment, one which exposed the limits of the public arena's ability to address the importance of family, health, and community. These labels were appropriated as the women saw that their emotionalism, a valued trait in the private sphere, could be transformed into a powerful weapon in the public arena:

> What's really so bad about showing your feelings? Emotions and intellect are not conflicting traits. In fact, emotions may well be the quality that makes women so effective in this movement. . . . They help us speak the truth.

Finally, through toxic waste protests, women discovered the power they wield as mothers to bring moral issues to the public, exposing the contradictions of a society that purports to value motherhood and family, yet creates social policies that undermine these values:

> We bring the authority of mother—who can condemn mothers? . . . It is a tool we have. Our crying brings the moral issues to the table. And when the public sees our children it brings a concrete, moral dimension to our experience. . . . They are not an abstract statistic.

White, working-class women's stories of their involvement in grass-roots toxic waste protests reveal their transformations of initial shyness and intimidation into the self-confidence to challenge the existing system. In reconceptualizing their traditional roles as mothers, these women discovered a new strength. As one activist from Arizona says of herself, "Now I like myself better. I am more assertive and aggressive." These women's role in the private world of family ultimately became a source of personal strength, empirical knowledge, and political strategy in the public sphere. It was a resource of political critique and empowerment which the women appropriated and used as they struggled to protect their families.

### Overcoming Obstacles to Participation: Gender Conflicts in the Family

In order to succeed in their fights against toxic wastes in their homes and communities, these women confronted and overcame obstacles not only in the public sphere, but also within the family itself, as their entry into the public arena disrupted both the power relationships and the highly traditional gender roles within the family. Divorce and separation were the manifestations of the crises these disruptions induced. All of the women I interviewed had been married when they first became active in the toxic waste movement. By the time of my interviews with them, more than half were divorced.

A central theme of these women's narratives is the tension created in their marriages by participation in toxic waste protests. This aspect of struggle, so particular to women's lives, is an especially hidden dimension of white, working-class women's activism. Noted one activist from New York:

> People are always talking to us about forming coalitions, but look at all we must deal with beyond the specific issue. How do you deal with the delicate balance of family versus issue, the flack that comes with it, the insecurity of your husband that you have outgrown him. Or how do you deal with your children's anger, when they say you love the fight more than me. In a blue-collar community that is very important.

For the most part, white, working-class women's acceptance of a traditional gendered division of labor has also led them to take for granted the power relations within the family. Penny Newman, who was the West

Coast director of CCHW, reflected on the beginnings of her community involvement:

> I had been married just a couple of years. My husband is a fireman. They have very strict ideas of what family life is in which the woman does not work, you stay at home. . . . I was so insecure, so shy, that when I finally got to join an organization, a woman's club, . . . it would take me two weeks to build up enough courage to ask my husband to watch the kids that night. I would really plan out my life a month ahead of time just to build in these little hints that there is a meeting coming up in two weeks, will you be available. Now, if he didn't want to do it, or had other plans, I didn't go to the meeting. (Zeff 1989, 183)

Involvement in toxic waste issues created a conflict between these traditional assumptions and women's concerns about protecting their children, and this conflict made visible the power relations within the family. The CCHW publication *Empowering Women* (1989, 33) noted that:

> Women's involvement in grassroots activism may change their views about the world and their relations with their husbands. Some husbands are actively supportive. Some take no stand: "Go ahead and do what you want. Just make sure you have dinner on the table and my shirts washed." Others forbid time away from the family.

Many of these women struggled to develop coping strategies to defuse conflict and accommodate traditional gender-based power relations in the family. The strategies included involving husbands in protest activities and minimizing their own leadership roles. As Lois Gibbs commented: "If you can bring a spouse in, if you can make them part of your growth, then the marriage is more likely to survive, but that is real hard to do sometimes." Will Collette, a former director at CCHW, relates the ways in which he has observed women avoiding acknowledged leadership roles. He described this encounter with women involved in a toxic waste protest in New York:

> I was sitting around a kitchen table with several women who were leading a protest. And they were complaining about how Lou and Joe did not do their homework and weren't able to handle reports and so on. I asked them why they were officers when the women

were doing all the work. They said, "That's what the guys like, it keeps them in and gives us a little peace at home."

In a similar vein, Collette recalled working with an activist from Texas to plan a large public hearing. Upon arriving at the meeting, he discovered that she was sitting in the back, while he was placed on the dais along with the male leadership, which had had no part in the planning process.

As the women became more active in the public arena, traditional assumptions about gender roles created further conflict in their marriages. Women who became visible community leaders experienced the greatest tension. In some cases, husbands were held responsible for their wives' activities, since they were supposed to be able to "control" their wives. For example, a woman who fought against an incinerator in Arkansas related:

When the mayor saw my husband, he wanted to know why he couldn't keep his pretty little wife's mouth shut. As I became more active and more outspoken, our marriage became rockier. My husband asked me to tone it down, which I didn't do.

In other cases, women's morals were often called into question by husbands or other community members. Collette relates the experience of an activist in North Dakota who was rumored to be having an affair. The basis for the rumor, as Collette describes, was that "an uppity woman has got to be promiscuous if she dares to organize. In this case, she was at a late-night meeting in another town, and she slept over, so of course she had to have had sex."

Toxic waste issues thus set the stage for tremendous conflict between these women and their husbands. Men saw their roles as providers threatened: the homes they had bought may have become valueless; their jobs may have been at risk; they were asked by their wives to take on housework and child care. Meanwhile, their wives' public activities increasingly challenged traditional views of gender roles. For the women, their husbands' negative response to their entry into the public sphere contradicted an assumption in the family that both husband and wife were equally concerned with the well-being of the children. In talking about Love Canal, Gibbs explained:

The husband in a blue-collar community is saying, get your ass home and cook me dinner, it's either me or the issue, make your choice. The woman says: How can I make a choice, you're telling me choose between the health of my children and your fucking dinner, how do I deal with that?

When women were asked to choose between their children and their husbands' needs, they began to see the ways in which the children had to be their primary concern.

At times this conflict resulted in more equal power relations within the marriages, a direction that CCHW tried to encourage by organizing family stress workshops. By and large, however, the families of activist women did not tolerate this stress well. Furthermore, as the women began openly to contest traditional power relations in the family, many found that their marriages could not withstand the challenges. As one activist from Arkansas described:

I thought [my husband] didn't care enough about our children to continue to expose them to this danger. I begged him to move. He wouldn't. So I moved my kids out of town to live with my mom.

All twenty women interviewed for this article were active leaders around toxic waste issues in their communities, but only two described the importance of their husband's continuing support. One white woman who formed an interracial coalition in Alabama credited her husband's support in sustaining her resolve:

I've had death threats. I was scared my husband would lose his job, afraid that somebody's going to kill me. If it weren't for my husband's support, I don't think I could get through all this.

In contrast, most of these activists described the ongoing conflict within their marriages, which often resulted in their abandoning their traditional role in the family, a process filled with inner turmoil. One woman described that turmoil as follows:

I had doubts about what I was doing, especially when my marriage was getting real rocky. I thought of getting out of [the protest]. I sat down and talked to God many, many times. I asked him to lead me in the right direction because I knew my marriage was failing and I found it hard leaving my kids when I had to go to meetings. I had to struggle to feel that I was doing the right thing. I said a prayer and went on.

Reflecting on the strength she felt as a mother, which empowered her to challenge her government and leave her marriage, she continued:

It's an amazing ordeal. You always know you would protect your children. But it's amazing to find out how far you will go to protect your own kids.

The disruption of the traditional family often reflected positive changes in women's empowerment. Women grew through the protest; they became stronger and more self-confident. In some cases they found new marriages with men who respected them as strong individuals. Children also came to see their mothers as outspoken and confident.

Thus, for these women, the particularistic issue of toxic waste made visible oppression not only in the public sphere, but also in the family itself. As the traditional organization of family life was disrupted, inequities in underlying power relations were revealed. In order to succeed in fighting a toxic waste issue, these women had also to engage in another level of struggle as they reconceptualized their traditional role in family life in order to carry out their responsibilities as mothers.

### Conclusion

The narratives of white, working-class women involved in toxic waste protests in the 1980s reveal the ways in which their subjective, particular experiences led them to analyses that extended beyond the particularistic issue to wider questions of power. Their broader environmental critique grew out of the concrete, immediate, everyday experience of struggling around survival issues. In the process of environmental protest, these women became engaged with specific governmental and corporate institutions and they were forced to reflect on the contradictions of their family life. To win a policy issue, they had to go through a process of developing an oppositional or critical consciousness which informed the direction of their actions and challenged the power of traditional policy makers. The contradiction between a government that claimed to act on behalf of the family and the actual environmental policies and actions of that government were unmasked. The inequities of power between white, working-class women and middle-class, male public officials were made visible. The reproduction within the family of traditional power relationships was also revealed. In the process of protest these women uncovered and confronted a world of political power shaped by gender and class. This enabled them to act politically around environmental issues, and in some measure to challenge the social relationships of power, inside and outside the home.

Ideologies of motherhood played a central role in the politicizing of white, working-class women around toxic waste issues. Their resistance grew out of an acceptance of a sexual division of labor that assigns to women responsibility for "sustaining the lives of their children and, in a broader sense, their families, including husband, relatives, elders and community."[6] In disproportionately displacing the environmental and social costs of growth into their communities, the political economy posed a direct threat to these communities and created everyday crises for working-class women. Toxic waste policies threatened the survival of children, family, and community, and prevented women from fulfilling their traditional responsibility for preserving life. These policies violated the assumption embedded in white, working-class women's acceptance of a gendered division of labor: that their right to carry out their role will be protected. In response, they fought to protect their families and communities and, in the process, appropriated and reshaped the cultural and material resources of everyday life into tools of a class-based resistance. Ideologies of motherhood, traditionally relegated to the private sphere, became political resources that these women used to initiate and justify their resistance and increasing politicization. Rejecting the separation of public and private arenas that renders invisible and insignificant the world of women's work, they developed a public, more politicized ideology of motherhood that became a resource to fight gender and class oppression.

Ideologies of democracy also played an important role in this politicizing process (Boyte 1980; Krauss 1989). White, working-class women entered the political arena with expectations that the modern democratic state will be responsive to the concerns of private citizens and protect their families from harm (Habermas 1973). As these women participated in political life, however, they found that the state supported the toxic waste policies of the private economy and excluded women's direct participation in political life. They experienced a contradiction between the state's democratic promise and the actual goals and policies the state pursued. Discovering that this structure of power violated their ability to fulfill their work as mothers, these women inserted themselves into the political arena and forced political leaders to make real the democratic rights they espoused. In this way, the ideology of democracy was appropriated and transformed into a resource of opposition, rooted in the necessity of realizing women's mothering role.

The analysis of white, working-class women's politicization through toxic waste protests reveals the contradictory role played by dominant ideologies about mothering and democracy in the shaping of these women's oppositional consciousness. The analysis these women developed was not a rejection of these ideologies. Rather, it was a reinterpretation, which became a source of power in the public arena. Their beliefs provided the initial impetus for involvement in toxic waste protests, and became a rich source of empowerment as they appropriated and reshaped traditional ideologies and meanings into an ideology of resistance.

An analysis of social change that starts with the everyday world of experience can make visible different processes of politicization. As we have seen, white, working-class women's involvement in toxic waste protests led to their politicization around issues of class and gender. In contrast, the toxic waste protests of women of color have been grounded in experiences, values, and beliefs that differ from those of the white, working-class women examined here, thereby resulting in different concepts of environmental justice (Krauss 1994a, 1994b). African American women, for example, have brought to their protests a political awareness grounded in race, and sharing none of the white, working-class women's initial trust in so-called democratic institutions. They have arrived at a concept of environmental justice that is linked to other social-justice concerns, such as jobs, housing, and crime. The subjective dimension of protest thus offers a lens through which to view the multiple analyses shaped by women in environmental movements throughout the world. Women's visions of environmental justice and social inequality are mediated by subjective experiences and interpretations and rooted in the political truths they construct out of their identities as mothers and members of specific communities.

### Notes

1. See Hamilton 1991; Pardo 1990b; Brown and Mikkelsen 1990; Cable 1992; Krauss 1990, 1993.
2. Susser 1982; Haywoode 1991; Naples 1992.

# Chapter 6

# Producing the Battered Woman

*Shelter Politics and the Power of the Feminist Voice*

## Karen Kendrick

My interest in the topic of domestic violence discourse and policy comes out of my own experiences of abuse. In doing this research, I was forced to confront the multiplicity of my own identity and the contradictions of being a feminist, a white, middle-class woman, an academic researcher, and a battered woman. In my earlier work on domestic violence services and discourse, my standpoint was conspicuously absent (Kendrick 1994), and my refusal to locate myself in that work was partly a result of my struggles around the experience of being abused and around claiming the identity of a battered woman. While I recognized that my relationship was abusive, and took steps to end the abuse, I was unable to speak to friends and family about the experience. I was afraid that if I admitted my abuse I would be told simply to leave the relationship. And since I was not willing "simply" to leave at that point, I believed that I would be exposed as too weak, too dependent, and as a bad feminist. In other words, I feared being identified and categorized as a "battered woman."

In the dominant discourse on domestic violence, battered women are constructed as either low-income women with no way to support themselves independently, as middle-class women with no job training or skills, or as women with a psychology of dependence and learned helplessness. As an educated, white, middle-class woman, I felt that I did not have access to an economic justification for staying with an abusive partner. I was also raised under a liberal mythology that I could and should be *both* completely independent *and* in a committed heterosexual relationship. Because I wasn't economically "trapped," I felt that I had failed to live up to the expectations of my feminist identity. Further, because battering is usually constructed as extreme and repeated physical violence, I also felt that the emotional abuse I faced was not "bad enough" to allow me to claim the status of battered woman.

At the time of my abuse, and even afterwards when I first began researching and writing about violence against women, I did not have this analysis of my situation. Instead I was confused, questioning my right to do research on domestic violence, rejecting the label battered woman, and failing to understand how race and class could fit into my analysis. I was privileging my own standpoint by keeping it invisible. It is only through reading works by women of color and Euro-American women extolling the need to pay attention to whiteness that I have been able to problematize my own standpoint, to make it visible.[1] Making my whiteness and "middle-classness" visible has not only enabled me to understand how race, class, and gender work together in domestic violence discourse and policy, but has also enabled me to understand the contradictions between my experiences of abuse and my construction of feminism.

When I began my research to identify variation in the construction of the category "battered women" in different service sites around South County, I expected to find a feminist analysis present in shelters that contrasted with the constructions of battered women in other locations. Contrary to my expectations, what I found was a surprising consistency in the construction of "battered women" across shelters, law enforcement, and other social and psychological services. This finding led me to explore the process by which feminist activists in the battered-women's movement have sometimes been forced to reposition their political analysis in response to pressures by funding agencies, mental-health professionals, and law enforcement.[2] In this chapter, I examine how "feminist voices have become themselves powerful and productive within a power/knowledge network" that constructs battered women as clients of a system of social and legal services (V. Bell 1993, 25; also see Loseke 1992). My analysis must be understood within the politics of this conservative southern California county and should not be taken as a generic critique of feminist practice in other settings. However, lessons learned in the course of this investigation may shed further light on the contradictions of feminist practice as it confronts processes of bureaucracy and professionalization and becomes increasingly reliant on state sanctioning and state funding (also see Ferree and Martin 1995).

### Fighting Domestic Violence in South County

In describing any social or political movement it is important to locate it within its specific geographical and political context. South County is a large county in southern California where the average household and family incomes are well above national averages[3], the county is geographically and economically segregated. There are cities made up of working-class and low-income people from Euro-American, Latino, Asian and Pacific Islander, and African American backgrounds.[4] The cities are connected to the mostly white and affluent suburban areas almost solely by the extensive southern California freeway system. Little public transportation is available.

One of the cities in South County has a special investigator for domestic violence and another is in the process of creating such a position. The criminal court system handles those cases of battering which have been defined as severe enough to warrant criminal prosecution, while the family court system handles restraining orders, violence involving children, and violence during divorce or separation proceedings. Both the criminal courts and the family courts may require that batterers receive psychological treatment. There are more than ten batterers' treatment programs in South County that are approved by the probation department to handle court-mandated offenders. In contrast, South County has only three shelters for women who have been abused. Women with or without children are allowed to stay from thirty to forty-five days.[5] Each shelter has a twenty-four-hour crisis hotline.[6] Workers at all three shelters told me that they have a continuous waiting list for women trying to get into the shelters.[7]

There are two formal South County coalitions established to address domestic violence. The first is the Coalition of Batterers Treatment Programs, which was started by the county probation department in order to provide approval for the programs serving offenders diverted to treatment by the court. The second is the Domestic Violence subgroup of the Social Service Providers Network (SSPN), an organization encompassing a broad range of social-service workers in the county.[8] In addition, there is an informal task force which was started by a superior-court judge in order to increase communication between the criminal and family courts, and between professionals in the legal and social-services professions. The Coalition of Southern California is a coalition of direct service providers which includes but is not limited to members from South County.

To understand how feminist activists participate in the construction of the "battered women" in this county in Southern California, I interviewed workers in domestic violence services, including members of coalitions organized to increase the coordination of responses to battering and to pressure for policy changes and legislative action, as well as shelter staff, legal and law-enforcement personnel, and therapists working in the area of domestic violence.[9] The shelter workers interviewed for this study all held at least a bachelor's degree in some aspect of social work, counseling, or social science. All but one of them was Euro-American. In this sense, it might be useful to distinguish them from battered women's movement activists more broadly. However, given the demands by state credentialing agencies, they may be similar in educational and professional background to others employed in California's battered-women's shelters. It is also important to remember that many shelter workers are unpaid staff and may bring greater diversity of training and experiences to their work than the paid staff I interviewed.

Unlike some other areas of the U.S., the services and coalitions designed to challenge the abuse of women in South County are highly professionalized, top-down approaches. The major portion of resources in South County goes towards legal action, counseling, and social services, particularly for batterers' treatment programs. There appear to be few, if any, grassroots efforts organized specifically around abuse in the county. While local community centers or other organizations may have people within them working on issues of violence against women in the home (for instance, the Vietnamese American Community Center), there appears to be no larger communication or networking among these local activists.

The shelter movement in South County arose and developed within this particular sociopolitical context. There has not been a strong feminist or liberal political community to provide support for radical action. Activists in South County have often come into the movement during or after professional training. However, feminists in other geographical contexts have self-consciously resisted professionalization. For example, Rodriguez (1988) describes a shelter in Hilo, Hawaii, which successfully harnessed the diversity and political commitment of its workers and volunteers to resist professionalization and bureaucratization.

## The Politics-of-Needs Interpretation

Interviews and observation for this study were conducted to explore two related issues: (1) the structure of the system of services in the county and the specific policy goals of, and services provided at, each location; and (2) the dominant discourse on domestic violence in the county and in each location. In order to understand the material and discursive struggles that have produced the "battered woman" of contemporary domestic violence discourse in South County, I utilized Nancy Fraser's analysis of "the politics of needs interpretation" (1990, 200). Activists in the battered women's movement develop "oppositional" discourses in order to make previously private needs political. The publicizing of needs is met with "reprivatizing" discourses that seek to recuperate the challenges of the oppositional discourse by depoliticizing the issue. Finally, activists, policy makers, and concerned professionals develop an "expert" discourse that can be used to articulate the oppositional movement to the state and to argue for the provision of services to meet the now publicized needs. The expert discourse is produced through the process of negotiation between activists, detractors, and the state, as well as through the contributions of established professionals in psychology and social services. In order to negotiate with the state for support of movement goals, activists must argue that their analysis of abuse should take precedence over both "common sense" beliefs and analyses presented by psychologists and mental-health workers (Fraser 1989). In this way, activists claim that they have more right to interpret battered-women's experiences and needs than other professionals and workers in the state (psychologists, police, legislators, and so one). While the claim to an expert status is necessary and powerful for the movement, it has had some unforseen and problematic consequences for feminist political analyses and actions around the abuse of women. In many cases, the claim to an expert voice displaced the voices the movement had initially sought to empower—the voices of women who experienced abuse.[10]

By claiming an expert voice, domestic violence professionals construct battered women as clients, not as experts of their own experiences and needs. Through the expert discourse, women who experience abuse become reified, naturalized as battered women, "always already" victims of either patriarchy or their own psychological problems. Accordingly, it becomes impossible to see the multiplicity of battered women's identities or the complexity of their lives. And finally, neither the oppositional discourse of the early battered women's movement, nor the expert discourse on domestic violence, made race, sexuality, and class salient issues in understanding the abuse of women and the contexts in which women live their lives. The battered women as client is discursively abstracted as a woman without any particular race or class, who is always and only heterosexual. Consequently, discussions of women's needs also become abstract, and politics based on these needs do not account for the material differences of women's lives.

While my analysis explores the abstract process by which expert discourses depoliticize or reprivatize oppositional discourses, it also explores how such a process occurs through the everyday practices of shelter staff. This case study attempts to explicate how radical feminist practice can, in some instances, be repositioned into an expert stance. It also attempts to find sites of resistance and to identify ways in which progressive forces can reinsert a more radical agenda.

## Early Struggles in the Politics-of-Needs Interpretation

Two activists interviewed for this study were involved in New Beginnings, the first shelter to be opened in South County in 1976. Both of these activists are white professionals who came to their involvement in the shelter movement through feminist politics and not by personal experiences of abuse. Joan Kearns and Margaret Pane both explained that when the New Beginnings shelter began to receive governmental funding, it led to increased outside control over the structure of the shelter's organization. Funding and certifying agencies were especially concerned that mental-health professionals play a central role in shelters. Both women challenged professional conceptualizations of abuse by asserting that women in abusive relationships were not psychologically sick, and that women and not professionals were the experts of their own experiences. Joan Kearns, a lawyer and one of the original Board members of the shelter recalled:

> Originally when we started New Beginnings . . . we were very very concerned that it not become institutionalized and the women treated like cases. There was a lot of controversy about the involvement of mental-health professionals.

In order to avoid institutionalization, Joan explained, New Beginnings was designed to be non-hierarchical, to rely on volunteer labor, and to enable survivors of abuse to teach and empower one another as experts of their own experiences. For example, voting Board members who were not necessarily survivors of abuse themselves were originally required to work a certain number of hours per month in the shelter. Joan explained:

> That was in order to keep the board from being so separated from the program and women, that we didn't think about them as institutional cases. . . . But it was basically impractical I guess. If the place had remained small, if you had that continuing pool of volunteers, if maybe somehow the women themselves could have made it self-sustaining on a very small basis, it could continue that way.

According to Joan, shelter workers opposed the hierarchical difference and distance between the expert and the client which would come from a professional approach to service provision in the shelter. They therefore took steps to avoid allowing a large gap to form between the Board members who had control over major policy decisions and funds, and the women who sought refuge in the shelter. However, the most telling element of this quote is the clause, "but it was basically impractical." If the shelter had remained "small," if it had become "self-sustaining," then the methods that New Beginnings had employed to resist institutionalization and professionalization might have succeeded. However, as the need for shelter space increased, the shelter, which was originally opened with money from federal block grants, did not move towards self-sustenance, but instead sought increased governmental assistance.

According to Joan and Margaret, the county began to regulate shelter practice through it's control over the funds it funneled to the shelter. Margaret Pane, who was a graduate student in sociology at the time, volunteered at the shelter during its first five years and sat on the Board for a short while. She discussed the pressure from the county:

> With the funding from the county and from the state . . . they demanded certain things, and they wanted us to bring in mental-health experts, et cetera, to do counseling, so it's been more or less mandated by society. And of course, we in the states have a lot of reverence . . . for credentials.

According to Margaret's analysis, the pressure to professionalize shelter practice came not only from the material force and coercion which the county was able to apply due to its control of block-grant funds, but also from the fact that the county valued the expert mental-health voice. The dominant discourse on the value of trained professionals in social services dictated that the county would pressure for the involvement of mental-health professionals.

During at least the first five years of this shelter's existence, workers struggled with the county over the conceptual basis and structural form of the organization. However, the struggle over shelter practice and philosophy was not only between the county and the shelter, but also went on within the shelter itself. Margaret and Joan both described an incident in which one of the first directors brought a psychiatrist into the shelter to interview potential residents "against the express wishes of the board." The role of the psychiatrist was to decide whether or not the women were "safe" enough to stay in the shelter. Eventually, the board was notified that the director had hired the psychiatrist without their approval, and both the director and psychiatrist were fired.

This incident demonstrates that the negotiation of the role of professionals in shelter work was not simply a struggle between an economically powerful county and a group of anti-professional shelter workers. From the beginning shelter volunteers were sometimes themselves women with, or working towards, professional degrees. Margaret explained how increasing numbers of professional women were hired into paid staff positions:

> You know, in the early days, there were a lot of professionals who were working free, doing what ever they could to help. But little by little they get chased out, and the women who were working in shelters because they were feminists may not have had the credentials, and they get kicked out because they didn't have the credentials.

While New Beginnings initially privileged the battered woman's voice as expert and argued that women needed safety not counseling, they still had to develop ways to negotiate the material pressures from the county and debates within their own ranks.

### Constructing and Serving Battered Women

In making the abuse of women a public issue, the battered-women's movement has often been challenged with the question "Why do women stay? Aren't they just asking for it if they stay in abusive relationships?" This attempt to blame the abuse of women on *women* rather than on men, or on the structure of the heterosexual family, has been so pervasive that a tremendous amount of feminist and non-feminist academic research has been devoted to it (Walker 1984; Barnett and La Violette 1993). Despite research that shows that women in fact do seek help to end their abuse, and many do eventually leave their abusers, the question "Why do women stay?" is still dominant in public discourse (Dobash and Dobash 1992).

Exploring how shelter discourse answers the question "Why do women stay?" gives a valuable insight into the construction of the "battered women" discourse. Shelter responses are made up of a contradictory combination of feminist and professional themes about abuse. Following feminist insights, shelter activists have attempted to explain "why women stay" in ways which will not implicate women in their own abuse; but they have relied upon descriptions of women's psychology to do so. The material conditions of women's lives are often treated as if they are only potential barriers to leaving an abusive relationship. The real hurdles that women need to overcome, according to the shelter workers I interviewed, are false beliefs about their circumstances. For example, Janet Bay, outreach coordinator for New Beginnings, spoke about the types of counseling women need once they reach the shelter:

> She needs to work on her issues, you know, how she's dealing with it, what she's going through, reasons why *she feels* she needs to stay, for example, economic, social, religious for some women. Lots of women have lots of family pressures [and] mothers or grandmothers will say, "Oh, you must stay with it, you know, I stayed with it, why can't you?" You know, that kind of thing, we're a real patriarchal society. [Emphasis added.]

In this case, Janet acknowledges that women stay in abusive relationships because of a host of outside forces, including economics and patriarchy. Yet, in her formulation, women are trapped primarily because they *feel* social pressures and not because they face real structural impediments to success. Furthermore, Janet does not include in her list the fact that the danger to women's lives increases when they attempt to leave physically abusive partners.

It is not a far step from asking why women stay in abusive relationships to asking if a woman somehow contributes to her own abuse by staying in the relationship. During a training session for counseling interns on how the patterns of abuse are established in a relationship, Janet Bay of New Beginnings described how women implicitly "condone" their own abuse:

> Let's say a shoving incident took place, and it may have startled you, but you say, "Oh gosh, well that's not gonna happen again." So, in a sense, you're condoning that kind of behavior. That in essence is giving permission to allow something like that or something even more severe to happen a second time.

In this description Janet does not allow for the possibility that there are diverse experiences and multiple definitions of abuse. It reinscribes the notion that abusive behavior always follows the same patterns, that it is easily labeled as domestic violence, and that women are suffering from a false consciousness about the truth of their situations.

When shelter workers explain women's behavior by reference to their psychological state, they contribute to themes in domestic violence discourse, which take abusive relationships out of the context of social relations and pathologize the individuals involved. The generic and undifferentiated battered woman develops "low self-esteem." She "believes" there is no way out. She is "unaware" of her options. Presumably, all battered women feel the same way and in actuality have the same options, and presumably shelter workers can teach women the truth about these feelings and these options. Within the shelter, women who experience abuse are no longer defined as the experts of their particular experiences. They must have their experience interpreted for them, in a singular way, by shelter experts. The abuse is de-contextualized to such an extent, and its gendered nature rendered so invisible, that once again women are blamed for their own abuse. In shelter talk, women may not be morally at fault for staying in abusive relationships, but they are implicated nonetheless. They are implicated because the act of staying in an abusive relationship continues to be pathologized, and because shelter discourse continue to answer the question "why do women stay" rather than questioning its underlying efficacy. By incorporating psychological theories into shelter talk about abuse, shelter workers contribute to shifting the focus of domestic violence discourse towards therapeutic concerns and away from social or political ones.

## Battered Women as Battered Mothers: The Intergenerational Theory of Abuse

In order to challenge dominant ideology about the sanctity of the two-parent heterosexual family, shelter activists have often constructed the abuse of women as extreme and repeated physical violence that is passed on from generation to generation. In a publicity and donation-seeking handout from New Beginnings, they write:

> Without intervention [domestic violence] does not go away on its own, but tends to get worse over time, becoming more frequent and more severe. . . . Domestic violence is intergenerational. Without intervention it can move from one generation into the next. Children who watch their mothers being abused frequently grow into abusers or they become abused. The solutions to the prevention of domestic violence are complex, but the first step is removing the women and children from the abusive environment. That's what New Beginnings does.

In this pamphlet, New Beginnings relies on the construction of abuse as intergenerational in order to justify the existence of the shelter as the "first step" to ending violence. This presentation legitimates the shelter's position as a social service provider for battered mothers, and the protection of children is now seen as a major focus of domestic violence discourse.

The main form of intervention in shelter work is the removal of women from abusive relationships. This puts the responsibility for ending abuse on women who must be convinced of the danger to themselves and more importantly to their children. In this scenario, women are often seen as morally responsible for protecting themselves and their children from abusive men. For example, Natalie Ramirez,[11] a head counselor at Family Alternatives, described that program's philosophy this way:

> To break the cycle of violence, to provide a safe haven for women to come and get out of a very dangerous life-threatening situation, and hopefully make an impression both on the kids and mom to eventually break that cycle of violence that seems to be continuing.

This intergenerational cycle of abuse, a cornerstone of professional descriptions of abuse, serves to place the blame for violence on families rather than society, and to place the responsibility for ending violence on mothers rather than fathers. By emphasizing "life-threatening" types of abuse, shelter workers create an urgency which justifies intervening in and "breaking up families." However, "to break the cycle of violence" is to "make an impression" on women and children, and not on men or society. Note that Natalie's statement does not even include an actor who is violent, but rather constructs abuse as a "situation" in which "the cycle of violence . . . seems to be continuing."

The legal and law-enforcement personnel I interviewed argued for intervention into abusive relationships because of the effects on children and society and not because of the effects on women. I asked Family Alternatives counselor Natalie how she felt about people measuring the effects of abuse in terms of children rather than women. Her response closely mirrored the explanations given by legal and law enforcement personnel:

> There's a lot of truth to it, and that's why our goal is to break the cycle of violence, because children exposed to violence in the home learn to cope with stresses in life with violence, and if . . . *mom is too busy . . . she's not there to raise the kids properly and morally,* and so they look for their acceptance elsewhere, and that's where you get the gang problem. . . . The little boys grow up. . . . They beat their wife because that's learned behavior. When girls grow up, they think that . . . when you get married, your husband's going to slap you around a little bit, and that's okay. . . . And so, *if you start showing the kids, through the mom,* that its not acceptable . . . then that's when you're seeing a lot of change. [Emphasis added.]

In Natalie's statement, the woman who is abused is *morally and practically implicated* in creating the "gang problem" and in the perpetuation of violence in later generations. The psychological explanations for abuse and for women's reactions to abuse are transformed here into judgements about women's moral culpability as mothers. In the contemporary discourse on abuse, the solution is not to address social and economic inequalities which contribute to gang activities, crime, or the abuse of women. The answer is not to change gendered patterns of power in heterosexual relationships. Instead, the answer is to "start showing the kids through the mom" that there are morally preferable, non-violent ways to live.

It is important to explore what kind of morality is implicated in Natalie's statement. The morality alluded to here comes directly out of the discourse on "proper families." In the "proper family" women have primary responsibility for their children. The failure to meet this responsibility will not only result in "problem" children, but will always be a result of the mother's failures and not the father's. Furthermore, any problems in the family originate in the family itself. Social structures of sexism, racism, and poverty are unimportant—violence in families and in society is a direct result of mothers' failures to protect and guide their children. The proper mother then, stays home with her children, protects them from abusive men, and guards against their involvement in crime. And finally, the proper family is implicitly coded white and middle class. The myth of the violent and deviant, poor, non-white family lingers heavily in the background of domestic violence discourse.

## Protecting White, Middle-Class Families

Shelter and coalition activists frequently have to challenge the notion that domestic violence happens only or mainly in non-white families and/or the lower classes. As Pleck (1987) demonstrates in her historical work on the development of domestic violence policies in the U.S., family violence has commonly been viewed as an outcome of the perceived lack of morality in working-class or low-income families or families of color. While few people educated about, or working in, the domestic violence field today would claim that abuse is only a problem in non-Euro-American families, the lawyers and law-enforcement personnel I interviewed expressed the belief that violence is more pervasive or acceptable in certain cultures. For example, Kevin Borden, a white, U.S.-born detective in charge of Spousal Abuse at one local police department explained:

> I'm working on a case right now, we work with a lot of Vietnamese. [They believe] it's okay to hit your wife occasionally, it keeps her in line. And the females grow up saying: "That's the way it is. I'm supposed to get hit if I get out of line." And the boys grow up saying, "she gets out of line, force her back in." I'm working with one case right now, and it's an Iranian family. And it's gotten pretty violent sometimes. She's an American, and that's why it's even brought to my attention, but he sees absolutely nothing wrong with just wail-

ing on her. And that's a repeat offender. You talk to him and he's got no remorse. He's [always] got an answer for you. You know that counseling's not gonna do him any good, cause he [thinks he] knows more than the counselor.

Implicit in this statement is that the cultural values of Vietnamese and Persian people differ greatly from white American cultural values. The assumption is that the only reason the wife of the Persian man even called the police is because she is "American." Implied in this formulation is that an "American" man, even if he beat his wife, would at least feel some "remorse," and would possibly be able to stop the behavior through counseling. In this way, the entire Persian culture is pathologized. While "Americans" have psychological problems that can be fixed, other cultures are unredeemable. The pathologizing of ethnic families serves to protect the myth of white, middle-class, heterosexual families as the more civilized family form.

The belief that non-white, working-class families are more abusive is challenged in "fact sheets" or "common myths about abuse" produced by organizations dealing with violence against women. The following excerpt from a pamphlet distributed by New Beginnings shows how they attempt to challenge this prevalent myth:

Demographic surveys indicate that battering happens in families that are Caucasian, Black, Hispanic, Asian, Native American, or from any culture. Battering also occurs in wealthy, middle-class and low-income neighborhoods. Well educated families are just as likely to have outbreaks of domestic violence as less educated families. Battering does not discriminate!

As mentioned above, activists in the battered women's movement have had some very important reasons for making the claim that "battering does not discriminate." However, while this claim is an attempt to challenge the racism and classism inherent in dominant constructions of domestic violence, it does not really counter the racist and class-based assumption that abuse stems from moral deficits or improper values. Instead, the claim that "battering does not discriminate" is constructed in order to gain support from white, middle- and upper-class political and legal authorities, and the dominant middle-class society. While activists rightly challenged the notion that abuse only happens in low-income and non-white families, they did so through a rhetorical strategy that reinscribes rather than challenges the discourse on moral difference. Left intact is the assumption that if battering *did not* happen to middle-class white women, we would not need to intervene.

The contradictory response to issues of race/ethnicity and class by shelter activists has led to dilemmas in current shelter policies, but also contains some hopeful signs. For instance, even though the dominant discourse on domestic violence makes the general claim that abuse crosses all boundaries, shelter activists in South County are learning that in order to assist different groups of women they need to develop understanding of how abuse affects women differently. For example, Grace Stone, the community outreach coordinator for Haven House, explained that after hiring a counselor who happened to speak Spanish, they realized that having a Spanish-speaking counselor brought more Latinas into the shelter. Haven House now has two Spanish-speaking staff members, plus one staff member from India who works "a lot with East Asian women," and they would like to hire a "Near Eastern" staff person. Thus, the staff at Haven House have become aware that women in the U.S. speak many different languages and will be less likely to go to a shelter where their language is not spoken. What is unclear is whether or not Grace feels the shelter needs to make any other programmatic changes in order to help women from different races and cultures, or if dealing with women from different cultures will cause the shelter to develop new analyses of abuse. Basic issues include: Is it enough to have one or two counselors who speak a particular language? Since many cultures and languages are represented by the geographical terms, "East Asian" and "Near Eastern," is one counselor in each group enough? Do women from different cultures need different types of counseling or do all battered women experience the same psychological issues? Are there particular material needs that should be met for different women? Should the shelter develop an ESL program?

New Beginnings established a "Multicultural Advisory Board" which has great potential for re-politicizing the shelter. However, contradictions arise from attempting to simply add-in attention to race and cultural difference without developing a new critical standpoint based in understanding how race, class, and gender oppression work together. Janet Bay explained the goals of the board: "What we wanted to do is have representatives from all the different cultures . . . to provide special skills and expertise . . . [and] guidance to the outreach programs development within the multicultural community to facilitate providing culturally sensitive intervention to families." The Multicultural Advisory

Board could become an important avenue for the shelter to develop an understanding of the ways in which racism and other material oppressions shape women's lives. It could also become a platform from which shelter workers could interrogate their own racism and the implicit racism of shelter practices.

However, when I asked Judy what *specifically* the Multicultural Advisory Board would do, she gave a troubling example. As one of their first projects, the board arranged for a Latino therapist to give a presentation to the staff on abuse in the Latino community. According to Judy, he talked about "how the abuse of women is more culturally acceptable" among Latinos. The therapist explained that Latino men feel they have to live up to a standard of "*machismo*" and that this includes controlling their wives. I do not know whether the therapist who addressed the staff actually said that abuse is more acceptable among Latinos, or if Judy simply interpreted the statement this way. Regardless, two problematic discursive constructions were reinscribed through the presentation. The first is the valuation of expert voices over experiential ones. While it was probably important to the board that the therapist who gave the presentation was a Latino, it is significant that they sought a professional therapist rather than a group of formerly battered Latinas. And secondly, the notion that non-white families and gender relations are essentially different than among whites, and that they are more accepting of abuse, was reinforced. As long as the board privileges professional voices and confines its programming to how domestic violence is differentially accepted in particular cultures, it will not create the space for shelter workers to develop a radical racial, class, or even gender politics.

### The Tension between Individualist and Structural Critiques

Among the shelter workers I interviewed, there was some variation in their understanding of the impact of battered women's different material circumstances on their specific needs. For instance, while Grace Stone seemed to marginalize the impact of women's economic resources on their ability to escape from abuse, Natalie Ramirez foregrounded women's economic needs. An emphasis in shelter work on women's emotional states over their material circumstances is particularly damaging for low-income women. Two workers at the Haven House shelter told me that the shelter conducted a survey and found that the single largest reason women gave for returning to an abusive partner after a shelter stay was that they could not find adequate and affordable housing. Grace also noted that the majority of the women in the shelter are "below the poverty line, because other women have money to go to a hotel or someplace else." Yet earlier in the interview, Grace discussed services which were not provided by the shelter:

> There's a fine line with these women as to how much you do with them and for them. One of the things we do not do is find them places to live after they leave the shelter. We will get them a *Pennysaver*, we have a pay phone at the shelter, they are encouraged to use the pay phone. . . . And that's because they've gotta learn to get out there and talk with the landlord themselves, negotiate that themselves, and of course, that's the hardest thing for them to do, after they leave the shelter.

If a lack of alternative housing is the number-one reason women give for returning to an abuser, we have to wonder why finding housing for women is not the number-one priority for the shelter. State and county agencies provide funds to shelters for each woman for a maximum of forty-five days, and according to Grace, Haven House will not allow women to exceed the maximum stay for which the shelter is funded.

Finding affordable housing in forty-five days is a near impossibility for some women, particularly women who are underemployed or unemployed and have young children. Although Haven House is the only area shelter that allows women to keep their jobs while at the shelter, they can not do so if their work schedule conflicts with mandatory group support meetings. Furthermore, because shelters prefer to take clients from outside of the communities in which they are located, transportation to their job could be a real barrier for many women. Differences based on a woman's immigrant status, class, race, ethnicity, or number of children might preclude the possibility of being able to acquire housing independently after a stay in the shelter. These factors are displaced by the assumption that battered women are suffering from psychological problems and that, through personal transformation, they will be able to leave their partners and meet their family's economic needs.

As the consequence of centering the individual psychological framework, the primary goal of shelter work, as defined by the activists I interviewed, is to help women understand their abuse as a function of their *feelings* of inadequacy, entrapment, and reliance on an abusive man, and not to help women understand and address their specific and varied socioeconomic and emotional needs. For example, I asked Grace what she thought was the major contributor to the changes she sees in women during their shelter stay. She responded:

> I think it is self-realization. Just realizing that she has some control over her own life . . . if a woman comes in and says, "hey, I'm here for thirty days, and I'm going back with him," we say, "fine, you stay here." It's because they know she's not going to leave the same way she came in. . . . There's something about making a woman understand that [she has options] that is very freeing. I mean, it sounds very simple, but I would say that that's the biggest change factor that we can offer these women, that you are in control of your life, and you always have choices, and here are some of those choices, and here are some social agencies or places that you can go. . . . And, interestingly, I don't think anyone could have told me this, [that] you can give that to a woman in thirty days. People can change drastically in that short a period of time.

There are a number of important issues raised by Grace's description of how the shelter helps women to change. First, Grace emphasizes change in terms of the way a woman *thinks* about her life. In this statement, the goal of the shelter shifts away from ending abuse and towards changing individual women. If a woman returns to an abuser she will still be experiencing abuse, but according to Grace, the important thing is that she will not leave the shelter "the same way that she came in."

According to Grace, Haven House helps women through the process of personal change by helping them to "realize" that they have some control over their lives, that they have choices. Thus, the shelter philosophy perpetuates the notion that women in abusive relationships are suffering from a false consciousness about their life options. Grace does not discuss the very real and different constraints on various women's life options. Accordingly, it is not *having* options that frees women, but *believing* that they have options. And finally, Grace defends the thirty-day limit as an adequate amount of time in which women can make changes in their lives. Because "people can change drastically in that short a period of time," and because the goal of the shelter is to change women's thinking and not their material circumstances, thirty days becomes long enough.

In contrast, Family Alternatives' policy allows women to stay up to sixty days, given certain extenuating circumstances. Natalie Ramirez explained:

> We have undocumented ladies who have maybe had one child who is a U.S. citizen and their sole income is welfare of $299 a month and where are you gonna find a place for that? So we realize that that's an obstacle which we have to overcome, so we might give her a little bit more time to accumulate enough money to move out. Or, we have women who have U.S.-born kids, but somewhere along the line, while they were with their spouse, they committed fraud, and the way that that happens is, they might have left him, applied for welfare, and he wheedles his way back into the relationship, likes the idea of free money. "Don't tell welfare I'm living back with you," and holds that over her head, "now you can't leave 'cause I'll tell welfare." Or, somewhere along the line it gets found out that he's living there, and somebody reports her and she's cut off. So she can't support herself. Or you get a woman with five kids, and she's got the income coming in, but nobody wants to rent to a family with a single lady with five kids.

In this case, Natalie is fully aware that low-income and immigrant women, and women with children, face issues beyond simply feeling trapped. She understands that shelter workers cannot ignore these issues if they want to help women succeed in living without an abuser. Natalie's alternative interpretation of the issues facing low-income women contrasts markedly with Grace's description of the Haven House policy. These different interpretations translate directly into policy. While Family Alternatives is willing to extend women's stays for a short period of time and is willing to pay for that using funding that does not come from the state, Haven House is not. This discrepancy may be due in part to the different social locations of the workers at the two shelters.

Haven House is located in a much more affluent section of South County than Family Alternatives and has a large volunteer corp made up of upper-middle-class women. In fact, Grace informed me that Haven House "had more volunteers than they knew what to do with" both in the administrative offices and in the shelter. In contrast, Family Alternatives was so understaffed at the time of this research that the outreach co-coordinator could not spare time for an interview. She was doing both her work and the work of an Assistant Director, and she informed me that the shelter was desperately in need of volunteers in the administrative office. Accordingly, it is possible that Family Alternatives staff are more aware of the difficulties facing low-income women and women of color than the staff at Haven House, because the shelter is located in a lower-income community with a larger percentage of people of color, and because the shelter itself does not have as many resources.

## Summary and Discussion

The major strategies of the battered-women's movement include working for the support of shelters and for changes in family law, criminal law, and police responses to domestic violence. In order to argue for these changes and for the support of shelters, activists in South County were forced to legitimate their voice as experts on the needs of battered women. In the process of arguing for public support for shelters, shelter activists developed their own expert voice on abuse and used this voice to respond to questions raised in the discourse on proper families. With increased state funding, shelters were pressured to professionalize their staffing. As more professionally trained women were hired into shelters, the expert voice developed by the South County movement shifted from the voices and experiences of women who experienced violence in their home to social workers, psychologists, and other mental-health professionals. The contemporary dominant discourse on domestic violence relies on therapeutic vocabularies to both deflect challenges to the shelter and to construct battered women as the proper and deserving clients of shelter work.

The "battered woman" as a singular and comprehensive identity is produced through domestic violence services in South County. Seldom were battered women constructed as a diverse group of women who face various oppressions and whose life options are limited in specific ways by their diverse social locations. Instead they were depicted primarily as women suffering from a uniform set of psychological and cognitive problems. As a result, the needs of women who experience forms of abuse ranging from emotional manipulation and coercion through sexual abuse and coercion to physical violence of diverse types were rarely centered in shelter practice.

Lacking any sustained attention to the experiences of women of color and low-income women, shelter activists in South County seldom questioned the notions of family, community, and identity upon which the dominant discourse was based. As a result, the shelter movement in this location has not successfully challenged the construction of the violent family as deviant, poor, and non-white. In South County, there has been no large-scale, concerted effort to explore how to create shelters and other services that would allow room for different perspectives and debates that would challenge race and class bias. Shelter workers interviewed for this study, for the most part, had not interrogated their own critical standpoint for privileging the white, middle-class heterosexual family form. Nor have they grappled with the implications of constructing an abstract "battered woman" who seemingly has no class or race or ethnicity and who is seen as suffering from a range of psychological problems.

While shelters today undoubtedly help thousands of women each year and while coalition activists have raised both public and state agency awareness of abuse and of issues facing women who are abused, I also believe that as a movement we need to find alternative approaches to fighting domestic violence. The first step should be to interrogate feminist claims-making practices, particularly around constructing categories such as the "battered woman." Our political strategies must recognize and explicitly state that women who are abused face diverse life challenges, have widely ranging life options, and experience many different forms of abuse. As long as the struggle against the abuse of women remains narrowly focused on helping individual women leave abusers by building self-esteem, the material conditions of women's lives cannot be explored and addressed.

By incorporating the experiences of women of color, immigrant women, poor women, and lesbians into feminist critical standpoints, the shelter activists might begin to question the efficacy of seeking increased legal and law-enforcement solutions to the exclusion of other strategies. These solutions force us to focus on extreme physical violence over lesser physical abuse or sexual and emotional abuse. More importantly, they ignore the oppressive ways that families of color, gay and lesbian families, and low-income families are treated through contemporary state policies. When arguing for increased criminal penalties for abuse, activists need to understand that these penalties will be applied selectively and will disproportionately affect families that are not white, middle-class, and heterosexual.

The battered women's movement has made great gains in exposing the reality of abuse and violence in women's lives. They have worked to change custody laws, to allow women to seek restraining orders, to provide hotlines and shelters that have helped thousands of women. The battered-women's movement developed from women's anger and specific women's concrete needs. By linking the personal experiences of women to a feminist political analysis, activists and researchers have been able to challenge the depoliticizing perspectives that women's problems are primarily psychological in origin. However, the power of the psychological discourse within professionalized shelters has begun to displace radical feminist political analyses in some locations. This is especially evident in conservative political environments like South County.

Anti-domestic violence struggles must also work to insure affordable low-cost housing, education, welfare rights, medical care, affirmative action, fair immigration policies, and so on. These issues cannot be seen as separate from violence against women. One necessary and obvious step is for shelter workers and feminist activists to go into the diverse communities around them and form coalitions with a broader range of individuals, groups, and organizations.

Through my own experiences of abuse, of seeking help to end it, and of doing this research, I have come to understand the limits of my previous feminist, class, and race politics. My earlier work was devoid of an understanding of how class, race, and heterosexuality shaped domestic violence discourse and policy as well as my own struggle. The ongoing process of exploring my standpoint and the epistemological limits of my experience has not been easy nor will it be easy for other anti-violence activists who try. However, we must be willing to expose and challenge the limits of our own experience and politics so that we can continue to challenge violence against women and sustain radical feminist political action.

**Author's Note:** I want to thank the two women who made this work possible. Nancy Naples for her patience, insight, and mentoring throughout the research and writing process. Her assistance has been invaluable. And my mother, Jean Kendrick, for teaching me to love reading and debating, for encouraging me to come to graduate school, and for always believing that I could be successful. I also want to acknowledge the emotional and intellectual community offered by fellow graduate students during the creation of this work: Lisa Jones, Chrisy Moutsatsos, Beth Quinn, Erica Bornstein, and Deborah Mindry.

## Notes

1. Martin and Mohanty 1986; Mohanty 1991a; Williams 1991.
2. Also see Schechter 1982; Loseke 1992; Matthews 1995; Reinelt 1995.
3. The average per capita income in this county of 2,410,556 residents is $19,890. The average household income is $45,922, while the average family income is $51,167.
4. According to the 1990 census, fifty-five percent of Orange County residents reported themselves as "white, non-Hispanic"; twenty-four percent "Hispanic"; ten percent "Asian and Pacific Islander"; and point-five percent "black."
5. Two shelters have "second step houses" which provide low-cost housing to a small number of women for up to a year or more after completing the shelter program.
6. The Orange County Sexual Assault Network recently closed down, but there is at least one remaining sexual-assault hotline open. There is also a crisis hotline for women operated independently of the shelters.
7. A program called "Safety Net," which provided hotel vouchers for women in case the shelters were full, recently lost its funding. Currently, the county funds two vouchers per shelter per month which they can give to women to stay for up to five days in a hotel when the shelter is full.
8. After I completed the research for this chapter, another coalition formed out of this subgroup of the Social Service Providers Network. The new coalition was organized to begin fundraising and planning for a new shelter in the southern region of South County.
9. I conducted at least four semi-structured interviews in each category for a total of nineteen formal interviews. I attended meetings of three area coalitions against battering, and conducted short, informal interviews with some attending members. Finally, I was able to attend a training on domestic violence for counseling interns conducted by the Community Outreach Coordinator of one of the shelters. All names of places, coalitions, shelters, and people in this paper are pseudonyms.
10. Schecter 1982; Fine 1985, 1989; Loseke 1992.
11. Natalie Ramirez is a Latina shelter worker who told me that she got involved in working at the shelter because of some kind of "personal experience" with abuse. She did not elaborate on whether she was a survivor herself.

# Chapter 7

# Navigating the Anti-Immigrant Wave

## *The Korean Women's Hotline and the Politics of Community*

**Lisa Sun-Hee Park**

The passage of California's Proposition 187 in November 1994 has produced dramatic tensions in immigrant communities across the country. This bill, which severely restricts the rights of immigrants, was just the beginning of a nation-wide wave of anti-immigrant sentiment.[1] The effects of such hostile policies were felt not only by the immigrant community as a whole, but also by immigrant families individually. One aspect of these repercussions is evident in the lives of battered immigrant women. In this chapter, I investigate the impact of anti-immigrant legislation on battered immigrant women by focusing on the relationship between a grassroots domestic violence hotline and the community it serves.[2] I argue that these policies shifted the community boundaries, creating unlikely alliances among adversaries, as well as forming distances between friends.

This chapter focuses on the politics of gender and ethnicity experienced by a nonprofit, community-based, battered women's organization, Korean Women's Hotline (KWH), located in "Koreatown," one of the largest Korean American communities in the nation.[3] Founded in 1990, the Hotline has struggled to survive as a "community-based" entity despite resistance by the larger Korean American community.[4] The tension within this Korean community does not necessarily signify a greater resistance toward domestic violence activists than in other communities.

Differences in culture and history may produce some differences in the manifestations of domestic abuse; however, there is no evidence to indicate a greater presence of wife battering in any one community, ethnic group, or class category. According to the Hotline, this resistance on the part of other Koreatown organizations toward KWH stemmed from the fact that KWH members endorsed an alternative model of family unity that challenged the traditional patriarchal and hierarchical Confucian definition of a stable and healthy family.

Four years after its inception, the Hotline found itself at an impasse with the passage of California's Proposition 187 and the subsequent proposal of federal and state anti-immigrant bills. But the threats to restrict immigration and deny documented and undocumented immigrants access to a variety of educational, health care, and social services shifted Koreatown's boundaries to include KWH for the first time. The leaders of this Korean community relaxed their opposition to the Hotline to some degree in an effort to present a united front against the anti-immigrant political climate.[5]

In this chapter, I argue that this shifting of boundaries in response to hostile policies moved KWH from the margin towards the center of the established Korean community. In the process, the Hotline members felt pressure to choose alliances between the Korean American community and the mainstream domestic violence movement. Pulled in two different directions, neither of which adequately encompassed the experiences of Asian immigrant feminist organizations, Hotline members expressed dissatisfaction with both options.

In addressing these topics, I first describe KWH's interaction with the local Korean community prior to the anti-immigrant legislation, and then focus on the Hotline's efforts to construct a women-centered definition of a healthy family and community unity. I also discuss local leaders' adverse reactions to this reconstruction of accepted cultural norms. The second part of the paper presents community life after the passage of anti-immigrant policies. I address the changes that immigrant families, battered immigrant women, and the battered women's hotline experienced, and conclude with a discussion of the implications of the changes for the mainstream domestic violence movement.

### Organic-Activist-Research

This paper is the result of three-and-a-half years of weekly involvement with KWH as a member of the organization. I attended Board meetings, accompanied women to domestic violence court, wrote grant proposals, provided child care, transportation, language translation, and community education, and directed a volunteer-training program. During my years of involvement with KWH, I gradually became a part of the organization and subsequently became privy to a great deal of "insider" information. My access in this organization was greatly influenced by my personal history as a Korean American woman and activist. As an "organic-activist-researcher," I work within my indigenous population, with which I share intimate cultural understandings and history (Park and Pellow 1996). In this way, my experiences expand the boundaries of participatory research (Stoecker and Bonacich 1992).

My affiliation with two often conflicting arenas of loyalty—the university and the community—provides a unique standpoint from which to witness social behavior (also see Collins 1990). This joint affiliation served as an advantage when interviewing members of the Korean American community, many of whom place significant value on higher education. They viewed their roles as teachers of sorts, helping me with my "schoolwork." Interestingly, this was not the case when I approached the Hotline. Most KWH members had attended a university in the U.S. and had no romantic notions of academia. In fact, they were initially suspicious of my intentions. In this situation, I overcame a burden of trust (Burawoy 1979) by behaving like a regular volunteer—refraining from interviewing or otherwise acting like a researcher—for eight months. I began the interview process once the KWH members became comfortable with me, and after I had established an identity apart from my researcher status.

My work began in February 1992 as a participant observer. I participated in KWH's annual forty-hour volunteer-training program. I then had the opportunity to attend community events and work as a volunteer at KWH. After five months of collecting fieldnotes and gaining trust from KWH, I began conducting formal interviews. I conducted fifty formal interviews ranging from one-half to two hours. Of the fifty community residents interviewed, thirty were KWH members, and ten were community leaders, including two Korean newspaper editors, a pastor, and several heads of Korean organizations. The remaining ten were identified by those previously interviewed in a process defined as "snowball sampling." All the other respondents were first-generation or had immigrated as children. Only one respondent was born in the United States.

The interview structure varied somewhat for Hotline members, community leaders, and community members, in accordance with each group's unique experience. In general, the open-ended questions were organized around five main topics, probing individual awareness and perception of the Korean Women's Hotline, domestic violence, Korean community concerns and problems, women's roles (specifically those of Korean women living in the United States), and the local power structure. I collected much of the data on immigration policy through follow-up interviews, participant observation, and written materials from community groups, as well as mainstream media reports. I conducted interviews in English, Korean, or both, depending upon what was more comfortable for the respondent. In keeping with my promises to respondents in my field research, pseudonyms are used for places, people, and organizations.

## Life Before The Anti-Immigrant Wave

### Korean Women's Hotline and Koreatown

The Korean Women's Hotline, founded by three Korean women, opened its phone lines in 1990 on Korean Independence Day—a symbol of the struggle to attain freedom from violence for Korean American women in the area—and is still operating today. KWH's services include not only crisis intervention, referrals, translation, legal advocacy, community education, and leadership development, but also domestic violence advocacy training for community volunteers, professional social workers, police officers, and health-care providers. The Hotline is located within a large metropolitan city, in an area called "Koreatown." Approximately 150,000 Koreans live in the city and surrounding suburbs. The Korean community is tightly connected and fairly self-sufficient, acting as a "micro-society" that offers much of the same services as the larger mainstream society. For instance, the community has a complex communications system, with three daily newspapers, five weekly newspapers, two television stations, and two radio stations. There are also sixteen Korean social service providers, merchants selling everything from Korean food and clothes to Korean movies, and several Korean-owned and -run banks. There are also more than 160 Korean churches in the larger metropolitan area.

The project initially began with hopes of providing a shelter, but after seeking advice from other Asian American social service agencies with similar objectives and evaluating their limited financial and human resources, the founders resolved to establish a hotline. KWH's mission statement and philosophy, in accordance with the philosophy of the founders, indicates a strong feminist leaning. Their brochure states,

> We, Korean Women's Hotline, are an all-woman, grassroots organization with a mission to empower Korean American women who have been abused and systematically neglected by our community and rendered powerless by our society. We try to provide an escape from an oppressive situation through intervention, advocacy, education, self-help, and by promoting leadership among Korean American women. (KWH Training Manual 1993, 1)

Similarly, their statement of philosophy is as follows:

> Korean Women's Hotline is rooted in the belief that all women have the right to live free from fear of violence, whether it be psychological, emotional, verbal, sexual or physical. We believe that violence against women is one symptom of subordination of women in society. As long as women are not recognized as equals, violence against them will be perpetuated and tolerated. Although those who commit acts of violence against women are ultimately responsible for its eradication, we feel that it is women who can best act on behalf of the interest of women. Our actions are based on non-hierarchical, egalitarian principles with decisions reached through consensus. (KWH Training Manual 1993, 1)

KWH rejects the Korean community's tradition of hierarchy and patriarchy. With a commitment to a democratic decision-making process, KWH helps promote a sense of leadership among members rather than rely on a top-down structure. As with many other mainstream feminist organizations, KWH functions to empower its members as well as to provide a social-service. One of the founders describes how the organization affected her and other women associated with the Hotline:

> I think KWH provided a way for a lot of us to focus more. It clarified a lot of issues and became a tool for a lot of us to understand the power structure and how things work. 'Cause you know, so

many people talk about race and have and have-nots, and all this, and many times it stays at a rhetorical level; but I think KWH got you to see how it gets to be played out, you know, ultimately. So you know, it clarified a lot of issues, at least for me. And I think it happened to a lot of other people, too, because through organizing when we didn't have any staff, we all did a lot of work, and it was hard, but we all learned a lot of skills—how to write a letter, how to take minutes, how to run meetings, how to contact other people, who the resources are—so, it was an eye-opening experience in a lot of different ways. . . .

KWH provides a forum for Korean women to engage beyond the boundaries prescribed by tradition. Within KWH, women act as pivotal decision-makers, learn new skills, build leadership capacities, and experience camaraderie with other Korean women.

The organization grew considerably in a short time. In three years, KWH hired a second staff member and the number of volunteers increased from zero to thirty. For fiscal year 1993–94, they reported an annual budget of $83,000, a significant increase from the $1,000 with which the organizers began.[6] From only fifteen to thirty calls a month at its beginning, this organization now receives more than one hundred fifty calls a month from the Korean American community.[7] They estimated a forty per cent increase in demand for their services in one year. In response to this increase, the organization moved from their small, one-room office to a larger, two-room office.

On the whole, the domestic violence cases have been severe. The Korean women who call have done so as a last resort. Having endured years of abuse and countless attempts to justify their husband's behavior, they risked family shame and severe retribution by contacting the Hotline. Some women are in their sixties calling after forty years of abuse, having waited for all their children to marry and have families of their own. However, since KWH does not keep uniform records of the callers to the Hotline, demographics of the callers are not available.

### Reconstructing a Healthy Family

KWH's continuing success challenges the Korean community's established norms. For local leaders, the Hotline's presence questions their ability to meet needs of the Korean Americans living in the community. One staff member noted that the dominant view on the pervasiveness of domestic violence within the Korean community's is one of denial and that interferes with the general acceptance of KWH. She explained:

> I think they are not ready to accept KWH. Some people appreciate us; but even those who do, do not understand KWH's substance. They don't know about the process and the structure of domestic violence. For example, they think, "Oh what miserable women and children; I cannot believe how the abuser can do that" but at the question of divorce, they always say, "Family is first. We have to save the family." And when they meet an abused woman, they say, "Oh, I cannot believe that. She must have deserved that."

Korean leaders appear apprehensive because KWH's existence may signify a lack of unity within the community. Unity is crucial to maintaining the status quo and a sense of nationalism. Its importance is rooted in Confucianism, a tradition that positions family cohesion as the basis of a larger community or state unity. In describing the Korean family system, Chungmoo Choi (1992, 106) writes,

> In Confucian culture, filial subordination to the household head is analogous to the subordination of the children-citizens to the father-king. The existence of gender and generational hierarchies within the home conditioned children to accept hierarchy as natural, reinforcing Confucian notions of filial piety and obedience to authority in general and fostering loyalty and obedience to the state.

In accordance with this Confucian philosophy, one community leader said, "[i]n order to have a healthy society, we have to have a healthy family, and the core of that is the mother." Accordingly, a lack of unity in the family is indicative of a breakdown in the ethnic community—a construction that places further blame on women.

One KWH volunteer, however, argues that the outward appearance of unity comes at the expense of women in a domestic violence situation:

> Let's say they have a daughter-in-law and a son and the son is beating the daughter-in-law and suddenly the daughter . . . decides that she is not going to live like this anymore. There won't be harmony in the family and order is going to break down. They just want to keep all the pieces together no matter if she's happy or

not. They don't really care about women's lives or happiness, they just want to keep all the pieces together.

A KWH board member adds: "We have to start looking into the fact that the daughter's happiness makes up part of the harmony."

Embedded in these statements is the reconstruction—by KWH members—of what a stable and healthy family and community must look like. KWH's survival legitimates the idea that domestic violence is a serious issue within the Korean American community, and challenges the long-standing ideology of family unity. For Hotline members, presenting this reconstruction of family and community has been an uphill struggle.

In many ways, KWH has had to start from scratch. Many of the significant advances made by mainstream feminists in the domestic violence movement have not been shared by the tightly knit Korean community. As a result of the strict patriarchal and hierarchical culture reinforced by centuries of Confucianism,[8] what constitutes abuse in mainstream American culture may not be viewed as such in Koreatown. What some Koreans define as reinforcing obedience, American culture might define as physical or mental abuse. Asian American activists Margaretta W. L. Lin and Cheng Imm Tan (1994, 323) write, "[m]ost people if asked would say that we should not tolerate domestic violence. Yet, many community leaders still say that a little discipline, an occasional beating now and then to teach the woman a lesson, is not domestic violence." KWH members have had to redefine as violence what a Confucian patriarch might view as discipline. As a "community-based" group with little support from the organized community itself, KWH must therefore maneuver carefully in both the Korean and mainstream communities.

KWH is aware that the domestic violence problem is a source of embarrassment, particularly in light of the expectations bestowed upon a community seen as part of a "model minority." According to this myth, Asian Americans are an ideal minority group by comparison to other people of color stereotyped with problems such as domestic violence, crime, and poverty. Much of mainstream American society maintains and accepts the myth with open arms, for if Asian Americans are indeed ideal, they then require no attention or financial support (Suzuki 1989). The myth makes KWH's work all the more difficult because to raise the issue of domestic violence is to air "dirty laundry" and consequently to explode the model-minority myth.

Airing "dirty laundry" is not taken lightly in Koreatown. Fear of embarrassment and shame perpetuates a system of silence. Not surprisingly, KWH's members experience great difficulty in speaking to others about domestic violence. Their actions breach valued rules that dictate "appropriate" behavior for young Korean women. Any deviation from these rules signifies disrespect toward the community elders. These rules create barriers for KWH in their efforts to expand. In fact, the members complain that responding and reacting to such ideology hinders them from fulfilling their mission to assist battered women. In addition to gender roles, KWH actively rejects a number of other norms, including the general perception of the domestic violence problem within Koreatown. This perception was apparent when eight out of the ten local leaders I interviewed acknowledged the existence of domestic violence in Koreatown, but countered that it was less urgent than other "more pressing" problems. They viewed domestic violence as a result of stress due to changes in the economy, rather than as institutionalized male violence: they believe that once a man's economic status improves, he will no longer abuse his wife. Others blamed abuse on mental illness or alcoholism. Although KWH acknowledges the many stresses of immigrant life, they view domestic violence as a persistent part of the community, irrespective of economic class. During a volunteer-training session, one member replied,

> Alcohol and the hardships of poverty may aggravate the situation, but the situation was there to begin with. Those who are rich also beat their wives—we just don't hear about them much because they have the resources to protect their privacy. Also, we found that some men who go to Alcoholics Anonymous and become sober continue their abuse.[9]

A community leader who described himself as the most powerful Korean person in the geographic region emphasized what he saw as the positive side to domestic violence:

> It's the oriental way—to be silent and to suffer. I think that's one of the reasons why women take punches from their husbands and still keep going—taking care of their children . . . and put[ting] them in a nice school. That's strength and that's power.

KWH members found this cultural explanation troubling. A board member responded:

We are trying to find an alternative source of power or empowerment for Korean women. It's pretty scary to think that the only way
we have power is to suffer. Such thinking doesn't benefit us. It
benefits abusers.

## The Politics of Community

The Hotline activists' rejection of accepted community ideology has
not gone unnoticed. The community has retaliated both directly and
indirectly with threats, denial, and negative rumors. For instance, telephone threats by a woman's abuser or an abuser's family members are
regular occurrences. In addition to accusations of "brainwashing"
women into divorce, KWH is accused of insensitivity to the plight of
immigrant Koreans. Not only are the callers angry about the Hotline's
interference in their private family lives, they denounce KWH as "Amer-
icanized" and as traitors. Threats of lawsuits are also not uncommon.

Local leaders often became hostile when the topic of domestic violence was raised. Several community members I approached for interviews refused to answer any questions directly related to domestic violence in Koreatown, and became angry when I mentioned this topic. In
an indirect way, community hostility is also shown through the absence
of monetary support for KWH. In its second year, the Hotline sent out a
mass mailing to all the Korean churches in the area asking for support
and offering to visit or conduct community-awareness programs. Only
two churches responded, one antagonistically. Interviews I conducted
with community members revealed that much of the Korean public is
unaware of KWH's activities. While all the community leaders were
familiar with KWH, they apparently did not pass this information along
to those they served. As it stands, the information passes largely through
informal, word-of-mouth means.

In general, Korean American community members avoid speaking of
domestic violence and the Hotline. As in the wider society, domestic violence is frequently defined as a "woman's issue." As the president of a
Korean organization with more than seven hundred members put it:

I don't know about [KWH]. I just read about that in the newspaper. It's a woman issue and I'm not a woman so I don't know what
its function is.

He said the topic came up during an association meeting as well: "We discussed that and . . . we thought it was a woman's problem and we just weren't interested about that." This comment presents a false dichotomy of "community" (read "men's") and "women's" issues. As a male, he and his organization see their concerns as separate from women's concerns. According to this organizational leader, economic discrimination against immigrant Korean businesses is the single most important problem—and one which lies only in the "man's" arena. His statements are indicative of the strict hierarchical division of gender roles and concerns in which the term "women's issue" conveniently dissolves any personal involvement.

Closely coupled with the above-mentioned strategy is the official neglect of domestic violence by decision-making and public-opinion-forming institutions in Koreatown. For example, I asked the director of the largest Korean organization (with ten thousand members)—which functions as an umbrella organization for all community groups as well as a representative in mainstream politics—"is domestic violence a community concern at all?" Sidetracking the question, he responded instead by listing the organization's four main goals for the community, which did not include domestic violence. He focused on the importance of community solidarity in achieving greater influence in mainstream politics, particularly in his efforts to combat recent surges in xenophobia. The director of this organization viewed racial/ethnic harmony as vital and the Hotline's goals as inconsistent with his organization's objectives. Unfortunately, without official recognition of the problem, it was unlikely that KWH's concerns would be included in the local agenda.

Rumors constitute the final category of retaliatory action by community leaders against KWH. This may be the most subtle yet most powerful strategy, for word spreads quickly in a close-knit community. Rumors can create a dangerous environment for KWH volunteers, particularly since KWH lacks institutional resources within the community and relies heavily on informal means of communication. While often used as a form of resistance from below (Scott 1990) in this case rumors were employed as tool of repression from above. Rumors that Hotline volunteers enforce divorce and adhere to radical, white, anti-family ideals harm their reputation as legitimate Korean American social service providers. The KWH staff has learned to be cautious. They do not give out their location to everyone who calls. A post office box is available for letters, and advertising is done as discreetly as possible. They leave their brochures in other social service offices and in police stations where the people most in need may obtain the phone number. According to the coordinator, the majority of volunteers became acquainted with KWH through word-of-mouth and personal networks.

### Immigrant Families Under Fire

Such defensive actions on the part of the Korean American community are understandable given the many stresses evident within immigrant families. The traditional hierarchical boundaries in which husband, wife, children, work, and family are categorized shifted as women entered the workforce upon immigration. In some cases, the women are the only wage earners, having found jobs, as low-paying and dangerous as they may be.[10] This role reversal has challenged the long-standing male authority that promised support and nurturance in exchange for power and control. Lin and Tan state that these factors have aggravated drinking problems and violence in the home, but they are careful to note that "[w]hile APA [Asian Pacific American] refugee and immigrant men do have struggles and challenges to cope with, as do the women, this is never an excuse for violence in the home" (Lin and Tan 1994, 330). KWH members reinforce this argument by stating that although immigration may exacerbate domestic violence, it does not make it inevitable: "There are plenty of immigrant men who don't batter."

Anti-immigrant policies can also exacerbate domestic violence as they limit family resources and disempower the male authority figure. These policies disempower the immigrant community in general and immigrant families in particular by forcing them to rely almost solely on informal networks for survival. With limited access to education, social services, health care, and jobs, the poor and undocumented immigrants may be further isolated.[11] The second half of this chapter will focus on anti-immigrant legislation that affects so many dimensions of immigrant family life, including the well-being of battered women.

### Life After the Anti-Immigrant Wave

The history of immigration policies in the United States documents the movement of Asian Americans from a despised to a model minority. Restrictive legislation such as the Chinese Exclusion Act of 1882, which ended the first wave of Asian immigration to the United States, is indicative of the portrayal of Asian Americans as the "yellow menace."[12] The doors reopened with the Immigration Act of 1965, creating the second wave of Asian immigration. With the current onslaught of anti-immigrant bills on state and federal legislative agendas, as well as increasing efforts to strengthen the borders of this country, it appears that this second wave is drawing to a close. Given the potential power of immigration policies over so many dimensions of immigrant communities, including the gender ratio (and subsequently the population growth), demographic and social characteristics, and employment patterns, it is not surprising that the mere proposal of an anti-immigrant bill significantly affects the daily routine of immigrant life (Hing 1993). One source of these effects is front-page newspaper articles that report a growing effort to strengthen the nation's borders by making life for those immigrants already here more difficult. For example, *The New York Times* recently reported: "With the public growing angry over illegal immigration, the Republican Congress is considering the adoption of the most restrictive changes in the country's immigration laws in 71 years" (Holmes 1995, A1).

Fear of anti-immigrant sentiments is evident among Korean Americans who arrived in significant numbers in the 1970s with the passage of the Immigration Act of 1965. Many newcomers were professionals who experienced initial downward mobility upon entering the United States. Many found a niche as small business entrepreneurs catering to Korean ethnic tastes, or entered the African American and Latino consumer markets after confronting job-market barriers, such as glass ceilings in white-collar occupations, difficulties with English proficiency and American customs, and persistent discrimination.[13] Thus, many recent immigrants already lead precarious lives. With anti-immigrant legislation, the family must endure new challenges that leave many immigrant families at risk, and with them the lives of battered immigrant women and the organizations created to assist them.

California's Proposition 187, the 1996 Welfare Reform Bill, and the Immigration Bill HR. 2202 increase the level of stress within immigrant families and communities. These recent U.S. policies affect both documented and undocumented immigrant families. While California's Proposition 187[14] denies education, health care (including emergency medical care), and social services to undocumented immigrants, the Senate Welfare Reform Bill bars immigrants, including U.S. citizens, from many federal and federally-funded needs-based programs. The HR. 2202 bill introduced by House Immigration chair Rep. Lamar Smith slashes family immigration by one-third, imposes tough restrictions on legal immigrants' access to all federal means-tested programs (school lunches, immunizations, battered women's shelters, Head Start

Programs, etc.), and requires hospitals to report undocumented immigrants who seek emergency services.

### Immigration Legislation and Battered Women

The sociopolitical context in which this anti-immigrant legislation emerged created a xenophobic reaction towards both documented and undocumented immigrants. The National Immigration Forum, based in Washington, D.C., reported a dramatic increase in discriminatory actions towards people of color one month after the passage of Proposition 187 in California. For instance, a grocery store clerk in Santa Clara examined a legal immigrant's driver's license and refused to sell her anything unless she could produce a social security card verifying her legal status. Other incidents included pharmacies refusing to fill prescriptions unless immigration documents were presented and school security guards barring students of color from entering schools one day after the passage of Prop. 187 (Otto 1994).

The implications of anti-immigrant policies are far-reaching for battered immigrant women. KWH members found that battered immigrant women are more fearful than ever of leaving their abusive households as access to legal, medical, and social services is threatened. Almost all the women who call the Hotline are immigrants with limited English proficiency. Most have lived in relative isolation within the Korean community. Their lives consist of home and work, and little else (Rimonte 1989).

Although there are no statistics on exactly how many Korean American women are battered, KWH volunteers agree with others in the battered women's movement that domestic violence knows no boundaries, as it cuts across cultural, racial, political, and socioeconomic divides (Rimonte 1989; Lin and Tan 1994). KWH members speculate that English-speaking Korean women may have other options and seek help from others outside the community, perhaps in an attempt to ensure anonymity. The immigrant women who call KWH, on the other hand, have limited resources and nowhere else to turn. KWH volunteers acknowledge the courage these women have, risking further abuse, family and community ostracism, and possibly deportation (for those whose residence in the U.S. is dependent on their marriage).

On several occasions, abusers have used threats of deportation as a means of control. In such instances, the law was deliberately misrepresented in order to deter the woman from seeking help, as well as to increase her dependence upon the abuser. In addition, ignorance of legal options, limited English skills, and meager economic resources deter many immigrants from seeking help (Peterson 1988; Abraham 1995). It is apparent that the hostility anti-immigrant policies foster threatens these women's already tenuous well-being.

## Immigration Legislation and KWH

As a small community-based organization serving immigrant women, KWH is experiencing a similar fate. Recent government actions have spawned internal strife and funding cuts and have resulted in greater numbers of KWH clientele reporting fear of formal and informal retaliation by mainstream social service providers. The impact of these policies demands a great deal of KWH's resources. Volunteers have recently focused more of their time and energy on KWH's role as an agent of social change. Members are active participants in anti-Proposition 187 rallies, letter-writing campaigns, and community-wide meetings, in addition to their regular duties. The biannual forty-hour volunteer-training sessions now includes a section on the effect of anti-immigration policy on Asian immigrant women. As mentioned earlier, funding is another major concern during these hostile times. More than one-third of KWH's budget comes from state and federal government sources, a dependence that is increasingly accompanied by official intrusions into KWH affairs. For example, a letter recently arrived from a government office requesting that KWH verify the legal status of all staff members. KWH members understood this letter as a sign of things to come—verification of the legal status of the women and clients who call the Hotline. The strain is apparent as KWH works to remain a strong community-based organization despite thinning resources and greater risks.

## Unlikely Alliances

These policies produced an unintended effect on the relationship between KWH and the community leaders. In light of the threats new immigration policies posed, Koreatown leaders developed a heightened awareness of their vulnerable position in the U.S. Consequently, concerned community activists drew upon KWH's identity as a Korean immigrant organization to fight against immigration policies. For the first time since the Hotline's founding, some of the community leaders invited KWH to participate in a number of events. The community's need for a unified front in the face of xenophobic legislation diminished the level of resistance toward KWH. One result of this newly formed coalition was the successful organization of a forum entitled, "Developing Effective Strategies in Response to the Recent Anti-Immigration Wave."[15] KWH and nineteen other Korean groups in the area hosted the event. Another unprecedented partnership that emerged in response to imminent government-assistance cuts was a collaboration between KWH and two other Korean social service agencies to diversify, increase, and pool funding sources.

Prior to the current anti-immigrant wave, community leaders tried to dismiss KWH as feminist and therefore foreign to Korean culture. The local leaders' retaliatory actions reflected an effort to place KWH outside of the Korean community—for distance from KWH means distance from domestic violence. In this environment, KWH activists used outside, mainstream sources to maintain a community-based organization and circumvent the barriers local leaders posed. For instance, KWH threatened to air community "dirty laundry" through the mainstream media and to use its legal connections in an effort to force community organizations to listen to its message.

With the introduction of anti-immigration policies, both the wider Korean American community and KWH acknowledged the importance of a unified identity as a defensive measure against powerful institutional forces. With an arrangement to agree to disagree, KWH and the community decided to set aside their differences—as least temporarily—in order to work together against a common enemy. It would be naive to suggest that anti-immigration policies dissolved all past animosities between KWH and other local actors. Despite the opening of the Korean American community boundaries, which have expanded to include KWH, the future of this coalition is uncertain at best.

### Creating Distances

The uncertainty that anti-immigrant legislation has caused affects not only KWH's relationship with the ethnic community, but also its relationship to mainstream domestic violence organizations. Increased contact with the Korean community has led to a distancing from the larger domestic violence movement. As part of a Korean feminist organization, the Hotline members felt forced to choose between their ethnic and nationalist identity and their feminist identity.

For instance, KWH recently experienced a dilemma when the lease for its office ended and the Hotline needed to find a new home. The Board members conducted a lengthy search involving much discussion among themselves, the women who call the Hotline, and KWH volunteers. Their dilemma centered on whether or not to move closer to other (mainstream) feminist-oriented organizations, or further into the

Korean community. Through consensus, the women at KWH decided to move into a building that houses other Korean American social service agencies, in order to sustain their weak but growing ties with the larger Korean community.[16] This move meant that, for the first time, the office would be open to the community. Since confidentiality remained their most important priority, KWH members also secured a private location away from the office where KWH volunteers could meet with Hotline callers should the occasion arise. The Hotline members reasoned that this move would allay some community members' suspicions toward KWH, and that confidentiality would remain intact since almost all of their crisis intervention is conducted by the telephone. On occasions when face-to-face meetings are necessary, they are held in courtrooms, shelters, or other, more private locations.

The Hotline's open-house reception in the new office was attended by more than a hundred individuals from various community groups. It was clear that KWH's move to create an "open" environment was well-received by Korean American community members. For the first time, people were welcome to view the office and attend a tour explaining the organization's functions. Also, for the first time, Korean newspaper reporters did not accuse KWH of hiding from the community. However, the reaction was less enthusiastic from some members of the local domestic violence movement. Several individuals, including some of KWH's funders, were openly skeptical about the Hotline's unconventional move. Despite KWH members' attempts to calm their fears, the skeptics remained uneasy about an "open" office.

To a certain extent, this uneasiness is understandable—particularly from the point of view of a funder who wants to protect her "investment." Those working in the domestic violence movement are aware of the importance of keeping shelters confidential, and it is logical to expect others to do the same. The difference here lies in the fact that KWH is a hotline and not a shelter. In addition, KWH is an ethnic, community-based organization that must incorporate lessons learned not only from mainstream domestic violence organizations, but also from its own ethnic community. In this way, KWH must find creative solutions to alleviate concerns from two at times opposing arenas of loyalty. The Hotline's move was an effort to take advantage of a fledgling relationship with the larger Korean community while maintaining past alliances with other feminist organizations. Unfortunately, KWH's expectations of better relations with some of the mainstream feminists and funding sources may prove to be ungrounded.

## Implications

Ironically, anti-immigrant legislation may present itself as an opportunity to strengthen past alliances as well as to form new ones. Without exaggerating the so-called "positive" side of hostile legislation, one can note that there is evidence that an initial—and temporary—bond created by force can be used productively in forming lasting relationships. In addition, state intervention may expose the gaps or differences between alliances, as is the case for the Hotline's relationship with domestic violence organizations. Nevertheless, this too can be used as an opportunity to explore differences and to find creative ways of working together and forming a closer relationship than that which existed before.

The effects of anti-immigrant legislation, as described in this chapter, are so pervasive in the lives of battered immigrant women that any occasion to strengthen their chances is a chance worth taking. Perhaps we could more easily identify such opportunities if we widened the notion of what constitutes a "woman's" issue or concern. In this respect, both the Korean American and the mainstream domestic violence communities need to expand their respective arenas of concern in order to realize the overlap of issues that they share. For those interviewed in the Korean community, domestic violence was strictly a woman's problem and not viewed as a community issue. In much of the anti-domestic violence community, immigration policy is not viewed as a central concern. As illustrated by the women who call the Hotline, such limitations can have detrimental effects.

It is immigration's embeddedness within economic relationships and institutional inequalities that certifies its status as a feminist issue. Some scholars may have difficulty linking immigration and feminism due to the subtle, pervasive nature of institutionalized phenomena. For example, Kathleen Ferraro (1983, 289) explains that "[w]hile there is no longer widespread explicit support for the use of violence to control wives, other macro-level conditions and ideologies perpetuate an environment in which escape from a violent marriage is difficult for women." In this way, immigration law is one such "macro-level condition" that keeps particular women captive in harmful situations.

Similarly, it is domestic violence's embeddedness within economic relationships and institutional inequalities that certifies its status as a Korean American community issue. The economic concerns expressed earlier by community leaders and members are intricately tied to domestic violence. The proposed immigration restrictions that affect the lives of battered immigrant women have a strong connection to economic conditions. This contemporary wave of immigrant scapegoating comes at a time of increasing layoffs and job shortages. It is apparent that immigration restrictions ebb and flow according to economic and political demands (Mohanty 1991a, 25) and that these economic and political hostilities are experienced, albeit differently, by the entire immigrant community. The difficulties experienced by the women who call KWH's Hotline are linked to the lives of those in the larger community.

In observing the implications of immigration legislation in the lives of battered Korean American women, the women who serve them, and their community, I have argued that government policies (whether or not a measure is passed) have the power to affect the everyday lives of individuals and to alter relationships with the target community. However, it is also evident that there is considerable activity at the community level in response to government legislation that may open new opportunities. The true test of community-level endurance lies in the ability to recognize allies in different communities, and to find creative methods of building a firm foundation of cooperation.

**Author's Note:** I would like to thank the women at KWH, Allan Schnaiberg, David N. Pellow, Nancy Naples, Elizabeth Clifford, Brett Stockdill, Patricia Zamudio, and Arlene Kaplan Daniels for their valuable comments and encouragement.

### Notes

1. A September 24, 1995, *New York Times* article reported: "Both [House and Senate Bills] would crack down on illegal immigration and end what has been a 30-year-old policy of welcoming legal immigrants. For the first time since 1924, there will be a reduction in the number of foreign-born people who are legally permitted to come to the United States" (Holmes 1995, A1).

2. There is no single definition of "community." The term may embody geographic, cultural, religious, and/or political boundaries (Suttles 1972; Hunter 1974; Stoecker 1995b). I use this term loosely to designate the boundaries around what I call "Koreatown." Similarly, my use of the term "community" in describing Koreatown denotes the established norms that guide the behavior of those who interact within its boundaries.

3. I use the words "Korean American" and "Korean" interchangeably.

4. My statements concerning Koreans, Korean women and the Korean community are limited to my arena of study. Statements are not necessarily generalizable to every Korean American person or community.

5. In this case, I make a distinction between community leaders and members. I define the leaders as those who head various Korean American organizations and/or hold an authoritative position within Koreatown. These individuals are almost all male, first-generation immigrants. (The second generation usually moves away from Koreatown.) When asked who holds power or is powerful among Koreans in the larger metropolitan area, my Korean American informants were remarkably consistent in their remarks. Wealthy businessmen (including heads of Korean newspapers) and clergy clearly topped the list. On the other hand, community members are Korean Americans who live, work, worship, or otherwise participate in Koreatown activities, but who do not necessarily hold positions of authority.

6. Approximately ninety-five percent of the Hotline's funding comes from outside sources such as government agencies and local philanthropists.

7. The number includes all types of calls—emergency and non-emergency.

8. Kim 1981; Chow 1987; Choi 1992.

9. Rimonte (1989, 329) explains, "The community's earlier explanation of domestic violence, blaming the circumstances, is only denying the problem. It also denies the victims the right to look for alternatives and ignores their need to seek help. It also does not question the man's assumed right to beat women during times of stress, or the woman's assumed obligation to respect that right."

10. A part of the reason for this shift may be the increasing decline of traditionally "masculine" unskilled workplaces, such as manufacturing, within the United States. More and more U.S. companies are taking advantage of a shifting global economy that provides lower labor costs in Third World countries (Rubin 1996). Also see Bonacich and Light 1988; Amott and Matthaei 1991; Zhou 1992; Hossfeld 1994.

11. Light 1972; Conzen 1979; Lamphere, Stepick, and Grenier 1994.

12. Miller 1969; Nee and Nee 1987; Takaki 1989; Zhou 1992; Hing 1993.

13. See Suzuki 1989; Yan-McLaughlin 1990; Hing 1993; Bonacich, Ong, and Cheng 1994.

14. Immediately following its passage, a federal restraining order was issued. The order explicitly prohibits state agencies from implementing any regulations until the more than one dozen court cases filed seeking to stop the proposition are resolved.

15. The forum was held on October 21, 1995.

16. The choice was between a building that housed other Korean American social service agencies, located in Koreatown, and a building run by a mainstream feminist organization, located outside of Koreatown.

**Appendix: Specific Strategies for Working with Immigrant Women**

An important preliminary step in working with immigrant women is to be prepared. For many organizations, time and resources are in short supply, but these services are well worth the initial expense. This initiative parallels efforts by proponents of the disabled who have successfully ensured appropriate services in many organizations. I have highlighted four of the most imperative strategies:

1. Language translations (verbal and written): Map out a list of possible resources where same-language counseling and written domestic violence literature are available. Particular ethnic communities (especially those in large cities) will have a variety of written materials.
2. History: To lessen the risk of cultural shock, research a variety of different historical and cultural backgrounds. This effort may ensure a greater mutual understanding. For instance, understanding the history of Korean Comfort Women and other more recent militarized sexual slavery campaigns in Asia may sensitize shelter workers to the reactions of Asian women to the military barracks-like environment of some shelters. These and other historical facts should be a part of training sessions.
3. Immigration law: Some basic knowledge of immigration law should also be a part of an ongoing training program. This is necessary to protect the rights of immigrant women and children who may not be aware or are misinformed.
4. Basic necessities: Get to know the ethnic communities that surround you and make a list of what is available. For example:
   - Food: identify the location of ethnic grocery stores where you can obtain "comfort food."
   - Churches: identify nearby or same-language churches, temples, or mosques.
   - Job search: identify same-language referrals who can assist survivors in finding a job—particularly those groups well-connected in the ethnic community.
   - Bus/mass transit: be prepared to start from the basics—many immigrant women have led very isolated lives.

# Part III

# Networking for Change

# Chapter 8

# Latina Immigrant Women and Paid Domestic Work*

## *Upgrading the Occupation*

## Pierrette Hondagneu-Sotelo

Until recently, the orientation of the scholarly literature on immigration and the activist immigrant rights movement shared one significant feature: a traditional androcentric bias that obscured issues concerning immigrant women. This began to change in the 1980s, with the proliferation of new scholarship on immigrant women, and 1991 saw the first national conference on immigrant and refugee women, where activists discussed a diverse array of issues, including alternative employment strategies for immigrant and refugee women.[1] A key breakthrough in these developments is understanding immigrant women as agents in their own right, as workers with their own particular migration trajectories and employment needs.

This chapter discusses the intersection of research on and activism with immigrant women who do paid domestic work. After discussing some of the limitations of both scholarship and activism on immigrant women's issues, I describe the methodology and research findings from a study I conducted in a San Francisco Bay Area community where many undocumented immigrant women are employed in domestic work. Participant observation was an integral method in developing an understanding of the issues facing Latina immigrant women who do paid domestic work, and it was also key in providing a framework for conducting community activism simultaneously with research. Research findings were later applied and disseminated in *fotonovelas*—didactic, illustrated leaflets—through an advocacy project aimed at Mexican and

*Originally published in *Clinical Sociology Review* Vol. 12, 1994, pp. 257–270. Reprinted by permission of the author and the Sociological Practice Association.

Central American immigrant women who do paid domestic work in Los Angeles.

The themes in this chapter reflect the convergence of concerns and issues drawn from three arenas: research on immigrant women and work, scholarship on paid domestic work, and the emergence of the immigrant rights movement. The section below examines the intersection of some of these issues in order to situate the subsequent discussion.

## Intersections: Immigrant Women, Immigrant Rights, and Paid Domestic Work

### Immigrant Women Work?

The myth that Latina women, and especially Mexican immigrant women, do not typically seek employment still persists in spite of evidence to the contrary.[2] This stereotype is perpetuated by research that implicitly characterizes Mexican immigrant women as "dependent migrants" who migrate principally for family reunification.[3] Typically, dependent migrants are posed dichotomously with independent labor migrants, but, in reality, even immigrant women who enter a country as "dependent" migrants often exhibit high rates of labor-force participation. Women often migrate both to be reunited with their families and for financial reasons. Since they work to help support their families, who may either remain behind in the country of origin or accompany them to the new country, family and employment are intrinsically linked.

The myth that immigrant women do not participate in the labor force is also contradicted by numerous cases of "female-first" migration streams to the United States and Western Europe, where women have in fact preceded men (Brettell and Simon 1986). Mexican immigration does not fit this pattern, because the temporary contract labor programs instituted during WWI and between 1942 and 1964 recruited primarily Mexican men for work in U. S. agriculture. Evidence suggests, however, that in other instances Latina women have pioneered labor migration streams. These female-led streams are often induced by immigration policies or practices that favor the entrance of paid domestic workers.[4] For example, sociologist Terry Repak (1990) discovered that in Washington, D.C., the pioneer settlers of the substantial Central American population that grew during the 1980s were women who came to the U. S. in the 1960s and 1970s as live-in domestic workers with families involved in the diplomatic corps.

Although immigrant women in the United States work in numerous sectors of the economy, most of them cluster in a few occupations: paid domestic work, the garment industry, family enterprises in the ethnic enclave, and highly skilled service-sector jobs, such as nursing (Pedraza 1991). Mexican undocumented immigrant women are faced with an even narrower set of alternatives. They are concentrated in work as factory operatives, domestic workers, in low-level service-sector jobs, and in informal sector jobs such as vending. This concentration reflects the labor-market interplay of race, class, gender, and legal status/citizenship, more than it does human capital resources. Due to discrimination, and the difficulty of obtaining legal permanent-resident status, work authorization, and the transfer of credentials, Mexican and other Latina immigrant women who were teachers and nurses in their home countries often find themselves working in the informal sector in the U.S., as street vendors, domestic workers, or garment assemblers. Increasingly, the particular employment issues of these women are becoming a focus for research and mobilization.

### Immigrant and Refugee-Rights Advocacy

Passage of the Immigration Reform and Control Act of 1986 (IRCA) signaled a new era in the immigrant rights movement in the United States. While IRCA offered amnesty-legalization for some undocumented immigrants, it also created problems for many by imposing employer sanctions. IRCA effectively criminalized employment of undocumented immigrant workers, since it prohibited the hiring of anyone without legal permission to work in the U. S. An unanticipated and paradoxical consequence of this legislation was that it generated and rejuvenated activism in defense of immigrant rights. In every major U. S. city with a large immigrant population, there are now large umbrella coalitions that include community, church, legal, and labor groups working to define, establish, and defend civil rights and workplace rights for immigrants and refugees. These advocacy groups are working outside the traditional and exclusive category of U. S. citizenship. Advocacy groups have developed many innovative strategic approaches but, until recently, many of these efforts were directed only at men.

Work is a key issue for immigrants and refugees, and on street corners in cities across the U. S., immigrant men congregate to find jobs in construction, packing, gardening, painting, or as temporary furniture movers. Day laborers wait for potential employers to hire them for a few hours, for a day, or for a week. Abuses by employers, police, and immigration authorities are rampant, and immigrant rights advocates in San Francisco, Los Angeles, and New York have responded by meeting with elected officials, local business owners, and police officers, by setting up hiring halls, and by attempting various organizing efforts.[5]

The plight of day laborers is certainly serious, and in the context of continued levels of immigration, the ongoing recession, and employer sanctions, the numbers of immigrant workers offering their services as day laborers appear to be increasing. Immigrant women, at least in California, do not gather or wait on street corners to be picked up by strangers for potential employment; nevertheless, like immigrant men, these women work in many unprotected, unregulated, informal-sector jobs. Immigrant women workers, and their jobs, are however often less visible than are their male peers. For various reasons, among them the "invisibility" of immigrant women's employment, immigrant rights advocates have been slower to defend immigrant women's labor rights. In the fall of 1990, I began meeting with a group of lawyers and community activists associated with the Coalition for Humane Immigrant Rights in Los Angeles (CHIRLA) to organize an advocacy program for paid domestic workers, the majority of whom in Los Angeles are Latina immigrant women. Some of the research findings from my project were integrated into this information and outreach program.

## Paid Domestic Work

The sociology of occupations has traditionally overlooked paid domestic work. This may be due to the belief that paid domestic work would soon become obsolete in modern society because the job is atavistic, based largely on ascribed status, and requires the performance of non-specialized, diffuse menial tasks (Coser 1974). Feminist scholarship, however, has drawn attention to this hidden occupation, and much of this research has been guided by efforts to examine the interlocking systems of race, class, and gender.[6]

Paid domestic work is currently organized in various ways. The dominant form of organization, however, has shifted historically from live-in employment to day work, and, ultimately, to job work (Romero 1988, 1992). In "job" work, the housecleaners work for different employers on different days, and are paid not by the hour, but a certain amount for performing agreed-upon tasks. Under these arrangements, domestic workers are able to position themselves as "experts," selling their labor services in much the same way a vendor sells a product to various customers; and since they work for several employers, they are less likely to become involved in deeply personalistic employer-employee relations (Romero 1988).

Regardless of these improvements, paid domestic work continues to occur in an isolated, largely unregulated and privatized environment. When paid domestic workers negotiate job terms and pay, they generally do so without the benefit of guidelines established by government, unions, employment agencies, or private firms. A labor agreement established by two lone individuals who are operating without standard guidelines heightens the asymmetry of the employer-employee relationship, and domestic workers must locate and secure multiple sources of employment to survive. Paid domestic work is increasingly performed by Latina and Caribbean immigrant women, a group of workers who, due to their class, race, gender, and legal status, are among the most disfranchised and vulnerable in our society. I examined and then later disseminated research findings on how immigrant women domestic workers strategize to improve their employment in job work. The research process itself was also contextualized by community activism.

### Research Description

My research on domestic employment comprises part of a larger study on changing gender relations among Mexican undocumented-immigrant women and men in a San Francisco Bay Area community (Hondagneu-Sotelo 1992). This well-defined immigrant barrio is bordered by middle-class and more affluent residential areas, and the women seek domestic employment in these surrounding communities, some of which are characterized by lavish suburban and semi-rural estate residences; three of the nearby cities rank among the top ten wealthiest cities in California, each of them surpassing the per capita income of Beverly Hills.[7]

I had not initially entered the field with the intention of examining how the women organize paid domestic work. In fact, as I started my research, numerous factors had led me to believe that most Mexican immigrant women in this community worked in laundries, hospital cafeterias, and convalescent homes. As it turned out, jobs located in these types of institutions were more typical of women who had secured legal permanent resident status. As I became immersed in many activities and groups in this community, I quickly learned that although undocumented immigrant women worked in numerous jobs, they typically held jobs as paid domestic workers in private households, usually working for different employers on different days.

I began the research in November 1986, just as the Immigration Reform and Control Act was signed into effect. At that time, I attended a large public forum held in a community center where I had once been employed. Several hundred undocumented immigrant women, men, and children had crammed into a multipurpose room to learn more about this highly publicized but poorly understood law, and it was on that evening that I accepted an invitation to join a small neighborhood service and advocacy organization that was forming to address many of the issues arising from IRCA. This group began meeting on a biweekly basis, on Friday evenings, in a classroom at a local elementary school. The meetings initially drew as many as forty people on a regular basis. We typically sat on folding chairs arranged in a circle, and at each meeting we educated ourselves about the new immigration law and discussed how it might impact the local community of undocumented immigrants. We planned various strategies for organizing community members and for disseminating information, and as employer sanctions went into effect, we monitored and tried to ensure the protection of civil liberties. The group also circulated petitions, sponsored public forums, and organized fund-raising events. Discussions of strategy and concrete tasks were sometimes superseded by conversation about everyday experiences, including shared employment and discrimination experiences. My participant observation extended to various other venues where people were also talking about the new immigration law and how it might affect their work and family lives. These topics dominated discussions at social events, in small clusters of individuals gathered to eat at taco trucks, in private homes, and in other organizations and church groups.

In these venues, I began to pay particular attention to what the women were saying. As a participant and a "known" observer in many settings, I saw women talking about how they managed paid domestic work. Everywhere, it seemed, employment issues and concerns surfaced as a popular, everyday topic of conversation. As I focused part of my research on these issues, I began to read broadly in the historical and sociological literature on the topic. The ideas and approaches used in these studies prompted new questions for me, and so my ethnographic and interview research emerged in dialogue with both the research literature and community activism.

Much has been written about the solitary quality of the housecleaning job, but the social interactions I observed among immigrant women domestic workers provided a sharp contrast to the portrait of privatized employment. In various social settings—at picnics, at baby showers, at a parish legalization clinic, and in people's homes—I observed immigrant women engaged in lively conversation about housecleaning work. Women traded cleaning tips; tactics about how best to negotiate pay; how to arrange jobs geographically so as to minimize daily travel; how to interact (or more often, avoid interaction) with clients; how to leave undesirable jobs; remedies for physical ailments caused by the work, and cleaning strategies to lessen these ailments. The women were quick to voice disapproval of one another's strategies and eager to recommend alternatives. These interactions were not embedded in formally organized cooperatives, as they are for some Latina immigrant women domestics (Salzinger 1991), but neither were the consultations as haphazard as those that have been described among some African American domestic workers (Rollins 1985; Kaplan 1987).

My discoveries about how the domestic-work occupation is organized derive mainly from participant-observation and informal conversations that occurred in various public and private locales. It is also supplemented by interviews with seventeen women who were at the time of interview working as non-live-in domestic housecleaners, or had done so in the recent past. The majority of the seventeen women interviewed were between thirty and fifty years old, although one woman had begun working as a domestic in the United States at the age of fifteen and another was still energetically working at the age of seventy-one. Fifteen of the seventeen women were currently married or living in consensual unions, and they came from diverse class and occupational backgrounds in Mexico. All interactions and interviews were conducted in Spanish.

To date, most studies of domestics are largely based on information gathered from interviews and historical materials.[8] An exception is Rollins's study (1985), which is based on interviews with domestic employers and employees, and on participant-observation material gathered by Rollins when she went "undercover" as a domestic worker— a method that provided a wealth of insights. The novelty and strength of participant-observation in the present study is that it occurred in tandem with community activism and was conducted in multiple settings. I participated with the women and gathered information at parties, church and community events, and in people's homes. Observing paid domestic workers in their daily social life reveals that many connections and exchanges undergird what appears to be a privatized economic relationship.

## Research Findings and Advocacy

Research findings from this study were disseminated in Los Angeles through an information and outreach project sponsored by an immigrant rights group, the Coalition for Humane Immigrant Rights in Los Angeles. The key people in this project are the outreach workers, who are Latina immigrant women who have experience doing paid domestic work. As they ride the public buses and visit certain Westside parks and bus stops to distribute the informational materials, these outreach workers advise domestic workers on their employment rights, and provide resource information on where to obtain legal assistance for job-related problems. The outreach workers also distribute small notebooks and encourage domestic workers to document all work hours, tasks performed, and pay received daily, so that if a labor dispute should arise in which they pursue a legal remedy, they will have documentation to present in court.

*Fotonovelas* are the key materials for disseminating information in this program. *Fotonovelas* consist of booklets with captioned photographs that tell a story, and in Latin America, where they are widely read for entertainment, they are typically aimed at working-class men and women. The Dignity for Domestic Workers advocacy group developed the text for several didactic *fotonovelas*, and hired an artist to draw the corresponding caricatures. Based on the research with paid domestic workers, I prepared a *fotonovela* that is primarily aimed at newcomer immigrant women who lack experience and peer information about the occupation. In this section, I summarize some of the major findings on occupational organization, and describe how these were applied in the production of *fotonovelas* for domestic workers in Los Angeles.

The ongoing activities and interactions among the undocumented Mexican immigrant women I observed in my study led me to develop the organizing concept of "domestics' networks," a concept that counters the view of the domestic occupation as an entirely privatized and individualized labor relation (Hondagneu-Sotelo 1994). Domestics' networks are immigrant women's social ties among family, friends, and acquaintances that intersect with housecleaning employment. These social networks are based on kinship, friendship, ethnicity, place of origin, and current residential locale, and they function on the basis of reciprocity, since there is an implicit obligation to repay favors of advice, information, and job contacts. In some cases these exchanges are monetarized, as when women sell "jobs" (i.e., leads for customers or clients) for a fee. Generally, however, more informal reciprocity characterizes these interactions. Immigrant domestics rely on their network resources to resist atomization and enhance their work, but the networks themselves can also be oppressive.

Although the domestics' networks played an important role in informally regulating the occupation, jobs were most often located through employers' informal networks. Personal references were very important to employers of domestic workers, and employers typically recommended a particular housecleaner to their own friends, neighbors, and coworkers. Although immigrant women helped one another sustain domestic employment, they were not always forthcoming with job referrals, since there was a scarcity of well-paid domestic work. Competition for a small number of jobs prevented the women from sharing job leads among themselves, but often male kin who worked as gardeners or as horse-stable hands provided initial connections. Many undocumented immigrant women were constantly on the lookout for more housecleaning jobs. Indeed, part of the occupation seems to be the search for more jobs, and for jobs with better working conditions and pay.

Since securing that first job is difficult, many newly arrived immigrant women find themselves subcontracting their services to other more experienced and well-established immigrant women who have steady customers for their services. In interviews and informal conversations, many women told me that this served as their entry into the occupation. In some cases, this arrangement provided an important apprenticeship and a potential springboard to independent contracting. The relationship established by the two women, however, was not characterized by altruism or harmony of interests.

While a subcontracted arrangement is informative and convenient, especially for an immigrant woman who lacks her own transportation or has minimal English-language skills, it can also be very exploitative, and one part of the didactic *fotonovelas* focuses on this aspect of the occupation. Through a series of caricature drawings, a simple comic strip narrates the story of a modestly dressed, newly arrived immigrant woman, who is picked up on the street by a more prosperous looking immigrant woman driving a large car. The woman with the car offers to take the newly arrived woman in as her housecleaning "helper," and in the subsequent drawings, we see that the newly arrived woman is indeed working, but her subcontracting employer is withholding her pay until she performs the job "correctly." The leaflet is intended to warn domestic workers, especially those who may be newly arrived immigrant women, of the dangers of this arrangement.

The pay for domestic work varies widely across different regions in the country and even within a given area. There are no unions, government regulations, corporate guidelines, or management policies to set wages. Instead, the pay for housecleaning work is generally informally negotiated between two women, the domestic and the employer. The pay scale for which domestics attempt to negotiate is influenced by the information they share among themselves, and by their ability to sustain a sufficient number of jobs, which is in turn also shaped by their English-language skills, legal status, and access to private transportation. Although the pay scale remains unregulated by state mechanisms, social interactions among the domestics themselves serve to informally regulate pay standards.[9]

Unlike employees in middle-class professions, most of the domestic workers I observed talked quite openly with one another about their level of pay. At informal gatherings, such as a child's birthday party or a community event, the women revealed what they earned with particular employers, and how they had achieved or been relegated to that particular level of pay. Working for low-level pay was typically met with murmurs of disapproval or pity, but no stronger sanctions were applied. Conversely, those women who earned at the high end were admired.

Since most women obtain jobs through employer referrals, in their new jobs they generally ask for at least the same rate they are presently earning elsewhere, or they ask for a slightly higher rate. Women at the upper end of the pay scale were able to clean more than one house a day, and they generally asked to be paid by the job. They wanted to be paid a fixed fee for the house cleaned, rather than by the hour. Women who could clean quickly, and who drove, found that they could clean two, sometimes even three houses a day, so their earnings put them into the upper levels of the occupation. Other women who lacked private transportation also often preferred to be paid by the job rather than by the hour because it allowed for greater scheduling flexibility and job autonomy. So another *fotonovela* was designed to advise domestic workers to charge by the house, not by the hour, and this leaflet shows a paid domestic worker negotiating for higher pay with a new employer.

Domestic work is a very unstable job. Paid domestic workers are always at risk of underemployment as some employers go on vacation, remodel their houses, or periodically decide that they can no longer afford cleaning services. Women who are not well connected to networks of employers who provide referrals, and to other domestics who offer strategic advice, run the risk of severe underemployment. One *fotonovela* shows several women chatting about their work as they watch their children play at a birthday party in the park, and advises the workers to share job information with their peers. In my study I found that information shared and transmitted through the informal social networks was critical to domestic workers' abilities to improve their jobs. These informational resources transformed the occupation from one of a single employee dealing with a single employer, to one where employees were informed by the collective experience of other domestic workers.

In the instance described in this article, community activism contextualized participant observation, and it was this method that led to a particular set of research findings about the domestic-work occupation, which were then later disseminated in an advocacy project. Domestic work is typically thought of as one of the least desirable occupations. It is a low-status, stigmatized, dead-end job with no avenues for promotions; there are no guaranteed benefits, written contracts are the exception rather than the rule, and the job requires hard physical labor for relatively low wages. Moreover, the legacy of slavery and servitude lingers in the occupation, since paid domestic workers are treated condescendingly and are often required to express deference in exchange for their employers' maternalism (Rollins 1985). Yet for many immigrant women, domestic work is not the worst possible job. In fact, when it is properly organized and compensated, many women view it as a relatively desirable job that offers more flexible hours, job autonomy, and potentially higher pay than other job alternatives.

Paid domestic workers have used various strategies to upgrade the occupation. Previous research has shown that Chicana women upgraded the occupation by claiming expertise (Romero 1988, 1992), Black women have sought to improve their working conditions and maintain their dignity by finding "one good employer" (Dill 1988), and Latina immigrant women have attempted to impose standards and allocate jobs by organizing in domestic-worker collectives (Salzinger 1991). My research focused on how Mexican undocumented immigrant women have improved their working conditions and pay by informally sharing job information and techniques among themselves (Hondagneu-Sotelo 1994). As transborder capital mobility and immigrant settlement signal the waning of nation-state borders, we see the emergence of membership rights and claims among those who are neither "insiders" with official citizenship status nor "outsiders" who work and reside elsewhere. Together with the increasing visibility of occupations such as domestic work, and the recognition of immigrant women as workers, this sphere has provided a rich arena for community activism and participatory research. The proliferation of new scholarship on immigrant women, and the immigrant rights movement, as well as the simultaneous increase in xenophobia, suggest new avenues and needs for innovative sociological research and practice.

### Notes

1. The first national conference on immigrant and refugee women drew more than three hundred women, most of them Latina and Asian immigrants representing a myriad of organizations and agencies. The conference, titled "Dreams Lost, Dreams Found: Women Organizing for Justice," was held in Berkeley, California, October 5–7, 1991, and was sponsored by the Family Violence Prevention Fund and the Coalition for Immigrant and Refugee Rights and Services, a San Francisco Bay Area coalition that includes more than eighty-five organizations.
2. See, e.g., Kossoudji and Ranney 1984; Simon and DeLey 1984; Fernandez-Kelly and Garcia 1990.
3. Studies that implicitly characterize women as dependent migrants generally examine only male heads of households who are assumed to be independent labor migrants. The two most highly acclaimed studies released in the late 1980s on Mexican immigration are based solely on responses from male immigrants. In Portes and Bach (1985), the researchers restricted their sample to "male family heads," and in Massey et al. (1987), the researchers interviewed heads of households as well as those with migration experience, whom they characterize as "a few older sons" (p. 19).
4. For similar instances in different international contexts, see the article by Foner, Caspari, and Giles in Brettell and Simon (1986).
5. See "Workers of the World on U. S. Street Corners," *Network News: Newsletter of the National Network for Immigrant and Refugee Rights*, Vol. 5, No. 3, April-May, 1992.
6. Clark-Lewis 1987; Glenn 1986; Rollins 1985; Chaney and Castro 1989; Romero 1992.
7. An article entitled "California Cities: Rich and Poor" in the *Los Angeles*

*Times,* July 6, 1992, reports that the 1990 census listed per capita income ranging from $55,721 to $68,236 for these three municipalities.

8. See Katzman 1981; Sudden 1983; Glenn 1986; Romero 1988, 1992.

9. In the study, I did not interview the employers of the domestic workers, although I know that they represented different socio-economic classes, because they included teachers, nurses, and secretaries as well as residents of very affluent, upper-income neighborhoods. Salzinger (1991) suggests that in paid domestic work there is a dual wage structure that is set according to the economic means of employers, so that high-income employers pay at the top of the scale, and single mothers or elderly people on fixed incomes pay toward the bottom of the scale. This proposition is contradicted by the reports of outreach workers in the Dignity for Domestic Workers program in Los Angeles. They found that many live-in domestic workers in exclusive residential areas such as Beverly Hills and Pacific Palisades were earning as little as $90–140 a week in 1992 and 1993.

# Chapter 9

# Class, Gender, and Resistance in the Appalachian Coalfields

## Virginia Rinaldo Seitz

This chapter is an account of working-class women in Appalachia who both created and emerged from a labor struggle that transformed their political analyses, social relations, and communities. In the late 1980s, as the "distant thunder" (Yancey 1990) of a coal strike was rumbling once again in the mountains of Southwest Virginia, women in the coal counties began to join together to form a labor support group, the Family Auxiliary of District 28 of the United Mineworkers of America (UMWA). Their story is one of collective and personal struggle for social agency, shaped by the structural forces of class, gender, and an ascribed ethnicity. In this historically specific moment and setting, these mostly white, working-class women constructed an understanding of class struggle from their particular standpoint as Appalachian women. Through consciousness-raising and public and private expressions of resistance, they challenged the coal company, the state, and, eventually, working-class men. While internal fractures within the group of women who became active during the coal-mining strike reveal that sharing the same "standpoint" or social location and set of experiences does not necessarily translate into shared political analyses, organizational strategies, and leadership style, I demonstrate the powerful ways in which these women drew upon their gender, class, and racialized ethnicity as "Appalachians" to help wage a successful strike against the powerful Pittston Coal Company.

The Family Auxiliary, also known during the strike as the "Daughters of Mother Jones," is a group of wives, widows, mothers, daughters, and sisters of coal miners. In the time before, during, and after the strike against the Pittston Coal Company, which lasted from April 1989 to February 1990, the women of the Auxiliary led a popular, union-based strug-gle that attracted national and international attention—suggesting that obituaries of the U.S. labor movement had been written prematurely.

## Studying Intersections of Class, Gender, and Ethnicity in Women's Activism

During a twenty-three-month period from June 1990 to April 1992, I collected data through participant observation, interviews, and inten-sive life-history interviews with members of the Family Auxiliary, as part of a larger study of women's empowerment through grassroots activism (Seitz 1995). In addition to attending meetings and informal gatherings with individuals and the group, I conducted interviews with twenty women and collected the life histories of three participants. Although there have been selective coal strikes in the region since the Pittston set-tlement, the interview data was collected before they occurred. My informal interactions with various members of the group continued into 1995.

The study was grounded in socialist feminist interpretations of stand-point theory, global political economy, and grassroots social movements. Socialist feminism locates women's oppression in the interdependent structures of capitalism and patriarchy[1] and allows for an analysis embedded in a "standpoint" shaped by experiences of class, gender, race, ethnicity, and other fault lines of social inequality.[2] For example, in these mountains, the ascription of negative characteristics to poor and working-class "Appalachian" people, historically couched in the subtext of biological inferiority, is reminiscent of the racist rhetoric used in communities where greater racial diversity brings racism to the forefront of identity and of discursive and political practices (Franken-berg 1993). Consequently, I use the women's consciousness of being "Appalachian" as an ascribed ethnicity that converges with gender and class in constructing a white, working-class, Appalachian women's stand-point.

Although this study highlights the perspectives of white Appalachian women, African Americans in the coalfields can also take on this iden-tity, suggesting the complexity of our understanding of race and ethnic-ity from an Appalachian women's "standpoint." The social construction of race in the coalfields took different forms than in other areas of the South because of the overwhelming commonality of class interests and the small number of Blacks within the population. Blacks from the deep South, as well as members of various immigrant ethnic groups, were recruited as laborers in the mines in hopes that working-class solidarity could be mitigated by racial/ethnic difference. Prejudice did ignite confrontations among union men, yet the coal companies could not completely quell class-based unity (Shifflett 1991).

While African American women supported the strike, none were part of the Auxiliary's core group of about twenty-five members in 1990. Although their lives are embedded in the racialized history of the region and the nation, white women in the core group of the Family Auxiliary tended to identify their African American friends and Auxiliary members in terms of class commonality rather than racial difference. Similarly, Black women I interviewed, although conscious of segregation in company housing and church membership, and of the more subtle forms of racism that have been the norm, also emphasized their class interests in concert with the white workers in the region. Today, African Americans hold leadership positions in the union, and may identify themselves as Appalachian as well as Black, sometimes citing Appalachian as a primary identity (Johnson 1985; Lewis and O'Donnell 1990a, 1990b).

The term "Appalachian" evokes far more than the mountainous geography of a region of the middle South. Even beyond the coalfields, to be identified as Appalachian carries with it negative stereotypical assumptions about the intellectual, moral, and physical inferiority of poor, white, working-class persons, signified through their language, food, housing, and familial arrangements. The most pervasive stereotypic representation of Appalachian communities is that there exists within them a *subculture*, a *culture of poverty*,[3] that explains deprivation as the result of internal deficiencies (Weller 1965; Loof 1971). Through this lens, "Hillbillies," like Blacks and the Third World poor, are victims of their own cultural inadequacy. In the sense that "Appalachian" carries a particular meaning in American metropolitan culture, it is an ascribed ethnicity, a social construction that operates similarly to race in marginalizing and demeaning "other" groups within the dominant ideology of the larger society. However, women activists in this case study drew upon their Appalachian "ethnicity" to develop a particular form of class and gender consciousness as they actively participated in the strike against Pittston.

### The Context for Activism From the Standpoint of Appalachian Women

Social inequality, deprivation, and class struggle are nothing new to coal miners and their families. In the 1980s, the coal counties of Southwest Virginia were characterized by higher-than-state-average unemployment, underemployment, undereducation, dependency on transfer incomes, and income insecurity (Kraybill, Johnson, and Deaton 1987). The trend continues, and the coal industry, its once-powerful union, and the secondary industries that coal once attracted, are on the decline. Manufacturing companies no longer stop in the mountains as they move south beyond U.S. borders (Gaventa 1990), and regional development authorities are hard-pressed to devise alternative strategies for economic development.

The centralization and bureaucratization of political and administrative authority (Clavel 1983), particularly in the last twenty-five years, has effectively excluded working-class participation in the public discourse of the region (Gaventa 1980), and the social-welfare benefits won with the struggles of the union and the War on Poverty (1964–1971) are all but lost in the current anti-welfare policy climate of the 1990s. Class antagonisms, once defused through public social investment, cyclical migration, or periodic booms in the coal industry, simmer in a contracting regional and national economy.

It is in this context that women from Southwest Virginia began organizing in the Fall of 1988 to support union miners and their families. These mothers, wives, and daughters came to the Auxiliary because it offered them a setting in which to support coal miners in challenging Pittston Coal Company's decision to cut health-care benefits to retired and disabled miners. This context reflects the contemporary tendency for working-class struggle to center around benefits rather than wages. In the women's analysis, the proximate cause of their activism was the company's betrayal of miners who had given their lives to the company; it was an affront to their sense of corporate responsibility, connection to community, and concern for the well-being of past and future generations. As one women explained:

> I remember when I was a little girl, my dad would always say that even though he may be poor, even though he may not always have a job, at least he's got his health card. And sure enough, they knew that when they got old and retired they would have their health care and could have their medicines. Taking that away—that was the biggest mistake that the company ever could make.

The "awesome toll of death, injury, and disease in the bituminous coal industry" (Shifflett 1991, 106) was validated by respondents in this study: I learned of a coal-miner husband whose chest was crushed, another whose spinal column was permanently damaged, a third who was mutilated by a beam that drove through his face and destroyed his palate, two grandfathers and a teenage husband who died in explosions, a father who was dying of pneumoconiosis ("black lung"), and another who had lost a leg in a mining accident. "Taking away the health care," as one women explained, "was what really set everything off, keyed everybody up, and put the fight in them."

The gendered division of labor has long been intensified in and around the coal camps and mining towns. Although family life was completely dominated by the coal companies through company-owned housing and stores, women were relegated to the home or, on occasion, to work in the sewing factories. Although women won the right to work underground in the 1970s, they faced enormous resistance and harassment from a cross-class alliance of miners and management (Seitz 1995). Traditionally, women have been prohibited from working in the mines, and their presence in and around the mines was considered bad luck. The coal towns were an "all-male world" where men released their frustrations and anger on themselves and other miners (Shifflett 1991), and, as the women in this study confirm, on their wives and children.

Although there is a history of militancy among miners' wives, class struggle in the past has been waged primarily by men. Women's activism has been circumscribed by their supportive role to their husbands in the union, or idealized through their domestic roles and in the persons of "exceptional" women, like Mary Harris "Mother" Jones. Called "the most dangerous woman in America" in 1902 (UMWA 1990, 21), Mother Jones was a founder of the Industrial Workers of the World, fought against child labor, and is best remembered for her work organizing coal miners (Jones 1972). One of her favorite mobilizing tactics during a strike was to organize a "bucket and broom brigade" of miners' wives.

The image of Mother Jones casts her shadow on contemporary Appalachian scholarship that, as Sally Maggard (1986, 100) notes, "attempt[s] to recover Appalachian women as historical actors, but which misrepresents their history as a collection of a few great women of courage." As in other liberal strategies for the inclusion of a few *exceptional* women in history (the add-women-and-stir approach), the stories of these women, "more revered than explained" (Hall 1986, 355), do not affirm *ordinary* women's place in the history of social change. Nevertheless, it was ordinary women in Southwest Virginia who founded the Family Auxiliary.

Without their identification of strategic *gender* interests,[4] formed within their standpoint as working-class Appalachians, the Auxiliary women's class-based activism could be viewed as "proxy" activism: they are acting for men's class interests to meet their own practical needs. When those needs are politicized as strategic within the structural nexus of gender, the agency of women can then be realized. For those women who have experienced such "conscientization" (Freire 1970) or politicization, the seemingly "age-old structures of male dominance and privilege," as Kate Young puts it, "are not sacrosanct, nor indeed given in the genetic inheritance, but are social impositions, and as such, amenable to change" (Young 1988, 8).

### "We could do a whole lot down here!"

Although the Family Auxiliary has been a membership organization from its beginning, its singular relationship with the UMWA has increasingly presented contradictions for the women who are its members. The Family Auxiliary began as a result of deliberate UMWA strategy: in the Spring of 1988 the union hired two unemployed female coal miners[5] to work part-time to organize women in the various locals of District 28 into a "ladies auxiliary." One of the organizers was also a founding member of the Coal Employment Project (CEP), now a support group of women miners. She had earlier attempted to organize women for the impending strike through the CEP, but was dissuaded by a previous director of that organization, who saw its mission exclusively as legal advocacy. As a part-time employee of CEP, this woman miner had worked in the early 1980s on an industrial and then the national Family Leave Campaign. When the UMWA looked for support for the impending strike, she was ready to work with another laid-off woman miner to rally women and their families over the issue of health benefits.

In February of 1988, the UMWA contract with the Pittston Coal Company expired, and most Southwest Virginians thought a strike was inevitable. For the union, the strike promised to be a major confrontation, and organizing the women was a way to be prepared. The women organizers hired by the union began reaching out to the women in UMWA District 28 within traditional lines of authority. Even with the sponsorship of the United Mineworkers, they knew that they had to go to the men before they could get to the women. As one organizer observed:

> You have to remember that Southwest Virginia is sort of traditional: the men took care of the job, the work, and the women took care of the home. They just didn't get involved in whatever happened on the job or anything. They just went to church, stayed at home, took care of the kids, and that was it.

The two women organizers met with the leadership of all of the locals in the District to begin the process of establishing branches of the Auxiliary with the goal of expanding the base of support for the strike. At first, some miners resisted their wives getting involved in the men's business of union politics, an attitude that did not completely disappear as the strike unfolded, so that auxiliaries were never formed in some locals. However, more and more women did come out to the Auxiliary meetings being held all over District 28 in 1988 and into 1989. Rather than one centralized organization, the women believed it was better to have separate auxiliaries for each local or for a few locals. That way, women would be working with their friends and neighbors and would not be expected to travel far to meetings.[6] Informants estimated that there were approximately fourteen locals that had auxiliaries, with 150 to 500 active women during the strike, and with fifty highly active members who regularly participated in the meetings and the decision-making process. One woman recalled how they effectively organized with the many auxiliaries:

> Getting information from one local to another about what was going on and keeping the flow got to be impossible, so we started calling a monthly District meeting so that *everybody* could come. . . . We held the meetings at District headquarters in Castlewood. That's how we got the word back. That became our planning stage, where we decided what to do next.

Initially, the small number of women in the local auxiliaries planned ways to educate themselves and their communities about the issues in the union dispute with Pittston, and about how women in other areas had become involved in strikes in the past. As one woman explained:

> [W]e went down to Kentucky where Pittston has a mine and we

met the women that was in the A.T. Massey strike. And we learned from those women!

They adopted strategies utilized effectively in other strikes. For example, one organizer stated that:

> We got talking to some women from Pennsylvania who had been in the Canterbury strike and a few others up there. One auxiliary had organized just around food banks, so we got some of them to come down. The women began to figure out that *we* could do *a whole lot* down here!

In discovering the history of women in their labor movement, members validated their right to act on labor issues. In the politics of gender, defining an ideological base for the strike and participating in making the decision to strike was in itself oppositional political practice.

The Auxiliary was open to anyone for membership, and during the strike (April 1989–February 1990), children and retired and disabled male miners were active members. However, the decision-making as well as most of the work was done by women. Gender expectations and responsibilities precluded some women in the UMWA Auxiliary from participating in picketing, travelling north to protest stockholders' meetings, blocking roads, taking over buildings, or getting sent to jail— all actions of other Auxiliary members during the strike. These women chose less confrontational forms of participation, such as cooking food for thousands of supporters at the union's "Camp Solidarity." This "Hill-billy Woodstock" (Yancey 1990, 2), located in an old rural camp leased to the union for a nominal fee, served as a gathering place and campsite for more than seventy thousand supporters from all over the U.S. and other countries. Members of the Auxiliary also sewed home fashions and clothing from union-identified camouflage fabric, cared for other women's children, and kept the phone chains going to facilitate their more militant sisters' activism. Yet, for more "traditional" women, participation and identification with the Auxiliary also led them to a growing recognition of their strategic needs.

### "It really put the radical in us"

At times, women's eagerness to become involved in the substantive issues of the strike was threatening to the miners. Their emerging strategic consciousness was an assertion of women's agency in class struggle, and constituted a shift from their former "proxy" position. The women's new understanding of class enabled them to affect positively the relationship of the miners with their union, and of the union with the community. As one member of the Auxiliary explained it:

> A lot of women lived pretty close to one another, but they hadn't been thinking about their husbands working for the same company. You don't think about it! The men always took care of their jobs and that was theirs, and we took care of the families. Then a lot of men, when we first started organizing, were totally against the women being involved, but the Auxiliary has the potential to make the union strong. . . . It's like when one of the women, before she got involved, had told her husband to go ahead and sign the contract. She had never been involved in nothing and she thought that every individual went in there and signed a contract. Some of the women felt that their husbands should not go out on strike because they were going to miss a paycheck. When they got into the Auxiliary, they started learning more about the union and a lot of them started educating their husbands.

The interests of the Auxiliary and union officials merged during the fourteen-month period before the strike, when miners continued to work without a contract (February 1988–April 1989). The women decided to keep a continuous presence, picketing two days a week in front of Pittston headquarters; approximately one hundred women walked the picket line regularly. They also decided to organize marches, to picket the homes of Pittston management and lawyers, and to pressure local businesses to take a stand on the union. One member described the effect of their activities in this period: "It was those things that really put the radical in us!"

Local businesspersons quickly realized that displaying support for the union was in their interest, even though none of the women would describe their actions as an attempt to boycott unsympathetic merchants. As one women firmly stated:

> Boycott? No! It's illegal to boycott! We were just taking our business to where we felt comfortable as individuals. That's where union people can help. If the store had a card in the window you went in and thanked them for supporting the unions. And if they didn't

have a card, you didn't buy. . . . No boycott. Boycott is when you write out pamphlets and stand on street corners and say: "Don't trade." But if I walk into this place with four other women and ask them to put up a sign and they wouldn't, or if they say right out: "We don't support the UMWA; all we want to do is to do business," well, all they're really saying is that all they want to do is make *money*. Now if *I* make money, it's up to me to decide where I want to spend it. It's a free choice, and I could tell my friends: "The best place to buy your groceries is Acme. They treat folks right."

The strategy worked. Local restaurants donated food and drinks or paper goods to the miners' "Camp Solidarity," and women as consumers exercised their economic power by avoiding non-supportive and non-union stores. One respondent told me that even though there were thousands of people at rallies in St. Paul, and even though many of the people at the rallies smoked cigarettes, they wouldn't cross the street to buy from the Food Lion store.

> Food Lion said they would shut their doors before they would support the UMWA, and we learned that Food Lion does not treat its employees right. . . . So, we'd get in our cars and drive back up to the Piggly-Wiggly to buy a pack of cigarettes or chewing gum, whatever we needed.

Support for the union may have been self-interested on the part of businesses that put up union signs, but the women succeeded in their campaign to develop a community basis for the strike:[7]

> So we'd be on the picket line. . . . And we'd talk to the merchants and get them to put our sign up: "We support the UMWA." And it really helped at Lebanon [the location of Pittston headquarters], because when we started the union was getting cussed at every turn. And it took the women to talk to people, to let them know that without the union in that part of the country, who was going to spend money with them [the merchants]? Other jobs don't make enough! . . . They started realizing that it was going to hurt them, too.

An important catalyst for building the membership of the Auxiliary occurred during a memorial service in June 1988. Auxiliary members were honoring the memory of miners, including a woman, Cat Counts, killed five years earlier in an explosion at the McClure mine. One member described the event:

> We did a caravan from Castlewood to Clintwood and stopped at McClure for the memorial service. And that was the one thing that really started cementing our work, because people saw that the Pittston company wouldn't even stop the trucks while we was having the memorial service for the people that got killed!

The behavior of the coal company, its transgression of social and religious norms and lack of respect for the miners killed, gravely offended the women.

Women activists were also angered by the company's attempt to push the men "to a quick temper." Both union leadership and the women in the Auxiliary wanted this strike to be nonviolent. When the strike began in April, 1989, the women would attempt to defuse the volatile emotions that usually ended in violent confrontation, to the benefit of the company. Another member described how they accomplished this:

> If some of the men got really upset if something was happening on the picket line, the women would start singing "Amazing Grace" and it would just sort of calm everything down. That was our goal—to keep the violence down.

The women also manipulated gender constructions to lessen the brutality of the police as well as the volatility of the miners: the women surrounded the men to protect them from a menacing group of state police. If the police wanted to attack the miners, they would have to force their way through a line of women:

> Because the women placed themselves on the front lines, they eventually got arrested, but the police really didn't want to cross the women. They did arrest them finally, but the police weren't as rough on the women. Then the men started seeing how the women being there could help, could keep our people from getting roughed up. How it could stop our people from getting an arm broke or even a bruise.

Union leadership also used assumptions about women's "nature" and appropriate gender roles to their advantage. Strike leader Marty Hudson told a reporter that "he used the women's audacity to prod the men and keep them committed to civil disobedience . . . throwing out reminders like 'the women did this'" (Yancey 1990, 4).

Gender ideology also influenced the response of Pittston management and the media when thirty-seven women in the Auxiliary took over Pittston headquarters on April 18, 1989. The takeover provided the symbolic content for the family-based and nonviolent character of this strike. Pittston President Mike Odum, for example, gave instructions to his staff that the women were to be treated politely, and conveyed his concern that there was a seven-months-pregnant woman in the group.

The next morning, newspapers around the state headlined the women's sit-down. Union leadership claimed a victory and the press dutifully reported: "On April 18, 37 wives, widows, and daughters of miners gathered in Lebanon for instructions from Marty Hudson, and then piled into vans and pickup trucks. . . . Just like that, the UMWA had seized Pittston headquarters—with women" (Yancey 1990, 4). Yet, from the standpoint of the women, this highly visible political action was not done *with* women but *by* women. Auxiliary members contradicted the reading that women were being herded into the front lines of the strike by the union:

> Well, we had been down there on the picket line for over a year and you know how people just get to talking. We were talking about how we would just *love* to go over there and just take it over, make them notice you, you know! We kept talking about it, and when the strike come, we started talking to [UMWA strike leader] Marty Hudson, and he kept saying: "I don't know, well, maybe." We wanted to do it before the strike but he didn't. Then we approached him one time and he said: "Well, do whatever you want to." I don't think he thought we would do it! But we did, and it was *fun*.

Exploring the subversive potential of the image of Mother Jones, women identified themselves to company officials and the media not by name, but by calling themselves by number, such as "Daughter 13" of the "Daughters of Mother Jones." Using a common name contributed to group solidarity, creating a bond among women who had little experience of themselves as subjects, little experience in women's groups, and no experience in civil disobedience. Fear of breaking laws and the fear of retribution by the company against family members was lessened because they did not identify themselves as individuals. One participant explained:

> If I went in there myself, I would have been scared to death! But when there's a whole group, I knew that everybody was there, that what happened to one was going to happen to the other.

For the Auxiliary, identification with the life and work of Mother Jones became a source of knowledge and critique, both of the power of capital and the power of the male-dominated union. Members argued that the union wanted control of the women's group in order to take credit for their highly visible actions. One member compared the women's problems with union leadership to those of Mother Jones:

> We're not set up as a *union*, we're set up to be with *whoever* is in need, whoever is in struggle. You see, Mother Jones fell out with the international president about this when she started. So you look back, and you see what you're going to have to deal with. And then you do just what you feel is right.

The Auxiliary also initiated a picket in the neighborhood of Pittston President, Mike Odum, in Abingdon. The women planned carefully, picketing on different days and at different times, to avoid arrest under a court injunction prohibiting picketing. As one activist recounted:

> You know, before the strike started the women got together and said: "You know what we'd like to do? Picket Mike Odum's house!" So we started thinking about it, figuring it out. We asked some people in the union and they really wouldn't give us no answer. We asked where he lived and nobody knew. We knew he lived in Abingdon, so we just looked it up in the phone book! . . . It was one of those exclusive subdivisions, big fancy houses. So we just went in there and parked our cars and started walking up and down. He called the union and said he was going to have us put in jail but he never did. But he didn't like it! You know they could have got an injunction, but the ruling wasn't that clear. We would picket two or three hours a day for six months. We didn't do it every day or at the same time, because if we did, he would have

had the cops out. We'd just pull up, start picketing, and before they could get it together, we'd be out of there.

The women recognized the psychological content of what they were doing. They also argued that it was morally appropriate to confront Mike Odum's wife and children at home: if the strike was a family issue for them,[8] it also must become an issue for the Odum family:

> From the time we started, they kept every shade in the house down. If his wife and children were there when we showed up, she put them in a vehicle and left. . . . One time we saw [the lawyer's family] sneak in through a neighbor's yard. A bunch of picketers is not going to hurt anyone physically, you know, but mentally. . . . Why do people in a little higher position feel that they have to hide? Because they know they're guilty! They know that they're not helping the working people get what they deserve. They know that they're taking it away from them.

### "It keeps on growing and growing"

Those women who had neither the inclination nor the opportunity for public protest—women who used privatized forms of expression like cooking, crafts, and caring for others—found that they could use these forms in subversive ways. They created a distinctive style of dress and home furnishings with a political message, as popular women's crafts became a vehicle for spreading support for the strike. For local people and for the thousands of weekly visitors to the union Camp Solidarity, women sewed and decorated household items, like wedding albums covered in camouflage fabric and trimmed in lace, and sold them at rallies and benefits.

For the time being, it seemed that to be Appalachian was to be praised rather than reviled, respected for your capacity for social action rather than trivialized for your social inadequacies. Filmmakers and the news media came to the region to document events surrounding the strike. At times, Camp Solidarity was a global village, as visitors and supporters descended on the hills and narrow valleys of Southwest Virginia: the Socialist Workers Party sponsored a caravan from New York City, and miners from Poland and the Soviet Union came to visit, as did labor leaders from Nicaragua and El Salvador.

Auxiliary members enthusiastically adopted camouflage T-shirts with blue jeans as their signifying dress, and sold T-shirts printed with strike slogans and as a fund-raiser. Fully accessorized with political buttons worn on vests, sashes, and blue-jean jackets, they also made and sold "jackrock" jewelry,[9] symbolically deflating assumptions about the superiority of metropolitan over Appalachian culture. The adoption of military camouflage was especially ironic in that this strike was less violent than previous strikes. There was widespread involvement by women and other supporters, but the primary oppositional tactic was nonviolent civil disobedience.

The consistent and visible oppositional presence of the women in the Auxiliary took new forms as the strike progressed. The local auxiliaries now had steering committees that met together regularly, and all of the women met informally quite often as the pace of events quickened and there were more and more mass mobilizations. Women were getting arrested, and sent to jail, and engaging in diversionary tactics against the local and state police. Respondents told stories of how local knowledge of back roads and dirt roads allowed them to escape police and their roadblocks. They also told of listening to police radio to learn of their plans, then switching rural route numbers to trick the police on their way to intervene in a strike action; as outsiders, the state police were unfamiliar with the mountain roads. Several women spoke of their personal experience in civil disobedience:[10] "I've always thought of myself as a law-abiding citizen," one women reported, "but being in the strike, getting on a bus and being taken to jail, it's hard not to see that the law can be used against you, against what's right."

Other women traveled out of the area and out of the state. They kept a noisy and combative vigil at the jails in Roanoke when strike leaders were imprisoned, and made several trips to Pittston's corporate headquarters in Greenwich, Connecticut, demonstrating at shareholder meetings and planting crosses on Pittston's lawn in memory of relatives who had died in the mines. Not only were they keeping the pressure on Pittston, they were building self-esteem and solidarity among the women along class and gender lines, and discovering a pride in their suffering as Appalachian people. As one woman expressed:

I just feel like I'm a lot better person, and I have a greater understanding. I have a whole lot better understanding of how the union works! Because before, I didn't give it a thought. My husband would go out to work and bring home a paycheck and I didn't give a thought to what our union was about or what it did. If anything, being part of this has made me a stronger person. . . . This was a grassroots project right from the beginning, because women had never done anything before, never played any active part or done anything out of the ordinary or daring! But we have built ourselves up since then, and it keeps on growing and growing.

## "The struggles are so many"

In February 1990, the UMWA and Pittston reached an agreement that formally ended the strike, yet the Auxiliary continued to meet to consider its past and future as an organization. Looking back, some women recalled with humor how company officials underestimated them:

We walked the picket line in front of the Pittston office in Lebanon for over a year before the strike ended. We put in two days a week. . . . No matter what, we would be there. It would rain, the temperature would soar up over a hundred [degrees], but *we would still be there* on them days. Pittston didn't think we would stay. They figured that when it got hot, we'd quit; that if it rained, we'd leave. But we didn't. We just set up a tent! When it came wintertime, we just boxed up the tent and set up a kerosene space heater and stayed right there. We even got so everyone would cook something and bring it to the picket line so anybody that came had something to eat.

But working-class solidarity became increasingly fractured along gender lines following the settlement of the strike, creating unresolvable tensions for some of the women. Members of the Auxiliary had been in the "center of the action" during the strike and had developed both the capacity and the expectation that they could analyze and act on their class interests. Leaving it to the men in the union—whether leadership or their husbands—was no longer an unexamined assumption. In part, women became disillusioned with their potential to have any influence in the union following the strike. One Auxiliary member, for example, attended the UMWA convention in Miami in 1990, following the settlement, expecting the work of the women to be acknowledged. She was angered that "the only woman on the stage was Elizabeth Dole," President George Bush's Secretary of Labor, who was involved in negotiations for settlement.

Some members of the Auxiliary came to see the vision of the union as narrow and self-serving. They felt that the union "sold them out" in its need for a victory in Southwest Virginia: "All they really wanted was a contract that they could say was won with the strike," one member observed. But many miners have *not* returned to work and more and more men are losing their jobs. Women fault the union for not seeing beyond the worker to the family, and further to the community. One member contrasted a *woman's* analysis of working-class unity to that of men in the UMWA. She said: "Men see their union brothers and sisters; women see their union brothers and sisters, but they also see their friends and their community." This expanded conceptualization of class interests, grounded in women's lived experience of family and community, emerged only after women in the Auxiliary had an authentic involvement in class politics—authentic in the sense that they were no longer "surrogates" for their husbands and men's gender/class assumptions. From the standpoint of these white, working-class women, the union alone could neither capture nor articulate their newly formed conceptualization of class.

The struggle to assert their authority as women with the men in the union was also a struggle to expand the agenda of the Auxiliary beyond conventional boundaries of union politics, sometimes with the knowledge that class and gender politics intersect: "The only way that you're going to deal with the problems within the home is to point out that [the company president's] job is in no way any more important that the coal miner's job, and that the coal miner's job is in no way any more important that what his wife is doing at home."

It is not surprising that such a realization could lead to the emergence of gender conflict in the home as well as the union: the women's growing authority within the strike challenged gender roles and boundaries. Sometimes, relationships with husbands were both transformed and strengthened:

> You'd be surprised at the women that before the strike *never* went out of the home, except to buy groceries with their husband or mother-in-law or sister. During the strike their husbands started seeing how good, how much work the women were doing, and they encouraged them. A lot of marriages was really strengthened.

For other marriages, the stress of the strike and its aftermath was exacerbated by the changes, and women reported recognizing, for the first time, painful contradictions in their marriages, contradictions that cannot easily be resolved within the material reality of the Appalachian working-class:

> I've changed a lot being part of the strike. That's why I see these things about him today. I think I'm a lot stronger, but I'm afraid that he's threatened by the things I do. He's changed a lot, too, but not in the same way. I think now that he sometimes uses me as some kind of a crutch. Before he didn't; everything was *his* way.

### "We don't want to own it, we want to pass it along"

Conflict, as well as solidarity, was also brewing within the Auxiliary, and it exploded in the weeks following the settlement of the strike. "It's kind of sad," a respondent from a different association told me about the break in the Auxiliary. "You see, women have been without power for so long, sometimes it's really difficult for them to deal with it when they get it." Although most of the women were readily able to reconceptualize power as an expansive capacity to engage others in making social change, it is possible to infer from the interviews that a few of the women held on to their new power as a scarce and individualized commodity, rejecting, for the moment, the collective dimensions of the process of empowerment.

The conflict within the Auxiliary, whose members proudly identified themselves as the Daughters of Mother Jones during the strike, became a subtext during my interviews with members on both sides of the dispute, revealing how fragile solidarity can be among women who share a particular social location or standpoint. Differences in leadership styles, organizational strategies, and political analyses led to a painful split in the organization. A small number of women who wanted to claim ownership of the group broke off from the majority of the members who held on to a more democratic leadership style (see Sacks 1988b). One member of the Auxillary explained:

> They let what they did, the publicity or any recognition they got, go to their heads. And they acted like they were above you, and would try to control you. They loved the limelight and the publicity and they would seek out after it. When we regrouped [after the strike], we still thought we had one organization, and they did that

[split off into a new group claiming the name of Daughters of Mother Jones] without telling us!

During the strike, women in the Auxiliary began to split over issues of leadership and accountability. Two factions emerged, associated with one or the other of the original organizers. The reasons for the split are complex and subject to highly contextualized interpretations, reflecting differences in personalities, in relationships to union leadership, and, most clearly, in the use of power and leadership styles. The division was also complicated by the extensive attention women received from the media during the strike. Each side accuses the other of wanting to dominate the Family Auxiliary, and each implied that funds were misappropriated by the other side. It is important, however, to acknowledge that the sides were not equally weighted: the clear majority of women remained with the Family Auxiliary.

The most hurtful event to the women in that larger group, which continued its affiliation with the union, was a secret bid by a breakaway faction of four women to successfully incorporate for themselves the name women used during the strike: Daughters of Mother Jones. The breakaway group was described by the others as caught up under the charisma of one woman leader, interested primarily in the public attention generated by their strike activities. The breakaway group was also accused of being dismissive of the contributions of the women who did *not* picket, go to jail, or engage in the more confrontational actions of the strike. Embedded in the critique of the Daughters faction was a comparison of this leader to the men in power in the union, who dismiss women on similar grounds.

A rapprochement among the women was achieved, in part, because of the decline in membership of the breakaway Daughters. As interest in the Daughters dwindled, some of them began meeting with the Auxiliary again in 1992 to plan a fund-raiser for miners who had not returned to work since the strike was settled. These meetings were facilitated by an African American man who was president of a union local and was described by an Auxiliary woman as "the only man in the union who really gave the women credit for what they did in the strike." "He doesn't tell the groups what to do," another member reported. "He won't tell one this and the other that. He says that we should all sit down and talk, and he wouldn't discuss nothing outside of an open meeting." This man's leadership style, as reported by the woman in the Auxiliary, was more congruent with the consensus-building methods observed in women's groups (Yudelman 1987; Leonard 1989) and in the Family Auxiliary itself, excluding the Daughters faction.

By Spring of 1993, the Daughters had just about disbanded and their leader had returned to work underground as a miner. Although incorporation rights to the name Daughters of Mother Jones were still held by one woman, one member of the Auxiliary planned to reclaim the name as soon as the former member neglected to pay corporate taxes—which many women I spoke with expected would happen in the near future. Speaking of the Daughters and the remaining member who still held legal claim to the name, this Auxiliary woman said: "She wants the name because she wanted control over other women. We don't want to own it, we want to pass it along."

If the breakaway Daughters' vision had been clouded by masks of power, their sisters in the Auxiliary recognized that the empowerment of working-class women and their families depended on an expansion rather than a contraction of power: a reinterpretation of power as a generative rather than coercive force. Although some of the Daughters thought that public attention during the strike was an entree into celebrity, they all finally learned that the "everyday world" (Smith 1987a)—still shaped by the structural inequities that helped politicize the women I interviewed—is not much improved. Several years since the "glory days" of the Pittston strike, membership has declined in the Auxiliary: approximately twenty women still participate, with "nine you can always count on," down considerably from the three hundred regulars at the peak of the strike.

Five years after the contract with Pittston was signed, the women still meet, monthly, when possible. Because both the names "Daughters of Mother Jones" and "Family Auxiliary" are loaded with memories of dissention and betrayal, the women are trying out the names "Freedom Fighters" and "Justice Fighters." These sweeping terms signal an expansion of their political analyses: the motivations for their political participation are now viewed as broad-based struggles of working-class Appalachians—over jobs, benefits, environmental pollution, and other community-development issues specific to the region.

The women claim that the victory over Pittston was illusory: many union miners have lost their jobs since the resolution of the strike, and many more never returned to work. Women also blame the union for being more interested in the symbolic content of their victory over Pittston than the actual terms of the settlement and how they affect people in the area. By enlarging the context for resistance—from the union to the family and community—the women implicitly and explicitly question the role of traditional unions as sole arbiters of their interests, yet are often immobilized in acting in alternative venues by the contradictions presented by their social responsibilities and material constraints. The threat of a new general strike continuously looms over the depletion of coal-industry health funds to retired miners and widows, and conditions for coal-mining families have deteriorated with continuing recession and contraction in all job markets. "How are we going to keep the organization together *and* keep the family together?" One member asked:

> I wish I could be optimistic, but if you look at the unemployment, at how many women were really active in the strike and all, and how many of their husbands [are] laid off, well—you know, no money coming in! Like me. There's quite a few women that have the knowledge to do it, but when you have to start worrying about day-to-day, about how to get food on the table. . .

## Conclusion

A social movement and the consciousness that both shapes and emerges from it are highly contextual and equally dynamic (Thompson 1963). The contextual reality of the women who made this movement—the Family Auxiliary, known during the Pittston strike as the Daughters of Mother Jones—is located within particular rather than universal constructs of class, ascribed ethnicity, and gender, giving form to how these women act as working-class Appalachian women in a particular historical movement. Internal fractures within the Daughters of Mother Jones demonstrate that the process of women's empowerment is highly complex and iterative.

This account of the Family Auxiliary began with a group of people whose experiences, contributions, concerns, and dreams were rarely acknowledged and little heard within the social, economic, and political arenas of life. The position and condition of that marginalzation (Young 1988) was constructed for them by subordinate female gender roles, the depressed socioeconomic conditions of the region, and a cultural ideology defining them as Appalachian. Yet the same constructs shape their standpoint in ways that have enabled them to create a "creative social conflict" through the Family Auxiliary, and to enter a process of empowerment.

Empowerment is a term often used to represent a positive material change in the condition of an individual, yet emphases on individualism and the separation of material and ideological dimensions of change through an economistic lens are problematic in feminist theory. In contrast, Morgen and Bookman (1988, 4) offer a feminist definition of the term. They define "empowerment" as "a process aimed at consolidating, maintaining, or changing the nature and distribution of power in a particular social context." This fits more closely with my assertion from this study that empowerment is both a process and an outcome of collective identity and political praxis, resulting in a capacity in thought and action to address the condition and position of marginalization (Molyneux 1986; Seitz 1995).

Although the material condition of mining families has not improved and may have worsened since the strike, the members of the Family Auxiliary will no longer unconsciously accept a subordinate position as working-class persons, as Appalachians, and as women. As one member said, when asked what would happen if there were another strike: "The next time, it's going to be even better!"

The Family Auxiliary has strained against the boundaries that separate domestic and market labor. Its members have challenged the union's definition of class politics, their men's definitions of their roles as women, and metropolitan assumptions about Appalachian people; they have found strength in mutual support and consensus-building. Despite internal conflict, the members are resolving their differences, building a collective leadership, and planning for the future. Their activism is expressed through a form of "creative social conflict" that Gilkes (1994, 229) sees as both "inevitable and necessary, if racial-ethnic, gender, and class inequities are to be eliminated and social justice achieved."

### Notes

1. Eisenstein 1979; Hartmann 1981a, 1981b; Sargent 1981; Beneria and Feldman 1992.
2. Hartsock 1983; Smith 1987; Collins 1990.
3. See Moynihan 1965; Inkeles 1969; Foster 1973.
4. Molyneux (1986) and Moser (1989, 1993) have contributed to a conceptual framework for analyzing women's collective activism by distinguishing

between "practical" and "strategic" gender interests and needs. As Moser (1989, 1803) has interpreted them, "practical gender needs are those which are formulated from the concrete conditions women experience, in their engendered position within the sexual division of labor, and deriving out of their practical gender interests for human survival." "Strategic gender needs," Moser states, "are those needs which are formulated from the analysis of women's subordination to men, and deriving out of their strategic gender interest . . . for an alternative, more equal and satisfactory organization of society than that which exists at present, in terms of both the structure and nature of relationships between women and men."

5. When their labor is needed as wage workers in times of labor shortage, women have been allowed to work underground as they did during World War II (Shifflett 1991, 81). In the 1970s and 1980s, an advocacy organization for women miners, the Coal Employment Project, successfully litigated for their rights as underground workers (Hall 1990). As mining jobs decrease, especially union jobs, women are pushed out, as they are the most recently hired workers. The justification of their exclusion is usually on the basis of gender, citing a need to protect women from unsafe labor conditions and to return them to where they are really needed, in the home (Kessler-Harris 1982).

6. If your husband worked at a mine a long distance from home and there was a closer local, you could join the auxiliary near your home rather than the auxiliary affiliated with your husband's union membership. An important constraint on an organization that spanned several counties was the cost of telephone calls. Long-distance charges, especially to women who would be facing the enforced frugality of a strike, were to be avoided. Setting up local auxiliaries that would meet together once a month cut down on telephone costs, especially later in the strike when phone chains were in use almost daily.

7. Yancey (1990, 2) reports that community support was so strong that "when state police brought the first busload of arrested strikers to the Dickenson County Jail on April 24 (1989), residents mobbed the streets, businesses shut their doors, and some miners escaped from the courthouse on a rope. On April 26, the crowds were so thick that troopers were afraid to unload arrested strikers. Instead, they took them on an eight-hour ride to Honaker."

8. In April 1989, the first month of the strike, high-school students in all of Dickenson County's three schools walked out in protest against the coal company, and the protests spread to other schools in the region. All summer, children joined their parents on the picket lines (Yancey 1990, 5).

9. Jackrocks are the miner's traditional weapon against strike-breaking coal trucks: two nails bent and welded together so that one point is always sticking up no matter which way it lands.

10. Two pro-labor coalfield lawyers, Frank Kilgore and Scott Mullins from St.

# Chapter 10

# Gender, Race, and Community Activism

## *Competing Strategies in the Struggle for Public Education*

Carolyn Howe

It is no secret that public education in the United States is in crisis. Theories of the local state and of social movements, informed by analyses of race, class, and gender, can go a long way toward informing struggles to save public education from fiscal crisis and attacks from the Right.

In this study, I examine two strategies for social change that developed on the same side of a local campaign to fund public education in Emerson,[1] Massachusetts, in the Spring of 1991. This campaign to influence a key aspect of the local state—the public funding of education—took place in the context of antitax conservatism coupled with widespread apathy toward local government.

The struggle involved organizing for a referendum election to override Proposition 2 1/2—Massachusetts' tax-limitation law—in order to raise $4.6 million for the Emerson Public Schools. Two groups of concerned citizens came together in what I refer to as the "education-override campaign" reflecting different strategies for social change. Both groups were composed largely of white, middle-class liberals.[2] The gender composition of the groups differed, however, as did the implicit perspectives on how to do politics at the level of the local state. One group, based in a core of local businessmen and politicians genuinely concerned about education, pursued a traditional electoral strategy aimed at (1) securing endorsements from key business, political, and religious organizations and (2) contacting voters likely to agree with the education override. The other group, based primarily in a group of mothers from a public elementary magnet school, but including parents from three or four other schools, pursued a school-based organizing strategy aimed at educating and mobilizing networks of people at their children's schools.

The education-override campaign was a success—the ballot measure was approved—and its success can be attributed to the high level of organizing that the two strategies together produced.[3] However, as an effort to impact the local state by changing the way education decisions are made in the city, the grassroots organizing campaign had little lasting impact. I argue that this was because the women's school-based organizing strategy became subsumed under the businessmen's electoral strategy, leaving intact the city's traditional white, male power structure and its way of doing politics.

### Perspectives on Struggle Over the Local State

As many state theorists have argued, the local state enjoys a degree of autonomy from the central state.[4] As a result of this autonomy, both local business interests and citizen groups can have a potentially major impact on politics at the local level. The nature of that impact varies, however.

Offe and Wiesenthal (1980, 94), make the distinction between "class conflict *within* political forms and class conflict *about* political forms." Traditional electoral campaigns are conflicts *within* existing political forms or rules of the game. A struggle to increase the capacities of subordinate groups to have their voices heard by the local state is a conflict *about* political forms—that is, a struggle over the rules of the game. When subordinate groups exercise an increased capacity to struggle, there is a realignment of the balance of power, and those changes become a part of the political landscape. But such changes are always contested. The continuing security of the local power elite depends, in part, on the absence of a politically active citizenry, and, thus, the former have no interest in helping to mobilize the latter. As Stoecker and Schmidbauer (1991, 101) argue, capitalists attempt to "depoliticize" the local state so as to camouflage their influence while restricting the access of oppressed groups to the state. Subordinate groups, on the other hand, try to "politicize" the state by making explicit the conflicting interests of the power elite and the citizenry.

While much of the literature on the local state and on struggles over tax policies in particular have focused on the struggle between capital and labor, little research has been done on the influence that interest groups representing women, people of color, or the elderly have on such struggles (Campbell 1993, 169). This study of the Emerson campaign to override Proposition 2 ½ helps to correct this imbalance. While business leaders, education leaders, the teacher's union, and organized parent groups were united in the desire to increase taxes to fund education, the *processes* by which the campaign to override Proposition 2 ½ was waged reflected different class, race, and gender interests. Such interests are tied to the standpoints of dominant and subordinate groups.[5]

When people from dominant groups attempt to mobilize others for a social cause, they are likely to pursue strategies based implicitly on utilitarian models of collective action that emphasize individual rather than bloc recruitment.[6] By mobilizing individuals, dominant groups are able to recruit the desired constituency without creating alternative—and potentially threatening—sources of collective power. The strategy of mobilizing individuals was the cornerstone of the electoral approach to the 2 ½ override campaign.

In contrast to the outlook of dominant groups, the experiences and standpoints of oppressed people can lead to an alternative understanding of society and increase the likelihood of an awareness that only through collective, not individual, action is liberation possible.[7] Ferree (1992, 37) notes that women, working-class people, and oppressed racial-ethnic groups may be especially likely to reject competitive individualism as a feasible value and put emphasis instead on maintaining viable networks of relationships. This emphasis shapes their strategies for organizing. Women are more likely than men to perform the informal and "invisible" work of building networks and linking them together to create a web of solidarity.[8] At the same time, such actions are racially coded, making the process of building multiracial alliances problematic. As Omi and Winant (1994, 60) note, ". . . our very ways of walking, talking, eating, and dreaming become racially coded simply because we live in a society where racial awareness is so pervasive." It is not possible, Omi and Winant (1994, 60) argue, "to organize, maintain, or transform social structures without simultaneously engaging . . . in racial signification." White women, Latina women, African American women, and other women of color will tend to develop networks within their own communities, most likely crossing boundaries only when racial-ethnic differences and power differentials are acknowledged and consciously addressed.

This study adds to the literature on the state and to feminist and social movement studies of community-based activism by being explicit about the class, race, and gender interests of the largely white, middle-class activists in this struggle—interests that ultimately contributed to the failure of the school-based organizing strategy.

## Methodological Considerations

On the morning of April 26, 1991, I sat in Westside Magnet School's library with nine other women who made up the school's Cultural Integration Committee. We were meeting to plan how to improve the bilingual and multicultural aspects of the school's curriculum when the principal walked into the room and announced that due to budget cuts there might not be a bilingual program the next year, and that several popular teachers and support staff would not be rehired. Furthermore, she said, class size would increase to forty children per classroom.

The next week involved a flurry of activity in which I and four other women emerged out of the parent group to become the core leadership, or "centerwomen" (see Sacks 1988b), for the school's organizing campaign to override Proposition 2 ½. Officially, we became the Westside Magnet steering committee. With the steering committee and support from the Parent Teacher Organization, the principal, and many Latino and Anglo teachers, I helped organize my daughter's school to pressure the City Council to hold a special election for a Proposition 2 ½-override vote. With more than seventy-five parent activists, our school emerged as the most active in the education-override campaign that resulted in a victory on election day.

In addition to my own participation, I kept notes on meetings and conversations and have subsequently interviewed a dozen men and women who were the key leaders and activists in the override campaign. In pursuing the research in the way I did, I have rejected "the assumption that maintaining a strict separation between researcher and research subject produces a more valid, objective account" (Cook and Fonow 1990, 76). I have been aware of my "conscious partiality" (Mies 1983) to the struggle I write about and the strategy I helped formulate. I am aware that my knowledge of social-movement literature helped to shape the strategy and tactics of the women at my daughter's school. While this kind of "praxis" research is certainly non-traditional, it is becoming more common in feminist and other kinds of radical research

(Cook and Fonow 1990). While there may be certain biases I cannot escape, my understanding of the campaign was deepened by my personal involvement, even as my personal involvement was shaped by my own class, race, and gender position in a community sharply but quietly divided along each of these lines.

The different origins and strategies of the education-override campaign illustrate gender, class, and racial-ethnic perspectives on the proper objectives of struggles at the local state level. An elaboration of the two strategies is presented below. I begin with a discussion of the businessmen's "depoliticizing" electoral strategy and then proceed to describe the mothers' "politicizing" school-based organizing strategy.

### The Coalition for Emerson's Future: The Electoral Strategy

In 1980, conservatives in Massachusetts rode the wave of the Reagan victory and passed Proposition 2 1/2—a law that prevented property taxes from increasing more than 2 1/2 percent per year. The law allowed citizens to "override" the tax limitation for a single year if a referendum election so mandates. With successive years of inflation, Proposition 2 1/2 cut into city budgets, and Governor Dukakis subsidized cities to make up the deficit. The election of a Republican governor in 1990 made it clear that cities could no longer rely on generous subsidies from the state.

In the Fall of 1990, a group of business, political, and education leaders in the city, aware that a school crisis was pending, met to discuss what it would take to override Proposition 2 1/2. When the crisis of funding became critical in April of 1991, Steve Davis, founder and Executive Director of the Business-Education Collaborative Group, and Don Porter, a financial administrator for a local college and president of the citizen group, Citizens for Quality Public Education, reassembled a coalition of business, religious, and teachers'-union leaders to help push for a 2 1/2-override election. Due to significant public pressure by parents and this leadership coalition, the City Council eventually agreed to call for an election.

Don Porter and Steve Davis's coalition became a registered political action group known as the Coalition for Emerson's Future. The Coalition reflected the class and racial makeup of the white power structure in the city. And, as the power elite seek to avoid challenges to their power, the Coalition's strategy in the campaign was not about organizing or challenging the structure of the local state. Rather, it was about getting and winning an election. As in a traditional election campaign that is run in a top-down, bureaucratic manner, Don Porter and Steve Davis assumed the position of co-chairs of the campaign, and, as Don said:

> We hit the ground running pretty well. We had money in the bank from the get-go and essentially Steve and I assumed the dictatorship role. And we said, "If you don't like it, that's too bad." And I think in a five-week campaign that was right. I don't have any qualms about that at all.

By the middle of May, two people who had prior experience running electoral campaigns, Mark O'Neil and Liz Nelson, were hired for six weeks to help run the campaign. Mark's job was to oversee the electoral campaign. Liz's job was to work with the press, and eventually she was assigned to work with the parent-organizing effort.

The centerpiece of the electoral strategy involved calling people from voter registration lists in precincts where voter turnout was high and where there was some record of prior liberal voting on education and tax issues. These tended to be the white, middle-class precincts on the west side of town. Using voter lists—known as "purge lists"— that had been donated by political candidates, volunteers at one of two phone bank locations called only those voters whose names had been checked off for having voted at the previous two city elections. The decision to go after these voters represented an implicit decision to avoid the white, working-class east side of town and the African American and Latino sections of the city.

The strategy outlined above is a common one for waging elections for local, state, and national offices. Had this been the only strategy in the campaign, there would be little theoretical interest in telling the story. However, this strategy was successful in part because it benefitted from the grassroots organizing done by the women who developed the school-based organizing strategy. While the teachers' union mobilized its members to make phone calls, and members of the Coalition steering committee also participated, the largest group of volunteers were mobilized by parent organizers at various schools. The story of that mobilizing effort is the story of the women's school-based organizing strategy.

## The School-Based Organizing Strategy

The school-based organizing strategy was similar to those employed by grassroots organizers in unions and in communities. The goal of the strategy is to build an alternative source of power to challenge traditional authority and to create a "politicized" context for local politics. The strategy itself emphasizes finding natural constituencies for the cause and organizing them, as blocs, into a coalition struggle. For groups that are not natural constituents, but are deemed to be potential allies, the strategy involves finding connections between the cause and the groups' interests. In the override campaign, parents were considered natural constituents, as their children would be adversely affected if the override did not pass. The objective was to reach parents through a contact person at their child's school who could explain how the decreased budget would affect their particular school. Other groups, like retired people, were considered potential allies even though they did not have an immediate stake in the override outcome. By appealing to their interests as grandparents and to their civic responsibility, we hoped to win over a significant sector of the elderly population.[9]

After learning about the imminent school budget crisis on April 26, Mary Marinello, the bilingual principal of Westside Magnet School, called a meeting for the following Monday night to which one hundred Anglo and Latino parents and teachers and twenty children came.[10] We organized classroom coordinators for each classroom to call every other parent in the class to encourage their attendance at key meetings and to inform them about the issues. Through this process we organized both Anglo and Latino parents at the school to attend key City Council and School Committee meetings, wearing blue "Westside Magnet School" T-shirts and sweatshirts—as we did for the next eight weeks—to draw attention to our presence and to make a statement that we were becoming organized.

We developed a mechanism for linking parents throughout the city, which came to be known as the "school phone tree." The Westside Magnet coordinators would call the main contact person for each school who, in turn, would call the classroom coordinators, who then would call each student's parent. Five women and two men (including one woman from a nearby neighborhood school) agreed to coordinate the efforts to find a contact person and to distribute a phone-tree packet to each school in the city. Bill Kelly, a Westside Magnet parent, agreed to coordinate our phone tree.[11] It was through the school phone tree that parents' questions and concerns about the override would be answered, absentee ballots could be sent out, and volunteers would be recruited for the campaign. Each individual parent was thus organized as a member of a bloc—the bloc of her or his child's school.

While phone trees are nothing new in organizing campaigns, this particular phone tree was an effort to organize an alternative power base in the city that would be independent of the traditional power structure of business and education leaders. The very creation and use of the phone tree was a mechanism for organizing parents who had long been accustomed to sitting back and letting school principals and the city's politicians, education administrators, and businessmen make the important educational decisions. The long-term goal of building an alternative source of power was seldom discussed as a group, although there was frequent talk of the problems with the way politics was done in the city, and an awareness that we were attempting something new. The level of commitment to this strategy varied, from those who primarily wanted to use it to win the override to those who saw the potential for a lasting alternative power base.

Through the phone tree, we tried to organize a city-wide meeting of parents. While only eight schools were represented at that meeting (a small number out of some fifty schools), it was nevertheless one of the first times so many schools had worked together to solve a problem, and we decided to double our efforts with the phone-tree organizing to get people out for a second city-wide meeting on May 20. Recognizing that a 2 1/2-override campaign required a broad coalition, the women at Westside Magnet School agreed that I should contact Don Porter, President of Citizens for Quality Public Education, to see what his group was doing about the school crisis. It was then that I learned that a coalition of business, political, religious, and union leaders was already meeting to discuss an override of Proposition 2 1/2. Don invited me to the next meeting of the Coalition, which three of us from Westside Magnet School attended. It was following this meeting that Don Porter and Steve Davis called to "appoint" Judy Samson, a member of Citizens for Quality Public Education and an active parent from Norton Street School, and me as co-chairs of the "parent-organizing committee" of the override effort. Judy became a bridge between the two strategies for, while she was a skilled electoral strategist and offered many of the key insights for that strategy, she also understood the importance of grassroots organizing.

## Class and Race Issues in the Override Campaign

At this point, organizing for the override had been going in two directions: the parent-organizing effort and the traditional electoral effort. Aside from the organizing taking place at Westside Magnet School, little was being done to mobilize in the Latino and African American communities, which, together with a small Southeast Asian population, represented forty percent of the public-school population.

At Westside Magnet School, a beginning alliance was being made between the Latino and Anglo parents. We recognized that Latino children in the city's bilingual programs would suffer the loss of bilingual classroom aides without the override, and so Latino parents were considered a special constituent for the campaign. The problem was that large numbers of Latino citizens were not registered to vote, so Mary Marinello, the principal, organized a Latino voter-registration day at City Hall and got several bilingual parents and teacher aides, including one other Anglo woman and myself, to help.

Carmen Sánchez, a Puerto Rican parent and teachers' aide at Westside Magnet School and an activist in the Latino community, had been interested in voter registration for some time and saw that first day's effort as a catalyst for kicking off a major voter registration drive among Latinos. Carmen soon became a centerwoman for the override effort in the Latino community. However, she was never formally brought into the meetings of the white women activists at the school or the Coalition for Emerson's Future. The reason for this goes back to the tendency, discussed above, for people to form networks within their own racial-ethnic comfort zone. Although meetings of the white women activists took place at the school, we were largely unaware of Carmen's involvement in the Latino community and we had no natural links with other Latino parents. Because I spoke Spanish, the other women left it to me and to Mary Marinello to do any outreach to the Latino community.[12]

Outside of the school-based effort, Carmen spent time talking to the Latino community about the override and helped to get the Spanish-language radio and television programs to emphasize the importance of the override for bilingual education and to urge people to get out and vote. This was a tactic that might not have worked in the dominant white community[13] although it was an effective tool among Latinos who viewed the Spanish-language programs as the people's voice in the community. These media spots were supplemented with door-to-door leafleting and discussions, according to Carmen. For our part, Mary

Marinello and I went to the Latino community center to talk about the override campaign. Friendship networks within Emerson's Latino community were drawn upon by school and community activists to register Latinos as voters in numbers unsurpassed by previous efforts, thus bringing in additional voters for the Proposition 2 ½-override election. Unfortunately, efforts begun by Mary Marinello and Carmen Sánchez to bring the Latino community into the override effort were not picked up by the Coalition for Emerson's Future. Efforts to reach the African American community and the white, working-class east side were also minimal. Aside from token efforts to invite an African American pastor, Rev. Samuel James, to the Coalition steering committee, little was done to reach out or listen to the needs of the minority community. As Don reflected:

> It wasn't discussed as a minority question. It was strictly a voting question. And it was not in a racist fashion. It was a voting fashion. We just said, "What areas of the city vote? What areas of the city are concerned with education. . . ?" We talked to Rev. James at St. John Baptist Church and the NAACP. The problem is that they don't bring any votes to the table. We also didn't go to the east side.

The intersection of race and class dynamics come together in Don's comments and are apparent in the overall strategies of the override campaign.

While some white activists wanted to pursue a racially-inclusive strategy, those in power determined that the campaign would focus on people with a history of liberal voting in city elections—largely excluding the African American and Latino populations (who were unregistered or don't vote) and the white working class (who were generally not "liberal" voters). The divisions of race and class—both structural and subjectively felt differences—were reinforced by the white, patriarchal power structure. The failure of the Coalition for Emerson's Future to extend the coalition to the African American and Latino communities, and its avoidance of the white, working-class east side of the city, is consistent with its gender-coded resistance to the grassroots organizing of the white, middle-class women who were attempting to mobilize a city-wide coalition of parents, which I discuss below. Mobilized and empowered African American and Latino communities would pose a clear threat to the existing power structure, and were thus viewed as a threat to the campaign itself. Throughout the campaign, Don Porter expressed concern that the parent-organizing effort not be viewed as "a Westside Magnet thing." While he never stated his concern directly, it was apparently related to the widespread suspicion of and racism towards this bilingual, multi ethnic school in the white community.[14] It was clear that Don and others did not want to alienate that white community.

Efforts by a few white women to work more closely with Latino parents, and Carmen Sánchez in particular, were constrained by the absence of prior ties between the two groups of women; this made efforts to work together seem forced. Although Westside Magnet School was a bilingual magnet school, the bilingual program maintained a de facto separation between English-dominant classrooms and Spanish-dominant classrooms, encouraging distance between both Anglo and Latino students and Anglo and Latino parents. Principal Mary Marinello seemed to cherish the power she held as the main liaison between the Anglo and Latino communities, and at times seemed to discourage collaboration between the two groups. For the most part, the Latina women worked independently in their own communities or directly with Mary Marinello.

In short, the failure to pursue closer ties with the Latino community and other communities of color stemmed in part from a racially-coded contest over the distribution of new resources that would arise with a Proposition 2 1/2 override[15] and in part from the awkwardness of breaking out of racially coded, "commonsense" ways of doing things that kept both the Coalition for Emerson's Future and the Westside Magnet steering committee from moving too far from the comfort zone of the white community. Both of these factors point to the difficulty of building multiracial and multiclass coalitions when the racism in our society so effectively keeps people apart. It is exactly such class- and racially-coded decisions and non-decisions that create the structure of institutionalized racism and class divisions—even when the key actors feel that they are anti-racist and aim to be class inclusive. These divisions, and the struggle between a politicizing and depoliticizing campaign effort, reached a climax at the second city-wide meeting called by the Westside Magnet steering committee.

### Strategies in Conflict: The City-Wide Parents' Meeting

In preparation for the May 20 meeting, our seven volunteers phoned parent representatives at every school. Don Porter came to one of the

Westside Magnet steering committee's weekly planning meetings and promised to help us prepare for the city-wide meeting. He asked us to delay our meeting a few days, however, in order to give us more time to prepare materials. He volunteered to have our materials typed up professionally and to duplicate two hundred copies for the meeting. We suggested a plan to sign up volunteers for specific tasks for the override effort, and Don said he would ask Mark O'Neil, the Coalition's paid organizer, to identify specific tasks and to prepare sign-up sheets. Exhausted and relieved to have the Coalition's help and cooperation, the women agreed to delay our meeting until Thursday, May 23, but insisted that it still be held in the Westside Magnet School auditorium. Our meeting with Don Porter thus marked the beginning of the tense coalition between the white women activists at Westside Magnet School and the Coalition for Emerson's Future.

At our second meeting with Don Porter, just before the scheduled May 23 meeting, Don asked if he could chair the city-wide meeting so that it would not look like "a Westside Magnet thing." In the interests of building a city-wide coalition, we reluctantly agreed, although most members of our group were angry at this turn of events. The Westside Magnet women wrote up a model for a parent phone tree, instructions on how to talk to parents in their children's classes about the override, and a list of questions and answers about the override effort. We expected Don to have this material duplicated. We hoped a contact person from each school would attend and learn how to identify volunteers and supporters and how to talk to people who were undecided or had questions about the override. We planned to distribute printed instructions and voter-identification material at the city-wide meeting of parents. When the night of the meeting arrived, none of the material given to Don had been duplicated. Instead, he had prepared a butcher-paper display with an overview of the history of Proposition $2\frac{1}{2}$ and the school budget. He asked Mark O'Neil to describe the strategy for the override campaign. Perhaps unaware that many of the two hundred people at the meeting were not yet convinced of the need for an override, Mark imprudently told of the Coalition's three-fold strategy: target likely supporters of the override: that is, the (white, middle-class) west side of town; do not try to persuade people; and, if people stated they were against the override, do not tell them the election date or to call to remind them to vote. This strategy seemed elitist to many of the Westside Magnet parents; some were appalled that the plan was to ignore potential opponents (including the east side residents); others were angry that this strategy was stated publicly. The women from the steering committee, who had organized this meeting, were outraged that the meeting did not even address our organizational strategy. Mark tried to explain the phone-tree idea, but, since he did not understand its purpose or organization, the presentation was unclear and inaccurate. Rather than sign people up for specific tasks, Mark brought a single yellow-paper pad on which people could sign their names if they were interested in volunteering to help with the override campaign. While West Side Magnet women caucused to debate whether to take over the agenda, Don dismissed the meeting.

Bill Kelly and the women who had worked on developing the phone-tree strategy were furious at the Coalition's presentation and at the absence of a list of specific tasks for which people could sign up. Following the meeting, the tensions between Westside Magnet parents and the Coalition spokesmen exploded. Later that night, I received several phone calls from parents, some of whom wondered if Don Porter and Mark O'Neil were really in favor of the override, or if they were trying to sabotage the campaign. One woman expressed anger that a meeting organized by women was taken over by two men who spoke for the entire two hours. As Jan Levoie, a Westside Magnet activist, said later:

> I think there was a lot of frustration at that point because we felt like the control was being taken away from us and we had actually started the ball rolling. . . . And the Coalition was taking credit for all the momentum here when actually it belonged to us. . . . [A]t several points [they] dropped the ball on things that they told us they were going to do and then didn't follow through on . . . and we kept saying, "Oh, we should have just done this ourselves."

The next morning, at a steering-committee meeting of the Coalition, Judy Samson, Claire Hannon—another Westside Magnet activist—and I vented our anger and frustration toward the previous night's meeting. The anger came from feeling patronized: the experience and planning that had gone into preparing for that meeting had been trivialized by the men at the head of the Coalition. The frustration came from feeling that a golden opportunity had been lost: an opportunity to show other parents that this was a *parent* effort, and to mobilize them into concrete tasks on behalf of the education-override campaign.

As a result of the May 23 meeting, all of the Westside Magnet women's planning and work of the previous weeks were lost, and, in a fundamental way, the momentum and organization were never regained. By building upon school-based connections, the women's strategy had the potential to reach out to working-class communities and communities of color which had previously been uninvolved in school politics. This then had the potential of becoming a base for a broad coalition that could work independently of the school hierarchy or the business community to place demands on the city for better schools.

In practice, however, the school-based organizing strategy became subsumed under the electoral strategy, and the networks that were created in the organizing effort were not nurtured. The Westside Magnet activists made several attempts to organize parents at other schools, but after the May 23 meeting the Coalition's electoral strategy achieved hegemony. The school-based organizing brought in volunteers for the electoral campaign, but not in a way that would facilitate the building of a lasting grassroots organizational structure. At the time, the Westside Magnet white women activists were angry that we did not get sufficient support from the Coalition; we thought they did not understand our strategy. In retrospect, it seems likely that they did understand, but opposed our strategy. While the two strategies were complementary in winning the override election, they were contradictory in fundamental ways: one approach attempted to win an election through a centralized and depoliticized campaign; the parents' approach attempted to politicize the campaign and win by building an alternative source of political power in the city.

### Conclusion

On June 25, 1991, citizens turned out in large numbers to vote their positions on the override. Out of six ballot measures, only the education override passed—by a vote of fifty-two to forty-eight percent. It passed even though the total amount requested in new taxes was more than the total of the other five override requests. In a community resistant to tax increases and skeptical of public spending, it appears to be the tremendous amount of organizing that went into the education-override campaign that explains why people voted for $4.6 million in new taxes for the public schools.

Coalition leaders thought that the six hundred volunteers for the override campaign could be easily mobilized for subsequent struggles; such mobilization, however, would occur within the traditional political forms that had long operated in the city. The Westside Magnet steering-committee women correctly felt, however, that without an organizational structure—which we had unsuccessfully attempted to put in place—the six hundred names were no more than a mailing list. After the override campaign, the same people held power in the city and in the school administration. While funding was restored to the public schools, education decisions were made in the same way and by the same people.

Rather than empowering people to take an active part in shaping the communities in which they live, the effort to save public-school funding reinforced traditional ways of doing politics centered around an elite core of businessmen, politicians, and party loyalists. What this story shows is the difficulty subordinate groups have trying to politicize struggles when they are in alliance with the very dominant groups they seek to challenge and whose interests are to prevent subordinate people from gaining power. The mistake the women at the center of the school-based organizing strategy made was in failing to recognize the camou-flaging and depoliticizing practices of the business Coalition. On the surface, the Proposition 2½-override campaign was what some social movement scholars have called a "consensus movement" (Lofland 1989; McCarthy and Wolfson 1992): there was no organized opposition to the 2½ override and there was broad consensus among grassroots activists and the city's power elite about the need to increase taxes for education. While the women organized within the framework of a "conflict movement" for the goal of seeking a shift in the balance of power in the community, our short-term goal—to win the override election—became part of the consensus movement. It was difficult to politicize the struggle while working within a consensus movement. By the time we were aware of a conflict between our politicization strategy and the depoliticization strategy of the Coalition, it was too late to focus on our long-term goal without sacrificing the short-term goal. It could also be argued that because our class and racial standpoint was one of privilege, we were more concerned at that moment with the immediate threat to our schools than with the chronic problems of racial-ethnic and class disunity. Without the 2½ override, our otherwise privileged children would definitely suffer; without our city-wide coalition of parents—that is, our new alternative source of power—things would go on as they had been and we would certainly suffer less than would other racial-ethnic and class groups in the city. Dolores James, an activist and wife of Rev. Samuel James, noted in regard to the override election:

> Black people do not perceive that [a Proposition 2 ½ override] is going to make any difference in terms of how their children are treated in schools or how their quality of life would be improved. Because there was a time when monies were not an issue—when the money was available—and a lot of Black people . . . were still not full participants in the system. There is not a relationship between money and the improvement of the quality of life in the Black community.

Because white, middle-class women experience both a race- and a class-based comfort level with traditional structures of political power, it is important for grassroot organizing efforts to have a truly multiracial or multiethnic, as well as cross-class, leadership structure. Working-class women of color would be less likely than middle-class white women to give up a politicizing strategy to transform political forms.

This story of the women's failure to fully implement a school-based organizing strategy and our inability to link successfully with the Latino community has implications for community-based organizing. We need to better understand the race and class structures and biases that impede cross-class and multiracial organizing. We need to understand the gender dynamics that, if unrecognized and left unchallenged, can destabilize grassroots organizing by women who are distant from the centers of power in a community. We need to understand the race, class, and gender biases inherent in traditional electoral strategies. Audre Lorde (1984, 123) writes that the future of all of us may depend on "the ability of all women to develop new definitions of power and new patterns of relating across difference." This means that we need to find new ways to organize, new ways to share power among ourselves when building alternative organizations, and new ways to recognize the entrapments used to divide us and to depoliticize our struggles.

**Author's Note:** Thanks to Jerry Lembcke and Nancy Naples for suggestions on previous drafts of this chapter.

## Notes

1. All names of locations, people, and organizations have been changed.
2. Most of the people involved held professional or administrative jobs or were married to someone with such a job. They generally voted for Democratic Party candidates and many were active in or supported community organizations that addressed concerns typically associated with liberal causes. Members of one group tended to be active in Democratic Party politics, and some were elected officials.
3. This claim is made on the grounds that of six ballot questions to override Proposition 2 ½ (for education, police, fire, library, public health, and elder affairs office) only the education override passed, despite the fact that the funds sought for education were more than the total of all of the other ballot questions put together. None of the other parties that stood to benefit directly from an override organized a grassroots campaign. The police and fire department ran radio adds and distributed lawn signs, but no grassroots organizing was done.
4. See Markusen 1984; Greer 1986–7; James 1988; Stoecker and Schmidbauer 1991.
5. See Hartsock 1983; Smith 1987a; Collins 1990. Patricia Hill Collins (1990, 26) notes that the struggle to develop a *self-defined* standpoint involves "tapping sources of everyday, unarticulated consciousness that have traditionally been denigrated in white, male-controlled institutions." She argues that race, class, and gender oppression can vary, yet generate some common epistemologies among subordinate groups (p. 207). The same argument can be made regarding dominant groups, who share similar experiences that conform to dominant institutional practices.
6. Offe and Wiesenthal 1980; Therborn 1983; Lembcke 1988; Ferree 1992.
7. Hartsock 1983; Smith 1987a; Collins 1990.
8. See Milkman 1985; Bookman and Morgen 1988b; Pardo 1990; Payne 1990; Naples 1992; Krauss 1993.
9. Westside Magnet parents organized a children's choir from the school that went to retirement homes to sing to assembled residents. One child made a brief plea on behalf of the override campaign. A principal from a different public school came along to answer any questions the senior citizens had about Proposition 2 ½ or the proposed override.
10. As throughout the campaign, videos, snacks, and games were provided for children who came to meetings.
11. To the frustration of the Westside Magnet steering-committee women, most members of the Coalition for Emerson's Future remember our school phone-tree plan as "Bill's idea" or "Bills's model for that parent phone tree organization."
12. This included the voter-registration drive, a talk at the Latino Community Center, putting out bilingual notices, and bilingual meetings at the school.

These were the only efforts in the city to build a multiethnic effort for the override of which I am aware.

13. The Massachusetts Teachers Association had found that a highly visible campaign would bring out the "no" vote on an override issue at twice the rate that it would bring out the "yes" vote. As a result, they cautioned against radio ads and lawn signs and urged a silent campaign that would go after natural constituents: parents, teachers, and liberal voters.

14. White people often cautioned me against sending my daughter to "that school where all those Puerto Rican kids go." Similar comments were received by other white parents at the school as well.

15. Nancy Barry, one of the Westside Magnet steering committee members, said in a casual conversation during the campaign that it was not fair for the bilingual program to get more money if the override won, because they already had smaller classes and classroom aides in each room.

# Part IV

# Constructing Community

# Chapter 11

# "The Community Needs to Be Built by Us"

## *Women Organizing in Chicago Public Housing*

Roberta M. Feldman, Susan Stall, and Patricia A. Wright

Since the mid 1950s, women residents of Wentworth Gardens, a public housing development in the South Armour neighborhood of Chicago, have worked on their own behalf and on behalf of their community to "socially reproduce" and improve their housing development, which is home to 1,264 residents, all of whom are African American. Like other Chicago Housing Authority family developments, Wentworth Gardens has been plagued by inept management and inefficient and inadequate maintenance and services. But its residents have not reacted passively to such government disinvestment; rather, Wentworth women have worked collectively toward altering living conditions that threaten their public housing development's viability. These women's political struggles over the material and spatial resources controlled by the city and the local housing authority prepared them to extend their appropriation of physical spaces beyond the geographic boundaries of their housing development into economic development activities in the surrounding community—specifically, a proposed sports arena.

With entry into economic development, community activists are forced to increase their reliance on outside "experts" to negotiate with state officials, real-estate developers, and other commercial interests. Analysts of grassroots movements caution that this shift into economic development undermines the democratic and participatory emphasis of local activism (Stoecker 1995a). In contrast, in this chapter we demonstrate that Wentworth women residents retained control over their organized actions and communal structures due to their long history of activism and the participatory relationships they had established with the technical assistants chosen to work with them. However, as we will also discuss, their efforts were compromised by the fracturing of alliances between the public-housing residents and their home-owning neighbors. Here we highlight the fragility of cross-class alliances as well as the power of organized community resistance.

Wentworth residents' actions to improve their housing environment and services are neither unique to Chicago nor to other public housing developments in the United States. Women residents have historically fought and continue to fight for their right for safe and decent shelter and adequate services.[1] And while affordable, safe, and decent shelter remains a necessary objective for public housing revitalization, calls for economic opportunities are also being heard (see Center for Community Change 1994). Community activists and their allies are increasingly aware that to improve public housing and disadvantaged communities in general, community-development processes must address not only the environmental and social viability of the community, but its economic viability as well.

In December 1989, Wentworth Gardens' women resident activists incorporated as a Resident Management Corporation (RMC) and negotiated a dual-management agreement with CHA.[2] Prior to their RMC incorporation, Wentworth Gardens activists had engaged in effective organizing campaigns, formed other organizational entities, and developed and managed several on-site service facilities to address their unmet community needs for child-care, laundry, and grocery services. Resident efforts to develop and manage these service facilities were motivated not only by a sense of necessity, but also by strong community ties. Mrs. Beatrice Harris,[3] a long-time community activist, explains how grassroots initiatives are accomplished:

> That's the way we do it. We all volunteer together, and without a working relationship like that you can't do anything. But if you get a good working relationship, baby, you can do wonders!

The concern that the shift from community organizing to economic development undermines local participatory democracy fails to recognize women's socially reproductive labor within their communities and the empowerment and skill building that flow from these activities (e.g. Bookman and Morgen 1988b; Haywoode 1991). This chapter outlines why and how the Wentworth Gardens activist women were gradually drawn into economic development activities. Furthermore, the chapter demonstrates how, through their history of activism, these women developed the relationships and the basic skills needed to work in partnership with the outside "experts" who became increasingly necessary as engagement in economic development grew. While the process is still unfolding, there is much to learn from the experiences of these low-income African American women activists.

## The Case Method and Activist Scholarship

The analysis reported in this chapter is part of an ongoing participatory research project in which two of us, Feldman and Stall, are using a multiple-method case-study approach (Henig 1982; Castells 1983) that includes in-depth interviews, direct observation, and surveys, media reports, archival files, and organizational records to create ongoing information on effective community activism for a variety of shifting academic and activist purposes. Our research is also informed by two of the authors', Feldman's and Wright's, experiences as technical assistants to the South Armour Square Neighborhood Coalition, a group that was established to fight against the location of the new White Sox Baseball Stadium in an area directly adjacent to Wentworth Gardens.

The participatory aspect of the research seeks understandings of social relations and social change through dialogue and social respect between the researchers and the residents of Wentworth Gardens (as reviewed in Petras and Porpora 1993). These understandings are intended to uncover and challenge the inequitable societal conditions faced by residents of this public housing project. As participatory researchers, we have shared research reports, articles, and scholarly papers with residents whose comments are incorporated into subsequent revisions. We have assisted activist residents by documenting and giving recognition to their achievements and sharing the successes of Wentworth women activists with nonactivist residents and potential community supporters. Our writings also provide formal documents for grant proposals.

## Social Reproduction and the Politics of Place

For nearly four decades, women activists of Wentworth Gardens have struggled against increasing state disinvestment and growing poverty in their community, and attempted to meet their own and their neighbors' everyday needs. Their efforts have ranged from arranging informal social gatherings with neighbors and providing neighborly support (such as information sharing, errand running, and child care), to organizing more formal resident-initiated service programs (including grounds clean-ups, garden plantings, food and clothing distributions, youth and senior programs, crime-prevention and education programs, and organized sports activities), as well as sponsoring yearly celebrations and fund-raising efforts (Feldman and Stall 1990).

Through these activities, women residents not only provided essential services, but also created a sense of social solidarity fundamental to the creation of community. In the organization of social gatherings and festivals, women engage in a distinctive type of social reproduction described by Daniels (1985, 363) as "sociability work." Women who organize community benefits and parties "make the aura of sociability that not only encourages people to give generously to a cause but also develops the esprit to create and shape a sense of community" (Daniels 1987, 408). Creating this ambience to elicit sociability requires ingenuity, organizational skills, and persistent effort. Through their social-reproduction work,[4] Wentworth women sustain the social fabric of community and help to foster a community identity, while at the same time they provide essential services. For example, the resident-operated laundromat not only offers needed service, but is also a place for "neighboring" and a primary recruitment ground for community activists. The laundromat volunteer operators express intense attachment to this space, and engage in rituals to reinforce solidarity, such as birthdays celebrated "right down here." Perhaps the high degree of social cohesion and interdependence generated through participation in this facility can best be illustrated by Lucille Burns, who, although she and her husband had moved out of Wentworth years before, still returned several times a week to volunteer in the laundromat.

While the empirical importance of women's social-reproduction work inside the home has been established and argued to be a source of social change,[5] only recently has women's social-reproduction labor in the community, often essential for survival in lower-income communities, been recognized as a type of resistance or political activity (Morgen and Bookman 1988b; Haywoode 1991) integral to the development and sustenance of social movements (Stoecker 1995b). In their attention to community activism, Sara Evans and Harry Boyte (1981) offer historical evidence that rootedness in communal settings and participation in communal structures "can serve as the arenas where people can distinguish themselves from elite [societal] definitions of who they are, [and] gain the skills and mutual regard necessary to act as a force for change" (p. 56). Communal structures and organized actions can serve as "social spaces," offering arenas outside of the family in which women can develop "a growing sense that they [have] the right to work—first in behalf of others, then in behalf of themselves" (p. 61). Within these social spaces, essential relationships are formed, and "participatory competence" (Kieffer 1984) is developed and sustained.

Traditional political theory neglects to explain how human "connectedness" in social networks and in communities is essential to politics (Ackelsberg 1988). Haywoode (1991, 76) argues that the realm of community which women create through their everyday activities becomes "the third element" that mediates between the public and private spheres and provides the base for a new politics. In fact, "women build political networks outward from their household, kinship and community connections" (Haywoode 1991, 75) and "demand of public institutions that they fulfill their obligations to citizens" (Ackelsberg 1988, 302).

Yet, despite the increased attention in feminist scholarship to the political dimensions of maintaining households and communities, the physical settings in which, and often over which, power struggles are waged are largely overlooked (Feldman and Stall 1994). Grassroots activism is implicitly place-bound; that is, the networks of relationships and the activism that they support more often than not are located in and may involve conflict over places. Feldman and Stall (1994) proposed that the foundation of individual and collective empowerment so vital to grassroots activism in low-income communities is not only substantially locally based, but often is intimately connected to ongoing struggles for rights and control over spatial resources to house social-reproduction activities that create and sustain these communities. Particularly for low-income women, the power to affect change is to be found in part in the empowering experiences of the everyday, ongoing struggles to appropriate the physical settings of their homes and communities. The struggles of women activists in public housing for the rights to and control over the physical settings of their housing environments not only mediate the satisfaction of everyday material needs for safe and decent shelter, but also facilitate the processes of community building, and contribute to nurturing individual residents' positive self-concept and self-confidence, local leadership, and collective skills and resources for social change (Feldman and Stall 1994).

At Wentworth Gardens, the struggles for spatial resources to house and support social-reproduction activities have been central to the residents' community activism. Below we briefly examine the residents' actions to develop and manage on-site and proposed neighboring service facilities. In particular, we describe their ongoing struggles to appropriate spaces in which to house these services, and the various strategies Wentworth activists have used to challenge the barriers to their rights to control and use these spaces.

According to Wentworth Gardens' women resident activists, all of the housing development and the surrounding development is their "home," a place they care deeply about and one in which they find nurturance. To appropriate the spaces of their housing development, they have been creative and tenacious, but they also have had to confront micro and macro obstacles that at times result in discouragement and interpersonal and organizational conflicts. Wentworth activists' struggles to reopen and maintain the field house for youth-related activities is, in particular, a telling, visible example of how personal and political concerns become closely intermingled at the community level (Haywoode 1991) in the struggles for rights and control over community spatial resources.

Wentworth women residents came to this struggle well organized. Resident activists managed in the mid 1950s, with the help of a tenant-relations representative from CHA, to organize four of the seven blocks in Wentworth and form a development-wide elected Resident Council in 1955 to contend with the unresponsiveness of CHA on-site management. A small core of volunteers expanded to fifteen committed activists. (During the last three decades, the core group has fluctuated between ten and twenty-five women.) Resident participation was encouraged by "centerwomen" such as Mrs. Hallie Amey, the sustainers of neighborhood networks (Sacks 1988).[6]

In the early 1960s, CHA threatened to close the field house that served as an important resource for the community and to dismantle its sponsored youth programs. According to Mrs. Amey, who was serving as the Resident Council President, it was a local youth protest against the lack of community recreational programs that mobilized her and several other Resident Council members into action. This incident initiated Wentworth women's first organized challenge to the governmental disinvestment in their public housing development. Mrs. Amey explained:

One day I looked out the window, I think we were giving a small fish fry or something, and there was a group of boys marching through the area with picket signs on them, picketing CHA [for closing the field house]. And I told the ladies, "They're picketing the wrong group. They [the boys] should be picketing us." I said, "If anything comes up in here for us, it's going to come through us. . . . So I'm just saying this to tell you, there just comes a point and a time when there's a need for something, and a group of people gather and decide that they are going to do this for the benefit of their community [and] they can do it.

At first, women resident activists, through the Resident Council, attempted to pressure the CHA on-site management to reopen the field house and provide youth programs. When continued appeals failed to make CHA accountable, Mrs. Amey and several other residents pressed management to allow them to run a program in the field house. But management declined. They deemed the residents unreliable and incapable. With no options left, these Wentworth women decided to act on their own, with the material resources they could count on as their own. Since the women were actively engaged in the social-reproduction work of child care, they decided to create a preschool program in one of the field house rooms. Mrs. Amey explained that "the only thing we had was a desire to start." Unpaid resident volunteers successfully operated the preschool program five days per week, serving between twenty-five and thirty children for about two years. When the program was well established, the CHA did officially grant the residents control of the field house facility. The Resident Council then mobilized other local groups to help pressure the Chicago Park District to assume responsibility for youth recreation programs.

In 1968, with no laundry facilities available within walking distance, resident activists worked with the CHA to obtain space and funds, and opened an on-site laundromat. Sustained through resident volunteers, all profits above maintenance, repair, and replacement costs are returned to the community for such things as yearly community festivals and scholarship funds (see Feldman and Stall 1994). In 1973, the residents opened and have since operated an on-site convenience store. Also managed by resident volunteers, this store not only offers items needed by residents on a daily basis, such as baby diapers, canned and paper goods, and cleaning supplies, but it is also a site for "neighboring." Both of these actions followed the successful organizing campaigns to keep the field house open.

In 1987, local organizing efforts were again required to ensure the continued existence of the field house, which was in such poor repair that the scheduled children's summer food program faced cancelation. Again, a core group of women activists working with a community organizer began to attend the weekly public CHA Board of Commissioners' meetings to pressure for the roof repair. Time and persistence resulted in CHA's approval of the roof repair, but no funds were allocated to make the repairs. Undaunted, Wentworth United women persevered and continued to press the CHA Regional Supervisor until repair monies were located and allocated, and the field house roof was not only repaired, but replaced. For the Wentworth United women, the replacement of the field house roof served their goal to provide a visible, tangible sign of their growing political effectiveness not only for themselves, but for all residents of the Wentworth Gardens development, and for CHA and municipal officials.

The Wentworth residents' ongoing struggles to maintain and improve the field house facility and its programs, the development and continued operation of the laundromat, and other facilities and services such as the on-site convenience store, illustrate the synergistic relationship among social-reproduction activities, individual and collective space-appropriation processes, and grassroots resistance. To secure and maintain activities supportive of child care, laundry, and food production, Wentworth women required and fought for hard-won rights to appropriate the spaces necessary to house these activities. In doing so, they defied CHA's definitions of who they were—unreliable and incapable—and what their rights were to develop, use, and manage the material and spatial resources of their housing development. In the process, they relied on and further developed the social cohesiveness and political effectiveness of their community to act as a force for social change. Wentworth activists organized the Residents Council, the first group in the development to represent all Wentworth residents in requests and disputes with the CHA; worked with and supported a subsequently established Local Advisory Council (LAC),[7] a CHA-mandated resident representative committee; and sought alliances with technical assistants, foundations, and neighboring universities. Through these efforts, and as visible evidence of their community organizing, Wentworth women gained the self-confidence, skills, and organizational base to take on new challenges, such as the White Sox stadium battle.

## The White Sox Stadium Battle

The proposed construction of the new Chicago White Sox Baseball Stadium immediately adjacent to Wentworth Gardens threatened the viability of Wentworth Gardens and other residences located in the neighborhood of South Armour Square. At the time, the surrounding South Armour community was a stable neighborhood of home-owning, working-class African American families, public housing residents, and senior citizens. Wentworth resident activists became involved in this conflict, which reached beyond the geographic boundaries of their immediate development, to oppose the baseball stadium development. The history of invisible struggles in which Wentworth women resident activists engaged to create and sustain their homeplace and promote community viability prepared them and their neighbors for visible action against powerful political actors—the Illinois Sports Facility Authority, the White Sox Corporation, and the City of Chicago. A resident-initiated on-site action committee had been meeting regularly for more than a year to support the LAC in their ongoing frustration with the failure of CHA to maintain the buildings and to meet the basic daily needs of the residents. This committee was moved to collective action by what they believed to be a "crisis" with an immediate, tangible impact on their community, as exhibited by a newspaper article showing the proposed site of the new White Sox Stadium engulfing much of Wentworth Gardens.

In 1987, the committee sought help from local community organizer, Sheila Radford-Hill. Radford-Hill, employed by a Chicago citywide not-for-profit organization, had worked previously in the community setting up a School Watch Program with Mrs. Amey. After meeting for several weeks, the committee selected a name for itself. Mrs. Amey recalled:

> . . . [I]t was decided and approved that we would choose the name—Wentworth Garden Residents United for Survival. . . . Because here were the White Sox right up on us threatening to take our home, and here's CHA doing nothing for us in here—it was the only name that really fit what we were about to be about!

The women members of Wentworth United provided leadership in the political and legal actions to stop the stadium construction. Their past activist efforts provided them with the experience and expertise that many of the home-owning residents of the wider community did not have. Members of Wentworth United were approached by their home-owning neighbors for organizing assistance. Mrs. Marcella Carter, a Wentworth United activist, explained:

> A group of residents [from the surrounding neighborhood] had come to us and asked us, would we help them, because the White Sox were going to tear their homes down. They didn't have any idea about a council or anything so we helped them. We got Sheila [Radford-Hill] to come out and we helped them to form the South Armour Square Coalition.

Wentworth Garden residents, along with 178 homeowners residing within the site of the proposed stadium, and residents in a neighboring senior housing development, the T. E. Brown Apartments (federally subsidized and owned and operated by a local Baptist church), and other renters in the area formed the South Armour Square Neighborhood Coalition (SASNC) to lead the fight. The Coalition voted to oppose the stadium construction because of the devastating effect it would have on the South Armour community (Wright 1988).

When Governor James Thompson and Acting Mayor Eugene Sawyer first announced the relocation of Comiskey Park in January 1987, the Wentworth United activists (now part of SASNC) organized and attempted to negotiate with the City of Chicago, the White Sox Corporations and the Illinois Sports Facility Authority to locate the stadium in an alternative site to save the housing and stores in their community. The Wentworth United activists, as members of SASNC, began the battle by lobbying appropriate public officials. They first attended Sports Authority meetings at the old ballpark, Comiskey Park. Mrs. Carter, at that time the South Armour Square Coalition's secretary, explained one effective strategy they used to make their presence known:

> There was one time when we went to the stadium, to the Sports Authority meeting, and we had little crickets [noise makers]. And every time they said something we didn't like, we'd crick them. . . . Naturally, they threw us out.

The SASNC organizing campaign lasted for two years and included demonstrations at White Sox games in June 1987 and April 1988, testimony of residents at the Chicago Planning Commission, meetings with Acting Mayor Sawyer in July 1988, and several demonstrations and meetings with the Board and staff of the Illinois Sports Facility Authority.

As Coalition members, Wentworth women also made four trips to lobby the state legislators, including the Black Caucus in Springfield, Illinois, to block a bill that supported the stadium construction at the proposed site.

In the middle of the SASNC campaign, however, the homeowners negotiated a separate deal with the Illinois Sports Facility Authority. The remaining members of SASNC, primarily Wentworth residents, believed they were "sold out." Mrs. Dorothy Larimore, a past resident of Wentworth Gardens and a SASNC activist, describes the predicament they found themselves in:

> But what really did it, was when we were sold out. . . . We heard about a big meeting that they [the White Sox Corporation representatives and many of the property owners] were having at Abbott School. We found out at the last minute. Mr. Marshall [SASNC President] came to our meeting [Wentworth residents] with a stack of papers, I bet you two inches thick, for us to read in half an hour.

According to Mrs. Larimore and other resident activists, they were not given adequate time to respond to the document, nor were they informed about the meeting in which the Sports Authority had reached an agreement with the property owners to purchase their homes, thus paving the way for the construction of the stadium. Since the Authority had "quick take" powers over the land, many of the property owners did not feel they had any choice but to negotiate the sale of their homes.[8] According to the dissenting Coalition Board members, however, this agreement was never ratified because it had not been properly approved by the full SASNC Board. The remaining SASNC members were particularly bitter because they believed SASNC had a chance to win the battle. As one member stated:

> If people stay together, you're gonna win. I don't care what it is. . . . If you stayed together with it, we would have won.

While the homeowners left the coalition, the remaining residents continued to oppose the stadium development (Wright 1988). The organizing campaign culminated in a community meeting on January 17, 1989, where the SASNC members staged a "memorial service," with a coffin as a prop, at the local elementary school. Many residents testified at the service and told their stories about growing up, raising families and making friends over the years in the South Armour community. A letter campaign also was organized to build support from other community groups from across the city.

On February 8, 1989, SASNC, now representing primarily residents of Wentworth Gardens and the T. E. Brown apartments, and with a new lawyer, filed a federal lawsuit against the City of Chicago, the Sports Facility Authority, and the White Sox Corporation, in order to stop the stadium construction. Forty-nine plaintiffs from the neighborhood charged that the stadium site was selected in violation of the civil rights of the members of the community. Despite their efforts, the stadium was built and opened in 1991.

Unsuccessful in their attempts to halt construction, the Coalition altered the demands of their suit to seek reparations to replace lost retail facilities (see Zhang and Wright [1992] for a description of the lawsuit). Current SASNC Secretary and former Wentworth resident, Yvonne Dwyer, explained the Coalition's motivation:

> We felt it was good to let the White Sox know, first of all, that we were still here. We were concerned about the people that had to stay here. They no longer had any stores, they hadn't anything. So, we said, well, we need to make sure these people realize that we are here. And even though we were not a part, you know of the settlement, that we had a legitimate gripe because they had destroyed our community and they had just left us behind a wall, an iron wall . . . [of] the ballpark.

The case presented the argument that the civil rights of South Armour Square neighborhood residents had been violated by the government and the private sector. Had the stadium been relocated to the north, rather than south of its previous location, there would have been less displacement of residences and businesses. However, the north site would have required the displacement of white families. For SASNC, as with many community organizations, a lawsuit is a strategy of last resort. It was so here. SASNC cannot rebuild their neighborhood without substantial funds—$1.5 million alone is needed to construct facilities to replace the lost retail businesses.

Despite the loss of their battle to halt the stadium's construction, in publicly confronting formidable political, economic, and legal adversaries to reappropriate their homes, Wentworth resident activists worked to empower themselves. They have acted independently of the CHA in the public domain. In the process, they have formalized their organizational structure, first in the formation of Wentworth Gardens Residents United for Survival, and then as part of the South Armour Square Neighborhood Coalition. Wentworth resident activists increased their knowledge of and responded to the functioning of the city and state political systems, while still elaborating upon and extending their women-centered organizing and protest strategies. Lastly, these women established new social, political, and technical networks vital to their present and future plans. One plan they hope to implement through SASNC is to design and develop a sorely needed retail shopping center in the South Armour Square neighborhood.

### Working Toward a SASNC Shopping Center

Eleven neighborhood businesses in the area, including two grocery stores, a gas station, a bar, and a restaurant, had been torn down to make way for the new Comiskey Park. Consequently, residents in the area were forced to travel a minimum of two miles to the nearest grocery store, posing quite a burden for the majority of the low-income residents who are either senior citizens, handicapped individuals, or single mothers with children. Two-thirds of the residents now have to rely on public transportation and the limited bus service in the area to meet their everyday shopping needs.

When asked what they would do first if they won the lawsuit, Mrs. Larimore represented the general sentiment of the Coalition: "Well, we would start right this minute. Give us the money so we could start building [the shopping center]." During the organizing campaign for the White Sox battle, SASNC had been working with a university technical-assistance center on an economic development strategy plan to outline the options the community might take to gain control over its future development. In a series of discussions at the monthly board meetings, SASNC decided to make the replacement of the commercial establishments their first development priority. Their objective was both to replace the stores that were demolished in locating the White Sox Stadium, and also to create entrepreneurial opportunities and jobs for neighborhood residents.

While in past community-building initiatives reliance on technical assistants has been minimal, given the scope of this project, Wentworth Gardens activist members recognized the need for technical skills and resources not available within their ranks. Yet Wentworth Gardens activists and SASNC do not have the economic resources to secure the necessary assistance. In fact, other than the modest $8,000 planning grant from the City of Chicago in 1994, all the technical assistance on the project thus far, including legal, architectural, economic development, community organizing, and funding application preparation and funds have been donated. SASNC has secured these services through their prior relationships with a community organizer, Sheila Radford-Hill, and two local university centers. The technical assistants, Feldman and Wright, readily agreed to work with SASNC, in part because of personal commitments gained through long-term involvements, and also because they had been impressed by the Wentworth Gardens activists' comradery, creativity, and tenacity in achieving their goals despite enormous economic and political obstacles.

The accomplishments thus far are numerous. The technical assistants have provided the necessary expertise to assist Coalition members to survey existing retail facilities in the market region and determine retail needs; to survey the neighborhood for locations for the center and investigate the ownership and zoning regulations; to identify desired entrepreneurial opportunities and cooperative ownership potentials; to hold planning and design workshops to assess the feasibility of the preferred site; to develop schematic design alternatives and project construction costs; and to procure the property. Despite their reliance on the expertise of the technical assistants, Wentworth Garden residents are playing an active, vital role in all aspects of the development process thus far, drawing on skills and resources gained through their past struggles to build community and appropriate spaces for purposes of meeting the everyday needs of social reproduction. SASNC committees were formed to work with the technical assistants to articulate the purpose of the market and design feasibility studies, develop the necessary survey instruments, and survey the community. Although the design and analysis of the market-feasibility study was the primary responsibility of the technical assistants, SASNC members' contributions were essential to the study's effectiveness. For example, SASNC decided that they wanted to distribute the survey to every household in Wentworth Gardens as a way to collect the needed information, and to inform their neighbors about the project. The result was a strong survey response rate—fifty-three percent of all the Wentworth Gardens residents.

Participatory design workshops, used to engage resident participation in architecture and planning decisions, resulted in the needed materials for the lawsuit and fundraising grant proposals. They also provided the mechanism through which residents could articulate their preferences for a range of options. On the whole, the workshops proved to be "exciting" for both Coalition members and technical assistants, and contributed to reinvigorating their interest during the protracted lawsuit and search for alternative funding to develop the shopping center. Participation in the design of the shopping center is particularly compelling because it represented a material expression of the SASNC development objectives.

In their efforts to develop the shopping center, Wentworth activists are reframing their objectives and strategies from a focus on relationship building and service provision to assessing the market and financial feasibility of the proposed retail businesses for their commercial development. Not surprisingly, Wentworth women tend to express preferences for businesses that bear similarity to those services they currently are providing using the skills they already have, those primarily developed to meet their social-reproduction needs.

The SASNC has not relied solely on winning the lawsuit as a way to develop the shopping center. Rather they have pursued alternative sources of funds, including local and federal empowerment-zone funds and grants from local foundations. And indeed, this has proven to be an important strategy, because in May 1996, the SASNC lawsuit was dismissed. While this dismissal was a great setback, the SASNC continues to move ahead. They meet monthly with the technical assistance team. They are setting up committees to develop business plans, and they are attempting to obtain the option to purchase the land for the shopping center.

### Conclusion

Wentworth activists have called upon all the resources they can muster, including legal means, technical assistance, and outside funding, to win reparations for the damage done to their community by the construction of the White Sox stadium, and to rebuild the community's retail facilities. It remains uncertain whether or not they will be successful in meeting their goals. The increasing reliance on outside organizations and technical assistance, however, has not undermined grassroots democracy at Wentworth Gardens. Wentworth resident activists have not allowed the design and economic development activities, nor the dismissal of their lawsuit, to overshadow or destroy the other essential work in which they are engaged. While the shift from residents' past engagement in social reproduction and community organizing to this recent real-estate and economic development initiative poses substantial technical, economic, and political demands, it has not impeded residents in their ongoing women-centered organizing efforts to sustain the viability of their housing development. In fact, their efforts to become resident managers of the public housing development may actually be strengthened by the activists' abilities to engage in economic development, as resident management corporations have the best track record of successful economic development within public housing (Center for Community Change 1994).

The continued investigation of the everyday, ongoing, and yet often invisible struggles of poor women of color to appropriate space in low-income communities becomes increasingly urgent as safe and decent shelter becomes more difficult to obtain. Local and federal housing policies have not provided sufficient and adequate quality housing for this particular population (Birch 1985; Brietbart and Pader 1995). Our research adds to the growing evidence that the empowering experiences of appropriating spatial resources provide a central, crucial means for low-income women of color to develop resources for collective power to improve their housing conditions and community's viability (also see Rabrenovic 1995). These place-based collective actions are increasingly relevant today, when shrinking resources and new political conflicts heighten the importance of the physical setting of the neighborhoods on which low-income women depend for the necessities of daily life.

We also recognize the limitations of the struggles of poor women of color against the deterioration and disinvestment in their community. Like Williams and Kornblum (1994, 19), we have found that "no matter how effective tenants were in organizing themselves, numerous social forces—among them drugs, unemployment, ill health, cuts in social services—too often negated their best efforts." The accomplishments of the residents of Wentworth Gardens, while they are remarkable and do empower individuals and groups, cannot resolve the larger problems of the public-housing crisis and of low-income communities more generally. These grassroots initiatives, while impressive, are too fragile and sporadic to supplant the role of state and federal programs and non-profit organizations in providing decent, safe, and affordable housing, and for supporting leadership and economic-development opportunities for residents of public housing in the United States. Yet government-funded and non-profit programs, although they are imperative for the survival of low-income individuals, may be more useful for these individuals if grounded in local conditions and responsive to the voices of local activists who know the needs of their communities. Efforts to wrest control from powerful government agencies and corporations are further constrained by different interests dividing the local communities. Fortunately, women like Mrs. Amey, Mrs. Harris, Mrs. Carter, Mrs. Larimore, and Yvonne Dwyer, along with activist women in other low-income communities, remain as an important political resource for challenging the oppressive forces that impinge on their lives.

### Notes

1. See, e.g. Lawson and Barton 1980; Leavitt and Saegert 1990; Leavitt 1992; Breitbart and Pader 1995.
2. One approach to economic development that has received much attention is the nationwide movement toward tenant management of individual housing developments (Monti 1989; Peterman 1989), including resident ownership of the housing developments. A profile of eleven resident management corporations (RMCs) showed that most seek improved management and social services, and also modest business-development activities and job-creation and -placement efforts (U.S. Department of Housing and Urban Development, undated). RMCs around the U.S. have initiated employment and training programs, and created new community businesses. For example, resident businesses have included: employment-training and job-creation programs directed to building maintenance and renovation; the development and management of day-care centers, food stores and co-ops, health and counseling centers, catering, laundry, janitorial, legal, employment, and transportation services, and summer youth job programs and business education workshops; and self-employment entrepreneurial businesses such as hairstyling, lawn maintenance, screen repair, sewing, and word processing (see Center for Community Change 1994). These are some of the resident-initiated efforts that have provided employment skills, jobs, and new community services in the context of public housing.
3. The real names of the Wentworth activists as well as the technical assistants are used in this chapter, as per their requests.
4. Social reproduction is a concept that was initially developed by feminists as a critique of Marxist theory's neglect to elaborate upon the notion of social-reproductive activities in the reproduction of labor power and its role in effecting historical change (Harding 1981; Brenner and Laslett

1986). Social reproduction refers to the everyday routine activities of maintaining individual households and communities as well as social arrangements that protect, enhance, and preserve the cultural experiences of all members of the community. Social reproduction activities include, for instance, the birth and care of children, housework, the maintenance of physical and mental health, cooking, personal services, and education.

5. See Luxton 1980; Hartmann 1981a; DeVault 1991.

6. In her study of a University Hospital organizing effort, Sacks (1988a) contrasted two aspects of leadership. Most generally recognized is the leader as public speaker and confrontational negotiator. Sacks argued that this is a limited view of leadership, which is inadvertently a "class, gender, and perhaps racially biased one" (p. 120). In equating leadership with speaking, we often miss "women's key leadership role as centerwomen" (p. 121), and equally importantly, we leave "the impression that people act as individuals following an articulate orator" (p. 214).

7. Officially, residents at each of the nineteen CHA developments are represented by a CHA designated structure called the Local Advisory Council (LAC). LAC officers are elected locally, but LACs vary widely across developments in terms both of their representativeness and of their effectiveness in dealing with on-site issues.

8. The Illinois Sports Facility Authority (ISFA) offered a settlement to owners and renters based on a supplemental appropriation from the State. Under the "quick take" powers given to IFSA, the homeowners, renters, and businesses had to enter into a contractual agreement with IFSA by September 15, 1988 in order to receive relocation assistance. If agreements were not reached by October 15, 1988, ISFA had the authority to take title to the property and negotiate compensation later. Most of the homeowners and renters settled before September 15th, 1988. All of the properties were vacated by March 1989 to make way for the bulldozers.

# Chapter 12

# Creating Community*

## Mexican American Women in Eastside Los Angeles

### Mary Pardo

*Resistance strategies employed in everyday life inform women's participation in those struggles traditionally recognized as resistance movements . . . it is about creating the conditions necessary for life and not intrinsically oppositional.* (Aptheker 1989)

### Introduction

How may Mexican American women's efforts to improve the quality of life in their communities be understood as work? No wages are earned, no profits reaped, nor commodities produced. However, the unpaid work that women do in meeting their socially assigned responsibilities extends beyond nurturing and reproducing families; it creates community and the conditions necessary for life. So, when we broaden our conception of work and "take seriously" women's unpaid community work, we advance a theory which may unify race, class, and gender.

Nineteenth-century historical accounts of urban communities suggest that women's unpaid work often compensated for meager wages and inadequate public services. The working poor, particularly children and women, used the public streets to supplement their economic base; in the process, they also created social networks (Stansell 1990).[1] Today, the quality and quantity of public services such as recreation centers and schools in working-class communities continue to lag behind the needs of densely populated neighborhoods. For many working-class women, the community is both a living space and a work site. While most women desire amiable surroundings in which to meet their

---

*Originally published in *Aztlán* vol. 20, no. 1/2, 1991, pp. 39–67. Reprinted by permission of the author and Chicano Studies Research Center Publications.

socially assigned responsibilities, not all know how to create them.

The life stories of Mexican American women who have developed successful strategies for community building provide the rich detail needed to explore how women link family concerns to a wider network of resources.[2] While their work outside the home influences conditions in their neighborhoods, it can also change household arrangements. Women's community activism can either change the traditional domestic division of labor or reinforce "traditional" gender expectations.

As individual cases, the women's stories convey a sense of movement from household to neighborhood institutions. In the movement from one set of social relations to another, women often bridge the social distance that separates residents. The following discussion begins by presenting the eastside Los Angeles community context, focusing on the cases of women's community work that bridge social distance between Latino immigrants and established residents.[3] The discussion then creates links between state resources and inadequate community infrastructure, and, finally, considers the relationship between women's community work and household organization.

### Continuity and Change: Latino Immigrants and the Native Born

Eastside Los Angeles residents share ethnic origins (ninety-four percent are Latino); however, generation in the United States, language, home ownership, and income stratify residents. This differentiation means that integration of new immigrants may occur with some difficulty. One of the few community studies of immigrant and native born social interaction suggests that immigrants and native-born Mexican Americans hold critical perceptions of each other. The study found no automatic incorporation of new immigrants into the Chicano community; instead, it found the absence of regular interaction between the two groups. Chicanos saw undocumented Mexicans as "rural and backward, 'rate-busters' afraid to stand up for their rights"; Mexicanos perceived Chicanos as "not being hard workers who despite citizenship were not doing well materially and did not control their children properly" (Rodriguez and Nunez 1986).

In eastside Los Angeles, school settings provide an instance where immigrants and the native born may experience daily observation, if not direct interaction. At Roosevelt High School, cliques of students habitually congregate in particular sections of the campus. English-speaking and Spanish-speaking students gather at opposite ends of the school grounds. The new immigrant students complain that the Mexican Americans call them pejorative names such as "wetbacks, *mojados*, 'TJs,' and *ranchos*."[4]

The interaction between immigrant and native-born adults is also fraught with some of the tensions observed among adolescents, and attitudes toward immigrants bear on how women establish community networks. The period between 1965 and 1980 marked one of the largest influxes of Latino immigrants into Los Angeles County; almost half of the over eight hundred thousand Latino residents in the City of Los Angeles are not citizens (U.S. Census 1980). Residential patterns indicate that new immigrants (post-1965) seem more likely to reside next to older immigrants (pre-1965) than to native-born residents (Garcia 1985).

As new immigrants cope with the economic and social demands of life in eastside Los Angeles, they often violate what established residents see as the neighborhood norm. Women active in the neighborhood expressed differing perceptions, ranging from annoyance to tolerance, about the living patterns of immigrants. While the native-born Mexicans reflect the second generation's immigrant past, *pochos* may represent a glimpse of the future for the children of native-born Mexicans. Mexicans call the second generation *pochos*, which means faded and, used colloquially, refers to assimilated Mexican Americans or "faded Mexicans." The social distance and familiarity between Mexican Americans and Mexican immigrants creates problems and possibilities for establishing neighborhood cohesiveness.

Mexican American women became acquainted with many new immigrants when they perceived the need to inform them about neighborhood norms. For the last twenty years, Rosa Villasenor, a fifty-one-year-old woman of Cuban and Puerto Rican descent, has rented a spacious three-bedroom apartment in a densely populated, privately owned 1950s housing tract called Wyvernwood.[5] Since 1970, she has observed the departure of most of the Anglo renters and second-generation Mexican Americans and the arrival of new immigrant Latinos. Her neighbors refer to her as "Doña Rosa," indicating respect for her as an influential person in the complex.[6]

Recognized by her neighbors as frank and outspoken, Rosa sternly scolds those who transgress neighborhood norms—adults littering, youth writing graffiti on the walls and young men racing cars through the small winding streets. Not one to mince her words, she says she thinks the new arrivals must be from "ranches" and she admonishes them until they stop the disruptive behavior. She shares with me her usual lecture to the unruly neighbors:

> When they race through here I tell them, "a car is not a horse and it is not a mule. Someday you are going to kill somebody, so you better stop." They say "Ay, Doña, don't talk to us that way!" But, they stop. I also threatened to make a citizen's arrest if I saw them in the street littering or doing worse things. But you know, I would never really have the heart to call the cops on them. But I tell them "really mean," so they think I am serious!

The assertion that someone is from the *rancho* or a *ranchito* suggests that a person is from a poor rural area and not fully accustomed to sophisticated metropolitan lifestyles. For established Mexican Americans, this helps explain behavioral differences between new immigrants and long-time residents. Rather than a matter of being Latino or Central American, differences are often linked to rural origins. In an alternative way, this attribute may be used to chastise a Latino, regardless of birthplace, who breeches etiquette.

Rosa balances the harshness of her scolding by sharing information on health clinics and "help hotlines" that offer rape and drug information. When the neighbors need to know how to reach public agencies or services, they call her. Rosa rather philosophically reflects on the activity just outside her doorway:

> See, in this community, you go out the door and you see everybody. Even if they are no good, they are out there! [Laughter] I think I would miss that. Here there is something happening all the time—it keeps me going!

Her husband, Frank, agrees about the problems of Wyvernwood and notes that Rosa's activism has helped to improve conditions. Then he explains that he had "not taken the opportunity to move in 1970 when he could afford it." Now in his mid-fifties, he carefully considers the burden of a mortgage. To compensate for the declining quality of life in the apartment complex, Rosa and an established immigrant woman from El Salvador formed an informal partnership. The Hollenbeck Police Station's Neighborhood Watch Liaison, Sgt. Frank Hurtado, calls them "his best activists."[7]

Increasingly overcrowded within the last decade, the Wyvernwood

Apartments lost their reputation for being relatively free of gang violence. Immediately after the murder of a young boy by rival gang members, Rosa circulated petitions asking for more police foot patrols (Stein 1989). She explains how she responded to the shock of the boy's murder:

> I never felt the need to get involved in this neighborhood because it was so peaceful. But after the shooting, I said I have to do something. So every night at six, after I made dinner, I would go from apartment to apartment to get people to sign the petitions.

As a result of her activity, Rosa knows all her immediate neighbors and many people throughout the hundreds of apartments. Rosa clearly set up her signature-gathering schedule after she prepared dinner for her husband. She also set up our interview appointment and other visits that I made to Wyvernwood, as she put it, "at about 7 P.M., after everybody is taken care of." As Susser notes, working-class women take on activism as an "extra job" (Susser 1988).

Rosa describes the strategies she used to convince the largely immigrant residents to sign a petition to bring in police foot patrols. Her bilingual fluency made possible her success in obtaining two hundred signatures. As she explained:

> It would take me about half an hour just to explain to the people! First, I would ask if they would want me to speak Spanish or English. They were scared of the gangs, of the police, or maybe, I thought, because they were doing something wrong. So a lot didn't want to sign. If they didn't sign I would go back the next day and tell them, "*Si firma esta nota, no va a pasar nada.*" [Nothing will happen if you sign.] I would tell them, "*La persona que no firma, es porque tiene miedo, porque sabe que está haciendo algo malo.*" [The person who does not sign must be afraid because he is doing something wrong] *Pero el que no esta haciendo nada malo no tiene miedo!*" [Laughing at her high-pressure tactics] See? [Confirming that I saw her strategy]. And, they would sign!

Rosa obtained the signatures by combining arguments in a sequence that illustrates her perceptions of material conditions and social relations in the housing complex. She understands immigrants have many fears: fear of deportation, fear of becoming crime victims, and fear of family members committing crimes. She addresses those fears by arguing that collective action will help.

She has observed and confronted the teenage sons of some residents in the act of removing the parts from stolen cars and selling them to other residents. Using this information, she reasoned with residents whose sons may have engaged in the activity that signing the petition would bring less "trouble" or "implication of wrongdoing" than refusing to sign.

Rosa's method represents a variation of how residents "manage" acts of violence and crime in their immediate neighborhoods. In a Mexican community in Chicago, Horowitz found that non-gang community residents coexisted with gang youth by avoiding contact with them. In a study of eastside Los Angeles, Moore noted that the United Neighborhood Organization refused to work with gangs and asked for stepped-up police patrols. However, she states:

> Community members were not hostile to gangs. In light of cutbacks in all community agency funding and the promotion of "law and order" solutions, requests for increased policing seem one of the few options offered to community residents. (Horowitz 1987 and Moore 1985)

Rosa speaks of the density of the housing and acknowledges that, given the cost of living, she understands why two and three families share one apartment. In some units she knows three Latino families share the $650 monthly rent for a two-bedroom unit. While she speaks with empathy about their plight, she sees it as no excuse to neglect the upkeep of gardens and apartments. She notes that the adjacent two bedroom apartment houses six adults and five children. She also remarks that the neighbors make frequent trips across the border for weddings, baptisms, birthdays, and other family-related events, and that frequent absences from the apartment lead to poor upkeep.

The neighborhood across Olympic Boulevard, one block north of the Wyvernwood Housing Complex, differs in dwelling styles, upkeep, and density. Typical of Boyle Heights, small, neat, wood-framed, single-family homes line the street. The newer immigrants and established residents live side-by-side but in lower density than at Wyvernwood Housing Complex. The practices of some of the new immigrants invoke various reactions among the women.

With some exasperation in her voice, one woman expressed slight annoyance at what she sees as a hallmark of some of the more recent Latino immigrant neighbors:

> Some of these [new immigrants] think they are living on a ranch over here. Sometimes all of a sudden in the morning when you are asleep, you hear roosters crowing and then the roosters are always walking around the street. . . .

However, not all women felt annoyed by the crowing roosters. I asked some of the other women how they felt about the roosters that typically walk casually down the middle of the asphalt street. Angie Flores answered in a way that drew on her memories of the Mexican American and African American neighborhood of her youth:

> Well, some people say [about the new immigrants], "*tantos perros, tantos gatos!*" [so many dogs, so many cats!] The roosters walk around here all the time. But I remember on 41st and Long Beach, "El Hoyo," where I lived in the '40s, they had roosters too. So, I am used to that. As for the dogs, I don't need to have one because I can hear the dogs barking as someone walks down the street.

Unlike some of her neighbors, she considered the barking dogs an advantage: they alerted her to the exact location of strangers walking down the block.

Angie emphasized that she had never seen "so much poverty." Moved by what she saw, for one full year she assisted her parish priest in his efforts to counsel undocumented workers regarding the Immigration Reform and Control Act of 1986 (IRCA).[8] Angie tells of her work with immigrants:

> We started helping the people fill out forms. First it was only on Wednesdays from eight to twelve, then it was two days a week for about four months because people would keep coming and coming. We would take their names, addresses, whether they were married and how many children. My *comadre* [child's godmother] lives across the street from the church, so she would keep the files in her house. In case someone gets picked up [by the Immigration and Naturalization Service], he [the priest] would call my *comadre* and she could look up the card and vouch for them. Her husband

just passed away, so she wants to keep active. Some would have only a place to pick up mail and I thought maybe they didn't have homes. They were so afraid their families would be separated because some children were born here and some born over there [in Mexico]. I felt so sorry for them that I wanted to do what I could for the "illegals" and for the community.

Angie's account illustrates a view of recent immigrants as the *pobrecitos* [unfortunate ones] that Rodriguez and Nunez refer to in their study of Chicano perceptions of the undocumented. Her immediate block is occupied by single family, owner-occupied homes similar to the one-story home she owns. Instead of simply blaming immigrants for the decline of city-sponsored services, such as a local post office, she links it to the influx of new Mexican immigrants, the exit of Jewish residents, and the lower socioeconomic status of new residents.

In largely immigrant communities, successful grassroots mobilization must overcome obstacles to communication. In some instances, long-time eastside residents share practical information about community resources and impart to immigrants the standards of community life in the neighborhood. Mexican American women say they have enhanced their Spanish fluency by communicating with new immigrants. Thus, women's bilingual skills as well as their understanding and perceptions of the immigrants' circumstances can either generate or hinder mobilization efforts.

### Linking Community Needs with Community Resources

In addition to overcoming communication obstacles between immigrants and established residents, the women also bridged the difference between what they perceived as community needs and existing resources. The remainder of the essay discusses three cases illustrative of how women's collective work created additional community resources.

In the first case, women worked to supplement the needs—books and equipment—of the parochial schools their children attended. In the second and third cases, women identified and communicated community needs to state and city representatives who allocate resources for recreation centers. One case required community mobilization; the others demanded persistent requests, communication, and some volunteer effort to garner city funds and control over a local recreation center. A holistic reading of all three cases offers a portrait of how women's community work connects the public and private spheres.

### Creating Resources: "Pillars of the Church."

In eastside Los Angeles, the parish boundaries may define one of the spaces within which community identity develops and associations flourish. Two general observations about the relationship between the Catholic Church and the Mexican community are appropriate at this point. First, the local parish pastor determines the degree of his community involvement. At the parish level, as Moore notes, "the church is not a monolith."[9] Second, a distinction exists between the Catholic Church as a formal institution and the parish as the neighborhood base for many families. The Church may be the site of schooling, family counseling, and a link with other institutions. Most of the women volunteered many years for parish fund-raising. Some volunteer work centered on fund-raising which generally benefitted the local parish; other volunteer work directly benefitted the parochial school children. Angie Flores also speaks of her forty years of volunteer work for the church:

> We helped for forty years to get the funds to build the church. *Jamaica* after *jamaica* [charity bazaar] . . . not just one *jamaica*, not two *jamaica*s, it was about three or four per year.

Angie's husband, Robert, who worked in construction, also donated his weekends to help build a garage and driveway for the church:

> My husband has been opening the church for twenty years. He also made the garage for the school and the driveway. He got all these construction guys to go work there. After it was done, the father asked how much is it going to be. My husband told him, you don't owe anything: everybody donated their work.

She commented that the priest calls her and her husband the "pillars of the church" because of all the work they have done. However, she says they now need to have time out. Her husband, who now walks with the aid of a cane, experiences some debilitation from arthritis, which Angie thinks resulted from standing in wet cement during the thirty years of his working days. Her son, who moved a few doors away from her, now assumes some of their former responsibilities at the church.

Children's educational needs led almost all the women into volunteer community work. Part of a mother's "traditional" responsibility includes overseeing her child's progress in school, interacting with school staff, and supporting school activities. Based on mutual concern for the welfare of their children, women met other mothers and developed a network of acquaintances and friendships. All the women interviewed had sent their children to parochial school (Dart 1990). Thus, their community activism was closely linked to the parish and often began with the entry of their children into school.

During the 1950s, the Catholic Church began building parochial schools attached to the parishes in eastside Los Angeles. Pastors established Mothers' Clubs and called them a "drawing card," noting that first-generation parents appeared more attracted to the parents' group than to other parish committees (McNamara 1957). Erlinda Robles, a Mexican American woman residing in a house on the street where she was born and raised, participated in the Mothers' Club throughout the 1960s. She describes her volunteer work and the tensions that existed among parents, priests, and nuns:

> I wanted my kids to go to Catholic school, and from the time my oldest one went there, I was there every day. I used to take my two little ones with me and I helped one way or another. I used to question things they did. And the other mothers would just watch me. Later, they would ask me, "Why do you do that? They are going to take it out on your kids." I'd say, "They'd better not." And before you knew it, we had a big group of mothers that were very involved.
>
> My husband used to call us the "*Tamaleras de Talpa*" [tamale-makers of the church] and the women would laugh. He called us that because once a week we would have a sale. Every Sunday we used to have a breakfast fund-raiser with eggs, burritos, and tamales. We used to start about Wednesday making tamales. Some would clean beans, others would clean the *hojas* [dried corn husks used to wrap *masa*—corn meal dough—for tamales]. We had enough women doing it so it worked out okay.

*Tamaleras*, literally translated, means "tamale makers." In Mexico, women who earn a living making tamales occupy low status in the national occupational hierarchy and they eke out a subsistence wage. So, when Valentin Robles jokingly labeled the women's work group *tamaleras,* he reflected the irony of continuity and change as Mexican American women in the U.S. produce tamales in order to create community resources, not individual or family subsistence.[10] As Erlinda described the traditional Mexican food women chose to prepare for the fund-raisers, I asked her how they arrived at the selection of items. She said ethnic food sold the best. After mass in the morning, people who attended the church wanted "their Mexican food." When women tried selling "Anglo food," such as hot dogs or ham and eggs, sales decreased and people complained. Breakfast in the parish hall after mass continues into the 1990s. Another woman confirmed that parishioners say they can easily make ham and eggs at home, and prefer to purchase Mexican food.

Brown and Mussell argue that food choices express more than group preference: they also provide a way to "bind an individual to a group." As in other cities and other ethnic communities, second-generation ethnics may purchase ethnic food and avoid time-consuming preparation. The preference for and preparation of Mexican food makes an identity statement about the common origins of immigrants and native-born Mexican Americans.

I commented that the preparation of food meant a lot of work and a very long work day. As Erlinda told the story, she had not stressed the labor that went into preparing the food for fund-raisers. The implication of my question, from the perspective of a woman who has reluctantly prepared tamales on three occasions, contrasted with her reply. She reflected on the meaning of the collective activity beyond material benefit for the school:

> It was a lot of fun now that I think about it. I made good friends—some of us are still friends to this day. The priest would give us the money to get the ingredients. We would prepare some of it on Saturday. On Sunday morning, someone would go at 5:00 and start heating the tamales, so by the end of the seven o'clock mass, the food would be warm. We would stay there until after twelve o'clock mass. Then we would stay until two-thirty and clean the kitchen.

The church kitchen became a place where Erlinda's husband, Valentin, then enlisted in the Navy and often stationed away from home, could be sure to find her. Thirty years later, Erlinda still meets with some of the other mothers from the Mothers' Club. The lasting friendships that she established through her participation in the collective work to create resources formed the "glue" that created a sense of community. So, women's unpaid work originated in their obligations as mothers and as members of a working-class, ethnic community.

Erlinda Robles volunteered for the Mothers' Club in the 1960s, when the parish did not mandate women's participation. Erlinda reflects that a small group of women usually carried out the work that benefitted many. By the late 1970s, the financial need of the parochial school increased and the church mandated parent participation in fund-raisers. The decreased participation of women may indicate the tensions between unpaid communitarian work and paid work as an increasing number of Mexican American women sought paid employment after 1970.

Although friendships continued to be established, the president of the now renamed Parents' Guild confronted increased difficulty in recruiting the volunteer labor needed to carry out weekly breakfasts. As president of the Parents' Guild, Rosa Villasenor spoke of how she had to demand participation of a single mother at one of the meetings:

> She said she could not afford to pay or participate because she was a single parent going to night school and working. I told her that it was not fair for her to get away with having all the other mothers doing her work. She was doing things to better herself and that was fine for her. I told her either she paid or she should come on Sunday mornings at least for the *desayunos* [breakfasts]. I couldn't let her get away with it because then the other women would say, "Well, why should I do it?" She wasn't too happy about it, but she started helping on Sunday mornings.

I reacted with sympathy to the story of a single working mother seeking higher education. From an individualistic point of view, the single mother could have used the free time to study. But, from Rosa's position of responsibility for the collective, the woman's release from collective efforts would work to the detriment of a system of volunteer labor. It would sabotage group cohesiveness and commitment; quite literally, Rosa could not "let her get away with it."

### "We did all the work and we had a 'say-so'!"

In the 1960s, parochial schools distinguished the positions to be held by priests and nuns. Nuns assumed the roles of teachers and counselors, and the priests assumed the administrative positions.[11] The gendered division of labor among community women, priests, and nuns led women to perceptions of what was "just" and then to press for a right to decide on the distribution of the fruits of their fund-raising efforts.

In one case, given the division of labor, some women thought nuns should be entitled to more authority in the parents' group. In another case, the women perceived that their volunteer work, which supplemented the costs of parochial schooling, justified their right to have a "say-so" about the use of funds. This meant they directly negotiated with the priest in charge of the school. Erlinda Robles speaks of her experiences working closely with a parochial school during the early 1960s:

> They [the priests] would invite the nuns who were the teachers only to the first meetings. So, the nuns didn't know anything about the mothers. They were left in the dark. Then we started insisting that the nuns start attending the meetings. They [the nuns] were so happy, you should have seen their faces. Then we wanted the fathers to attend too. That way they could feel they were part of it. So then they changed the name to the Parents' Club. After the nuns started attending, the priests knew when they were outnumbered. We had nuns who were ahead of their time. The nuns lived in the convent next to the school and a lot of mothers would go to them for counseling. There were always kids and mothers going to the place they lived. The priests didn't like everyone going to see the nuns. But I told him, they are always available to the people; you are not. From twelve to two you take a nap and are not be disturbed! The nuns don't do that.

In many working-class communities, the church may be one of the few places immediately accessible and trusted for the everyday problems of the community.[12] It may also serve as a bridge to local secular institutions. Erlinda continued to differentiate the services provided by priests versus those provided by the nuns:

> They [the nuns] used to drive a lot of mothers and kids around and they had an old station wagon. So we told the priests, we think the nuns deserve to get a new station wagon and we will do the food sales to earn the money. The nuns didn't want the priest to think they put us up to the idea, so they tried to say no, they didn't need a new station wagon. But we insisted. And they got it after all.

Erlinda's description captures a complex set of social relations in the parish. The "patriarchal" character of the Catholic Church reflected in the division of labor among priests and nuns created a situation women questioned. Guided by their own observations and perceptions of "equity" and their practical concerns, the women carefully challenged existing decision-making practices that excluded nuns. Similarly, the women used their volunteer work to enhance the effectiveness of the nun's activities by suggesting the purchase of a new station wagon.

Erlinda Robles also spoke of strategies they used to draw men as fathers and husbands into the enterprise:

> At the beginning, the priests used to say who the president of the Mothers' Club would be; they used to pick 'em. But, we wanted elections, so we got elections. Then we wanted the fathers to be involved and the nuns suggested that a father should be president and a mother would be secretary or be involved there [at the school site].

Of course, this comment piqued my curiosity because it seemed contradictory that women should want a man for president when women ran the guild. So, I asked if the mothers agreed with the nuns' suggestion. The answer was simple and instructive:

> At the time we thought it was a "natural" way to get the fathers involved because they weren't involved; it was just the mothers. Everybody [the women] agreed on them [the fathers] being president of the Parents' Guild because they worked all day and they couldn't be involved in a lot of daily activities like food sales and whatever. A mother was vice-president and took care of all the food sales. The president presided over all the meetings. During the week a steering committee of work used to make all the plans for the group and then meet with the president and let him know. One time the president did make a decision on his own to have a fund-raiser that required the group to cook on Mother's Day. At the general meeting the group opposed him . . . because he didn't have the right to decide that. Nobody showed up that day to cook except him, his kids, and his wife. So he learned he wasn't going to get away with that. But now that I think about it, a woman could have been president and done the job just as well!

The group demonstrated dissatisfaction by boycotting the event and effectively conveyed the message that decisions needed collective approval. And the 1990s gave Erlinda a new perspective on her 1960s perception of what was a "natural" order for men and women. Women also got men into the group by giving them a position they could manage. The men may have held the title of "president," but they were not making day-to-day decisions about the work, nor were they dictating the direction of the group. This should alert researchers against measuring power and influence by looking solely at those who hold titles.

Juana Gutierrez, another community activist who worked with an adjacent parish school, complements Erlinda's accounts of the mothers' work to supplement the quality of education received by their children:

> I worked at Santa Isabelle. The first year when I was the vice-president, I did all the work for the president too because he was a man and he worked [for wages]. I moved the people to make breakfasts every Sunday. At the end of the year, I gave the father [priest] $7,000. He was very happy. The school needed a new refrigerator and air conditioning, so they were able to get them.
>
> Every weekend I got three or four different mothers from the school. I was there every weekend. I would go buy everything—the sisters would give me a blank check and my husband would help a lot. After I bought the food, I gave the sister the receipts and after the sale, we would figure the profits. We would make about $400 to $500 profit!

Parish and parochial school activities occupied a significant portion, but not all, of the women's community activities. Outside of the church arena, the core activists also shaped conditions in their communities by making use of state resources. In each case, the women stated that the work they did bettered the community in general.

### Gaining State Resources through Collective Action

The work of bridging the gaps between the community's needs and the community's resources may require different actions. In order to bring needed resources into the community, eastside women have used several strategies. In the first case discussed, community mobilization was necessary. In the second case, a small group of neighbors persistently communicated needs to a city commission, and, after volunteering time to keep a recreational area open, successfully gained city resources to develop recreational services.

### The Case of Driver's Training Instruction

In 1966, Erlinda Robles chaired the Evergreen Parents Steering Committee and worked to obtain an adult driver's training program through the recreation center (*Eastside Journal* 1964). Erlinda described the situation:

> I would take my kids to the Evergreen Recreation Center, and a temporary director, a Russian man who had grown up in this neighborhood, asked the ladies who went there what kind of programs they would like. One lady from Talpa [church] said, "Driving, I want to learn how to drive." But as hard as he tried, he couldn't get the classes for us. Then one day there was a representative from the Urban Affairs office and he told me, "Don't start at the bottom; start at the top." So we got about 150 women together and went to the Board of Education and made our request for a driver's training class.

The strategy of using mass numbers—150 people taking buses to the Board of Education—to stress a "request" speaks to the context of 1960s protest tactics. For most of the women in the group, this was a novel experience. The presentations to the board, letter writing, and phone calls finally led to success. Erlinda continued:

> They finally said we could have a pilot program for driver's training. We got about 150 women and two men to sign up for the course, but they wouldn't give us behind-the-wheel training. We never had a formal group. We just went and met with a few other women and Henry Ronquillo. I remember my phone would be ringing constantly. Sometimes, I would just start crying. . . . Especially when the California Driving School started attacking us on the news and saying bad things against the program, like "a little knowledge is dangerous." If kids could get behind the wheel, why couldn't we? The California Driving School said they were going to put a bunch of women behind the wheel and let them free. We chartered two buses two times and got the women enrolled in the course to go before the Board of Education and ask for the program.

The women opposed the driving school's degrading portrayal of women as incompetent, dangerous, and less responsible than teens, and argued that their access to driver's training, at minimum, should be commensurate with that offered to youths.

Erlinda always enjoyed being involved in community issues, but never liked speaking in front of large groups. As one of the key organizers, she was pushed by a community liaison with the Office of Urban Affairs to make a presentation before the Board of Education:

> Henry Ronquillo would make me speak. I think when I get mad things come out of me. I spoke in front of the Board of Education and told them we wanted this program for the last ten years and that we were limited in our school and community volunteer activities because we didn't know how to drive. We could not afford to enroll in a private driving school; at that time they charged between nine and twelve dollars per hour.

Erlinda argued that the ability to drive would contribute to the women's effectiveness as volunteers and also allow some to seek work outside the home:

> A lot of those ladies wanted to work but the work was too far by a bus. A lot of ladies got jobs after they got their licenses. The women really needed to drive and the recreation director backed us up because they needed more people to be able to drive the kids to field trips. The mothers wanted to learn for the kids, for jobs, and to help around the community. Everything we said was true—a lot of those women began driving other kids around too. It was not a luxury; it was a necessity.

Thus, the women who participated as mothers and unwaged community workers gained community resources that would give them options to enter the labor force. They argued from the standpoint of women who were fulfilling the needs of their children and of their community.

After an eleven-week battle, the parents' group composed of women won a victory over a group of determined private driving-school owners. The driving schools blasted the program, "as big government again throttling private enterprise" (Kaywood 1967). In a unanimous decision, the Los Angeles Board of Education authorized pilot programs at two adult schools and added driver's training programs to the regular adult classroom instruction. Later, Erlinda found out that social services incorporated driver's training into a work incentive and training program for women on welfare. They actually brought the driver's education instructor who taught the Evergreen pilot program out of retirement so he could develop the program.

The issue of driver's training may sound insignificant in the context of 1990. But in 1970, the community's population was described as highly transit-dependent because of a high percentage of young people (forty percent of the population under twenty years of age), a significant percentage of elderly (twelve percent over sixty years of age), and low income (median family income forty to seventy percent below the city-wide average). More than one-third of the families did not own autos and forty-two percent owned only one auto (Escobedo 1979).

Erlinda Robles and several other women completed the driver's training course and decided to celebrate their success by having a potluck and inviting the instructors and other community members. As a main course, they planned to make tamales for everyone. The priest hesitated upon the first request to use the church facilities. There were similarities in the way the women promoted the purchase of the station wagon for the nuns and the way they obtained access to church facilities for a non-church-related event. Erlinda explains how they used their extensive volunteer work for the church as leverage to use the church hall to celebrate their victory:

> The majority of the ladies who worked on getting driver's training classes were the ones who always did all the cooking for the church fund-raisers at Talpa Church. Since the church had a large kitchen available, we asked the priest for permission to use it, but he said no at first. But we reminded him that we used to cook in the church about once month and if he didn't let us he wouldn't see us around anymore. So he changed his mind.

The collective work of women in the parish and their efforts in local political arenas merged. They combined the two spheres of activity when they demanded the use of the church facilities to cook for a celebration not directly church-based.

### The Case of the Boyle Heights Recreation Center

Juana Gutierrez lives across the street from a recreation center exactly one block square. The conditions of her immediate living space stood in direct relation to the small neglected park across a narrow street from her home. She expressed her concern for the safety of her children and illustrated another way women mobilize to gain state resources. Juana describes the problem as it existed in the mid 1980s:

> We had a lot of problems with drug dealers in the park across the street. I didn't want my kids or my neighbors' kids involved in drugs. I made Neighborhood Watch meetings with the police and city commissioners. At the time Councilman Snyder was in office. He answered when we called. Not like the one we have now. We told him about the problems in the park. He could not believe it because he had never been to the park. I told him to go right down there and see the burned car that is parked in the middle of the park. When it happened, we called the police and nothing happened.

Juana's efforts gained small concessions from the Parks and Recreation Department. Juana continued:

> So, the park commissioner finally ordered lights for the park. Then, he came and talked to me. He said, "Mrs. Gutierrez, I know because of the budget, we don't have anyone to turn on the lights at night or open the restrooms. Would you like to have the keys and do it?" I said, I will do it, not for pay, but as a volunteer. I will open the restrooms every morning and close them at night. Someone else would come and clean them. Sometimes my husband or my kids would turn on the lights at night.

When I mentioned that this must have been a tiresome job for her, she answered:

> Yes, but for my community and my kids, I did it. You know some nights, I would say, I am not going to turn on the lights; I am tired. Then the phone would ring and the neighbors would tell me, "Mrs. Gutierrez, *no va a poner las luces?*" [Aren't you going to turn on the lights?] For five years I did it.

Instead of stressing the sacrifice, Juana's account stressed the necessity

of her work, much as did Erlinda's story about the "*Tamaleras de Talpa*."
Juana further explained how her diligence won stable staffing for the
park.

When Assemblywoman Lucille Roybal-Allard informed Juana about
some monies available for hiring recreation directors in the local parks,
she mobilized her neighbors:

> When I heard the city had the money for other parks, I called to
> see if we could get some for our park. They told me they didn't
> have the money for Boyle Heights [a neighborhood in eastside
> Los Angeles]. I got the people together and went to talk to the
> Parks and Recreation Commissioners. For two years, about eight
> neighbors and I tried to get the position for a recreation director
> for the park. We called the office, we sent letters, and we went to
> the office of parks and recreation. Finally we got a position. Now
> the kids get trips to the beach and other places.

Juana Gutierrez took me on a walking tour of the park where about sixty
children and some adults played and relaxed well before four o'clock in
the afternoon. As we walked through the park, I took for granted the
green grass and newly planted shrubs. Juana recalled the brown and
barren untended hillsides of the previous years. Quite fittingly, the
newly hired young Latina gardener planted cuttings from Juana's rose
bushes and they now grow in the park. Juana commented on how well
the park is doing and saw her job as complete, "Now we have a director
and four or five helpers and thank goodness I don't have to do anything
over there."

These two examples—the acquisition of driver's training for community members and the staffing of the park—illustrate how the community
activism of the women extended beyond the simply defensive or reactive.
The accounts illustrate the women's conscious proactive use of power in
garnering additional resources and services sorely needed in their immediate neighborhoods. In the case of the driver's training classes and the
subsequent celebration at the church, the women combined access to
resources from secular and sacred volunteer activities. Furthermore, they
clarify how family units may often form a network in blue-collar neighborhoods and reach out for state resources.

### Household Organization: "As long as his meals are ready. . . "

Approximately half of the women interviewed worked for wages only during brief periods of time. Among the married women I interviewed who were over fifty years old, none currently worked for wages. A few had worked intermittently when school tuition increased beyond the capacity of their husbands' earnings. Most women stated they preferred to care for their children rather than work and have to send them to day care. Since their husbands had stable employment and salaries sufficient to support the family, they chose to stay home after they married.

The women's husbands worked in a variety of predominantly unionized blue-collar jobs—baker, construction worker, machinist, armed services member and plant maintenance person. None of the women stated that their husbands did not allow them to work. Sociological studies often attribute the lower labor-force participation rates of Mexican American women to the cultural inclinations of jealous husbands (Sowell 1981). The freedom of movement in the wider community of nonemployed Mexican American women certainly contradicts the notion that their husbands controlled them. The women, several of retirement age now, often referred to the decision not to work in relation to the types of jobs for which their education prepared them.

Angie Flores, a sixty-five-year-old mother of three sons, speaks of her experiences at Roosevelt High School in 1941:

> In my senior year [of high school], I had to go to Roosevelt, but they didn't have room in "Commercial" [clerical track]. They wanted me to take "Home Economics." I said, "Well, in that case, I wanted to quit school because I already now how to cook and sew!" Then, the war broke out and we moved and later in my senior year I lacked the money for graduation clothes and I quit high school.

She worked for a short time in a spinach-packing house next door to her home, then quit work when she married. When I asked if her husband preferred she not work, she recalled his words, "Well, Angie, if you want to go on working, go ahead; but, I married you so I could support you. . . ." According to Angie, she quit work because her husband earned good wages as a construction worker.

The married women who did work for wages were a bit younger than the other women—just turning forty. For the younger women in the group, increasing inflation eliminated the option to remain home and raise children. According to these women, the current cost of living required two salaries. Other married women entered the labor force only at particular points in family life when the need was great—particularly when their children entered high school and tuition escalated beyond what one wage could cover. As soon as the children graduated, the women left work. One woman worked so that her son, attending college out of state, could afford the trips back home.

Women who took an active part in their communities accepted the management of the household as first priority. Once they completed household work, they attended to community work outside of the home. The husbands of the majority of the active women worked at blue-collar jobs that often demanded rising before dawn. For example, Angie Flores's husband, Robert, worked laying cement. I asked Angie how he felt about her extensive volunteer work and how she balanced out her household responsibilities. She recalled that her mother, who lived with her at the time, shared her wisdom regarding the proper way to treat a husband:

> My mother used to live here with me and she used to help take care of the kids. She would say, "Just have his [Angie's husband] food already set up so he can serve himself when he comes home at night." And, he wouldn't say anything as long as he didn't have to change diapers. . . . We [Angie and her mother] used to take the kids with us when we went shopping or to the movies in the evening.

Angie's husband did not dictate the conditions under which she could go out on evening entertainment excursions, and she felt they had worked out a mutual agreement about responsibilities. The agreement allowed her flexibility. She recognized and respected "changing diapers" as his absolute outer limit. He accepted a self-serve dinner waiting for him on top of the stove, rather than demanding she be home to serve him.

Rosa Villasenor, now fifty-one years old, described similar household arrangements. She has two daughters in their early twenties who are attending college and living at home. She described her husband as very dedicated to their daughters; so, just in case something happened, he stayed home when she went to meetings:

> Like I said, my husband used to work two jobs—sixteen hours a day for about five years. Poor thing. Now he gets up at four a.m. and like most of these guys [in eastside Los Angeles] he doesn't have an easy job. When they come home, they take a shower and want

to relax. The men you find at meetings are retired or they don't even work. He never objected to me doing anything. As long as I feed him and do his clothes. I had to take care of that if I wanted to do what I wanted to do!

Clearly, the dominant theme throughout the passages above is that the women did community work while continuing to do the "private" household work of mothers and wives. The women recognized that maintaining household stability allowed them to do the work in the community. So the exchange may be understood not simply as women's compliance, but rather as a way to assert independent activity in the public sphere.

The organization of households tells much about the flexibility of women's time and their assertiveness in defining the boundaries of their work. The intensity of volunteer community work and activism ebbed and flowed in relation to the time they spent working for wages. Some community members explain, and in essence make trivial women's volunteer work, by saying, "They do it because they have the time."[13] Having the time may be a necessary condition for doing volunteer work, but not all women and men who are not employed engage in unpaid work for community betterment.

### Conclusion

When feminists coined the slogan "the personal is political," they expressed the relation between the private sphere of family and the public sphere of community. While these are conceptualized as separate spheres by some social scientists, the work women do to mediate between family and community institutions clearly reveals how the two are interconnected (Thiele 1986; Ackelsberg 1988). Although the women explain their community work in relation to family responsibilities, class and ethnicity further specify the work they do to create kinship networks (di Leonardo 1987 and Harley 1990). If we ignore class, we miss the complexity and meaning of women's work under particular economic circumstances and in particular community contexts.

Similar to other women of color, the Mexican American women described above suggest that everyday life and organized politics overlap in eastside Los Angeles. The women expressed a sense of belonging to the community and to their families; conversely, they perceived their families and their communities as belonging to them. Their activities and their life stories support a strong notion of integration and membership in the larger community. The neighborhood comprised the immediate physical and social space for the family and the women devised ways to influence its formation with limited resources.

In some instances, the women do not identify their community work as "political"; for them, the work holds a kind of middle ground and reveals the integrated character of the "social" and "political" spheres. The women's volunteer work in local parishes, on blocks, and in neighborhoods demonstrated a civic consciousness intertwined with, not solely defined by, family responsibilities. In practical everyday life, women who are mothers do carry out gender-specific responsibilities. But this is only part of the story, not the entire story.

The church, priests, and nuns were all significant resources in the community. The women negotiated with priests to have input into the expenditure of resources, the use of space, and the administrative procedures that affected their children's education. The women worked to include the participation of nuns and get them the resources to purchase what they needed, e.g., the station wagon. Women expressed a consciousness rooted in collective goals and work. Instead of individual advancement, they pressured to maintain the system of volunteer labor necessary to create collective resources.

Gender identity, ethnic identity, and class/community identity gave meaning to their community work. When they spent endless hours preparing the Mexican food preferred for parish fund-raisers, they did so as women who were members of a Mexican community.

Symbols of Mexican culture color the community and social relations. Food and bilingual communication stand as obvious expressions of Mexican American culture; volunteer work for immigrant rights signifies an empathy for new Latino immigrants derived from a common cultural past. Although these relations were sometimes characterized by tension, women used language and social skills to establish communication between immigrants and long-established residents.

Through unpaid community work, women gained skills and experience fund-raising, organizing neighborhood groups, negotiating with authority figures such as priests, husbands, and city officials, and managing households and family. The gendered nature of women's community work informed the strategies they used to create neighborhood networks that significantly improved the quality of life in their communities. The women implicitly expressed their conception of civic membership as they bridged the spaces between their homes and the community.

## Notes

1. Also see Evans (1989) for a historical account of how women in the U.S. redefined the boundaries between the private sphere of home and the public sphere of the larger community.
2. The data is drawn from a larger study of Mexican American women community activists. Mary Pardo (1990a). For a discussion of life history methods, see Daniel Bertaux and Martin Kohli (1984) and Susan Geiger (1992).
3. The designations "eastside" Los Angeles and East Los Angeles are used to refer to the area east of the downtown Civic Center. Often used interchangeably and similarly in demographic profiles, eastside Los Angeles, immediately east of the Los Angeles river, is part of the City of Los Angeles and represented by the same political structure; the geographical area East Los Angeles proper is unincorporated. The neighborhoods immediately east of the river include Boyle Heights, Lincoln Heights, and El Sereno. The statistics used in this section are for Boyle Heights, Lincoln Heights, and El Sereno. All have historically shared public services and territory.
4. The Spanish word for "wetbacks" is *mojados*; "TJ " refers to Tijuana, a city that borders California. *Ranchos* suggests the new immigrants' rural origins and connotes that they are country bumpkins. See Sahagun 1983.
5. The Wyvernwood complex includes 130 two story building housing 1,100 units with spacious rooms, which discriminated against the Latinos until the mid 1960s. See Acuna 1984.
6. Of the possible alternatives in Spanish for prefacing a woman's name, "*Doña*" denotes respect, often indicating moral authority, and sometimes affection.
7. Sgt. Hurtado of Hollenbeck Police Station, L.A.P.D., stated that women outnumbered men in Neighborhood Watch groups about five to one. Along with three men and fifteen women who belong to Neighborhood Watch, I visited the L.A.P.D. Dispatch Center.
8. The sponsors of IRCA, termed an amnesty law, designed it to "regain control of our borders," legalize perhaps millions of undocumented workers who came to the U.S. before the cut-off date of January 1, 1982, and impose harsh sanctions on employers who knowingly hire undocumented immigrants. The cut-off date is particularly punitive for the bulk of Central American refugees whose numbers began increasing in 1982. See Fuentes 1990.
9. The older women observed that increasing tuition fees result in fewer families being able to afford to send their children to parochial school. This has implications for community cohesiveness. The Los Angeles Archdiocese acknowledged that school tuition is beyond the reach of most Latino families and established a new education tuition fund for the 1990–91 school year. See also Dart 1990.

10. Williams (1984) describes the labor-intensive work of making tamales—buying, cleaning, cooking, stuffing, wrapping, and steaming. She discusses how Mexican American migrant women workers in Texas and Illinois blur the boundaries between family and public affairs by preparing and distributing tamales in the interest of promoting kinship cohesiveness and channels of reciprocity among non-family members.

11. Until the 1970s, nuns formed the teaching force for parochial schools. Because the nuns were paid literally room and board, the cost of parochial schooling was accessible to the poor. As fewer women became nuns, the teaching force changed over to predominantly laypersons, increasing the costs and the tuition.

12. Religious order priests, Claretian Fathers from Spain, have come to Los Angeles since the early 1900s. Many of the Spanish priests served at several East L.A. churches, including the one above. According to one interviewee, they were accustomed to a midday *siesta* and did not want to be disturbed by parishioners from 12 to 2 P.M.

13. Also see Dabrowski (1983) for a study of working-class white women and civic action that documents the contribution of the "civic activities and presence" of the women then attributes it to the "personal lifestyles of women which are conducive to community work."

# Chapter 13

# Work, Politics, and Coalition Building

## *Hmong Women's Activism In a Central California Town*

### Sharon Bays

Before I actually began to interview Hmong women in the Central California town of Visalia[1] I was told by Hmong and non-Hmong alike to talk to the Hmong clan leaders in the community. If they agreed to my project, then people would talk to me. When I stated my desire to talk to women, some non-Hmong men and women eyed me sympathetically. "They don't have much to say," one man warned me. "They won't talk to you without the go-ahead from their husbands," another promised. But when the women did start talking to me, what they had to say could not have been more different from what I was told to expect. And when Hmong women began to organize themselves with other ethnic Laotian and non-Laotian women the following year, their actions decisively and irrevocably changed public sexual politics in Tulare County. After June of 1992, when the Asian American Women's Advancement Coalition (AAWAC, pronounced "awake")[2] was formed, people no longer suggested to me what I might expect from Hmong women.

I had known that my findings about Hmong women's activism and their new forms of politics would probably cause a stir among researchers, because they lacked precedence in the literature about Hmong life, here and in Laos. I asked myself, and my data: had women changed so radically because of their life in the United States? Then, early in 1994, I received a copy of Dia Cha's and Jacquelyn Chagnon's study, *Farmer, War-Wife, Refugee, Repatriate: A Needs Assessment of Women*

*Repatriating to Laos* (1993), the goal of which was to learn about women's perspectives in the repatriation process. Cha and Chagnon's work about women still in refugee camps helped to connect my data from women's histories in Laos and in the camps to their work and action in Visalia. Other than Lynellyn Long's (1988, 1993) study, which explored the changing familial relations in the Ban Vinai refugee camp that established the underpinnings for gendered troubles, there were no studies that suggested Hmong women who were still in Southeast Asia wanted their oppositional voices heard, or that they were unhappy with the male-dominated political organization. Because researchers often write about the Hmong as more homogenous than they in fact really are, there was no research that delineated gender differences over issues like income earnings, political empowerment, polygyny, birth control, and cultural preservation, as clearly and compellingly as Cha and Chagnon's. In her book, *Changing Lives of Refugee Hmong Women* (1994, 14), Nancy Donnelly hints at why this might be when she writes that "all the works published about the Hmong in Southeast Asia so far have been written by men, who have little access to the conversation of Hmong women even though they have sometimes been interested in it."

In this chapter I want to show that Hmong women are creating new political styles and networks that differ from men's political organizations, and that women's new forms are connected by two historical practices: their exclusion from traditional power and leadership circles, and their experience, in the camps and in Visalia, of engaging in cross-cultural social and economic interactions. To do this I will tell the story of AAWAC, describe the geopolitical environments from which it emerged, and show how this multiethnic group changed Tulare County Laotian community politics. Because the women in all four Laotian ethnic groups—Hmong, Lao, Mien, and Lahu— saw their problems as similar, including struggles both within their cultures and with the surrounding society, they chose a Laotian alliance that bridged ethnic distinctions and de-emphasized clan membership. This style of Laotian unity was, and continues to be, unfamiliar to Laotian men's politics in Tulare County. The profile of one Visalia activist, Pajhoua Her, presented below, at once illustrates women's centrality to adaptation processes and underscores the links between women's workplace networks and their political alliances. Her story enriches the broader one told here, while it shows how one woman works to overcome what Martha Ackelsberg calls the "fragmented consciousness that constrains political action in the U.S." (1988, 305).

The next section briefly outlines the reasons Hmong refugees have come to the San Joaquin Valley, where I was born and raised, and describes how I came to conduct ethnographic research in their communities. I will also broadly sketch the relationship between the refugee communities and the dominant one, and suggest how refugee programs designed by county government, informed only by a handful of men from the communities, helped to foster an activist sense of *Laotianhood* on the part of women.

### Geopolitical Background and the Politics of Fieldwork

Hmong military assistance to American forces and to the Central Intelligence Agency during our "secret war" in Laos marked Hmong for reeducation or death after the communist takeover. To escape this end, most Hmong made the treacherous trek across the Mekong into Thailand refugee camps in the mid 1970s. Initially widely dispersed in this country by refugee resettlement policy in the late 1970s and throughout the 1980s, approximately one hundred thousand Hmong and other ethnic Laotians have made second and third migrations to the San Joaquin Valley in Central California. The valley region now has the largest concentration of Laotian Hmong refugees in the United States. Like a long line of agricultural migrants before them, many Hmong harbored the desire to farm in the rural valley (Viviano 1986; Kitano and Daniels 1988). It was the notion of family reunification (Finck 1986), and the corollary idea of work in the country's most agriculturally productive counties, that inspired men and women who were once farmers in Laos to resettle in the San Joaquin Valley from the mid 1980s to the early 1990s. Only a relative few Hmong, however, could afford the investment required for a successful farming venture in California's competitive agribusiness environment. In spite of a depressed job market and discouragement by government agencies, the migrations developed a dynamic of their own.

The majority of the valley's diverse peoples, overwhelmingly of immigrant and migrant origin, have little to do with, and know little about, Laotian newcomers. The vast majority of Hmong and other ethnic Laotians in Tulare County continue to live in ethnic communities marked by poverty and distanced from the broader population. This distance has encouraged misunderstanding and fear, which feed on the struggle over what are often perceived as scarce and ever dwindling resources. Most adult Laotians in the San Joaquin Valley are or have been enrolled, often for years, in California's workfare program, Greater Avenues for Independence, or GAIN. In spite of their active participation in workfare programs, seventy percent of the Laotian population in Tulare County remains on some kind of public assistance (Tulare County DPSS 1992). Many of these are job trainees or job seekers who may also work part-time. Because a typical Tulare County job acquired through refugee workfare programs is low-wage and without health insurance, most part-time workers continue needing public assistance for their families' health benefits. The county unemployment rate throughout the early 1990s among the general population averaged around fifteen percent—more than twice the national average. This condition has only added fuel to the slow burn of anti-immigrant sentiment in Tulare County. California "natives" spin contradictory myths about new immigrants: they have either come for the higher welfare payments and are unwilling to work, or they take jobs away from citizens. Refugees, whatever their reasons for living in this country, have not been excluded from this homegrown brand of xenophobia.

In this contentious environment, I explored questions of identity among Hmong immigrants—how it is formed and reformed, what these changes have to do with the processes of adaptation and political action, and how these processes are in turn shaped by the experience of gender, race/ethnicity, generation, class, and region. I gathered data about work and welfare, youthful marriages, and the public gardens where Hmong find themselves in regular conflict with dominant practices, and, often enough, at odds with one another. On one level, my analysis examined adults' interaction with government job programs and the content of these programs. On another level, I looked at how members of the Hmong community—men and women, adults and children—differently described their culture.

While gardening at the Laotian Garden Farm was my primary way of meeting Hmong women during my first year of field work, I also joined the Tulare County Forum on Refugee Affairs in the Fall of 1991. Membership in this refugee advocacy organization and problem clearinghouse is open to any interested community person. Representatives from agencies such as Visalia Unified Schools, Welfare, Workfare, Child Protective Services, Health and Mental Health, and Police, and leaders from the Laotian communities sat at the Forum roundtable. I expected that becoming a member would broaden my knowledge of the interaction between government and the Hmong community, and of the nature of their encounters. The Forum was a site for learning about immediate problems in the refugee communities and the considerable discord between agency representatives who argued about the ways in which Refugee Programs were structured. To learn what troubled Laotian women about government programs and the Laotian spokesmen for their communities at that time, I had to go elsewhere.

My primary source of learning about women's discontent was direct interviews. I talked with most of the women in their own homes or in the gardens when others were present, but eight women volunteered to be interviewed in my apartment. It was clear that they spoke more freely with just the two of us in the room. These eight were women in their teens, twenties, and thirties, whose command of English was good.

There is an extensive discussion in feminist anthropological work about the insider/outsider position of the researcher when interviewing women of other cultures or from within the same culture.[3] Important issues feminists explore are the power relationships between researcher and subject, and the problematizing of the simplistic insider/outsider dichotomy. For example, Patricia Zavella's discussion of one aspect of difference, between her and Chicana informants, her education, is illustrative of the multitextured relationships anthropological research generates. Depending on the context, her status as a university-educated Chicana acted as a barrier or helped her to gain entry (1987, 20–29).

Why would Hmong women want to talk with me? Why would they trust me with the intimate stories of their lives? The answer requires a look at what Scott and Shah (1993) call the "politics of positionality"—at my political positioning in the Visalia context, in the Hmong community, and with Hmong women. Although I no longer live permanently in Visalia, I am an insider in the broader community, tied by family, friends, and work to local issues and events. On the one hand, I conducted research on very familiar turf. This facilitated my entrance to areas of my research that, for instance, examined government programs affecting refugee families. On the other hand, my Visalia insider's position did not necessarily allow easy access to Hmong families.

In this effort, three interrelated arenas of my research also became much more than sites of participant observation and data gathering. Through my work and exchange relationships in the garden with older garden women activists who led the debate in water use disputes, my growing political and social alliances among younger Hmong women, and my close friendships formed through a project in which I taught photography to children, I was no longer limited to the fringes of Hmong communal debates. I had joined the fray. Having joined, I was challenged primarily by the women and children with whom I worked: Where do I stand? What can I do about this or that issue? Can I write a letter on behalf of a family to the school district? Would I write grants for fledgling nonprofits? Will I leave when my time is up? Pajhoua Her's question to me at the first AAWAC meeting was typical of the inquiries that brought into question the nature of my fieldwork. She asked, "What about you? Will you be here for us two years from now, or will you stop when you become a professor or whatever you go on to be?" I considered this challenge significant, since it crucially constructed both my research questions once I was in Visalia and the way in which I went about doing my research: I was held accountable almost immediately for my actions and writings.

My research placed me in a variety of contexts in which I could view women's lives and they, in turn, could view me. However much men scrutinized my presence in the community, I was more aware that women studied and measured my actions. On the basis of their multi-contextualized information, they would choose to talk to me or not. I was also aware that women and girls with whom I worked used my more privileged position within the broader community as a resource. I wrote letters to schools on behalf of parents, accompanied women to the welfare office, wrote letters to county supervisors and local newspapers criticizing workfare programs and the ways in which they were created, wrote grants, and shuttled kids around Visalia. In this way, I felt a measure of reciprocity in the process of participant observation that served to mitigate the inherent intrusiveness of doing ethnography.

After my first year of fieldwork, and as I became aware of the different ways in which I was viewed by Hmong men, women, and children, the diversity within the Hmong community became clearer to me. While I discovered that competing claims characterized the Hmong community, and that it was a relative few Hmong men's representations of Hmong culture that held sway with local schools and government social service agencies. I asked the question: *whose culture is it?* When several influential spokesmen for the Hmong community objected to the school district's inquiries into the marriages of eleven-, twelve-, and thirteen-year-old Hmong girls[4]—often to older men—school officials reluctantly agreed to not make early marriages an issue. Was the school district protecting one way of Hmong life over another? When government monies funded the exclusively male Mutual Assistance Associations (MAAs) whose board of directors excluded women, what cultural customs were being safeguarded? As I came to understand that clan leaders were angered by the federal government's new requirement to include women on their MAA's board, and frustrated by social service agencies' attempted manipulations of their organizations, it also became clear that some Hmong women were tiring of both groups interpreting their needs for them.[5]

The standard developed and used for both men and women in Visalia was the male experience. In an effort to act in a culturally appropriate way, state, county, and city government representatives consulted the male, mostly older, heads of clans in Visalia as the keepers of custom and tradition, in spite of the existence of more diverse and inclusive forms of Laotian leadership emerging in the area. What it meant for women and girls to be Hmong living in Visalia was a puzzle to social welfare agencies and ignored by Hmong men's organizations. It seemed obvious, not just for research objectives but also for public policy, that the voices of the women must also be incorporated into the information that shapes government-funded refugee-employment projects. Yet, throughout the two-year duration of my fieldwork in the area, the mythology that explained women's and girl's lives was widely repeated and thus easily believed by social worker, school administrator, and refugee coordinator alike.

Descriptions of Hmong women as "housewives," uninterested in working outside the home or in community politics, misrepresented the reality of working Laotian women in Tulare County and their emergent voices as community leaders.[6] These simple descriptions also misrepresented Hmong women's rich and varied work histories in refugee camps and in Laos. Traditional Laotian village life is described by a complementarity of roles between men and women where Hmong families engaged in work based on rice or opium cultivation, gardening, and animal husbandry.[7] With the increased warfare in Laos, women's and men's roles changed in different ways. Men gained more prestige and authority in their various warring roles, and women found their farming and home front responsibilities dramatically increased (Cha and Chagnon 1993). Several older women whose life histories I recorded told of families of related women who periodically handled Hmong agricultural production, gardening for family sustenance and cultural maintenance when husbands and fathers were absent as soldiers. With no corresponding gain in authority, women shouldered much of the burden of Hmong cultural survival.

In the refugee camps, household and economic roles changed once again, but this time more dramatically for men. Cha and Chagnon

(1993, 12) describe how women became the primary full-time income earners of their families as embroiderers, weavers, seamstresses, and basketmakers. Because of their enterprise they more actively engaged in social and economic interaction with other camp ethnic groups. Their findings concur with Long's study of Ban Vinai camp life during the 1980s. At this camp as well, it was primarily women who earned an income from traditional needlework sold in the United States. This economic advantage did not necessarily translate into political or household power for women, since camp life itself, Long writes, created tensions between men and women that often resulted in increased women's subordination and abuse (1993, 189).

The undermining of Hmong ways of life by a protracted war, and refugee-camp and aid-agency experiences, is crucial to understanding the circumstances of Hmong daily life in the United States (Long 1988; Takaki 1989). Although Southeast Asians are now the fastest-growing segment of our population on welfare (Leadership Education for Asian Pacific America 1993), adult Hmong immigrants in Tulare County rely on a mix of welfare, workfare, and work for survival. Men and women there (many of whom worked elsewhere in the States before moving to the central valley) are temporarily or longtime unemployed, part-time employed (sometimes with several jobs), recipients of government assistance who train for employment, and, less commonly, full-time employed. Most families I knew combined part-time work and aid such as food stamps and/or Aid to Families with Dependent Children (AFDC) as a part of their economic strategies. Other categories of work include informal economic entrepreneurial activities such as concessions at regional celebrations run by family members, women's arts, women's daily traveling food concessions, and, most significantly, women's garden work, which yields produce for family consumption, exchange commodities, and some money when vegetables are sold at local Asian markets.

My intention is not to undermine or misrepresent men's efforts to ensure a better life for their families here in the United States. Indeed, men's lives have been made more difficult by the dramatic changes in role expectations which deemed them (unfairly) to be the "breadwinners" in the job-depressed San Joaquin Valley. In spite of their Laotian agricultural working history with women as more cooperative, and women's roles as the income earners in the camps, the rigid gender roles imposed by the American welfare/workfare system, and the exclusively male, mostly military-influenced Hmong leadership system, has helped to shape more rigidly defined roles in Hmong families here. While women's diverse work patterns have remained fairly consistent through the village, camp, and migration years, welfare officials attempted to force the role of dependent homemaker on them—a role the women had never held.[8]

County officials ignored that part of Hmong culture which women had preserved and brought with them and that had assisted in their families' adaptation in a variety of settings. Women's work culture brought a measure of continuity to their lives and was vital to their political networks in Tulare County. Pajhoua Her's story illustrates how central women are to both material and cultural maintenance and to the processes of change and adaptation here in the U.S.

## Pajhoua Her: Refashioning Hmong Leadership

Pajhoua was fourteen when Laos fell to communist troops, ending what she describes as a fairly idyllic childhood. She remembers roaming the mountains around her village, feeding the animals her family raised, and working at her mother's side in the rice fields. The news of approaching troops caused her family hurriedly to pack up all belongings that could be carried on their own backs and by hand. Pajhoua and her extended family walked for a month to Vientiane, the country's capital. From there they crossed the Mekong River to a Thai refugee camp.

At the camp, Pajhoua met and was proposed to by the man who would soon become her husband. She accepted his offer of marriage since this man, ten years her senior and with a good command of English, was educated and the leader of a youth group. Since her new husband was well connected to the camp hierarchy, they were among the first to leave for the United States; she spent a relatively short time, only one year, in the camp. Pajhoua and her husband were the second Hmong family sponsored by a coalition of churches to resettle in Denver, Colorado. It was 1976, she was fifteen, pregnant with the first of her three children, and spoke no English.

After the birth of her daughter, Pajhoua spent three months in ESL classes but quit to work in a bakery making English pastries. By 1978, she had learned to speak basic English from interacting at the workplace, watching television, and talking with her sponsoring family. More refugee families were coming to the area, creating a need for translators to assist them in learning about the schools, health care, and the welfare system in particular. While her mother-in-law watched the children,

Pajhoua volunteered to help new refugee parents register their children in school, fill out forms, and familiarize themselves with the town. At this time, the Denver public school system was ready to hire someone who could assist them with refugee parents and children. Pajhoua was soon earning $4.50 an hour performing the same tasks for which she had previously volunteered. She also began accompanying the school nurse on home visits, translating and talking to Hmong women about their own and their family's health needs and problems. Pajhoua describes her years in American public school classes, where she translated for Hmong students, as critical to her own education in English and in American history and culture.

For the next sixteen years, in Denver, Fresno, California, and then Visalia, Pajhoua was in continuous contact with every institutional system that affected Hmong life—health services, schools, courts, and the welfare system. In her various roles, she made institutions intelligible to Hmong families while she educated American workers in those institutions about Hmong culture. This educating/brokering role remains one of her primary tasks in Tulare County.

Like other Hmong women I interviewed, Pajhoua had shared work environments with Anglos, Latinos, African Americans, and Asians. Her work experience at the Refugee Health Center in Tulare County put her in close contact with other ethnic Laotians—Lahu, Lao, and Mien—as well as Hmong and non-Laotians. As a Refugee Health community health technician, she focused on outreach to new immigrants to the area, made health assessments of entire families, and discussed problems with the Center's director and at staff meetings. At twice-monthly roundtable staff meetings and monthly community discussion/workshop gatherings, the health technicians learned about the different Laotian communities other than their own. Pajhoua told me soon after she began working there, "when I see Mai or Malee, I don't see Mien or Lahu, I see another woman who has had experiences like me."

Pajhoua brought this multiethnic perspective to community politics. Her ideas of coalition building and her own desire to "build bridges between ethnicities" has earned her considerable criticism from other Hmong leaders. They point to these characteristics in her political style as an example of her "Americanization" and her abandonment of "Hmongness," since her agenda has expanded beyond just Hmong issues. She dismisses these often repeated accusations as the leaders' attempts to exert power over her. Instead, she explains that she came of age in the ethnic diversity of her workplace environments, and that her previous exclusion from clan politics created in her a manner of political action that had little to do with Hmong clan arrangements. Pajhoua said that many clan leaders who are adept at problem solving within the Hmong community cannot make the switch to what she calls "external politics"—dealings with institutions and people other than Hmong. She cites the issue of Hmong articulation with the welfare bureaucracy as one area where the elder clan leaders are less effective, in part because most do not speak English and have yet to grasp the complexities of the system.

To aid her own understanding of refugee life vis-à-vis government programs such as welfare, Pajhoua became a member of the Tulare County Forum for Refugee Affairs when she came to Visalia in 1992. The Forum also acted as an advisory body for new Department of Public Social Services refugee policy.[9] Pajhoua learned that there were two clear obstacles regarding the identification of refugee family problems at Forum meetings in the early 1990s. First, the few Laotian women who were members rarely spoke because of the presence of male Laotian leaders, their own inexperience at public expression, and, significantly, because women's opinions were rarely sought by other Forum members (Laotian or non-Laotian). Second, although the Forum was a site for learning about the ways service agencies handle problems in the refugee communities, it was not a place to find resolution of these problems. Pajhoua, the other Hmong women, and several non-Laotian women began to understand that refugee families' problems could not be successfully identified, understood, or resolved by social service agencies until women's input was included in the Laotian community knowledge that informed county policies regarding their families.

Refugee policy generated by planners at DPSS was distorted for several reasons. Because they presumed that men were Hmong leaders in Tulare County, Refugee Services program designers relied for information concerning the refugee family and community. The view that women could not articulate the needs of their families and that men understood children's, family, and community needs better was widely held when I began attending Forum meetings in September of 1991 and still dominant when Pajhoua joined. These views were then incorporated into the body of the Refugee Services Plan in the form of employment programs that primarily focused on the men of the community, since they were considered to be the heads of household. Laotian women who were already in the workforce were referred to as "supplemental" earners at several meetings I attended. County planners also viewed the fact that women received the AFDC check in their name as "familial role reversal" (Tulare County 1993, 37), ignoring women's history of work and clearly basing these assessments on outdated American gender roles. These correlated neatly with Hmong men's beliefs about women's place. Pajhoua and the other working Hmong women on the Forum began to resist the depictions of who they were supposed to be. They were dismayed to learn that the historical exclusion of women from Hmong community politics was continuing among Tulare County policy makers.

### Organizing: The Rise of a Women's Multiethnic Coalition

On June 11, 1992, Pajhoua came together with six other Laotian women and three non-Laotian women who worked in refugee programs to counter this exclusion. They came to explore the problems experienced by Laotian women and their families that had previously been ignored by both social service agencies and traditional men's political organizations. Among those present, there was a core group of Hmong women whose interest was to form a group that "empowers refugee women," as one Hmong woman declared, and challenge the reigning representations of themselves among policy makers. Six of the ten women, including myself, came fresh from frustrating encounters with DPSS officials at Forum meetings. A few younger women, students at the community college, heard through word of mouth about a new "women's club." A majority of the Laotian women who joined the women's club worked at Refugee Health, where outreach work had helped to foster a sense of *Laotianhood* among the women who worked there. Three of these Refugee Health workers were also members of the Forum.

The Refugee Health work environment that fostered a sense of commonality and solidarity among its Hmong, Lao, Mien, and Lahu technician/translators was a crucial ingredient in the emergence of the women's political networking. Tulare County Health had, just six months prior to this June meeting, received a grant from the Office of Refugee Resettlement (ORR) to hire Laotians to work in its public-health and outreach program for new refugees. The health administrator who designed the grant and the Public Health nurse who directed the Refugee Health Center (both non-Laotian women) understood the importance for refugee women's health of hiring women technicians and translators who were refugees. The Refugee Health community-outreach model developed together by the Director and the technicians was an important component in the shared sense of history growing among Laotian women.

In order to discover what the health needs of women in each Laotian group were, Refugee Health community technicians would organize monthly discussion/workshops. For example, the Mien technician would encourage and recruit women and men from the Mien community to come to the Center to air problems, seek treatment, and receive information. Rotating turns, the Lahu, Lao, and Hmong technicians would do the same. The staff, representative of all groups, was present for all other ethnic groups. Certainly, women recognized some differences between the groups. However, the needs and constraints of most refugee women here were so similar that the bonds of commonality were firmly established and cultural distinctions seemed slight. Six Refugee Health women brought this powerful perspective to the June 11 meeting.

Pajhoua Her, one of the Refugee Health technicians, was integral to the establishment of a women's insurgent politics in the valley region. She came to Visalia fresh from the besieged ranks of the Denver Refugee Women's Coalition, a Hmong women's group struggling, under community criticism (including threats of violence), to focus on women's needs. Unlike any of the others present, she was armed with the experience of co-organizing a women's group against hostile Hmong community public opinion. This experience, rare for a Hmong woman, combined with her vision of a cross-cultural coalition, gave her a powerful voice. She became the group's political-action guide, especially in relation to the Laotian communities. Visalian Laotian women's bonds of friendship and kinship, strategically forged with politically active non-Laotian women, were central to the "communications network" (Freeman 1983, 8) necessary for movement's formation.

The experience that galvanized the non-Laotian women (including myself) and connected them to Laotian women's objectives was a deep frustration with the way government agencies, with the exception of Refugee Health, approached the "refugee problem." As members of the Tulare County Forum on Refugee Affairs, we were critical of new government plans that were poorly conceived and inefficiently structured. In the Tulare County scheme of Refugee Services (housed under the DPSS) in 1991, not one refugee woman's voice informed those plans that would greatly effect their lives. At this time, my own activism was stirred on several fronts of my fieldwork. The experience of following the county's process of creating a refugee job program that would find few Laotians employment was discouraging. It was particularly so since I had grown close to families whose adults earnestly participated in work-fare programs. After these programs for refugees were established, the great folly of DPSS policy was that there was no provision for hiring Lao-tians. Since the majority of Laotian workfare participants in the county were not proficient in English, hiring a bilingual Laotian staff would have helped to make programs understandable to Laotian job seekers. But no one working with them at DPSS or GAIN was proficient in any Laotian language.

There was no specific event that allied Laotian and non-Laotian women; rather, it was the shared experience of working together at the Forum that lit the fire that fueled women's organizing. We had seen Office of Refugee Resettlement monies intended for refugees go to cre-ating programs and a final Refugee Plan which, in the end, had very lit-tle to do with the lives of Laotian people.

These were the regional ingredients that gave rise to a multiethnic coalition: (1) the recognition that women's voices were absent in mak-ing government policy that affected refugee lives; (2) the women's refusal to continue being excluded from important political and deci-sion-making processes, (3) the rejection of misinterpretations of Laot-ian women's needs and identities; (4) the understanding of common Laotian cross-cultural constraints through workplace networks and community outreach work; (5) the inspiration and guidance from an experienced Hmong political fighter; and (6) the uniting with non-Laotian activists who served as a bridge to the dominant community. These processes included what other social movement theorists call the familistic idiom of kin and social networking (Sacks 1988a; Wei 1993), the generational construction of oppositional consciousness (Gluck 1987; Dill 1988; Hall 1990), the political uniting of diverse factions (Ack-elsberg 1988), and the importance of social and physical spaces for insurgent thought (Moore 1978; Jenkins 1985). Jo Freeman's investiga-tion of "the spark of life by which the mass is to cross the threshold of organizational life" (1983, 8) led her to identify recurring elements in movement formation. Among these were a communications network of persons who begin to organize around new ideas. Key among the new ideas explored by AAWAC was that group members would assist in rewriting or influencing refugee policy, since what had been recently written was "irrelevant to refugee lives" (Yang 1993a). The following sec-tion describes the process by which women made this happen.

## AAWAC: "Leading from the Center"

At the second meeting, fourteen (nine Laotian and five non-Laotian) women met to explore further the ideas proposed the week before, to identify refugee problems in general and women's issues specifically, to discuss the effect of these on families, and to design plans to aid in their resolution. The concerns expressed commonly clustered around gender, generational conflicts, and health issues. Women named the growing disparity between refugee parents and their children and the increasing discord between men and women as the issues that most concerned them. The isolation and depression felt by many women in the community and the lack of assistance for these conditions in the county, were also a priority. Refugee Health members stressed that the scarcity of women translators to represent women in medical contexts and family disputes needed to be changed. We learned that most women who sought aid at Mental Health had to rely on husbands or other relatives for their translations—often with less than helpful results. For example, AAWAC women explained that Laotian men have trouble speaking about issues related to women's reproductive systems, especially in the presence of women. If these were associated with a woman's depression, the health care worker would not learn about crucial patient history to make an appropriate evaluation. At the same time, the women were reluctant to discuss marital problems through a male interpreter.

These first meetings engendered an environment in which, slowly, women voiced their fears, debated issues, received and recycled information, and, most significantly, related personal histories. These expressions of self, family, and community were central to the emergent political awareness and the educational process for all of us. "We need each other," Pajhoua Her told the gathering about the alliance of ethnic groups. "Alone we would not be the same. And this is also what sets us apart from the others [i.e. other Laotian political organizations]."

In telling their personal stories to one another, Laotian women discovered that they shared many common exile, refugee-camp, and U.S. resettlement and multi-migrational experiences. Their emotional stories were inspiring and instructive to the rest of us. In hearing non-Laotian women's political and personal stories of defiance and/or negotiation, Laotian women also found a sense of camaraderie. Not only had they found a bridge to the surrounding community, but they understood many experiences of struggle related by those of us who were born and raised in California. Most of us had been active in other civil rights movements. Our discussions about the sustained and long-term nature of the women's and farmworker's movements, for example, helped Laotian women to situate their own struggle for justice in California's history.

My journal notes recorded after the fourth meeting (July 25, 1992) reflected on a few of the challenges AAWAC had immediately encountered, the issues that confronted us, and the divergent views held by different Lao ethnic groups.[10] The divisions in AAWAC, however, were seldom ethnic and more often generational, between young college women and forty-year-old mothers of seven, and between the married and the unmarried. For example, one discussion revealed that Lao women were more likely than Hmong to use birth control. Older Hmong women often fear their husband's disapproval or his leaving when they stop bearing children. Younger Hmong women, however, express their interest in a variety of contraceptives. Several non-Laotian women, in an effort to encourage the younger women, asserted that it is a woman's right to decide what she will do with her body. These kinds of declarations were met with silence by most of the Laotian women—even when they may have agreed with the assertion. One Hmong woman explained that Laotian women cannot decide on their own about when not to have children. "It can't work that way in Asian families," she told us, "problems like that are worked out in the family unit."

The non-Laotian women were told to keep in mind that family unity must be emphasized, not women's empowerment, although empowerment as a group goal was raised by several younger Laotian women first. If we settled on women's issues instead of family issues, argued some Laotian and non-Laotian members, the group would surely come under attack and efforts to change conditions for women would be obstructed. An outspoken Lao woman offered that we would meet with criticism either way, it didn't matter. The problem with one approach or the other, this argument went, was that family unity and a woman's well-being in that family may be at odds with one another, as some women's stories of abuse revealed. These problems are worked out in the extended family context, the Laotian women stressed to the rest of us. The non-Laotian women's biggest task was to listen well and to resist imposing their agenda on other AAWAC members.

The apparent contradiction that confronted Laotian women was their view that both change and protection of traditional values were essential to their well-being. The task for the group was effectively to incorporate both without diminishing one or the other—a seemingly impossible goal. We tried to maintain a delicate balance at every meeting. The discussions, however, were always the expression of an interplay between urgency about community problems and the politically appropriate manner in which these should be handled. The non-Laotian women's political mode of operation by choice was often more confrontational and radical than what many of the Laotian women were comfortable with. And so, we eventually began to act in what Pajhoua Her termed an "appropriate and gentle" manner.

"Appropriate and gentle" became a buzzword in the group for dealings with the Laotian male leadership, a few of whom were relatives of AAWAC women. It was at once a term of respect and one of political expediency. While Laotian women wanted to begin to express themselves publicly, they did not want to appear to undermine the authority of influential traditional leaders and venerable elders who continued to play a valuable cultural role in the community. Younger Hmong women expressed uneasiness at this tact and were frustrated by the restrictions it placed on their behavior. One nineteen-year-old student asked me: "What do the leaders have to do with us women? Why can't we stand on our own. . . ?"

AAWAC Laotian activists, primarily older women in their thirties and forties, described themselves as "centerpeople," or more commonly as "leading from the center," when speaking of community politics and their leadership roles.[11] The notion of centerpeople springs from AAWAC women's understanding that their roles as mothers, wives, household managers, and culture brokers often place them at the center of family debates and three-generation households with very divergent views on American life. Importantly, a whole organization of centerpersons would counter the structure of the more hierarchically run men's groups in the region. At the same time, their declared "leading from the center" was also intended to avoid publicly undermining Laotian men's positions of power. Much like the "appropriate and gentle" approach, this central stance acknowledged constraints and made those an integral part of the political strategy.

### Should AAWAC Become a Mutual Assistance Association?

In its first six months, AAWAC had learned the procedure of nonprofit incorporation, and by December of 1992, it was about to attain nonprofit status, sought in order to meet the requirements of most funding agencies. Our goal was to create and support alternative refugee programs for families in Tulare County. A debate emerged from this process that proved to be central to the creation of both members' solidarity and their empowerment. The question was, should AAWAC become a Mutual Assistance Association (MAA)? MAAs are informal voluntary organizations that aid in refugees' adjustment in the U.S., which began to incorporate formally as nonprofits in the 1980s and to take advantage of federal funding earmarked for such community-based groups (Olney 1993). In January 1992, the federal government required that all MAAs have both men and women serve on their boards of directors (none of the four MAAs in Tulare County had complied by June). Our group was divided because becoming a MAA that sought public funding required including a man or men on the governing board and possibly at weekly meetings. On this issue there were two clearly opposing arguments. One side asserted that by going after both public and private monies, AAWAC would expand its financial base and, by admitting men to the group, would broaden its community support base as well. The other side argued that once men were admitted, the very reason AAWAC formed in the first place—to confront the decisions of both traditional Laotian leadership and county social service systems—would be undermined. Could AAWAC still be a place where women articulate their ideas if a man were at the table? On the other hand, could AAWAC establish its programs for Laotian families without the boost from ORR funds allocated for MAAs? The women, including the non-Laotian members, were sharply divided on this defining issue.

AAWAC women differed in this debate by generation and political experience. The inclusionist side was led by two Hmong women who were experienced in public discourse, had represented Hmong women politically in the community and at national conventions, and had been verbally threatened and criticized by individuals in the Hmong community for their positions, which often contradicted notions about "decent" Asian women. They had both run the risks of being publicly outspoken and urged members to take advantage of all opportunities in the course of "stepping out" politically. Including men was, for them, part of an appropriate strategy.

Among those who opposed opening AAWAC to men, there were two distinct constituencies. The first was married women of all four Laotian groups who were new to the public political process. The second was young, unmarried, high school and college students who lived with parents in households where issues like relationships with boys, curfews, phone use, and fashion were contested. Both of these groups had declared AAWAC a safe place to speak, and both possessed a new-found sense of autonomy. They were protective of this forum and fearful of losing what they had only recently gained. I asked the group, in the middle of one of these dialogues, if a discussion on contraception would take place with a man at the table. After the initial silence, a Lao woman slowly shook her head, symbolically holding her lips tightly together. Most women made it clear that rather than express what would be perceived as ideas disloyal to the Laotian cultures in the presence of a man, they would choose silence. A young unmarried Hmong woman fumed about this privately to me afterward. "It's a women's club. This is the time for us to say anything we want. . . . This is our club." Because of such sentiments, the non-Laotian women sided with those who wanted AAWAC to remain strictly a women's organization. Several women pointed out that unlike men's groups, which were then weakened by clan and ethnic disputes, AAWAC sought to build Laotian unity and open communications with the broader communities. On the strength of these arguments, AAWAC women decided not to become a MAA.[12]

From AAWAC's frequently raucous discussions came the common ground that helped to forge a new Laotian identity based on common exclusion, common economic and social constraints within the broader community, and common fear that the problems they struggled with would pass on to their children. What gave AAWAC its force in the community (and provoked fear there) was its recognition of women as political beings, its insistence on the reinterpretation of Laotian women as vital to their families' support and adaptation, and its challenge to the politics-as-usual of both traditional Laotian organizations and government refugee policy makers.

By the beginning of 1993, AAWAC women had attained nonprofit status, begun to write proposals as a group for program funding, and continued to challenge Refugee Services policy. At the same time, the group prompted and advised county facilitators of court-mandated parenting programs to include Laotian perspectives. This ultimately influenced the Tulare County Department of Education (DOE) to hire two Laotians, a man and a woman (an AAWAC member), to work as liaisons between the DOE and Laotian families. AAWAC women worked in the community to change DPSS hiring policies that excluded Laotians, contested the efficacy of GAIN refugee job programs, and challenged both agencies' misspending of government monies intended for refugees. Taking on the DPSS and GAIN was the defining action in the Laotian communities for AAWAC women. Most refugees had long complained about their status with GAIN, but AAWAC had presented the first organized challenge to the program.[13]

In part, Laotian women's success is due to the breakdown of Laotian consortiums made up of older men, primarily ex-soldiers and veterans from our war in Laos. These leaders became disillusioned and exhausted in their fight with DPSS bureaucrats, which required an increasingly specialized language to obtain contracts and grants for their MAAs. They were also politically divided internally and embroiled in financial wangling with county officials who allocate ORR money.

As this happened, AAWAC worked at the grassroots level to include the elder leaders and MAAs in the challenge, for example, to the DPSS refugee programs. The process of getting consensus within AAWAC was often laborious and time-consuming. Follow-up meetings with the MAAs would take place weeks and sometimes months later, after they held further meetings to discuss what AAWAC had brought to the table. AAWAC also gained a firmer position in Visalia politics when an AAWAC program, the Asian Families Empowerment Project (AFEP) ultimately served the entire community.[14] The majority served by AFEP programs were women with children. After the first two years of programming, however, there were several hundred Laotian men who had independently or with family members sought advice or help from AFEP services. It was in this context, then, that Laotians and non-Laotians began to see AAWAC as representing all Laotians.

## Conclusion

My exploration of the "spark of life" that ignites community movement highlighted politicking and networking by Laotian women. In Visalia, women were not just individually challenging cultural canons and expectations, they were presenting the only collective and often public challenge from their communities to institutions of power in the broader community. To understand why this is so, I have called attention to three important aspects of Hmong life in Tulare County. First, Hmong women are creating their own political styles and networks that are clearly different from men's. Second, women's work is historically and presently crucial to Hmong material and cultural survival. In spite of the prominence of these patterns in Hmong cultural history, they were largely overlooked in the creation of programs designed to employ Hmong and to preserve Hmong culture in Tulare County. Third, women's new political and leadership styles and their work culture are connected by two historical practices. First, women were excluded from traditional power and leadership circles, and second, where relations with others were necessary and often demanded (as in the camps), women were more likely than men to engage in cross-cultural social and economic interaction and integration.

Women's past exclusion from politics may not have been a hindrance in developing political networks here. Perhaps they were more open to creating new forms of leadership because they were not encumbered by the old ones. And because Hmong women were outside of men's power arrangements, women had no political or economic stake in erecting barriers or maintaining tensions between themselves and non-Hmong. In fact, they found it more advantageous in the camps and in Visalia to build on interactions with others than to focus only on internal community politics.

The discourse about "cultural preservation" that developed between Laotian men and refugee agencies in the camps, and in the San Joaquin Valley, selectively reinforced some aspects of Hmong culture at the expense of others.[15] I found that this practice justified government support for a Hmong politics centered around men. When I first came to Tulare County in the Spring of 1991, women were nowhere in the Refugee Services program picture. Government-funded MAAs were under men's exclusive control, and men were the primary targets of Hmong workfare programs. Government agencies' practice of interviewing the men in the family as experts on child and household affairs had the effect of putting men at the center of government programming. If we are to understand refugee communities and the key role of women we have to stop this neglect of women in the public policy process.

As several Hmong women participated in the Forum for Refugee Affairs, they heard plans being made that would affect their families' lives with no input from themselves or any other Laotian woman. Through Hmong and other ethnic Laotian women's experiences in the workplace generally, and more specifically in jobs that emphasized community outreach, women understood one another's common constraints and needs. Women began to reject others' interpretations of who they were, how they were supposed to act, and what they needed. The knowledge and guidance from an experienced Hmong woman political fighter aided in shaping women's activism and their emergent political organization, the Asian American Women's Advancement Coalition.

Women who confront the status quo in the Hmong community here are accused of being "unHmong-like," even though their stories revealed that they drew on Hmong traditions in constructing their activism. This activism was also shaped by their interaction with Hmong leadership here, their work within Tulare County organizations, and their discourse with the broader community. Women's integrative social and economic roles in the camps stem directly from their refugee camp work patterns. Before that their work culture in Laos combined the duties of farming, gardening, craftwork, child care, cooking, and animal husbandry. The significance of this work, particularly while men were absent soldiering, has been largely overlooked. When I began my research, I wondered whether a prolonged period of taking household and Hmong economy into their own hands would change women's ideas about how they see themselves within their family and community. Although changes are not always immediate, I was fortunate enough to witness both the ongoing reconstruction of these models of agency and the flowering of political consciousness in Visalia, California, among young women and their mothers within the besieged ethnic community there.

My work with Visalia's newest agricultural immigrants contributes to understandings of cultural identity as heterogenous, shaped by the specific experience of gender, class, and generation as well as ethnicity, and foregrounds women's central role in cultural maintenance and grassroots mobilization. This position challenges the generic "he" assumed by most previous literature on the Hmong, and grows from and joins with the project that finds us all living gendered lives. My concentration on Laotian women's new politics and its connection to women's work culture also adds gendered perspectives to anthropological theories on adaptation among immigrants, and contributes to feminist investigations of work, identity, and struggle.

**Author's Note:** This article is a revision of a chapter from my dissertation, *Cultural Politics and Identity Formation In a San Joaquin Valley Hmong Community*. I want to acknowledge and thank the National Science Foundation and the UCLA Anthropology Department for their financial support throughout my doctoral fieldwork and the writing process. I also want to thank Karen Brodkin Sacks, my chair and mentor, for her guidance and support.

## Notes

1. The great San Joaquin Valley stretches through the middle of the state from Bakersfield to north of Stockton. Tulare County is located in the southeastern section of the central valley. Visalia, one of my hometowns, is its county seat.

2. AAWAC was the first Laotian-women-led, community-based organization in Tulare County. The group is unique in the country because it is a coalition of Hmong, Lao, Lahu, and Mien women with non-Laotian women who work closely with the Laotian communities, including myself. In 1993, AAWAC created the Asian Families Empowerment Project (AFEP), a cluster of social and educational programs for Laotian families, especially for the women and girls in them. The AFEP is directed by a Hmong woman, Pajhoua Her, who is profiled here.

3. Zavella 1987, 1993; Bell, Caplan and Karim 1993; Joseph 1993.

4. While some men claimed that the marriage of eleven- and twelve-year-old girls is traditional, I could not validate this through interviews with Hmong women or in the literature that discusses Hmong marriages in Laos (Donnelly 1989, 98; Geddes 1976, 80–81; Meredith and Rowe 1986), where the common ages of marriage documented by these researchers (fourteen through twenty) confirm data from my interviews. Instead, I found that these marriages were more an adaptation to socioeconomic factors that leave men with few options. Because older teenaged girls are beginning to resist men, some men seek out eleven- through fourteen-year-old wives. Many of these girls lack the knowledge or strength of age and experience with which to resist an older man's will and/or their family's arrangements.

5. In her book *Unruly Practices: Power, Discourse and Gender in Contemporary Social Theory* (1989, 153), Nancy Fraser elaborates the idea that welfare programs are not only unresponsive to women's needs, but also that the "identities and needs that the social-welfare system fashions for its recipients are interpreted identities and needs."

6. Hmong women indeed do most of the housework, but in Tulare County they also commonly work outside the home. Mimi Abramovitz (1988) may help to explain Hmong men's and the welfare bureaucracy's label of women as "housewives" even when they work. She describes social welfare policy's "preoccupation with the nuclear family unit featuring a male breadwinner and an economically dependent female homemaker . . . social welfare programs have consistently favored the conventional family model that uncritically freezes women and men into rigid gender roles" (Abramovitz 1988, 2). Gail Paradise Kelly (1994, 505) discusses Vietnamese immigrant women "housewives" in a similar fashion as socialized by American institutions, teachers, and refugee camp officials. "Housewife" was the required role for living in America, even when most women had worked in

Vietnam. In Visalia, DPSS workfare emphasis on men's employment as the "head of household" was misguided because it discounted Hmong women's work histories and the fact that it takes two or more paychecks for a family to be able to sustain itself once off of welfare. So, although men were targeted by government employment programs, the reality was that wives and older children often worked as well. Even then, families could not become "self-sufficient" (the county's goal for refugee families), since most jobs obtained through county workfare programs were low-paying and/or part-time.

7. Barney 1961; Cha and Chagnon 1993, Donnelly 1994.

8. Women's work in Laos—farming, gardening, animal husbandry, sewing, stitchery, cooking, cleaning, and child rearing—their craftwork for income combined with household chores, garden work, and child rearing in the camps, and their varied work histories in the U.S., which also combine housework, craftwork, and garden work, follow a distinctly diverse pattern. By this I mean that women do different subsistence, paid, and unpaid work as key economic sustainers of their households.

9. The Forum did serve as an advisory body to the designers of the DPSS/GAIN Refugee Services Plan. However, the advice was rarely incorporated into the body of plans, since many Forum members offered what could be described as vociferous criticisms of those plans.

10. The number of Laotian and non-Laotian women present varied every week. There was a core group, though, of about fifteen members, most of whom were Laotian. I use the term non-Laotian since those of us who were not Laotian varied ethnically.

11. The use of the term "centerperson" by Laotian women was an interesting development, coined by Pajhoua Her to describe women's reluctance to declare themselves "leaders" vis-à-vis Hmong men. I was particularly interested since my advisor, feminist anthropologist Karen Brodkin Sacks (1988b, 79–80), used the term to describe women who sustained workplace networks but who did not view themselves as leaders.

12. From the beginning, AAWAC women voted to seat several Laotian men on the AAWAC Board of Advisors, who meet once a year. In mid-1995 one Hmong man was asked to sit on the Board of Directors because, after three years of activism in the community, women felt confident that a man's presence would not change their political expression. AAWAC has not become a MAA, but the reasoning is different now from what it was in 1992. If AAWAC became a MAA, AAWAC would compete for MAA monies from ORR set aside especially for refugee-led MAAs. This would place us in direct competition with Lao Family of Tulare County. Pajhoua Her has stated that this would be a very unwise choice for a very small pot of money.

13. This is ongoing and often contentious. AAWAC has organized petitions signed by all the leaders from all Laotian groups to make programs relevant to refugee lives. AAWAC members have met many times with the

heads of DPSS and Refugee Services and with certain members of the County Board of Supervisors to list community complaints to refugee programs and to offer advice. We have written letters to local newspapers where they were published (see Yang 1993a; Bays 1994b) and have presented the Tulare County case at national conferences (Her 1995; Bays 1995). The case is simply this: Refugee Programs funded by ORR should be "culturally and linguistically compatible" (ORR 1992) with refugee communities. In Tulare County they are not.

14. The AFEP goals are: (1) systems workshops for Laotian parents to better understand schools, judiciary, police and social services; (2) parenting skills workshops in intergenerational conflict resolution; (3) mentoring young girls in educational options; and, (4) translators for Laotian women seeking help from Tulare County Mental Health. AFEP activities include weekly women's support groups and translation services at Mental Health, tutoring at-risk children, youth peer support groups, and educating the broader communities about Laotian community needs. The AFEP operates on a variety of county, state and federal grants, and to a lesser degree, with private foundation grants.

15. I found that Visalia Hmong peoples' accounts of cultural traditions and what it meant to them to be Hmong were often contradictory. These alternative ways of being Hmong, which differed most by gender and generation, resonated with Cha and Chagnon's (1993, 25) findings about camp life: "What one is seeing and preserving is not centuries-old traditions but refugee camp realities developed since 1975." They found that "cultural preservation" issues, which maintained hierarchies and kept women out of leadership roles, were antithetical to social change.

# Chapter 14

# Women's Community Activism

## *Exploring the Dynamics of Politicization and Diversity*

Nancy A. Naples

Paula Sands, whose parents were born in Japan, moved to West Harlem when she took a job at a nearby university. The apartment was afford-able, the location was convenient, and, given what she described as her "sheltered" life, she did not readily understand the disadvantages. She became active in her Harlem community when she enrolled her child in an overcrowded public school in the late 1960s. She was appalled by the conditions she found in the school. As someone from the middle class, she was unprepared for the way racism operated within the low-income and predominantly Black and Puerto Rican school district. When she and her husband went to discuss the problems with the principal, she found that:

> The principal was insulting. My husband was disgusted with his attitude and wouldn't go back. It was up to me. The attitudes of the teachers and principals [were appalling]. There was an assumption that minority parents did not give breakfast . . . (it was an excuse for not teaching) and that these children would not go on to college. [In fact,] the issues were not about education [at all].

Paula finally took her daughter out of the school when a seven-year-old child was raped during lunchtime. The teachers explained that they were not responsible for the children during lunch. Her early activism against the racist and irresponsible school district led her into other struggles, against absentee landlords and police harassment, for welfare rights and bilingual education, to increase voter registration of low-income residents, and to expand library services. She emphasized that as a Japanese American, she felt particularly moved to participate in protests against nuclear weapons and nuclear energy.

For the fifteen years that bridged her initial activism and our interview, Paula devoted much of her career and political activism to multicultural education and antiracist work. From her complicated position as both insider and outsider to the Harlem community in which she lived, and as a professionally educated middle-class Japanese American woman struggling alongside predominantly low-income African American and Puerto Rican mothers, Paula developed a complex analysis of how power dynamics and institutional practices in education and other spheres served to reproduce gender, race, and class inequalities. The firm distinction she drew between the dynamics within middle-class neighborhoods and those of poor neighborhoods is captured in the following quote.

> In your average middle-class suburban community you have children, parents, teachers all living in the same community. You all have a stake in making the school good because you're all part of the community; but in the segregated districts the predominant education program is run by an absentee staff who don't live in the community. It's not their community and a perfect example was one of the schools where we had to stop the teachers from parking their cars in the school yard and the children had to play in the street because the teachers wanted to have their cars, because they drove to the community, [the teachers] wanted them protected so they locked them in the school yard. It was a lack of concern for the youngsters and there was no reason for it! There were a lot of issues that came up which constantly pointed up the inability of the staff to recognize the legitimate claims of parents.

While Paula paints a much more coherent picture of school politics in middle-class neighborhoods than is, in fact, the case, she does convey her own complicated sense of community, one that clearly challenges any essentialized notions of "belonging," for she shared neither the race nor the class of those with whom she identified.

Paula's understanding of community is simultaneously geographic and gendered. Paula worked across race and class differences in women-powered struggles that were not defined in gender-specific terms, but in actuality were quite gender-specific. In fighting for educational equity, the women community activists in Harlem during the late 1960s drew upon their social experiences as mothers. They did so in both essentializing and strategic ways. In other words, they described their motivations for political action as a natural extension of their identities as mothers as well as understood that such claims increased their credibility as political actors. As activist mothers (Naples 1992), they taught their children and others in their community about how racism and class oppression worked to limit the opportunities of people of color from low-income neighborhoods. They also modeled for all in their social milieu how to fight against discrimination and oppression. Many felt it their duty as mothers or their mission as Christian women to fight on behalf of their children and their defined racial-ethnic[1] and geographic communities. For a number of years they were successful in wresting control of the school system from insensitive and racist administrators, in helping to hire African American and bilingual teachers, and in creating local school boards that were, at one point in time, community-led and community-controlled. Like Paula, many of the women involved in the movement for community control of schools who I interviewed in the 1980s (for a study of community workers in the War on Poverty) remained active in a variety of local struggles into the 1990s, although the content of their political actions did change along with the growing political conservatism and state disinvestment in their urban neighborhoods (Naples forthcoming a).

### Studying the Diversity of Women's Community Activism

For over a decade I have been exploring the ways in which women from different low-income communities in the United States come to identify and then challenge the relations of power that circumscribe their lives. What contributes to the process of politicization and what strategies are effective for fighting social and economic oppression at the local community level? Why do women of different racial, ethnic, class, cultural, and geographic backgrounds engage in these struggles, and what keeps certain women fighting despite minimal gains or even further devastation of their neighborhoods or towns? I began this work as I left related struggles as a social worker in New York City in 1980. The more personal motivation for this research was to try and understand how the many women with whom I had worked during the 1970s could continue community activism in low-income neighborhoods, often for decades. In this chapter, I explain how I came to understand the complex ways women of different racial, ethnic, class, and regional backgrounds are motivated to participate as community activists in struggles for progressive social change.[2]

In presenting this work, I draw on research with activists in two very different contexts: (1) from community workers in low-income neighborhoods in New York City and Philadelphia who I interviewed in the mid 1980s and mid 1990s,[3] and (2) rural residents in a small town in Iowa where I have been conducting research since 1990.[4] In both the urban and rural contexts, I investigated the ways in which women of different racial, ethnic, and class backgrounds developed their political analyses and engaged in diverse political struggles. My research on women's community activism highlights the complex dynamics of race, class, gender, and local cultural and political-economic context as they form both the grounds for women's politicization and political analyses as well as the structural matrix against which women wage their battles for social justice and economic security. The goal of this research is to explicate these complex relationships and to ground analyses of political action in women's constructions of themselves as women, as members of self-defined racial-ethnic groups and class-based communities, and as agents of their own lives. Space limitation prohibits me from presenting more complete histories of the few women I have chosen to feature in this chapter.[5] However, excerpts from their stories illustrate the power of analyses that begin from the standpoint of women activists.

### Outline of the Chapter

Authors in this collection as well as others who explore the dynamics of women's community-based activism discuss how starting inquiry from the standpoint of diverse women's lives deepens feminist analyses (also see Haywoode 1991). This chapter also illustrates some of the challenges faced in shifting the standpoint of inquiry to the everyday lives of women community activists. Ethnographic investigation of women's political praxis has been especially sensitive to the complex processes that contribute to the politicization of everyday life. This research highlights how racialization processes contour women's political experiences and political action (see, e.g., Morgen 1988). Michael Omi and Howard Winant (1986) argue that the concept of "racialization" accents the fluidity of racial-ethnic formation and allows us to observe changes in racial structures and race relations over time and space. It also helps us go beyond simple reified categories typically used to describe race so that we can focus on shifts in identities as well as the processes through which racial categories are created and maintained. The process of racialization, of course, must also be understood in relationship to shifting class, gender, cultural, and geographic dynamics.[6] Further explication of the relationship between racialization and politicization of everyday life forms the topic of the next section of this chapter.

Feminist identities are also contoured by these processes. How women develop feminist political analyses that differ from dominant perspectives to form what has been termed "oppositional consciousness"[7] is a central question raised in literature on women's political activism (see, e.g., Sandoval 1991). In the next section, I explore this concern with reference to women community activists' relationship to the Women's Movement of the 1970s and to feminism more broadly.

One of the most consistent themes to emerge from feminist analyses of women's political praxis is the significance of constructions of community for women's politicization and social action. However, as I illustrate below, constructions of community are ever shifting social formations that serve to exclude as well as redefine who "belongs" and who can be considered allies in specific struggles. To capture the complex ways women construct and experience community, I return to the concept of "standpoint" and explore the value of a multidimensional understanding of the term for the ethnographic investigation of women's political praxis. I conclude by stressing the significance of the wider political-economic context and highlight the contradictory role of the state as a catalyst for women's community activism.

### Racialization and Politicization of Everyday Life

Elena Calero, the twenty-eight-year-old daughter of Puerto Rican community worker Maria Calero, described in a 1995 interview how her mother's support helped her negotiate the racism she faced as a student in a predominantly white, upper-class private school in New York City:

And then I went to this high school and . . . had a really . . . bad experience and just felt very much like "other" the whole time I was there. . . . [A]nd the fact that I was validated at home [was especially important]. You know, it wasn't like [my mother] would say: "Oh, no, no, no, you're just overreacting!" You know, if I came home and said I heard this terrible joke, or this was said in class, you know, [my mother] would acknowledge that yeah, I was in this basically all-white environment of rich, rich kids and I wasn't going to fit in. So I [was] . . . being raised in a kind of a politicized environment that confirmed my own [experience]. . . . And . . . I think the lesson of being "other" is so profound that, you know, . . . it . . . changes your whole perspective on life and the world. . . . So I really think the fact that I had a politicized home base enabled me to kind of get through it by [becoming a political activist]. . . . Because I became [a major organizer] . . . I tried to organize the few [students of color] in high school, . . . and that was very hard for many of us.

Community activists develop their political sensibilities in community with others and, as Elena illustrates, the process of politicization is influenced by early childhood socialization as well as the social networks in which they circulate as they age. Their socialization and social networks are shaped by their structural positions as women with specific racial-ethnic and class backgrounds as they are embedded in different regional and shifting cultural contexts. How activists come to identify themselves as part of varying communities that shape their "coming of age" and their daily lives is one important key to understanding how and why certain women become aware of the relations of domination that shape their lives and subsequently form a commitment to fight injustice and inequality.

Women community activists are also politicized through specific experiences or struggles that they must first reflect upon before they can take effective action. While self-reflection opens one avenue for discovering how personal problems or discrimination is organized by processes that go beyond particular encounters or experiences, activists are more likely to develop a deeper understanding of these processes in dialogue with others who may be experiencing similar troubles or who have otherwise developed a broadened analysis of specific problems.[8] This interaction between the everyday life experiences of injustice, inequality, and abuse and processes of reflection occurring within localized networks with specific gender, race, and class dynamics opens spaces for oppositional consciousness and activism. The broader cultural, political, and economic environment also forms a powerful material context framing their lives and profoundly shapes how activists define their relationship to specific struggles, what political actions might be effective, and what resources are available. It also structures the very grounds upon which many of their experiences are built as Elena's discussion illustrates.

Paula Sand's narrative also powerfully illuminates the ways that racialization processes position people of different racial and ethnic backgrounds differently, and how class forms an important feature of race formation. Through dialogue and debate, as well as in encounters with racist educators and administrators, Paula began to deepen her understanding of these processes, which in turn fueled her commitment to join in struggles against racism and other forms of oppression (also see Stern, chapter 4 in this volume). However, while Paula and most of the community workers I interviewed in the mid-1980s offered careful gendered analyses of specific struggles in which they were engaged, few women had worked directly with organizations most identified with the Women's Movement of the 1970s (see Naples forthcoming a).

## Toward Oppositional Class-Conscious and Multiracial Feminist Praxis

Elena's mother, Maria, was employed as a community worker in New York City when I interviewed her in 1984. She was especially articulate about the tensions between Women's Movement activists and women of color who were participating in community-based struggles in the 1970s. She explained:

> I remember . . . one day [in 1970] somebody asking me to an interview at WBAI [a public radio station in New York City] and being terrified that this lady was going to ask me the inevitable question, "Are you a feminist?" Which eventually she did, and I had to—a moment of consciousness for me—I had to say, "Yes." But I was scared to death. And that was the first time I publicly said it, "Yes." I was scared that now I was going to go back to the Lower East Side [of Manhattan] and I was going to be banned from the Hispanic community. But of course I'm a feminist! The Black women in that program were pretty upset that she broached the question and they didn't want the question to be asked.

Maria and other Latinas who were active in struggles to protect and improve the lives of family and neighbors in the Lower East Side during the early 1970s were aware of the gender inequalities within their community. They developed a feminist consciousness through their organizing work. Yet, because of the saliency of race and class in their analyses, their feminism differed from that defined by those who were identified with the dominant Women's Movement. They also feared that their identification as feminists would undermine their credibility within the Latino community. Fortunately, much has changed in both arenas: as a result of the critiques by women of color and working-class women, "Women's Movement" activists have developed deeper sensitivity to the multiplicity of women's lives and, again due to the work of women of color in their own racial-ethnic communities, African American women and Latina activists now play a more visible role in prominent community institutions. New York City community worker Carlotta Mendez, interviewed in 1995, noted the shift within the Puerto Rican community:

> I may have been seen as an oddball in the '60s or '70s when I began to relate to the Women's Movement as a Puerto Rican woman, but in the 1990s it's not strange. We have a new generation of women who also [are] feminists . . . and the guys themselves have been educated. So it's not that I have an easy life if I'm doing the feminist bit for the Puerto Rican community but certainly it's not where it was twenty or thirty years ago.

Many of the Latinas interested in building a feminist movement did not find a site for their concerns within the existing framework of the Women's Movement of the 1970s. As a consequence of their dissatisfaction with the white Women's Movement, Maria Calero and Carlotta Mendez played important roles in the creation of the National Conference of Puerto Rican Women, the National Council of Puerto Rican Women, National Puerto Rican Women's Caucus, and the National Latina Caucus, among other organizations and networks.

As Maria and Carlotta both emphasized, constructions of feminist identities are profoundly influenced by the dynamics of race and class. Maxine Baca Zinn and Bonnie Thornton Dill (1996, 323–324) suggest the designation of "multiracial feminism" to capture approaches that locate both men and women "in multiple systems of domination." They trace the development of "multiracial feminism" to the theoretical work of: "African Americans, Latinas, Asian Americans, Native Americans, women whose analyses are shaped by their unique perspectives as 'outsiders within'—intellectuals whose social locations provide them with a particular perspective on self and society" (p. 324). Multiracial feminists, they argue, treat race "as a basic social division, a structure of power, a focus of political struggle, and hence a fundamental force in shaping women's and men's lives" (p. 324). Yet, despite their intent, the term "multiracial feminism" does not explicitly incorporate the dimension of class—although in reviewing the relevant literature, it is clear that most of the authors within this designated tradition do, in fact, take class as a fundamental material condition through which they examine the multiracial diversity of women's experiences. Furthermore, the term is an academic product, rather than a product of some broad-based political struggle. This is not to say that the struggle within Women's Studies to create more inclusive feminisms is not a highly charged political enterprise; in fact, that struggle is waged within a limited community that itself often lacks diversity, especially in class and race terms. How are we to broaden our analysis of feminisms if many women do not see themselves in the category, and if the terms we use are not taken up in political practice? I see a partial strategy in exploring how different women construct and experience community.

### Shifting & Sifting Sands of Community

In order to understand how women of different race and class backgrounds develop oppositional consciousness or an awareness of the dynamic relations of ruling that shape their lives in different contexts, and how the processes of political engagement transform their political analyses, we must learn how women construct and experience community[9]—that is, the localized context (and I do not mean the term only in the geographic sense) in which politicization and political action takes place—and how this localized context is itself a product of external negotiations.[10]

How community activists resist externally imposed constructions of community as well as draw upon them as resources is influenced by the dynamic relationship between the local context and the broader political economy, and by their own relationship to, and constructions of, community. Anna Ortega, a Mexican American community worker from Midtown, Iowa, interviewed in 1993, offered the following analysis of such external pressures:

> But a lot of the Americans think that because we're brown every-
> body comes from Mexico and it's not like that, you know. Because
> you can be Mexican, Hispanic, and you can come from Texas.
> You can come from Chicago. . . . You can be born and raised in
> California. . . . [They think]: "They're from Mexico. They're all
> illegals."

Anna Ortega is a U.S. citizen in her thirties who moved from Laredo
with her family for a job in the newly expanded food-processing plant in
rural Iowa. Anna distinguished herself from her white North European
American neighbors who she defined as "Americans." Racialization
processes create a division between "real Americans" (read: white European Americans) and other Americans. These divisions are sustained by
ideological constructions as well as material practices and institutional
arrangements. Those who do not fit the restricted definition of "American" feel outside the category despite their legal status as citizens.

The power of racialization processes to maintain a boundary between
constructed racial-ethnic groups, to push people with different histories
into one identifiable and controllable group, is part of our painful history. The enslavement of African peoples from different regions of
Africa with different languages and traditions, and the creation of the
category of "Indians" from the many diverse indigenous peoples in
North America, were accomplished first by force and then by denying
them their languages, religions, and cultural traditions. Anna Ortega's
narrative also illustrates how the process of placing externally defined
boundaries around peoples from different nations, with different languages, and different cultural backgrounds, continues as a practice of
social control in the U.S. today. It also underscores the care with which
community activists must proceed in working with people who do not
define themselves as part of a singular "community." All constructions of
community are political constructions no matter who defines the
boundaries.

The Mexicans and Mexican Americans who moved to Midtown, Iowa,
came with very different histories, and most did not see themselves as
part of the same "community." As Margarita Muñoz, the community
organizer hired by a statewide nonprofit organization in Des Moines,
tried to organize Latinos in Midtown to fight against police harassment
and unfair employment practices, she quickly discovered a major schism
between those born in Mexico and those born in the U.S. She also
found major differences between those who had lived in larger cities in

the U.S. and those whose experiences were shaped by small-town or rural life. For many women, gender expectations about woman's role in the home frequently interfered with their participation in the organizing efforts regardless of their backgrounds. After nine months, the initial organizing efforts had failed to produce any collective action that effectively involved Latino residents from the diverse "communities." The mobility of the Latino residents that resulted from the police harassment and the difficult working conditions further undermined the organizing efforts. Living and working far from Midtown and with commitments to organize in other communities, Margarita had difficulty keeping the organizing effort alive, especially when local activists moved away or were dealing with personal crises.

Missing in small, rural Iowa was the extended network of women with longer-term residency in the town who could communicate with new immigrants and migrants and integrate them into the "community," as I had found in my urban-based research. Acting through their gendered roles as mothers, as volunteers for the church, and as community caretakers, the urban community workers strengthened their kinship and friendship networks to form and sustain that sense of political community needed for effective community action.[11]

As case studies of women's community-based activism demonstrate, community is created in and through struggles against violence and for social justice and economic security, as well as through casual interactions with people who share some aspects of our daily lives, and by external pressures such as those identified by Anna Ortega. As a dynamic process, the social construction of community offers the possibility for redefinition of boundaries, for broadened constituencies, and for seemingly unlikely alliances. Such fluidity renders any single definition or experience of community suspect.

Women of color often find themselves on the borders of multiple communities—each claiming their allegiance and each with different definitions of what political actions are correct and which demonstrate betrayal. However, boundaries drawn around particular communities are also fluid constructions that shift with differing political, social, and economic pressures. Raids in Midtown, Iowa, by the INS repositioned many of the Mexican and Mexican American residents as community "insiders" to white residents who did not approve of the INS tactics and deportations of their neighbors and coworkers. Residents defined the tactics used by the INS (for example, forcefully picking up people outside their workplaces and homes, immediately removing them to the regional INS office in Omaha with no opportunity to arrange for their children's care or for funds to return to Iowa if released) as unnecessarily harsh. These actions repositioned INS workers as "outsiders" to the "community" and increased many white residents' sympathies for their Latino neighbors and co-workers (see Naples 1996).

For example, Anglo resident Bernice Poster, who was born in the area and plays an informal community work role in Midtown, Iowa, described how her consciousness shifted when she tried to help a young Mexican man who was unfairly arrested and deported after he recovered from an accident. She explained:

> I used to think that they [INS] were the good guys, that they were doing a good job. But after what I've been through and seen [in trying to help a young Latino] I think they're all a bunch of rats. I've seen how they treat the Mexicans and no one should be treated like that. They're like the Gestapo.

While the INS officials were "strangers" to the residents in Midtown, Iowa, the local police lived in the town. However, they too were redefined by many white residents as outsiders as a result of their harassment of Latino residents—behavior that many felt violated "community values."

Community activists also participate in constructing "community values" in ways that serve to include as well as exclude. For example, few of the urban community activists I interviewed included gays and lesbians in their definition of community. Angela Garcia, a Puerto Rican community worker from Harlem, emphasized:

> The issue of gay rights is not an issue in our community. It happens, it's there, and it gets taken care of. But it doesn't become a public issue—which is the problem that many of us have [as practicing Catholics.]

In defining gay rights outside her community's values, Angela rendered gay and lesbian Puerto Ricans outside her political circle. She also narrowly defined who she felt were legitimate members of her "community," thus inhibiting coalition-building with potential allies. I explore how women construct community and define themselves in relation to others in their social context with reference to the notions of "standpoint" and "positionality." It is to these interrelated concepts that I now turn.

## Relating Standpoint, Positionality, and Women's Community Activism

Ann Robinson, an African American community worker from New York City who I interviewed in 1984, related a key experience that helped fuel her community activism. She recalled a very cold winter when many of the young babies living in her tenement became ill due to lack of heat in their building. When the children did not receive adequate medical attention from the city-run hospital, several died. Anna exclaimed:

> What had happened is wrong! All the little babies . . . born that year died that winter in those houses, except one little boy. And we took the babies to Metropolitan Hospital, and they bathed the babies in alcohol and gave them some aspirin and told us to take them home. And I started fighting them, the Health Department, and others, to get the heat in the house, and other things like that. I knew that life didn't have to be like that. There's no reason that my children or anybody else's had to live like that. So when my kids started school I tried to organize the parents.

Women of color like Ann Robinson and Paula Sands who parent in low-income neighborhoods confront the manifestations of racism and class oppression in their everyday lives. For activist mothers, struggles on behalf of their children's education, health, and safety often require taking up political positions and speaking out in a variety of forums. White women activists in the anti-toxic waste movement also describe their motivation to participate through their identities and experiences as mothers trying to protect their children (see Krauss, chapter five in this volume). Taking such political actions is not a natural extension of these experiences, but does form a consistent feature of the stories told by activists across different racial-ethnic communities (see Naples 1991a, 1992). Women's class, race, ethnicity, country of origin, sexuality, and geographic location intersect to produce a vantage point, a location from which women experience different social problems in different ways (see, e.g., Crenshaw 1991b).

Feminist theorists interested in exploring the intersections of gender, race, ethnicity, class, and other social-structural aspects of social life have generated a diverse set of theories categorized under the rubric of "feminist standpoint epistemology."[12] Standpoint epistemology represents a crucial theoretical move in feminist theory, one that brings the modernist project of feminism up against the postmodern critiques of subjectivity and identity politics.[13] Yet such a complicated epistemological move leaves many contradictory tensions especially for those of us engaged in feminist activist research. Postmodern critics charge that by equating "women's ways of knowing" (Belenky et al., 1986) with their social identities, feminist standpoint theorists fail to articulate how identities are ongoing and unstable achievements. For example, feminists scholars who center the role of mothering practices in generating different political knowledges as Sara Ruddick (1989) does in her work on "maternal thinking" have been criticized for equating such gendered differences with an essentialized female identity (also see Giligan 1982). Further, as highlighted by Nancy Fraser and Linda Nicholson (1990) and Judith Butler (1992) among others, postmodern critiques of standpoint methodologies also raise important questions regarding the possibility of developing knowledges for an emancipatory politics for women.[14]

While postmodern critiques pose challenges from outside the frame, standpoint theories contain within them further challenges, tensions, and contradictions. To begin with, little agreement exists on how we might define and locate a standpoint. A number of authors in this volume (Wittner, Stall, Krauss, Kendrick, Park, Seitz, Howe, Pardo) make reference to feminist standpoint theories or use the term when explaining how women's social identities or social locations—as women, as mothers, as low-income people, as immigrants, as racial-ethnic minorities, as "insiders" among other identities—provided particular vantage points from which to experience and then begin to understand how relations of power contour their everyday lives. While some of the authors use the term to refer to particular individuals' experiences and vantage points, others like Stern and Krauss (in this volume) emphasize that standpoints are achieved in critical dialogue among those sharing similar experiences (also see Hartsock, 1987). These two approaches to standpoint analysis (standpoint defined as embodied in the social identities of particular actors and standpoint understood through critical conversations among "community" members) are often criticized by postmodern theorists who argue that individual identities and constructions of community are so fluid and shifting that any "knowledge" gained from these vantage points is too partial and fleeting to be "trusted" for feminist analyses. Viewing intersections of gender, class, race, and ethnicity as shifting and fleeting moments of sociality shakes up any belief in the permanence of knowledge generated from one social location.[15] Even more troubling is the way in which racialization processes mask dimensions of whiteness that contour standpoints however we define them.

One corrective to these dilemmas is found in Dorothy Smith's "everyday world" approach which views standpoint as a site of inquiry rather than property of individual "knowers." Her approach to standpoint analysis offers a methodological strategy for understanding "the social relations and organization pervading her [woman's] world but invisible in it" (Smith 1992, 91). Smith's approach is illustrated in Judith Wittner's chapter in which she explores how battered women use the court in ways not visible to those working inside the court system, including feminist advocates (also see Cambell and Manicom 1995).

However, rather than view standpoint from one angle, I find all three approaches to standpoint analysis (as embodied in social identites, as constructed in community, and as a site of inquiry) central to investigation of women's political praxis. For example, the centrality of mothering experiences for many community activists reveals the difficulty in separating standpoint as embodied in ones race, class, or gender identities from one grounded in particular communities from one defined as the site of inquiry (see Smith, 1987a). Community activists who were also mothers often characterized their process of politicization through caring for their children's needs. Yet the political actions and political analyses they developed in struggle and in dialogue with other community activists reshaped their gendered identities; in these cases, standpoints are both embodied and constructed in community. As they redefined their gendered expectations, some activists met with resistance from their husbands who did not relish their wives' demands for equality in the home or claims to a more public role. In some instances, marriages did not survive these struggles. By starting inquiry from the standpoint of women community activists, we are also, by necessity, exploring the ways in which gendered, class, and racialized social relations are put together, and how they organize women's everyday lives, as Smith (1987a) recommends.

In some ways, this multidimensional approach to standpoint has much in common with analyses of some postmodern feminists who draw upon the concept of "positionality" to describe:

> the subject as nonessentialized and emergent from a historical experience . . . [to] say at one and the same time that gender is not natural, biological, universal, ahistorical, or essential and yet still

claim that gender is relevant because we are taking gender as a position from which to act politically (Alcoff 1988, 433).

However, as analyses of women's community activism demonstrate, how women use gender as "a position from which to act politically" varies by race, ethnicity, class, sexuality, and region, among other dynamics that must be further contextualized and understood as relational, contested and changing over time. In this regard, as Mary Pardo (in this volume) reveals, what may appear "natural" at one point in time (e.g, that men should be placed in leadership roles when women are doing most of the day-to-day community work) can change as women redefine their gendered expectations.

As the above discussion of Latinos in Midtown, Iowa, highlights, differences exist within racial-ethnic groups as well as between them. African American women or Latinas are themselves diverse groups containing within them individuals who hold divergent perspectives and utilize disparate political practices as a consequence of differing class positions, or sexual orientations, or regional locations, among other factors (see, for example, E. F. White 1990). Remaining sensitive to the complexity of such differences, we can revisit Sara Ruddick's analysis of "maternal thinking as a feminist standpoint" (Ruddick 1989) not as a general and unchanging set of knowledges, but as a "place to begin" to explore how women's everyday life is "put together" (Smith 1992, 88). However, Ruddick's analysis remains bounded by a limited definition of family-based work. While she demonstrates that "maternal practice" influences women's disproportionate support for a "politics of peace," she neglects class, racial, ethnic, historic, and regional dimensions of social experience that also shape "maternal practice" and may contribute to different forms of political activism (also see Morgen and Bookman 1988b). The community workers whose lives were shaped by experiences of racism, sexism, and poverty learned to mother as activists fighting in their homes and communities against the debilitating and demoralizing effects of oppression. When we limit our analysis of mothering practices to those activities that occur within the confines of a nuclear family, we miss the material conditions that contribute to differing family forms, as well as the social construction of gender, mothering, and politics.

## Highlighting Economic and Political Context

The shifting conceptualizations of standpoint and positionality high-light the agency of the community activists whose experiences form the basis for my analysis. Inquiries from their standpoints also reveal hidden dimensions of the powerful political-economic forces that are structuring the grounds upon which they must organize their community-based responses. Economic restructuring and political conservatism are creating new crises in poor neighborhoods and for immigrant groups, people of color, and working-class residents in many different regions of this country. While these forces are not always evident to the activists as they fight specific campaigns at the local level, the process of analyzing such actions reveals how these sometimes global structural dimensions are manifest in the specific struggles against racism, homophobia, toxic waste, and wife abuse, and for living wages, quality education, safe housing, and community control. And, as emphasized by the many community activists who I have worked with and interviewed it is vital to keep the struggles as well as the analyses alive.

Many of these struggles take place in response to actions or inactions of government agencies and officials of the state, broadly defined. Official policies or informal and discriminatory practices of public school personnel, government officials, police, agents from the INS, public health care workers, social service staff, etc., are often catalysts for women's politicization and resistance strategies. Since the organization of the state and the implementation of state policies are shaped by inequities based on race, ethnicity, class, and region, women's experiences with the state also varies dramatically. As Aida Hurtado (1989) points out, "by the time women of color reach adulthood . . . [they] have developed informal political skills to deal with State intervention" (quoted in Sandoval 1991, 14). These skills are sharpened through interactions with state bureaucrats and other representatives of the state, as well as by racist and sexist constructions of immigrants, the poor, single mothers, welfare recipients, adolescent parents, and other state-targeted categories.

Analysis of women's community activism also reveals how the state not only supports the reproduction of gender, racial-ethnic, and class inequality, but also provides avenues through which these patterns can be challenged (also see Naples 1991a). The contradictory role of the state as both a catalyst for, and site of, women's politization forms another significant theme in research on women community activism.

For example, during the War on Poverty, state-funded community action agencies hired low income residents like Maria Calero, Carlotta Mendez, and Ann Robinson to assess community needs and provide diverse services to their neighbors. The state's sponsorship of indigenous community work affirmed the ongoing community work of African American women and Latinas from low-income urban neighborhoods. The community action agencies also served as sites in which other low-income residents could learn how to become effective community activists. These community-based organizations acted as a conduit for funds used to organize community residents more broadly, and became places where the community activists could wage campaigns against the state for better services and additional resources. These campaigns helped legitimate demands for decent housing, welfare rights, quality education, and safe and environmentally-sound neighborhoods. While the political activities of community workers were quickly circumscribed by funding cutbacks and bureaucratic mandates, experiences in community organizing and the political analyses developed by the community workers in the course of their employment in these organizations continue to benefit the women personally, as well as the low-income neighborhoods more generally.

## Summary and Discussion

Women are politicized and drawn into local political battles in a myriad of ways that reflect a wide diversity of personal and political concerns as well as varying constructions of community and social identities. Regional political economy and cultural practices woven in and through racial-ethnic and class formations also structure how women engage in community activism and what successes they achieve. Exploration of how women from different racial-ethnic, class, cultural, and regional backgrounds confront different constellations of power that differentially shapes their political consciousness and oppositional political practice enriches feminist scholarship. However, emphasis on differences among women could render invisible the processes by which relations of domination constitute these differences (see Gordon 1991b). Feminist standpoint analyses must confront the dilemma of how to remain sensitive to the diversity of women's experiences while acknowledging some "common differences" (Joseph and Lewis 1981). Without such comparative standpoint strategies, analysis of women's community activism might produce only isolated accounts of fleeting moments of resistance.

The literature on populist struggles stresses the limits of community-based action to transcend local boundaries and form larger political movements.[16] The rightward shift in the political climate, the decline in union membership and union-protected employment, and the growth in poverty, unemployment, and underemployment that accompany economic restructuring in this country pose further challenges to any efforts designed to link local struggles with more broad-based social movements. With the ascension of anti-poor and anti-immigrant political discourse and a decline in the state's support for economically poor urban and rural areas in the U.S., activists in poor communities must negotiate increased demands for legal aid and direct services while also finding alternative funding to replace the state's financial support for vital community organizations.

Many activists who I interviewed in the mid-1990s in both urban and rural contexts explained that they had, by necessity, shifted many of their efforts from critical political organizing to campaigns for basic survival. By 1996, Margarita Muñoz devoted most of her time and energy to responding to the increasing number of INS raids in small Iowa towns and finding legal assistance for non-English-speaking immigrant workers and their families. Her attention to more sustained community-based organizing efforts had diminished in the short time frame of one year that spanned her paid community work in Iowa. New York City activists reported that their involvement in the provision of food banks and legal services expanded between the mid-1980s and mid-1990s, often displacing political organizing efforts.[17] As health care services and housing assistance declined, these workers faced further pressures to address basic survival needs of the poor.

Furthermore, as immigrants and poor women are attacked both ideologically and materially in political discourse and social policy, they are, not surprisingly, discouraged from participation in community action. With the restructuring of citizenship enacted through contemporary immigration and welfare legislation and a narrowing in the ways in which people can make claims on the state for social justice and economic support, activists in low-income communities are also finding it more difficult to frame political actions in ways that effectively challenge the anti-state rhetoric. To end on such a note may detract from recognition of the continued significance of women's activism for the survival of many residing in low-income communities across the U.S. However, it is also a reminder that the struggle against economic inequality and social injustice must be fought on many levels.

Women's community activism does provide necessary building blocks from which to generate more broad-based movements for social change, as was evident during the Civil Rights Movement. Lessons learned in the process of fighting against state disinvestment; violence against women; homophobia; racial, ethnic, and gender discrimination; and class oppression can fuel broader movements for social change. The challenge is to provide for the continuity of these lessons over time, especially during periods of conservative backlash. I remain convinced that progressive social change requires envisioning a "just society" as well as drawing upon contemporary political practices based on participatory democracy, antiracism, and deep understanding of, as well as respect for, our many differences. I believe that women community activists from diverse racial, ethnic, class, and regional backgrounds have much to teach us about achieving such a vision.

## Notes

1. Following Glenn (1991) and Amott and Matthaei (1991), I use the term "race-ethnicity" to avoid the biological determinism associated with the concept "*race*" and to highlight the ways in which race and ethnicity intertwine in processes of "racialization" (Omi and Winant 1986).

2. While I do not examine the political engagement of women who participate in struggles to reinscribe racial, gender, and class inequality, the framework I offer might also be useful in exploring women's political participation more generally (see for example Ginsburg 1988; Klatch 1992; McCourt 1977). For example, Kathleen Blee (1996) explores the process by which women become racists and actively participate in Ku Klux Klan and Neo-Nazi groups. Factors that prove important included many of those that seem to motivate antiracist activists; namely a combination of socialization, community context, and specific "transformative" experiences defined through "racial" lenses. Blee explains:

   > As converts to racial activism, these women construct their stories of their lives as narratives of passage from racial naïveté to racist enlightenment. In such conversion stories, the more mundane details of actual recruitment to racist groups fall to the wayside. [However, s]uch racial 'awareness' is more often a *consequence* of association with members of racist groups than a *cause* motivating participation" [emphasis in original].

   Here Blee points out the central importance of racist ideological framing as woven through specific social locations and constructions of community. Blee's analysis includes some significant parallels with analyses of women's political activism more generally. As I have found in my interviews with community workers in rural and urban settings, once the process of politicization took place, or when the activists became aware of the patterns of oppression, they felt compelled to act. They could not remain "aware" and inactive. Racist activists interviewed by Blee also describe their active political engagement in racist groups as a logical extension of their becoming "aware" of racial dynamics. However, once motivated to participate, Blee reports, women who join racist groups "selectively disregard aspects of the ideologies and agendas of racial groups that are at variance with their personal goals or allegiances" (p. 693). While antiracist activists I interviewed often defined their participation as both personally empowering and politically beneficial to their communities, racist activists expressed a sense of "resignation" and lack of agency. Blee explains that "the declarations of resignation convey both hopelessness in the face of outside social or political forces and powerlessness to reconcile the contradiction between what they see as lofty movement goals of white, Aryan supremacy and the actual experiences of white, Aryan women within the racist movement" (p. 697).

3. In the first study (see Naples 1991a, 1993), I gathered oral histories from women who were employed by the community action programs funded during the War on Poverty in order to examine their motivation for community work, the political analyses and political strategies they developed over time, and the ways in which the changing political economy influenced their work. I utilized the "oral narratives" to explore the experiences of community workers employed in the late 1960s and early 1970s by the community action programs funded by the Economic Opportunity Act of 1964, and who remained in related employment in the mid 1980s. Of the sixty-four activists interviewed, forty-two were living in low income neighborhoods when they were hired as community workers in community action programs; twenty-two were non-residents. Seventeen of the sixty-four community workers interviewed in the mid-1980s were reinterviewed in 1995 when I also interviewed three of the community activists' daughters and four city, state and federal officials responsible for designing and overseeing CAPs.

4. In the second study (see Naples 1994, 1996), I explored the social restructuring of gender, race, and class that occurs alongside economic restructuring, and examined ways in which community workers (broadly defined) serve to help build alliances or broaden the gap between the white, European American residents and the Mexican and Mexican American newcomers in Midtown, Iowa, (the pseudonym for a small town in southwest Iowa with a population of approximately 1250). Until the early 1990s Midtown, Iowa, was almost exclusively comprised of white European Ameri-

cans. The town has experienced a growth in the number of Mexican and Mexican American residents since 1990, when a food-processing plant expanded and the company began recruiting workers from several towns in Mexico and later Laredo, Texas, among other locations in the U.S. By 1996, Latinos comprised almost over ten percent of the town's population.

5. I illustrate my analysis with oral narratives gathered from the following activists who I have interviewed between 1984 and 1996. All names used here are pseudonyms. They are listed in order of appearance in the chapter.

Paula Sands, Japanese American, age 47 in 1984, West Harlem, New York

Elena Calero, Puerto Rican/Anglo, age 28 in 1995, Boston, Massachusetts

Maria Calero, Puerto Rican, age 46 in 1984, Lower East Side of Manhattan, New York

Carlotta Mendez, Puerto Rican, age 58 in 1984, Manhattan, New York

Anna Ortego, Mexican American, age 38 in 1993, Midtown, Iowa

Margarita Muñoz, Mexican, age 32 in 1996, Des Moines, Iowa

Bernice Poster, Anglo-American, age 40 in 1993, Midtown, Iowa

Ann Robinson, African American, age 55 in 1984, East Harlem, New York

Josephine Carson, African American, age 51 in 1985, East Harlem, New York

6. See, e.g., Mohanty, Russo and Torres 1991; Rocheleau, Thomas-Slayter, and Wangari 1996.

7. Drawing upon Antonio Gramsci (1971), Aldon Morris (1992, 363) contrasts "oppositional consciousness" with "hegemonic consciousness" (or "the ideas of the ruling class") as follows:

> A crucial feature of hegemonic consciousness is that it always presents itself as a set of values and beliefs that serve the general welfare. . . . Its organizational expression enables it to wrap itself in institutional garments bearing labels proclaiming its universality.
>
> In contrast, oppositional consciousness is that set of insurgent ideas and beliefs constructed and developed by an oppressed group for the purposes of guiding its struggle to undermine, reform, or overthrow a system of domination. . . . [O]ppositional consciousness usually does not claim to represent the general interests of a society but only those of the oppressed group seeking to overthrow the system of domination perceived to be responsible for its oppression.

The power of "oppositional consciousness" lies in its ability "to strip away the garments of universality from hegemonic consciousness, revealing its essentialist characteristics" (p. 370).

8. This process is similar to that which occurred in consciousness-raising groups utilized within the Women's Movement of the 1970s to break down isolation, shift the site of knowledge creation, and help build a community of resistance (Peattie and Rein 1983). Consciousness-raising techniques drew from "the Chinese revolutionary practice of 'speaking bitterness' in which peasants began to reject the inevitability of their predicaments" through collective discussions about their experiences (Stern 1994, 512; also see Mitchell 1971). Freire (1985) discusses a similar process in his conceptualization of "conscientization," a process by which individuals become aware of how systems of domination structure their lives. Also see Morris 1992.

9. See, e.g., Haywoode 1991; Martin and Mohanty 1986; hooks 1990; Weiss and Friedman 1995.

10. In fact, advances in computer and communication technology have contributed to a new mode of organizing that does not require face-to-face interaction. For example, Elizabeth Ribet, a graduate student member of the National Women's Studies Association (NWSA) helped organize a protest against the organization's decision to co-sponsor a 1996 conference on girls with a mental-health facility that, she and others claimed, mistreated girls who were patients in this facility. Through the internet, she helped generate testimony from girls who had been locked up in the institution and put pressure on NWSA to, at the very least, include girls in any future decision making that related directly to them.

11. Rurality need not connote the absence of a strong network of women activists, as Virginia Seitz's study (in this volume) of the "Daughters of Mother Jones" demonstrates.

12. See especially Hartsock 1983; Harding 1986; Smith 1987, 1990; Collins 1990, 1991.

13. See Fraser and Nicholson 1990; Hennessy 1993.

14. Also see Flax 1990; Hennessy 1993; Nicholson and Seidman 1995.

15. Also see Spivack 1987; Haraway 1988; Mohanty 1991b.

16. See Kling and Posner 1990a; Ritchie 1990; R. Fisher 1994.

17. However, as one food advocate pointed out, her understanding of the specific needs of the poor increased with the expansion of the service component of her organization. She believed that the knowledge gained through direct service to poor New Yorkers enhanced her political advocacy on their behalf.

# References

Abbott, Sidney, and Barbara Love. 1972. *Sappho Was a Right-on Woman: A Liberated View of Lesbianism.* New York, NY: Stein & Day.

Abraham, Margaret. 1995. "Ethnicity, Gender, and Marital Violence: South Asian Women's Organizations in the United States." *Gender & Society* 9:450–468.

Abramovitz, Mimi. 1988. *Regulating the Lives of Women: Social Welfare Policy from Colonial Times to the Present.* Boston, MA: South End Press.

Ackelsberg, Martha. 1988. "Communities, Resistance and Women's Activism: Some Implications for a Democratic Polity." Pp. 297–313 in *Women and the Politics of Empowerment,* edited by Ann Bookman and Sandra Morgen. Philadelphia, PA: Temple University Press.

Acuna, Rodolfo F. 1984. *Community Under Siege: A Chronicle of Chicanos East of the Los Angeles River: 1945–1975.* Los Angeles: Chicano Studies Research Center Publications.

Aguilar-San Juan, Karen ed. 1994. *The State of Asian American Activism and Resistance in the 1990's.* Boston, MA: South End Press.

Alarcon, Norma. 1990. "The Theoretical Subject(s) of *This Bridge Called My Back* and Anglo-American Feminism." Pp. 356–369 in *Making Face, Making Soul— Haciendo Caras: Creative and Critical Perspectives by Women of Color,* edited by Gloria Anzaldúa. San Francisco, CA: Aunt Lute.

Albrecht, Lisa, and Rose M. Brewer. 1990a. "Bridges of Power: Women's Multicultural Alliances for Social Change." Pp. 2–22 in *Bridges of Power: Women's Multicultural Alliances,* edited by Lisa Albrecht and Rose Brewer. Philadelphia, PA: New Society Publishers.

Albrecht, Lisa, and Rose M. Brewer, eds. 1990b. *Bridges of Power: Women's Multicultural Alliances.* Philadelphia, PA: New Society Publishers.

Alcoff, Linda. 1988. "Cultural Feminism versus Post-Structuralism: The Identity Crisis in Feminist Theory." *Signs: Journal of Women in Culture and Society* 13(3):405–436.

Alcoff, Linda, and Laura Gray. 1993. "Survivor Discourse: Transgression or Recuperation?" *Signs: Journal of Women in Culture and Society* 18(2): 260–290.

Alexander, M. Jacqui, and Chandra Talpade Mohanty. 1997. "Introduction: Genealogies, Legacies, Movements." Pp. xiii–xlii in *Feminist Genealogies, Colonial Legacies, Democratic Futures,* edited by M. Jacqui Alexander and Chandra Talpade Mohanty. New York, NY: Routledge.

Allen, Paula Gunn. 1986. *The Sacred Hoop: Recovering the Feminine in American Indian Traditions.* Boston, MA: Beacon Press.

Amott, Teresa L., and Julie A. Matthaei. 1991. *Race, Gender & Work: A Multicultural Economic History of Women in the United States.* Boston, MA: South End Press.

Anzaldúa, Gloria. 1981. "La Prieta." Pp. 198–209 in *This Bridge Called My Back:*

*Writings by Radical Women of Color*, edited by Cherríe Moraga and Gloria Anzaldúa. Watertown, MA: Persephone Press.

Anzaldúa, Gloria. 1987 *Borderlands/La Frontera: The New Mestiza*. San Francisco, CA: Spinsters/Aunt Lute.

Anzaldúa, Gloria. 1990a. "Bridge, Drawbridge, Sandbar or Island: Lesbians-of-Color *Hacienda Alianzas*." Pp. 216-233 in *Bridges of Power: Women's Multicultural Alliances*, edited by Lisa Albrecht and Rose Brewer. Philadelphia, PA: New Society Publishers.

Anzaldúa, Gloria, ed. 1990b. *Making Face, Making Soul—Haciendo Caras: Creative and Critical Perspectives by Women of Color*. San Francisco, CA: Aunt Lute.

Apple, Michael W. 1982. "Education and Cultural Reproduction." Pp. 503-541 in *The Public School Monopoly*, edited by Robert B. Everhart. Cambridge, MA: Ballinger.

Aptheker, Bettina. 1989. *Tapestries of Life: Women's Work Women's Consciousness, and the Meaning of Daily Experience*. Amherst, MA: University of Massachusetts Press.

Arygris, Chris, and Donald Schön. 1991. "Participatory Action Research and Action Science Compared: A Commentary." Pp. 85-96 in *Participatory Action Research*, edited by William Foote Whyte. Newbury Park, CA: Sage.

Atkinson, Ti-Grace. 1973. "Lesbianism and Feminism." Pp. 11-14 in *Amazon Expedition: A Lesbian Feminist Anthology*, edited by Phyllis Birkby et al. New York, NY: Times Change Press.

Barnett, Ola, and Alyce La Violette. 1993. *It Could Happen To Anyone: Why Battered Women Stay*. Newbury Park, CA: Sage.

Barney, George. 1961. *The Meo of Xieng Khouang Province*. Minneapolis, MN: University of Minnesota Press.

Bart, Pauline B. 1993. "Protean Woman: The Liquidity of Female Sexuality and the Tenaciousness of Lesbian Identity." Pp. 246-252 in *Heterosexuality: A Feminism and Psychology Reader*, edited by Sue Wilkinson and Celia Kitzinger. London: Sage.

Bays, Sharon. 1994a. *Cultural Politics and Identity Formation In A San Joaquin Valley Hmong Community*. Ph.D. dissertation. UCLA.

Bays, Sharon. 1994b. "Hmong GAIN Protest Justified." *The Fresno Bee* 5/21, B7.

Bays, Sharon. 1995. "'A Bone to Gnaw On...': Workfare, Racism and Hmong Insurgency In Central California." Paper presented at the Hmong National Education Conference in St. Paul, Minnesota, April 6-8.

Beck, Evelyn Torton. 1980. *Nice Jewish Girls: A Lesbian Anthology*. Watertown, MA: Persephone Press.

Bell, Diane. 1993. "Introduction 1." Pp. 28-43 in *Gendered Fields: Women, Men and Ethnography*, edited by Diane Bell, Pat Caplan, and Wazir Jahan Karim. London: Routledge.

Bell, Diane, Pat Caplan, Wazir Jahan Karim, eds. 1993. *Gendered Fields: Women, Men and Ethnography*. London: Routledge.

Bell, Vikki. 1993. *Interrogating Incest: Feminism, Foucault and the Law.* London: Routledge.

Beneria, Lourdes, and Shelly Feldman, eds. 1992. *Unequal Burden: Economic Crises, Persistent Poverty, and Women's Work.* Boulder, CO: Westview Press.

Benmayor, Rina. 1991. "Testimony, Action Research, and Empowerment: Puerto Rican Women and Popular Education." Pp. 159–174 in *Women's Words: The Feminist Practice of Oral History,* edited Sherna B. Gluck and Daphne Patai. New York, NY: Routledge.

Bertaux, Daniel, and Martin Kohli. 1984. "The Life Story Approach: A Continental View." *Annual Review of Sociology* 10:215–37.

Birch, Eugenie L., ed. 1985. *The Unsheltered Woman: Women and Housing in the 80's.* New Brunswick, NJ: Center for Urban Policy Research.

Blackwell, Maylei. 1991. "Anna Nieto-Gomez and Las Hijas de Cuauhtemoc." Unpublished working paper, Women's Studies Seminar, California State University, Long Beach.

Blackwell, Maylei. 1996. "Retrofitted Memory: History, Identity Formation and the Struggle for the Chicana Feminisms in and through Nationalism." *Inscription* v.8. Center for Cultural Studies, University of California, Santa Cruz.

Blee, Kathleen M. 1996. "Becoming a Racist: Women in Contemporary Ku Klux Klan and Neo-Nazi Groups." *Gender & Society* 10(6):680–702.

Boles, Janet K. 1991. "Form Follows Function: The Evolution of Feminist Strategies." *Annals of the American Academy of Political and Social Science* 515 (May): 38–49.

Bolotin, Susan. 1982. "Voices from the Post-Feminist Generation." *New York Times Magazine,* October 17, 28–31+.

Bonacich, Edna, and Ivan Light. 1988. *Immigrant Entrepreneurs: Koreans in Los Angeles, 1965–1982.* Berkeley, CA: University of California Press.

Bonacich, Edna, Paul Ong, and Lucie Cheng. 1994. *The New Asian Immigration in Los Angeles and Global Restructuring.* Philadelphia, PA: Temple University Press.

Bookman, Ann, and Sandra Morgen. 1988a. "Rethinking Women and Politics: An Introductory Essay." Pp. 3–32 in *Women and the Politics of Empowerment,* edited by Ann Bookman and Sandra Morgen. Philadelphia, PA: Temple University Press.

Bookman, Ann, and Sandra Morgen, eds. 1988b. *Women and the Politics of Empowerment.* Philadelphia, PA: Temple University Press.

Borland, Katherine. 1991. "'That's Not What I Said': Interpretive Conflict in Oral Narrative Research." Pp. 63–75 in *Women's Words: The Feminist Practice of Oral History,* edited by Sherna Berger Gluck and Daphne Patai. New York, NY: Routledge.

Bowles, Samuel, and Herbert Gintis. 1976. *Schooling in Capitalist America.* New York, NY: Basic Books.

Boyte, Harry. 1980. *The Backyard Revolution: Understanding the New Citizen Movement.* Philadelphia, PA: Temple University Press.

Brecher, Jeremy, and Tim Costello, eds. 1990. *Building Bridges: Emerging Grassroots Coalition of Labor and Community.* New York, N.Y.: Monthly Review Press.

Breitbart, Myrna M., and Ellen J. Pader. 1995. "Establishing Ground: Representing Gender and Race in a Mixed Housing Development." *Gender, Place and Culture* 2(1):5-20.

Brenner, Johanna, and Barbara Laslett. 1986. "Social Reproduction and the Family." Pp. 116-131 in *Sociology From Crisis to Science? The Social Reproduction of Organization and Culture Vol.2,* edited by Ulf Himmelstrand. London: Sage.

Brettell, Caroline B., and Rita James Simon. 1986. "Immigrant Women: An Introduction." Pp. 3-20 in *International Migration: The Female Experience,* edited by Rita James Simon and Caroline B. Brettell. NJ: Rowman and Allanheld.

Broom, L. and J. H. Smith. 1963. "Bridging Occupations." *British Journal of Sociology* 14:321-334.

Brown, Phil, and Edwin J. Mikkelsen. 1990. *No Safe Place: Toxic Waste, Leukemia, and Community Action.* Berkeley, CA: University of California Press.

Bryant, Bunyan, and Paul Mohai. 1990. "Can the environmental movement attract and maintain the support of minorities." The Proceedings of the Michigan Conference on Race and the Incidences of Environmental Hazards.

Buechler, Steven M. 1990. *Women's Movements in the United States.* New Brunswick, N.J.: Rutgers University Press.

Bulkin, Elly, Minnie Bruce Pratt, and Barbara Smith. 1984. *Yours in Struggle: Three Feminist Perspectives on Anti-Semitism and Racism.* Brooklyn, N.Y.: Long Haul Press.

Bullard, Robert D. 1990. *Dumping in Dixie: Race, Class, and Environmental Quality.* Boulder, CO: Westview Press.

Bullard, Robert D. 1993. *Confronting Environmental Racism.* Boston, MA: South End Press.

Bullard, Robert D. 1994. *Communities of Color and Environmental Justice.* California: Sierra Club Books.

Bulkin, Wily, Minnie Bruce Pratt, and Barbara Smith. 1984. *Yours in Struggle: Three Feminist Perspectives on Anti-Semitism and Racism.* Brooklyn, N.Y.: Long Haul Press.

Bumiller, Kristin. 1987. "Victims in the Shadow of the Law: A Critique of the Model of Legal Protection." *Signs: Journal of Women in Culture and Society* 12: 421-439.

Bunch, Charlotte. 1990. "Making Common Cause: Diversity and Coalitions." Pp. 49-56 in *Bridges of Power: Women's Multicultural Alliances,* edited by Lisa Albrecht and Rose Brewer. Philadelphia, PA: New Society Publishers.

Burawoy, Michael. 1979. *Manufacturing Consent.* Chicago, IL: University of Chicago Press.

Butler, Judith. 1992. "Contingent Foundations: Feminism and the Question of

'Postmodernism'." Pp. 3-21 in *Feminists Theorize the Political*, edited by Judith Butler and Joan Scott. New York, NY: Routledge.

Butler, Judith. 1993. *Bodies That Matter*. New York, NY: Routledge.

Cable, Sherry. 1992. "Women's Social Movement Involvement: the Role of Structural Availability in Recruitment and Participation Processes." *Sociological Quarterly* 33(1):35-50.

Califia, Pat. 1979. "A Secret Side of Lesbian Sexuality." *Advocate* December 27, 19-23.

Califia, Pat. 1980. *Sapphistry: The Book of Lesbian Sexuality*. Tallahassee, FL: Naiad.

Califia, Pat. 1981. "Feminism and Sadomasochism." *Heresies* 12:30-34.

Cameron, Cindia. 1990. "Noon at 9 to 5: Reflections on a Decade of Organizing." Pp. 177-185 in *Building Bridges: The Emerging Grassroots Coalition of Labor and Community*, edited by Jeremy Brecher and Tim Costello. New York, N.Y.: Monthly Review Press.

Campbell, Marie, and Ann Manicom, eds. 1995. *Knowledge, Experience, and Ruling Relations: Studies in the Social Organization of Knowledge*. Toronto: University of Toronto Press.

Campbell, John L. 1993. "The State and Fiscal Sociology." Pp. 163-85 in *Annual Review of Sociology*.

Cancian, Francesca. 1996. "Participatory Research and Alternative Strategies for Activist Scholarship." Pp. 187-205 in *Feminism and Social Change: Bridging Theory and Practice*, edited by Heidi Gottfried. Urbana and Chicago, IL: University of Illinois Press.

Carillo, Roxanna. 1990. "Feminist Alliances: A View from Peru." Pp. 199-205 in *Bridges of Power: Women's Multicultural Alliances*, edited by Albrecht and Brewer. Philadelphia, PA: New Society Publishers.

Cassell, Joan. 1977. *A Group Called Women: Sisterhood and Symbolism in the Feminist Movement*. New York, NY: McKay.

Castells, Manuel. 1983. *The City and the Grassroots*. Berkeley, CA: University of California Press.

Castillo, Ana. 1994. *Massacre of the Dreamers*. Albuquerque, NM: University of New Mexico Press.

Cavin, Susan. 1985. *Lesbian Origins*. San Francisco, CA: Ism Press.

Cavin, Susan. 1990. "The Invisible Army of Women: Lesbian Social Protests, 1969-1988." Pp. 321-32 in *Women and Social Protest*, edited by Guida West and Rhoda Lois Blumberg. New York, NY: Oxford University Press.

Center for Community Change. 1994. *How to Save and Improve Public Housing: An Action Guide*. Washington, DC: Center for Community Change.

Cha, Dia, and Jacquelyn Chagnon. 1993. *Farmer, War-Wife, Refugee, Repatriate: A Needs Assessment of Women Repatriating to Laos*. Washington D.C.: Asian Resource Center.

Chaney, Elsa M., and Mary Garcia Castro, eds. 1989. *Muchachas No More: Household Workers in Latin America and the Caribbean*. Philadelphia, PA: Temple University Press.

Chen, May. 1992. Oral History Interview Conducted by Karen harper.

Chinchilla, Norma Stoltz, and Martha E. Giminez. 1991. Guest Editor's Introduction. *Gender & Society* 5(3):286–290.

Chodorow, Nancy. 1978. *The Reproduction of Mothering: Psychoanalysis and the Sociology of Gender*. Berkeley, CA: University of California Press.

Choi, Chungmoo. 1992. "Korean Women in a Culture of Inequality." Pp. 97–116 in *Korea Briefing*, edited by Donald N. Clark. Boulder, CO: Westview Press.

Chow, Esther Ngan-Ling. 1987. "The Development of Feminist Consciousness Among Asian American Women." *Gender & Society* 1:284–296.

Chow, Esther Ngan-Ling, Doris Wilkinson, Maxine Baca Zinn, eds. 1996. *Race, Class, & Gender: Common Bonds, Different Voices*. Thousands Oaks, CA: Sage.

Citizen's Clearinghouse for Hazardous Wastes. 1989. *Empowering Women*. Washington, D.C.: Citizen's Clearinghouse for Hazardous Wastes.

Clark-Lewis, Elizabeth. 1987. "From Servants to Household Workers." Pp.213–259 in *To Toil the Livelong Day: America's Women at Work 1780–1980*, edited by Mary Beth Norton and Carol Groneman. Ithaca, NY: Cornell University Press.

Clausen, Jan. 1990. "My Interesting Condition." *Outlook* 7 (Winter): 10–21.

Clausen, Jan. 1992. "A Craving for Community." *Women's Review of Books* 9 (March): 8–9.

Clavel, Pierre. 1983. *Opposition Planning in Wales and Appalachia*. Philadelphia, PA: Temple University Press.

Code, Lorraine. 1991. *What Can She Know: Feminist Theory and the Construction of Knowledge*. Ithaca, NY: Cornell University Press.

Collins, Patricia Hill. 1990. *Black Feminist Thought: Knowledge, Consciousness, and the Politics of Empowerment*. Cambridge, MA: Unwin Hyman.

Collins, Patricia Hill. 1991. "Learning From the Outsider Within: The Sociological Significance of Black Feminist Thought." Pp. 35–59 in *Beyond Methodology: Feminist Scholarship as Lived Experience*, edited by Mary Margaret Fonow and Judith A. Cook. Bloomington, IN: Indiana University Press.

Community Action Strategies to Stop Rape. 1978. "Freeing Our Lives: A Feminist Analysis of Rape Prevention." Community Action Strategies to Stop Rape, Women Against Rape, Columbus, Ohio.

Conzen, Kathleen N. 1979. "Immigrants, Immigrant Neighborhoods, and Ethnic Identity: Historical Issues." *Journal of American History* 66:603–15.

Cook, Blanche Wiesen. 1977. "Female Support Networks and Political Activism: Lillian Wald, Crystal Eastman, Emma Goldman." *Chrysalis* 3:43–61.

Cook, Judith A., and Mary Margaret Fonow. 1990. "Knowledge and Women's Interests: Issues of Epistemology and Methodology in Feminist Sociological Research." Pp. 69–93 in *Feminist Research Methods*, edited by Joyce McCarl Nielsen. Boulder, CO: Westview Press.

Coser, Lewis. 1974. "Servants: The Obsolescence of an Occupational Role." *Social Forces* 52:31–40.

Cotera, Marta P. 1976. *Diosa y Hembra: The History and Heritage Chicanas in the U.S.* Austin, TX: Information Systems Development.

Cotera, Marta P. 1977. *The Chicana Feminist.* Austin, TX: Information Systems Development.

Cotrell, Sharon. 1991a. "An Investigation of Contemporary American Indian Women and Feminism: Methodology and an Oral History of Otoe Woman Mary Cleghorn-Vann," Unpublished working paper, Women's Studies seminar, California State University, Long Beach.

Cotrell, Sharon. 1991b. Informal Seminar Report on Conversations with Anna Christiansen, American Indian activist, California State University, Long Beach.

Cotrell, Sharon. 1995. "Debating Feminism Within the American Indian Community," Unpublished working paper, Women's Studies seminar, California State University, Long Beach.

Cott, Nancy F. 1989. "What's in a Name? The Limits of 'Social Feminism'; or, Expanding the Vocabulary of Women's History." *Journal of American History* 76(3):809-29.

Crenshaw, Kimberle. 1991a. "Demarginalizing the Intersection of Race and Sex: A Black Feminist Critique of Anti-discrimination Doctrine, Feminist Theory, and Antiracist Politics." Pp. 57–80 in *Feminist Legal Theory: Readings in Law and Gender*, edited by Katharine Bartlett and Rosanne Kennedy. Boulder, CO: Westview Press.

Crenshaw, Kimberle. 1991b. "Mapping the Margins: Intersectionality, Identity Politics, and Violence Against Women of Color." *Stanford Law Review* 43(6):1241-1299.

Dabrowski, Irene. 1983. "Working Class Women and Civic Action: A Case Study of an Innovative Community Role." *Policy Studies Journal* 11(3):427-35.

Daniels, Arlene K. 1985. "Good Times and Good Works: The Place of Sociability in the Work of Women Volunteers." *Social Problems* 32(3):363-374.

Daniels, Arlene Kaplan. 1987. "Invisible Work." *Social Problems* 34(5)(December):403-415.

Daniels, Roger. 1988. *Asian America.* Seattle: University of Washington Press.

Dart, John. 1990. "Outreach Plan for Catholic Latinos Has Mixed Success." *Los Angeles Times* 5 June, sec. A, p. 3.

Dasgupta, Shamita Das, and Sujata Warrier. 1996. "In the Footsteps of "Arundhati": Asian Indian Women's Experience of Domestic Violence in the United States." *Violence Against Women* 2(3):238-259.

Davis, Angela. 1981. *Women, Race & Class.* New York, NY: Random House.

Davis, Flora. 1991. *Moving the Mountain: The Women's Movement in America Since 1960.* New York, NY: Simon & Schuster.

Davis, Sally Ogle. 1989. "Is Feminism Dead?" *Los Angeles* February.

DeVault, Marjorie L. 1991. *Feeding the Family: The Social Organization of Caring and Gendered Work.* Chicago, IL: University of Chicago Press.

Delgado, David. 1996. "How the Empress Gets Her Clothes: Asian Immigrant Women Fight Fashion Designer Jessica McClintock." Pp. 81–94 in *Beyond Identity Politics. Emerging Social Justice Movements in Communities of Color*, edited by John Anner. Boston, MA: South End Press.

Delgado, Gary. 1992. *Anti-Racist Work: An Examination and Assessment of Organizational Activity*. Oakland, CA: Applied Research Center.

Delgado, Gary. 1994. *Beyond the Politics of Place: New Directions in Community Organizing in the 1990s*. Oakland, CA: Applied Research Center.

Devault, Marjorie L. 1991. *Feeding the Family: The Social Organization of Caring and Gendered Work*. Chicago, IL: University of Chicago Press.

Devor, Holly. 1989. *Gender Blending: Confronting the Limits of Duality*. Bloomington, IN: Indiana University Press.

Dewey, John. 1966. *Democracy and Education*. New York, NY: The Free Press.

di Leonardo, Micaela. 1987. "Female World of Cards and Holidays: Women, Families and the Work of Kinship." *Signs: Journal of Women in Culture and Society* 12(3):440–53.

Dill, Bonnie Thornton. 1988. "Making the Job Good Yourself: Domestic Service and the Construction of Personal Identity." Pp. 33–52 in *Women and the Politics of Empowerment*, edited by Ann Bookman and Sandra Morgen. Philadelphia, PA: Temple University Press.

Dill, Kim. 1989. "Qualified Feminism and Its Influence on College Women's Identification with the Women's Movement." Unpublished manuscript, Columbus, Ohio.

Dill, Kim. 1991. "Feminism in the Nineties: The Influence of Collective Identity and Community on Young Feminist Activists." M.A. thesis, Ohio State University.

Dimen, Muriel. 1984. "Politically Correct? Politically Incorrect?" Pp. 138–148 in *Pleasure and Danger: Exploring Female Sexuality*, edited by Carol S. Vance. London: Pandora Press.

Direen, Brenda. 1991. "The Politics of Recovery." *Feminisms* (newsletter of the Center for Women's Studies, Ohio State University) 4 (March/April): 6–7.

Dobash, R. Emerson, and Russell P. Dobash. 1992. *Women, Violence and Social Change*. London: Routledge.

Donnelly, Nancy D. 1989. *The Changing Lives of Refugee Hmong Women*. Ph.D. Dissertation. University of Washington.

Donnelly, Nancy D. 1994. *Changing Lives of Refugee Hmong Women*. Seattle, WA: University of Washington Press.

Donovan, Josephine. 1985. *Feminist Theory: The Intellectual Traditions of American Feminism*. New York, NY: Ungar.

DuBois, Ellen, Mari Jo Buhle, Temma Kaplan, Gerda Lerner, and Carroll Smith-Rosenberg. 1980. "Politics and Culture in Women's History." *Feminist Studies* 6(1):26–64.

Dubois, Ellen Carol and Vicki L. Ruiz, eds. 1990. *Unequal Sisters: A Multicultural Reader in U.S. Women's History*. New York, NY: Routledge.

Duggan, Lisa. 1992. "Making It Perfectly Queer." *Socialist Review* 22(1):11-31.

"Dyke Manifesto." 1993. Flyer Handed Out at the March on Washington for Lesbian, Gay, and Bisexual Rights and Liberation, April 25, 1993, in possession of the authors.

*Eastside Journal.* 1964. "Congressman Lauds CSO Service," 28 May:1.

Ebeling, Kay. 1990. "The Failure of Feminism." *Newsweek* 116 (November 19): 9.

Echols, Alice. 1983a. "Cultural Feminism and the Anti-Pornography Movement." *Social Text* 7:34-53.

Echols, Alice. 1983b. "The New Feminism of Yin and Yang." Pp. 439-59 in *Powers of Desire: The Politics of Sexuality*, edited by Ann Snitow, Christine Stansell, and Sharon Thompson. New York, NY: Monthly Review Press.

Echols, Alice. 1984. "The Taming of the Id: Feminist Sexual Politics, 1968-83." Pp. 50-72 in *Pleasure and Danger: Exploring Female Sexuality*, edited by Carol S. Vance. London: Pandora Press.

Echols, Alice. 1989. *Daring to Be Bad: Radical Feminism in America, 1967-1975.* Minneapolis, MN: University of Minnesota Press.

Echols, Alice. 1991. "Justifying Our Love? The Evolution of Lesbianism through Feminism and Gay Male Politics." *Advocate* March 26, 48-53.

Edin, Kathryn. 1996. "Real-Life Choices: Low-Income Mothers and the Devolution of Welfare." Paper presented at the Research Network on Gender, State, and Society Annual Workshop held at the Social Science History Association Meetings, New Orleans, Lousiana, October 10.

Eisenstein, Hester. 1983. *Contemporary Feminist Thought.* Boston, MA: G. K. Hall.

Eisenstein, Zillah. 1981. *The Radical Future of Liberal Feminism.* New York, NY: Longman.

Eisenstein, Zillah R., ed. 1979. *Capitalist Patriarchy and the Case for Socialist Feminism.* New York, NY: Monthly Review Press.

Elden, Max, and Morten Levin. 1991. "Cogenerative Learning: Bringing Participation into Action Research." Pp. 127-142 in *Participatory Action Research*, edited by William Foote Whyte. Newbury Park, CA: Sage.

Epstein, Barbara. 1991. *Political Protest and Cultural Revolution: Nonviolent Direct Action in the 1970s and 1980s.* Berkeley and Los Angeles, CA: University of California Press.

Escobedo, Raul. 1979. *Boyle Heights Community Plan.* Department of City Planning, Los Angeles.

Evans, Sara. 1979. *Personal Politics: The Roots of Women's Liberation in the Civil Rights Movement and the New Left.* New York, NY: Knopf.

Evans, Sara. 1989. *Born for Liberty.* New York, NY: The Free Press.

Evans, Sara M., and Harry C. Boyte. 1981. "Schools for Social Action: Radical Uses of Social Space." *Democracy* (Summer):55-65.

Evans, Sara M., and Harry C, Boyte. 1986. *Free Spaces: The Sources of Democratic Change in America.* New York, NY: Harper and Row Publishers.

Ewing, Charles, and Moss Aubrey. 1987. "Black Women and Public Opinion: Some Realities About the Myths." *Journal of Family Violence* 2(3): 257-64.

Faderman, Lillian. 1981. *Surpassing the Love of Men.* New York, NY: Morrow.

Faderman, Lillian. 1991. *Odd Girls and Twilight Lovers: A History of Lesbian Life in Twentieth-Century America.* New York, NY: Columbia University Press.

Fanon, Frantz. 1966. *The Wretched of the Earth.* New York, NY: Grove Press.

Fantasia, Rick. 1988. *Cultures of Solidarity: Consciousness, Action, and Contemporary American Workers.* Berkeley and Los Angeles, CA: University of California Press.

Fay, Brian. 1987. *Critical Social Science: Liberation and its Limits.* Ithaca, NY: Cornell University Press.

Feldman, Roberta M., and Susan Stall. 1989. "Women in Public Housing: 'There just comes a point. . . .'" *The Neighborhood Works* (June–July):4–6.

Feldman, Roberta M., and Susan Stall. 1990. "Resident Activism in Public Housing: A Case Study of Women's Invisible Work of Building Community." Pp. 11–119 in *Coming of Age,* edited by Robert I. Selby, Katherine H. Anthony, Jaepil Choi and Brian Orland. The Proceedings of the Environmental Design Research Association Annual Conference, Urbana-Champaign, Illinois.

Feldman, Roberta M., and Susan Stall. 1994. "The Politics of Space Appropriation: A Case Study of Women's Struggles for Homeplace in Chicago Public Housing." Pp. 167–199 in *Women and the Environment,* edited by Irwin Altman and Arza Churchman. New York, NY: Plenum Press.

Fernandez-Kelly, M. Patricia, and Anna Garcia. 1990. "Power Surrendered, Power Restored: The Politics of Work and Family Among Hispanic Garment Workers in California and Florida." Pp. 130–149 in *Women, Politics, and Change,* edited by Louise A. Tilly and Patricia Gurin. New York, NY: Russell Sage Foundation.

Ferraro, Kathleen J. 1983. "Negotiating Trouble in a Battered Women's Shelter." *Urban Life* 12:287–306.

Ferree, Myra Marx. 1992. "The Political Context of Rationality: Rational Choice Theory and Resource Mobilization." Pp. 29–52 in *Frontiers in Social Movement Theory,* edited by Aldon D. Morris and Carol McClurg Mueller. New Haven, CT: Yale University Press.

Ferree, Myra Marx, and Patricia Yancey Martin. 1995. "Doing the Work of the Movement: Feminist Organizations." Pp. 3–23 in *Feminist Organizations: Harvest of the New Women's Movement.* Philadelphia, PA: Temple University Press, 1995.

Finck, John. 1986. "Secondary Migration to California's Central Valley." Pp. 184–187 in *The Hmong in Transition,* edited Glenn L. Hendricks, Bruce T. Downing, and Amos S. Deinard. New York, NY. The Center for Migration Studies.

Fine, Michelle. 1985. "Unearthing Contradictions: An Essay Inspired by Women and Male Violence." *Feminist Studies* 11:391–407.

Fine, Michelle. 1989. "The Politics of Research and Activism: Violence Against Women." *Gender & Society* 3:549–58.

Fine, Michelle. 1992. *Disruptive Voices: The Possibilities of Feminist Research.* Ann Arbor, MI: The University of Michigan Press.

Fine, Michelle, and Lois Weis. 1996. "Writing the 'Wrongs' of Fieldwork: Confronting Our Own Research/Writing Dilemmas in Urban Ethnographies." *Qualitative Inquiry* 2(3):251–274.

Fisher, Sue. 1993. "Gender, Power, Resistance: Is Care the Remedy?" Pp. 87–121 in *Negotiating at the Margins: The Gendered Discourses of Power and Resistance.* New Brunswick, NJ: Rutgers.

Fisher, Robert. 1994. *Let the People Decide: Neighborhood Organizing in America.* New York, NY: Twayne.

Fisher, Robert, and Joseph M. Kling. 1990. "Leading the People: Two Approaches to the Role of Ideology in Community Organizing." Pp. 71–90 in *Dilemmas of Activism: Class, Community, and the Politics of Local Mobilization,* edited by Joseph M. Kling and Prudence S. Posner. Philadelphia, PA: Temple University Press.

Flax, Nancy. 1990. *Thinking Fragments: Psychoanalysis, Feminism, & Postmodernism in the Contemporary West.* Berkeley, CA: University of California Press.

Fonow, Mary Margaret, and Judith A Cook, eds. 1991. *Beyond Methodology: Feminist Scholarship as Lived Research.* Bloomington, IN: Indiana University Press.

Foster, George McClelland 1973. *Traditional Societies and Technological Change* (second edition). New York, NY: Harper and Row.

Foucault, Michel. 1980. *The History of Sexuality: Volume One, An Introduction.* New York, NY: Vintage Books.

Frankenberg, Ruth. 1993. *White Women, Race Matters: The Social Construction of Whiteness.* Minneapolis, MN: University of Minnesota Press.

Fraser, Nancy. 1989. *Unruly Practices: Power, Discourse, and Gender in Contemporary Social Theory.* Minneapolis, MN: University of Minnesota Press.

Fraser, Nancy. 1990. "Struggle Over Needs: Outline of a Socialist-Feminist Critical Theory of Late-Capitalist Political Culture." Pp. 199–225 in *Women, the State, and Welfare,* edited by Linda Gordon. Madison, WI: University of Wisconsin Press.

Fraser, Nancy, and Linda J. Nicholson. 1990. "Social Criticism Without Philosophy: An Encounter Between Feminism and Postmodernism." Pp. 19–38 in *Feminism/Postmodernism,* edited by Linda J. Nicholson. New York, NY: Routledge.

Freedman, Estelle. 1979. "Separatism as Strategy: Female Institution Building and American Feminism, 1870–1930." *Feminist Studies* 5(3):512–52.

Freeman, Jo. 1983. *Social Movements of the Sixties and Seventies.* New York, NY: Longman.

Freire, Paulo. 1970. *Pedagogy of the Oppressed.* New York, NY: Continuum.

Freire, Paulo. 1985. *The Politics of Education: Culture, Power, and Liberation.* South Hadley, MA: Bergin and Garvey.

Friedan, Betty. 1985. "How to Get the Women's Movement Moving Again." *New York Times Magazine,* November 3, 26–29 +.

Frye, Marilyn. 1983. "Some Reflections on Separatism and Power." Pp. 95–109 in *The Politics of Reality: Essays in Feminist Theory*. Trumansburg, N.Y.: Crossing Press.

Frye, Marilyn. 1990. "Do You Have to Be a Lesbian to Be a Feminist?" *off our backs* 20 (August/September): 21–23.

Fuentes, Annette. 1990. "Immigration Reform: Heaviest Burden on Women." Philadelphia, PA: Publication of the American Friends Service Committee.

Galst, Liz. 1991. "Overcoming Silence." *Advocate* December 3, 60–63.

Gamson, Joshua. 1995. "Must Identity Movements Self-Destruct?" *Social Problems* 42(3):390–407.

Gamson, William A. 1968. *Power and Discontent*. Homewood, IL: Dorsey.

Gamson, William A. 1975. *The Strategy of Social Protest*. Homewood, IL: Dorsey.

Gaventa, John. 1980. *Power and Powerlessness: Quiescence and Rebellion in an Appalachian Valley*. Urbana, IL: University of Illinois Press.

Gaventa, John. 1990. "From the Mountains to the Maquiladoras: A Case Study of Capital Flight and Its Impact on Workers." Pp. 85–95 in *Communities is Economic Crisis: Appalachia and the South*, edited by John Gaventa et al. Philadelphia, PA: Temple University Press.

Gaventa, John, and Billy Horton. 1981. "A Citizen's Research Project in Appalachia, U.S.A." *Convergence* 14(3):30–40.

Gaventa, John, Barbara Ellen Smith, and Alex Willingham, eds. 1990. *Communities in Economic Crisis: Appalachia and the South*. Philadelphia, PA: Temple University Press.

Garcia, Alma. 1989. "The Development of Chicana Feminist Discourse, 1970–1980." *Gender & Society* 3(2):217–238.

Garcia, Phillip. 1985. "Immigration Issues in Urban Ecology: The Case of Los Angeles." Pp. 73–100 in *Urban Ethnicity in the United States*, edited by Lionel Maldonado and Joan Moore. Beverly Hills, CA: Sage.

Geddes, W.R. 1976. *Migrants of the Mountains: The Cultural Ecology of the Blue Miao (Hmong Njua) of Thailand*. Oxford: Oxford University Press.

Geiger, Susan. 1982. "Women's Life Histories: Method and Content," *Signs: Journal of Women in Culture and Society* 11(2):334–51.

Gibbs, Lois. 1982. *Love Canal: My Story*. Albany, NY: State University Press of New York.

Giddings, Paula. 1984. *When and Where I Enter: The Impact of Black Women on Race and Sex in America*. New York, NY: William Morrow.

Gilkes, Cheryl Townsend. 1980. "'Holding Back the Ocean With a Broom': Black Women and Their Community Work." Pp. 217–231 in *The Black Woman*, edited by L. R. Rose. Beverly Hills, CA: Sage.

Gilkes, Cheryl Townsend. 1983. "Going Up for the Oppressed: The Career Mobility of Black Women Community Workers." *Journal of Social Issues* 39(3):115–139.

Gilkes, Cheryl Townsend. 1988. "Building in Many Places: Multiple Commitments and Ideologies in Black Women's Community Work." Pp. 53–76 in *Women and the Politics of Empowerment*, edited by Ann Bookman and Sandra Morgen. Philadelphia, PA: Temple University Press.

Gilkes, Cheryl Townsend. 1994. "'If It Wasn't for the Women . . .': African American Women, Community Work, and Social Change." Pp. 229–246 in *Women of Color in U.S. Society*, edited by Maxine Baca Zinn and Bonnie Thornton Dill. Philadelphia, PA: Temple University Press.

Ginsburg, Faye. 1988. *Contested Lives: The Abortion Debate in an American Community*. Berkeley, CA: University of California Press.

Gittings, Barbara. 1976. "Founding of the New York Daughters of Bilitis." Pp. 420–433 in *Gay American History*, edited by Jonathan Katz. New York, NY: Avon.

Glenn, Evelyn Nakano. 1986. *Issei, Nisei, Warbride*. Philadelphia, PA: Temple University Press.

Glenn, Evelyn Nakano. 1991. "White Women/Women of Color: Historical Continuities in the Racial Division of Women's Work." Paper presented at the American Sociological Association, annual meetings, Cincinnati, Ohio, 24 August.

Glenn, Evelyn Nakano. 1994. "Social Constructions of Mothering: A Thematic Overview." Pp. 1–29 in *Mothering: Ideology, Experience, and Agency*. New York, NY: Routledge.

Glenn, Evelyn Nakano, Grace Chang, and Linda Rennie Forcey, eds. 1994. *Mothering: Ideology, Experience, and Agency*. New York, NY: Routledge.

Gluck, Sherna Berger. 1987. *Rosie the Riveter Revisited*. New York, NY: New American Library.

Gordon, Linda. 1986. "What's New in Women's History." Pp. 20–30 in *Feminist Studies/Critical Studies*, edited by Teresa de Lauretis. Bloomington, IN: Indiana University Press.

Gordon, Linda. 1990. "Family Violence, Feminism, and Social Control." Pp. 178–198 in *Women, the State, and Welfare*, edited by Linda Gordon. Madison, WI: University of Wisconsin Press.

Gordon, Linda. 1991a. *Black and White Visions of Welfare: Women's Welfare Activism, 1890–1945*. Madison, WI: Institute for Research on Poverty.

Gordon, Linda. 1991b. "On 'Difference.'" *Genders* 10 (Spring): 91–111.

Gorman, Phyllis. 1992. "The Ohio AIDS Movement: Competition and Cooperation between Grassroots Activists and Professionally Sponsored Organizations." Ph.D. dissertation, Ohio State University.

Gottfried, Heidi, ed. 1996. *Feminism and Social Change: Bridging Theory and Practice*. Urbana and Chicago, IL: University of Illinois Press.

Gramsci, Antonio. 1971. *Selections from the Prison Notebooks*, edited by Quintin Hoare and Geoffery N. Smith. New York, NY: International Publishers.

Grant, Jaime M. 1996. "Building Community-Based Coalitions from Academe: The Union Institute and the Kitchen Table: Women of Color Press Transition Coalition." *Signs: Journal of Women in Culture and Society* 21 (4): 1024–1033.

Green, Rayna. 1979. "American Indian Women Meet in Lawrence." *Women's Studies Newsletter* 7 (3).

Green, Rayna. 1980. "Native American Women: The Leadership Paradox." *Women's Educational Equity Communications Network News and Notes* 1 (4).

Green, Rayna. 1982. "Diary of a Native American Feminist." *Ms* v. 11 (July/August), pp 170–172, 211–13.

Green, Rayna. 1983. *Native American Women: A Contextual Bibliography.* Bloomington: Indiana University Press.

Green, Rayna. 1990. "American Indian Women: Diverse Leadership for Social Change." Pp. 61–73 in *Bridges of Power: Women's Multicultural Alliances,* edited by Lisa Albrecht and Rose Brewer. Philadelphia, PA: New Society Publishers.

Greenhouse, Carol J. 1988. "Courting Difference: Issues of Interpretation and Comparison in the Study of Legal Ideologies." *Law and Society Review* 88 (4): 687–708.

Greer, James L. 1986–7. "The Political Economy of the Local State." *Politics & Society* 15 (4):513–38.

Guthrie, James W., George B. Kleindorfer, Henry M. Levin, and Robert T. Stout. 1971. *Schools and Inequality.* Cambridge, MA: MIT Press.

Habermas, Jürgen. 1973. *Legitimate Crisis.* Boston, MA: Beacon Press.

Hale, Sondra. 1996. *Gender Politics in Sudan: Islamism, Socialism, and the State.* Boulder, CO: Westview Press.

Hall, Jacquelyn Dowd. 1986. "Disorderly Women: Gender and Labor Militancy in the Appalachian South." *Journal of American History* 73:354–382.

Hall, Jacquelyn Dowd. 1990. "Disorderly Women: Gender and Labor Militancy in the Appalachian South." Pp. 298–321 in *Unequal Sisters: A Multi-Cultural Reader in U.S. Women's History,* edited by Ellen DuBois and Vicki L. Ruiz. New York, NY: Routledge.

Haller, Mary. 1984. "Decline of a Social Movement Organization: The Women's Action Collective." Unpublished manuscript, Columbus, Ohio.

Hamilton, Amy. 1991. "Women in A.I.D.S. Activism." *off our backs* 21 (November): 4–5.

Hamilton, Cynthia. 1991. "Women, Home, and Community." *Woman of Power* 20:42–45.

Hanisch, Carol. 1978. "The Personal Is Political." Pp. 204–15 in *Feminist Revolution,* edited by Redstockings of the Women's Liberation Movement. New York, NY: Random House.

Haraway, Donna. 1988. "Situated Knowledges: The Science Question in Feminism and the Privilege of Partial Perspective." *Feminist Studies* 14 (3): 575–599.

Harding, Sandra. 1981. "What is the Real Material Base of Patriarchy and Capital?" Pp. 135–163 in *Women and Revolution: A Discussion of the Unhappy Marriage of Marxism and Feminism,* edited by Lydia Sargent. Boston, MA: South End Press.

Harding, Sandra. 1986. *The Science Question in Feminism.* Ithaca, NY: Cornell University Press.

Harding, Sandra. 1991. *Whose Science? Whose Knowledge?* Ithaca, NY: Cornell University Press.

Harding, Sandra. 1993. "Rethinking Standpoint Epistemology": What is 'Strong Objectivity'?" Pp. 49–82 in *Feminist Epistemologies,* edited by Linda Alcoff and Elizabeth Potter. New York, NY: Routledge.

Harley, Sharon. 1990. "For the Good of Family and Race: Gender, Work and Domestic Roles in the Black Community, 1880–1930." *Signs: Journal of Women in Culture and Society* 15(2):336–49.

harper, Karen. 1991. "The Awakened Volcano: Asian Women in L.A." Unpublished seminar paper. California State University, Long Beach.

harper, Karen. 1992. "I Never Embraced Separatism: Miya Iwataki, An Asian American Feminist Activist." Unpublished manuscript. California State University, Long Beach.

Hartmann, Heidi. 1981a. "The Family as the Locus of Gender, Class, and Political Struggle: The Example of Housework." *Signs: Journal of Women in Culture and Society* 6:366–394.

Hartmann, Heidi. 1981b. "The Unhappy Marriage of Marxism and Feminism: Toward a More Progressive Union." Pp. 1–41 in *Women and Revolution,* edited by Lydia Sargent. Boston, MA: South End Press.

Hartmann, Heidi, Ellen Bravo, Charlotte Bunch, Nancy Hartsock, Roberta Spalter-Roth, Linda Williams, and Maria Blanco. 1996. "Bringing Together Theory and Practice: A Collective Interview." *Signs: Journal of Women in Culture and Society* 21(4):917–951.

Hartsock, Nancy. 1981. "Staying Alive." Pp. 111–122 in *Building Feminist Theory: Essays from Quest,* edited by Charlotte Bunch, et al. New York, NY: Longman.

Hartsock, Nancy. 1983. *Money, Sex and Power: Toward a Feminist Historical Materialism.* Boston, MA: Northeastern University.

Haywoode, Terry. 1991. "Working Class Feminism: Creating a Politics of Community, Connection, and Concern." Ph.D. dissertation, The City University of New York.

Henig, Jeffrey R. 1982. *Neighborhood Mobilization: Redevelopment and Response.* New Brunswick, NJ: Rutgers University Press.

Hennessy, Rosemary. 1993. *Materialist Feminism and the Politics of Discourse.* New York, NY: Routledge.

Her, Pajhoua. 1995. "Women's Issues: AAWAC and Women's Coalitions." A paper presented at Southeast Asian Economic Exposition in Fresno, California. May.

Hertz, Susan. 1981. *The Welfare Mothers Movement.* Washington, D.C: University Press of America.

Hewitt, Nancy A. 1985. "Beyond the Search for Sisterhood: American Women's History in the 1980s." *Social History* 10(3):299–321.

Hing, Bill Ong. 1993. *Making and Remaking Asian America Through Immigration Policy 1850–1990.* Stanford, CA: Stanford University Press.

Ho, Chi-Kwan A. 1990. "Opportunities and Challenges: The Role of Feminists for Social Change in Hong Kong." Pp. 182–198 in *Bridges of Power: Women's Multicultural Alliances,* edited by Albrecht and Brewer. Philadelphia, PA: New Society Publishers.

Hoagland, Sarah Lucia, and Julia Penelope. 1988. *For Lesbians Only: A Separatist Anthology.* London: Onlywomen.

Holmes, Steven A. 1995. "Congress Plans Stiff New Curb On Immigration." *The New York Times* Sept. 25:A1.

Hondagneu-Sotelo, Pierrette. 1992. "Overcoming Patriarchal Constraints: The Reconstruction of Gender Relations Among Mexican Immigrant Women and Men." *Gender & Society* 6:393–415.

Hondagneu-Sotelo, Pierrette. 1994. "Regulating the Unregulated? Domestic Workers' Social Networks." *Social Problems* 41:201–215.

hooks, bell. 1981. *Ain't I a Woman: Black Women and Feminism.* Boston, MA: South End Press.

hooks, bell. 1984. *Feminist Theory: From Margin to Center.* Boston, MA: South End Press.

hooks, bell. 1990. *Yearning: Race, Gender, and Cultural Politics.* Boston, MA: South End Press.

Horowitz, Ruth. 1987. "Community Tolerance of Gang Violence." *Social Problems* 34(5):437–50.

Hossfeld, Karen J. 1994. "Hiring Immigrant Women: Silicon Valley's 'simple formula'." Pp. 65–93 in *Women of Color in U.S. Society,* edited by Maxine Baca Zinn and Bonnie Thornton Dill. Philadelphia, PA: Temple University Press.

Houppert, Karen. 1991. "Wildflowers Among the Ivy: New Campus Radicals." *Ms.* 2 (September/October): 52–58.

Huisman, Kimberly A. 1996. "Wife Battering in Asian American Communities: Identifying the Service Needs of an Overlooked Segment of the U.S. Population." *Violence Against Women* 2(3):260–283.

Huizer, Gerrit, and Bruce Mannheim, eds. 1979. *The Politics of Anthropology: From Colonialism and Sexism Toward a View from Below.* The Hague: Mouton Publishers.

Hull, Gloria T., Patricia Bell Scott, and Barbara Smith, eds. 1982. *All the Women Are White, All the Blacks Are Men, but Some of Us Are Brave: Black Women's Studies.* Old Westbury, N.Y.: The Feminist Press.

Humm, Maggie, ed. 1992. *Modern Feminisms: Political, Literary, Cultural.* New York, NY: Columbia University Press.

Hunter, Albert. 1974. *Symbolic Communities: The Persistence and Change of Chicago Local Communities.* Chicago, IL: University of Chicago Press.

Hurtado, Aida. 1989. "Relating to Privilege: Seduction and Rejection in the Subordination of White Women and Women of Color." *Signs: Journal of Women in Culture and Society* 14(4):833–856.

Ignatiev, Noel. 1995. *How the Irish Became White.* New York, NY: Routledge.

Inkeles, Alex. 1969. "Making Men Modern: On the Causes and Consequences of Individual Change in Six Developing Countries." *American Journal of Sociology* 75: 208-225.

Iwataki, Miya. 1983. "The Asian Women's Movement: A Retrospective." *East Wind* (Spring/Summer):35-41.

Iwataki, Miya. 1991. Oral History Interviews Conducted by Karen harper.

Jaggar, Alison. 1983. *Feminist Politics and Human Nature.* Totowa, N.J.: Rowman & Allanheld.

Jaggar, Alison M., and Rothenberg, Paula S., eds. 1993. *Feminist Frameworks: Alternative Theoretical Accounts of the Relations between Women and Men.* New York, NY: McGraw-Hill.

James, David R. 1988. "The Transformation of the Southern Racial State: Class and Race Determinants of Local-State Structures." *American Sociological Review* 53 (April): 191-208.

James, Stanlie M. 1993. "Mothering: A Possible Black Feminist Link to Social Transformation?" Pp. 44-54 in *Theorizing Black Feminisms: The Visionary Pragmatism of Black Women,* edited by Stanlie M. James and A. P. A. Busia. New York, NY: Routledge.

Jaquette, Jane, ed. 1994. *The Women's Movement in Latin America: Participation and Democracy.* Boulder, CO: Westview.

Jenkins, Craig. 1985. *The Politics of Insurgency.* New York, NY: Columbia University Press.

Johnson, Ann. 1985 (film). *Mabel Parker Hardison Smith.* Whitesburg, KY: Appalshop.

Johnson-Odim, Cheryl. 1991. "Common Themes, Different Contexts." Pp. 314-27 in *Third World Women and the Politics of Feminism,* edited by Chandra Talpade Mohanty, Ann Russo, and Lourdes Torres. Bloomington, IN: Indiana University Press.

Jones, Jacqueline. 1985. *Labor of Love, Labor of Sorrow: Black Women, Work, and the Family From Slavery to the Present.* New York, NY: Basic Books.

Jones, Mary Harris. 1972. *Autobiography of Mother Jones,* edited by Mary Field Parton. (1925. Chicago: Charles Kerr.) Reprint. Chicago, IL: Illinois Labor Historical Society.

Joseph, Gloria. 1981. "The Incompatible Menage a Trois: Marxism, Feminism, and Racism. Pp. 91-100 in *Women and Revolution,* edited by Lydia Sargent. Boston, MA: South End Press.

Joseph, Gloria, and Jill Lewis, eds. 1981. *Common Differences: Conflicts in Black and White Feminist Perspectives.* New York, NY: Anchor.

Joseph, Suad. 1993. "Fieldwork and Psychosocial Dynamics of Personhood." *Frontiers* 13(3): 9-32.

Jule, Ilsa, and Laurie Marin. 1993. "The Lesbian Avengers." *Deneuve* May/June, 42-44.

Kahn, Si. 1982. *Organizing: A Guide for Grassroots Leaders.* New York, NY: McGraw-Hill Book Company.

Kamen, Paula. 1991. *Feminist Fatale: Voices from the "Twentysomething" Generation*

*Explore the Future of the Women's Movement.* New York, NY: Donald I. Fine.

Kaplan, Elaine Bell. 1987. "'I Don't Do No Windows': Competition Between the Domestic Worker and the Housewife." Pp. 92-105 in *Competition: A Feminist Taboo?*, edited by Valerie Miner and Helen Longino. New York, NY: The Feminist Press.

Kaplan, Temma. 1982. "Female Consciousness and Collective Action: The Case of Barcelona, 1910-1918." *Signs: Journal of Women in Culture and Society* 7(3):545-566.

Kaplan, Temma. 1997. *Crazy for Democracy: Women in Grassroots Movements.* New York, NY: Routledge.

Katzman, David M. 1981. *Seven Days a Week: Women and Domestic Service in Industrializing America.* Urbana and Chicago, IL: University of Illinois Press.

Katznelson, Ira. 1981. *City Trenches: Urban Politics and the Patterning of Class in the United States.* Chicago, IL: University of Chicago Press.

Kaye/Kantrowitz, Melanie. 1992. *The Issue is Power: Essays on Women, Jews, Violence and Resistence.* San Francisco, CA: Aunt Lute.

Kaywood, Richard. 1967. "The Los Angeles Board Authorized Driver Training." *CALDEA Calendar* (January):4.

Kelly, Gail Paradise. 1994. "To Become an American Woman: Education and Sex Role Socialization of the Vietnamese Immigrant Woman." Pp. 497-507 in *Unequal Sisters: A Multicultural Reader in U.S. Women's History*, edited by Vicki L. Ruiz and Ellen Carol Dubois. New York, NY: Routledge.

Kendrick, Karen. 1994. "Tangled in the Webs of Practice: Discursive Struggles in the Treatment, Policing, and Politics of the Abuse of Women." Paper presented at the Annual Meeting of The Pacific Sociological Association. San Diego, April 1994.

Kennedy, Elizabeth Lapovsky, and Madeline D. Davis. 1993. *Boots of Leather, Slippers of Gold: The History of a Lesbian Community.* New York, NY: Routledge.

Kessler-Harris, Alice. 1982. *Out to Work: A History of Wage-Earning Women in the United States.* New York, NY: Oxford University Press.

Kieffer, Charles H. 1984. "Citizen Empowerment: A Developmental Perspective. Pp. 9-36 in *Studies in Empowerment: Steps Toward Understanding Action*, edited by J. Rappaport, C. Swift and R. Hess. New York, NY: Haworth.

Kim, Illsoo. 1981. *New Urban Immigrants: The Korean Community in New York.* Princeton, NJ: Princeton University Press.

King, Katie. 1994. *Theory in its Feminist Travels: Conversations in US Women's Movements.* Bloomington, IN: Indiana University Press.

Kitano, Harry, and Roger Daniel. 1988. *Asian Americans: Emerging Minorities.* NJ: Prentice Hall.

Klatch, Rebecca. 1992. "The Two Worlds of Women of the New Right." Pp. 529-552 in *Women, Politics, and Change*, edited by Louise A. Tilly and Patricia Gurin. New York, NY: Russell Sage.

Kling, Joseph M., and Prudence S. Posner. 1990a. "Class and Community in an Era of Urban Transformation." Pp. 23-45 in *Dilemmas of Activism: Class,*

*Community and the Politics of Local Mobilization*, edited by Joseph M. Kling and Prudence S. Posner. Philadelphia, PA: Temple University Press.

Kling, Joseph M., and Prudence S. Posner, eds. 1990b. *Dilemmas of Activism: Class, Community, and the Politics of Local Mobilization*. Philadelphia, PA: Temple University Press.

Koedt, Anne. 1973. "Lesbianism and Feminism." Pp. 246–58 in *Radical Feminism*, edited by Anne Koedt, Ellen Levine, and Anita Rapone. New York, NY: Quadrangle.

Korean Women's Hotline [KWH]. 1993. Training Manual.

Kossoudji, Sherrie A., and Susan 1. Ranney. 1984. "The Labor Market Experience of Female Migrants: The Case of Temporary Mexican Migration to the U. S." *International Migration Review* 18:1120–1143.

Koven, Seth, and Sonya Michel, eds. 1993. *Mothers of a New World: Maternalist Politics and the Origins of Welfare States*. New York, NY: Routledge.

Krauss, Celene. 1989. "Community Struggles and the Shaping of Democratic Consciousness." *Sociological Forum* 4:227–238.

Krauss, Celene. 1990. "Blue-Collar Women and Toxic Waste Protests." The Proceedings of the Second Annual Women's Policy Research Conference.

Krauss, Celene. 1993. "Women and Toxic Waste Protests: Race, Class and Gender as Resources of Resistance." *Qualitative Sociology* 16(3):247–262.

Krauss, Celene. 1994a. "Commonalities and Differences, Privilege and Oppression: Women's Experience in Toxic Waste Protests." Paper presented at the Annual Meeting of the American Sociological Association, August, Los Angeles, CA.

Krauss, Celene. 1994b. "Women of Color at the Front." Pp. 256–271 in *Communities of Color and Environmental Justice*, edited by Robert Bullard. CA: Sierra Club Books

Kraybill, David S., Thomas G. Johnson, and Brady J. Deaton. 1987. *Income Uncertainty and the Quality of Life: A Socio-Economic Study of Virginia's Coal Counties*. Virginia Agricultural Experiment Station Bulletin 87(4). Blacksburg, VA: Virginia Polytechnic Institute and State University.

Krieger, Susan. 1983. *The Mirror Dance: Identity in a Woman's Community*. Philadelphia, PA: Temple University Press.

Lam, Maivân Clech. 1994. "Feeling Foreign in Feminism." *Signs: Journal of Women in Culture and Society* 19: 864–893.

Lamphere, Louise, Alex Stepick and Guillermo Grenier, eds. 1994. *Newcomers in the Workplace: Immigrants and the Restructuring of the U.S. Economy*. Philadelphia, PA: Temple University Press.

Landry, Donna, and Gerald MacLean. 1993. *Materialist Feminisms*. Cambridge, MA: Blackwell.

Lather, Patti. 1986. "Issues of Validity in Openly Ideological Research: Between a Rock and a Soft Place." *Interchange* 17(4):63–84.

Lather, Patti. 1988. "Feminist Research Perspectives on Empowering Research Methodologies." *Women's Studies International Forum* 11(6):569–82.

Lather, Patti. 1991. *Getting Smart: Feminist Research and Pedagogy With/in the Postmodern*. New York, NY: Routledge.

Lawson, Ronald, and Stephen E. Barton. 1980. "Sex Roles in Social Movements: A Case Study of the Tenant Movement in New York City." *Signs: Journal of Women in Culture and Society* 6:230–247.

Leadership Education for Asian Pacifics and the UCLA Asian American Studies Center. 1993. *The State of Asian Pacific America: Economic Diversity, Issues, and Policies. Executive Summary*. UCLA Asian American Studies Center.

Leavitt, Jacqueline. 1992. "Women Under Fire: Public Housing Activism in Los Angeles." *Frontiers* 13(2):109–130.

Leavitt, Jacqueline, and Susan Saegert. 1990. *From Abandonment to Hope: The Community-Household in Harlem*. New York, NY: Columbia University Press.

Lee, Jee Yeun. 1995. "Beyond Bean Counting." Pp. 205–211 in *Listen Up: Voices from the Next Feminist Generation*, edited by B. Findlen. Seattle, WA: Seal Press.

Lembcke, Jerry. 1988. *Capitalist Development and Class Capacities: Marxist Theory and Union*. New York, NY: Greenwood Press.

Lembcke, Jerry, and Carolyn Howe. 1986. "Organizational Structure and the Logic of Collective Action in Unions." Pp. 1–28 in *Current Perspectives in Social Theory v.7*, edited by Scott McNall. Greenwich, CT: JAI Press.

Leonard, Ann, ed. 1989. *Seeds: Supporting Women's Work in the Third World*. New York, NY: The Feminist Press (CUNY).

Levine, Adeline. 1982. *Love Canal: Science, Politics, and People*. Lexington: Health.

Lewis, Helen, and Susanna O'Donnell. 1990a. *Remembering Our Past, Building Our Future*. Ivanhoe, VA: Ivanhoe Civic League.

Lewis, Helen, and Susanna O'Donnell. 1990b. *Telling Our Stories, Sharing Our Lives*. Ivanhoe, VA: Ivanhoe Civic League.

Light, Ivan H. 1972. *Ethnic Enterprises in America: Business and Welfare Among Chinese, Japanese and Blacks*. Berkeley, CA: University of California Press.

Light, Linda, and Nancy Kleiber. 1988. "Interactive Research in a Feminist Setting: The Vancouver Women's Health Collective." Pp. 185–201 in Donald A. Messerschmidt, *Anthropologists at Home in North America: Methods and Issues in the Study of One's Own Society*, edited by Donald A. Messerschmidt. New York, NY: Cambridge University Press.

Lin, Margaretta Wan Ling, and Cheng Imm Tan. 1994. "Holding Up More Than Half the Heavens: Domestic Violence in our Communities, A Call for Justice." Pp. 321–334 in *The State of Asian America: Activism and Resistance in the 1990's*, edited by Karin Aguilar-San Juan. Boston, MA: South End Press.

Linden, Robin Ruth, Darlene R. Pagano, Diana E. H. Russell, and Susan Leigh Star. 1982. *Against Sadomasochism: A Radical Feminist Analysis*. East Palo Alto, CA: Frog in the Well.

Lofland, John. 1989. "Consensus Movements: City Twinning and Derailed Dissent in the American Eighties." Pp. 163–96 in *Research in Social Movements: Conflict and Change*, Vol. 11. Greenwich, CN: JAI Press.

Loof, David H. 1971. *Appalachia's Children: The Challenge of Mental Health*. Lexington, KY: University of Kentucky Press.

Long, Lynellyn D. 1988. *The Floating World: Laotian Refugee Camp Life in Thailand*. Ph.D. Dissertation. Stanford University.

Long, Lynellyn D. 1993. *Ban Vinai: The Refugee Camp*. New York, NY: Columbia University Press.

Lorber, Judith. 1994. *Paradoxes of Gender*. New Haven, CT: Yale University Press.

Lorde, Audre. 1984a. "An Open Letter to Mary Daly," Pp. 66-71 in *Sister Outsider: Eassays and Speeches*. Trumansburg, N.Y.: Crossing Press.

Lorde, Audre, 1984b. "The Master's Tools Will Never Dismantle the Master's House." Pp. 110-13 in *Sister Outsider: Eassays and Speeches*. Trumansburg, N.Y.: Crossing Press.

Lorde, Audre. 1984c. *Sister Outsider*. Freedom, CA: Crossing Press.

Loseke, Donileen. 1992. *The Battered Woman and Shelters: The Social Construction of Wife Abuse*. NY: State University of New York Press.

Loulan, JoAnn Gardner. 1990. *The Lesbian Erotic Dance: Butch, Femme, Androgyny, and Other Rhythms*. San Francisco, CA: Spinsters.

Luttrell, Wendy. 1988. "Working-Class Women, Social Protest, and Changing Ideologies." Pp. 257-271 in *Women and the Politics of Empowerment*, edited by Sandra Morgen and Ann Bookman. Philadelphia, PA: Temple University Press.

Luxton, Meg. 1980. *More Than A Labour of Love: Three Generations of Women's Work in the Home*. Toronto: Women's Press.

MacKinnon, Catharine A. 1987. *Feminism Unmodified: Discourses on Life and Law*. Cambridge, MA: Harvard University Press.

Maggard, Sally Ward. 1986. "Class and Gender: New Theoretical Priorities in Appalachian Studies." Pp. 100-113 in *The Impact of Institutions in Appalachia*, edited by Jim Lloyd and Ann G. Campbell. Boone, NC: Appalachian Consortium Press.

Maguire, Patricia. 1987. *Doing Participatory Research: A Feminist Approach*. Amherst, MA: Center for International Education, School of Education, University of Massachusetts.

Mansbridge, Jane. 1993. "The Role of Discourse in the Feminist Movement." Paper presented at the Annual Meeting of the American Political Science Association, Washington, D.C.

Markusen, Ann. 1984. "Class and Urban Social Expenditure: A Marxist Theory of Metropolitan Government." Pp. 90-111 in *Marxism and the Metropolis*, edited by William Tabb and Larry Sawer. New York, NY: Oxford University Press.

Martin, Biddy, and Chandra Talpade Mohanty. 1986. "Feminist Politics: What's Home Got to Do with It?" Pp. 191-212 in *Feminist Studies/Critical Studies*, edited by Teresa de Lauretis. Bloomington, IN: Indiana University Press.

Massey, Douglas et al. 1987. *Return to Aztlan: The Social Process of International*

*Migration from Western Mexico.* Berkeley and Los Angeles, CA: University of California Press.

Matteson, Gretchen. 1989. "The History of the Women's Action Collective, a Successful Social Movement Organization, 1971–1984." Unpublished manuscript, Columbus, Ohio.

Matthews, Nancy. 1995. "Feminist Clashes With the State: Tactical Choices by State-Funded Rape Crisis Centers." Pp. 291–305 in *Feminist Organizations: Harvest of the New Women's Movement*, edited by Myra Marx Ferree and Patricia Yancey Martin. Philadelphia, PA: Temple University Press.

McCarthy, John D., and Mark Wolfson. 1992. "Consensus Movements, Conflict Movements, and the Co-optation of Civic and State Infrastructures." Pp. 273–97 in *Frontiers in Social Movement Theory*, edited by Aldon D. Morris and Carol McClurg Mueller. New Haven, CT: Yale University Press.

McCarthy, John D., and Mayer N. Zald. 1977. "Resource Mobilization and Social Movements: A Partial Theory." *American Journal of Sociology* 82(6): 1212–1241.

McCarthy, Kathleen D., ed. 1990. *Lady Bountiful Revisited: Women, Philanthropy, and Power.* New Brunswick, NJ: Rutgers University Press.

McCormick, Kelly. 1992. "Moms Without Dads: Women Choosing Children." Ph.D. dissertation, Ohio State University.

McCourt, Kathleen. 1977. *Working Class Women and Grass Roots Politics.* Bloomington, IN: Indiana University Press.

McNamara, Patrick Hayes. 1957. "Mexican Americans in Los Angeles County: A Study in Acculturation," M.A. Thesis, St. Louis University.

Melucci, Alberto. 1989. *Nomads of the Present: Social Movements and Individual Needs in Contemporary Society.* Philadelphia, PA: Temple University Press.

Meredith, William H., and George P. Rowe. 1986. "Changes in Hmong Refugee Marital Attitudes in America." Pp. 135–144 in *The Hmong in Transition.* New York, NY: Center for Migration Studies.

Merry, Sally Engle. 1990. *Getting Justice and Getting Even: Legal Consciousness among Working-Class Americans.* Chicago, IL: University of Chicago Press.

Mies, Maria. 1983. "Towards a Methodology of Feminist Research." Pp. 117–139 in *Theories of Women's Studies*, edited by Gloria Bowles and Renate Duelli Klein. London: Routledge and Kegan Paul.

Mies, Maria. 1991. "Women's Research or Feminist Research? The Debate Surrounding Feminist Science and Methodology." Pp. 60–84 in *Beyond Methodology: Feminist Scholarship as Lived Research*, edited by Mary Margaret Fonow and Judith A. Cook. Bloomington, IN: Indiana University Press.

Miles, Angela. 1996. *Integrative Feminisms: Building Global Visions, 1960s–1990s.* New York, NY: Routledge.

Milkman, Ruth, ed. 1985. *Women, Work and Protest: A Century of U.S. Women's Labor History.* London: Routledge & Kegan Paul.

Miller, Stuart Creighton. 1969. *The Unwelcome Immigrants: The American Image of the Chinese, 1785–1882.* Berkeley, CA: University of California Press.

Milwaukee County Welfare Rights Organization. 1972. *Welfare Mothers Speak Out: "We Ain't Gonna Shuffle Anymore.* New York, NY: Norton.

Minkowitz, Donna. 1992. "The Newsroom Becomes a Battleground." *Advocate* May 19, 31–37.

Mitchell, Juliet. 1971. *Woman's Estate.* New York, NY: Pantheon Books.

Mohanty, Chandra Talpade. 1991a. "Cartographies of Struggle: Third World Women and the Politics of Feminism." Pp. 1–47 in *Third World Women and the Politics of Feminism,* edited by Chandra T. Mohanty, Ann Russo, and Lourdes Torres. Bloomington, IN: Indiana University Press.

Mohanty, Chandra Talpade. 1991b. "Under Western Eyes: Feminist Scholarship and Colonial Discourses." Pp. 51–80 in *Third World Women and the Politics of Feminism,* edited by Chandra Talpade Mohanty, Ann Russo and Lourdes Torres. Bloomington, IN: Indiana University Press.

Mohanty, Chandra Talpade. 1995. "Feminist Encounters: Locating the Politics of Experience." Pp. 68–86 in *Social Postmodernism: Beyond Identity Politics,* edited by Linda Nicholson and Steven Seidman. Cambridge: Cambridge University Press.

Mohanty, Chandra Talpade. 1997. "Women Workers and Capitalist Scripts: Ideologies of Domination, Common Interests, and the Politics of Solidarity." Pp. 3–29 in *Feminist Genealogies, Colonial Legacies, Democratic Futures,* edited by M. Jacqui Alexander and Chandra Talpade Mohanty. New York, NY: Routledge.

Mohanty, Chandra Talpade, Ann Russo, and Lourdes Torres, eds. 1991. *Third World Women and the Politics of Feminism.* Bloomington, IN: Indiana University Press.

Molyneux, Maxine. 1986. "Mobilization Without Emancipation? Women's Interests, State and Revolution in Nicaragua." Pp. 280–302 in *Transition and Development: Problems of Third World Socialism,* edited by Richard R. Fagen, Carmen Diana Deere, and Jose Luis Goraggio. New York, NY: Monthly Review Press and Center for the Study of the Americas.

Molyneux, Maxine. 1985. "Mobilization Without Emancipation: Women's Interests, the State and Revolution in Nicaragua." *Feminist Studies* 11:227–54.

Momsen, Janet, and Janet Townsend. 1987. *Geography of Gender in the Third World.* Albany, NY: State University of New York.

Monti, Daniel J. 1989. "The Organizational Strengths and Weaknesses of Resident-Managed Public Housing Sites in the United States." *Journal of Urban Affairs* 11(1):39–52.

Moore, Barrington Jr. 1978. *Injustice: The Social Basis of Obedience and Revolt.* New York, NY: M.E. Sharpe.

Moore, Joan. 1966. *Mexican Americans: Problems and Prospects.* Institute for Research on Poverty, University of Wisconsin, Madison.

Moore, Joan. 1985. "Isolation, Stigmatization in the Development of an Underclass: The Case of Chicano Gangs in East L.A." *Social Problems* 33(1):1–12.

Moraga, Cherríe. 1981. "Preface." Pp. xiii–xix in *This Bridge Called My Back: Writ-*

*ings by Radical Women of Color,* edited by Cherríe Moraga and Gloria Anzaldúa. Watertown, MA: Persephone Press.

Moraga, Cherríe, and Gloria Anzaldúa, eds. 1981. *This Bridge Called My Back: Writings by Radical Women of Color.* Watertown, MA: Persephone Press.

Morgen, Sandra. 1988. "'It's the Whole Power of the City Against Us!'": The Development of Political Consciousness in a Women's Health Care Coalition." Pp. 97–115 in *Women and the Politics of Empowerment,* edited by Sandra Morgen and Ann Bookman. Philadelphia, PA: Temple University Press.

Morgen, Sandra, and Ann Bookman. 1988. "Rethinking Women and Politics: An Introductory Essay." Pp. 3–29 in *Women and the Politics of Empowerment,* edited by Sandra Morgen and Ann Bookman. Philadelphia, PA: Temple University Press.

Morris, Aldon D. 1992. "Political Consciousness and Collective Action." Pp. 351–373 in *Frontiers in Social Movement Theory,* edited by Aldon D. Morris and Carol McClurg Mueller. New Haven, CT: Yale University Press.

Moschkovich, Judit. 1981. "'But I Know You, American Woman.'" Pp. 79–84 in *This Bridge Called My Back: A Collection of Writings by Radical Women of Color,* edited by Cherríe Moraga and Gloria Anzaldúa. Watertown, MA: Persephone Press.

Moser, Caroline O.N. 1989. "Gender Planning in the Third World: Meeting Practical and Strategic Gender Needs." *World Development* 8(11):1799–1825.

Moser, Caroline O.N. 1993. *Gender Planning and Development: Theory, Practice, and Training.* New York, NY: Routledge.

Moya, Paula M. L. 1997. "Postmodernism, 'Realism,' and the Politics of Identity: Cherríe Moraga and Chicana Feminism." Pp. 125–150 in *Feminist Genealogies, Colonial Legacies, Democratic Futures,* edited by M. Jacqui Alexander and Chandra Talpade Mohanty. New York, NY: Routledge.

Moynihan, Daniel Patrick. 1965. *The Negro Family: The Case for National Action.* Washington, D.C.: Government Printing Office.

Naples, Nancy. 1991a. "Contradictions in the Gender Subtext of the War on Poverty: The Community Work and Resistance of Women from Low Income Communities." *Social Problems* 38(3): 316–332.

Naples, Nancy. 1991b. "'Just What Needed to Be Done': The Political Practice of Women Community Workers in Low-Income Neighborhoods." *Gender & Society* 5(4): 478–94.

Naples, Nancy A. 1992. "Activist Mothering: Cross-Generational Continuity in the Community Work of Women From Low-Income Urban Neighborhoods." *Gender & Society* 6(3):441–463.

Naples, Nancy A. 1994. "Contradictions in Agrarian Ideology: Restructuring Gender, Race-ethnicity, and Class in Rural Iowa." *Rural Sociology* 59(1):110–135.

Naples, Nancy A. 1996. "A Feminist Revisiting of the Insider/Outsider Debate: The 'Outsider Phenomenon' in Rural Iowa." *Qualitative Sociology* 19(1): 83–106.

Naples, Nancy A. 1997. "Contested Needs: Shifting the Standpoint on Rural Economic Development." *Feminist Economics* 3(2): 315–350.

Naples, Nancy A. Forthcoming a. *Grassroots Warriors: Activist Mothering, Community Work, and the War on Poverty*. New York, NY: Routledge.

Naples, Nancy A. Forthcoming b. "Towards a Comparative Standpoint Methodology: Explicating Dilemmas of Feminist Ethnography for Women's Political Praxis." *Women and Politics*.

Naples, Nancy A., with Emily Clark. 1996. "Feminist Participatory Research and Empowerment: Going Public as Survivors of Childhood Sexual Abuse." Pp. 160–183 in *Feminism and Social Change: Bridging Theory and Practice*, edited by Heidi Gottfried. Champagne-Urbana, IL: Illinois University Press.

National Council of Negro Women. 1975. *Women and Housing: A Report on Sex Discrimination in Five American Cities*. Commissioned by the U.S. Department of Housing and Urban Development, Office of the Assistant Secretary for Fair Housing and Equal Opportunity. Washington, D.C.: U.S. Government Printing Office. (June):33.

Near, Holly. 1990. *Fire in the Rain, Singer in the Storm*. New York, NY: Morrow.

Near, Holly. 1992a. "The News That 'Rocked the Feminist Community.'" *off our backs* 22 (January): 2.

Near, Holly. 1992b. "Queer Notions." *off our backs* (October):12–15.

Nee, Victor, and Brett de Bary Nee. 1987. *Longtime Californ': A Study of an American Chinatown*. Stanford, CA: Stanford University Press.

Nelson, Lynn Hankinson. 1993. "Epistemological Communities." Pp. 121–160 in *Feminist Epistemologies*, edited by Linda Alcoff and Elizabeth Potter. New York, NY: Routledge.

*Network News*. 1992. "Workers of the World on U.S. Street Corners," *Network News: Newsletter of the National Network for Immigrant and Refugee Rights*, Vol. 5, No. 3, April–May, 1992.

Newman, Penny. 1991. "Women and the Environment in the United States of America." Paper presented at the Conference of Women and Environment, Bangalore, India.

Nicholson, Linda, and Seven Seidman. 1996. *Social Postmodernism: Beyond Identity Politics*. Cambridge: Cambridge University Press.

Nieto-Gomez, Ana. 1974. "La Feminista." *Encuentro Feminil: The First Chicana Feminist Journal* 1(2).

Nieto-Gomez, Ana. 1991. Oral History Interviews Conducted by Maylei Blackwell.

Nishio, Alan. 1993. Oral History Interview Conducted by Sherna Berger Gluck and Karen harper.

Oakes, Jeannie. 1985. *Keeping Track*. New Haven, CT: Yale University Press.

Oboler, Suzanne. 1995. *Ethnic Labels, Latino Lives: Identity and the Politics of (Re)Presentation in the United States*. Minneapolis, MN: University of Minnesota Press.

Offe, Claus, and Helmut Wiesenthal. 1980. "Two Logics of Collective Action: Theoretical Notes on Social Class and Organizational Form." Pp. 67–115 in

*Political Power and Social Theory Vol. 1*, edited by Maurice Zeitlin. Greenwich, CT: JAI Press.

Office of Refugee Resettlement. 1985. *The Hmong Resettlement Study*, Vol.1. Washington, D.C.: U.S. Dept. of Health and Human Resources.

Office of Refugee Resettlement. 1984. *The Hmong Resettlement Study: Economic Development and Employment Projects*, Vol. 11. Washington, D.C.: U.S. Dept. of Health and Human Services.

Office of Refugee Resettlement. 1985. *The Hmong Resettlement Study: Exemplary Projects and Projects with Unique Features of Programmatic Interest*, Vol. 111. Washington D.C.: U.S. Dept. of Health and Human Services.

*off our backs*. 1992a. "The News That 'Rocked the Feminist Community'." *off our backs*. 22 (January): 2.

*off our backs*. 1992b. "Queer Notions." *off our backs*. October: 12–15.

Ohoyo Resource Center. 1981. *Words of Today's American Indian Women: (Ohoyo Makachi)*. Washington, D.C.: U.S. Department of Education.

Olney, Douglas Philip. 1993. *We Must Be Organized: Dual Organizations in an American Hmong Community*. Ph.D. Dissertation, University of Minnesota.

Omi, Michael, and Howard Winant. 1986. *Racial Formation in the United States from the 1960s to the 1980s* . New York, NY: Routledge.

Omi, Michael, and Howard Winant. 1994. *Racial Formation in the United Statesw from the 1960s to the 1980s*, Second Edition. New York, NY: Routledge.

Omolade, Barbara. 1994. *The Rising Song of African American Women*. New York, NY: Routledge.

Orleck, Annelise. 1993. "'We Are That Mythical Thing Called the Public': Militant Housewives during the Great Depression." *Feminist Studies* 19(1): 147–72.

Otto, Nancy. 1994. Fax Memorandum. National Immigration Forum, Dec. 5.

Pardo, Mary. 1990a. "Identity and Resistance: Mexican American Women and Grassroots Activism in Two Los Angeles Communities." Ph.D. Dissertation, University of California, Los Angeles.

Pardo, Mary. 1990b. "Mexican American Women Grassroots Community Activists: Mothers of East Los Angeles." *Frontiers* 11(1):1–7.

Pardo, Mary. 1995. "Doing It for the Kids: Mexican American Community Activists, Border Feminists?" Pp. 356–371 in *Feminist Organizations: Harvest of the New Women's Movement*. Philadelphia, PA: Temple University Press.

Park, Lisa Sun-Hee, and David Naguib Pellow. 1996. "Washing Dirty Laundry: Organic-Activist-Research Inside Two Social Movement Organizations." *Sociological Imagination* 33:138–153.

Park, Peter. 1992. "The Discovery of Participatory Research as a New Scientific Paradigm: Personal and Intellectual Accounts." *The American Sociologist* 23(4):29–42.

Pascoe, Peggy. 1990. *Relations of Rescue: The Search for Female Moral Authority in the American West, 1874–1939*. New York, NY: Oxford University Press.

Pateman, Carolyn. 1970. *Participation and Democratic Theory*. Cambridge: Cambridge University Press.

Payne, Charles. 1990. "Men Led, But Women Organized: Movement Participation of Women in the Mississippi Delta." Pp. 156–165 in *Women and Social Protest*, edited by Guida West and Rhoda Lois Blumberg. New York, NY: Oxford University Press.

Peattie, Lisa, and Martin Rein. 1983. *Women's Claims: A Study in Political Economy*. London: Oxford University Press.

Pedraza, Silvia. 1991. "Women and Migration: The Social Consequences of Gender." *Annual Review of Sociology* 17:303–325.

Persell, Caroline. 1977. *Education and Inequality: The Roots and Results of Stratification in American Schools*. New York, NY: The Free Press.

Peterman William. 1989. "Options to Conventional Public Housing Management." *Journal of Urban Affairs* 11(1):53–58.

Peterson, Corinne. 1988. Volunteer Manual. Greehouse Shelter/Chicago Abused Women's Coalition.

Petras, Elizabeth M., and Douglas V. Porpora. 1993. "Participatory Research: Three Models and an Analysis." *The American Sociologist* 24(1):107–126.

Phelan, Shane. 1993. "(Be)Coming Out: Lesbian Identity and Politics." *Signs: Journal of Women in Culture and Society* 18(4): 764–790.

Piven, Frances Fox, and Richard A. Cloward. 1977. *Poor People's Movements: Why They Succeed, How They Fail*. New York, NY: Pantheon.

Piven, Frances Fox, and Richard A. Cloward. 1979. *Poor People's Movements: Why They Succeed, How They Fail*. New York, NY: Vintage Books (Random House).

Pleck, Elizabeth. 1987. *Domestic Tyranny: The Making of Social Policy Against Family Violence from Colonial Times to the Present*. New York, NY: Oxford University Press.

Pousada, Alicia. 1984. "Community Participation in Bilingual Education: The Puerto Rican Community of East Harlem." Ph.D. Dissertation, University of Pennsylvania.

Portes, Alejandro and Robert Bach. 1985. *Latin Journey: Cuban and Mexican Immigrants in the United States*. Berkeley and Los Angeles, CA: University of California Press.

Ptacek, James. 1988. "Why Do Men Batter Their Wives?" Pp. 133–157 in *Feminist Perspectives on Wife Abuse*, edited by Kersti Yllo and Michele Bograd. Beverly Hills, CA: Sage.

Quest Staff, eds. 1981. *Building Feminist Theory: Essays from Quest*. New York, NY: Longman.

Quon, Merilyn Hamano. 1984. Oral History Conducted by Susie Ling, UCLA.

Rabrenovic, Gordana. 1995. "Women and Collective Action in Urban Neighborhoods." Pp. 77–96 in *Gender in Urban Research*, edited by Judith A. Garber and Robyne S. Turner. Thousand Oaks, CA: Sage.

Reagon, Bernice Johnson. 1983. "Coalition Politics: Turning the Century," Pp. 356–368 in *Home Girls: A Black Feminist Anthology*, edited by Barbara Smith. New York, NY: Kitchen Table, Women of Color Press.

Reinelt, Claire. 1995. "Moving onto the Terrain of the State: The Battered Women's Movement and the Politics of Engagement." Pp. 84–104 in *Feminist Organizations: Harvest of the New Women's Movement*, edited by Myra Marx Ferree and Patricia Yancey Martin. Philadelphia, PA: Temple University Press.

Reinharz, Shulamit. 1992. *Feminist Methods in Social Research*. New York, NY: Oxford University Press.

Repak, Terry. 1990. "Economic Change and International Migration: The Case of Central Americans in Washington, D.C." Unpublished paper.

Retail Chicago Advisory Panel. Undated. "Retail Chicago: A Neighborhood Commercial Development Initiative." A discussion paper for the Department of Planning and Development in Partnership with the Local Initiative Support Corporation and the Chicago Association of Neighborhood Development Organizations.

Rich, Andrienne. 1976. *Of Woman Born*. New York, NY: Norton.

Rich, Adrienne. 1980. "Compulsory Heterosexuality and Lesbian Existence." *Signs: Journal of Women in Culture and Society* 5(4):631–60.

Rich, Adrienne. 1986. *Blood, Bread, and Poetry: Selected Prose, 1979–1985*. New York, NY: Norton.

Rimonte, Nilda. 1989. "Domestic Violence Amng Pacific Asians." In *Making Waves*, edited by Asian Women United of California. Boston, MA: Beacon Press.

Ringelheim, Joan. 1985. "Women and the Holocaust: A Reconsideration of Research." *Signs: Journal of Women in Culture and Society* 10(4):741–61.

Ritchie, Mark. 1990. "Rural-Urban Cooperation: Our Populist History and Future." Pp. 291–301 in *Building Bridges: The Emerging Grassroots Coalition of Labor and Community*, edited by Jeremy Brecher and Tim Costello. New York, N.Y.: Monthly Review Press.

Roberts, Dorothy. 1995. "Race, Gender, and the Value of Mother's Work." *Social Politics* 2:195–207.

Rocheleau, Dianne, Barbara Thomas-Slayter, and Esther Wangari, eds. 1996. *Feminist Political Ecology: Global Issues and Local Experiences*. New York, NY: Routledge.

Rodriguez, Nestor, and Rogelio T. Nunez. 1986. "An Exploration of Factors That Contribute to Differentiation Between Chicanos and Indocumentados." Pp. 138–56 in *Mexican Immigrants and Mexican Americans: An Evolving Relation*, edited by Harley L. Browning and R. O. de la Garza. Austin, TX: Center for Mexican American Studies, University of Texas Austin.

Rodriguez, Noelie Maria. 1988. "Transcending Bureaucracy: Feminist Politics at a Shelter for Battered Women." *Gender & Society* 2(2):214–27.

Roediger, David R. 1991. *The Wages of Whiteness: Race and the American Working Class*. London and New York: Verso.

Rollins, Judith. 1985. *Between Women: Domestics and Their Employers.* Philadelphia, PA: Temple University Press.

Romero, Mary. 1988. "Chicanas Modernize Domestic Service." *Qualitative Sociology* 11:319–334.

Romero, Mary. 1992. *Maid in the U.S.A.* New York and London: Routledge.

Ronai, Carol Rambo. 1995. "Multiple Reflections of Child Sex Abuse: An Argument for a Layered Account." *Journal of Contemporary Ethnography* 23(4):395–426.

Rose, Margaret. 1990. "Traditional and Nontraditional Patterns of Female Activism in the United Farm Workers of America, 1962 to 1980." *Frontiers* 11(1):26–32.

Rosenthal, Robert, and Lenore F. Jacobson. 1968. *Pygmalion in the Classroom: Teacher Expectation and Pupils' Intellectual Development.* New York, NY: Holt, Rinehart, & Winston.

Rubin, Beth A. 1996. *Shifts in the Social Contract: Understanding Change in American Society.* Thousand Oaks, CA: Pine Forge Press.

Ruby, Jennie, Farar Elliott, and Carol Anne Douglas. 1990. "NWSA: Troubles Surface at Conference." *off our backs* 1 (August/September): 1016.

Ruddick, Sara. 1989. *Maternal Thinking: Towards a Politics of Peace.* New York, NY: Ballantine Books.

Rudé, George. 1980. *Ideology and Popular Protest.* New York, NY: Pantheon.

Ruiz, Vicki L. 1987. "By the Day or the Week: Mexicana Domestic Workers in El Paso." Pp. 61–76 in *Women on the U. S.-Mexico Border: Responses to Change,* edited by Vicki L. Ruiz and Susan Tiano. Boston, MA: Allen and Unwin.

Rupp, Leila J., and Verta Taylor. 1987. *Survival in the Doldrums: The American Women's Rights Movement, 1945 to the 1960s.* New York, NY: Oxford University Press.

Russell, Michelle. 1981. "An Open Letter to the Academy." Pp. 101–110 in *Building Feminist Theory: Essays from Quest,* edited by Quest Staff. New York, NY: Longman.

Ryan, Barbara. 1992. *Feminism and the Women's Movement.* New York, NY: Harper Collins.

Sachs, Carolyn. 1996. *Gendered Fields: Rural Women, Agriculture, and Environment.* Boulder, CO: Westview.

Sacks, Karen Brodkin. 1988a. *Caring by the Hour: Women, Work, and Organizing at Duke Medical Center.* Urbana, IL: University of Illinois Press.

Sacks, Karen Brodkin. 1988b. "Gender and Grassroots Leadership." Pp. 77–94 in *Women and the Politics of Empowerment,* edited by Ann Bookman and Sandra Morgen. Philadelphia, PA: Temple University Press.

Sacks, Karen Brodkin. 1989. "Toward a Unified Theory of Class, Race, and Gender." *American Ethnologist* 16(3):534–50.

Sacks, Karen Brodkin. 1994. "How Did Jews Become White Folks?" Pp. 78–102 in *Race,* edited by Steven Gregory and Roger Sanjek. New Brunswick, NJ: Rutgers University Press.

Sahagun, Louis. 1983. "Boyle Heights: Problems, Pride and Promise." *Los Angeles Times* 31 July, p. 1.

Said, Edward W. 1978. *Orientalism.* New York, NY: Vintage Books.

Salzinger, Leslie. 1991. "A Maid by Any Other Name: The Transformation of 'Dirty Work' by Central American Immigrants." Pp. 139–160 in *Ethnography Unbound: Power and Resistance in the Modern Metropolis,* edited by Michael Burawoy et al. Berkeley, CA: University of California Press.

Sandoval, Chela. 1982. "Feminism and Racism: A Report on the 1981 National Women's Studies Association Conference," Oakland, CA: Center for Third World Organizing. Reprinted in 1991, *Making Face, Making Soul—Haciendo Caras: Creative and Critical Perspectives by Women of Color,* edited by Gloria Anzaldúa. San Francisco, CA: Aunt Lute.

Sandoval, Chela. 1991. "U.S. Third World Feminism: The Theory and Method of Oppositional Consciousness in the Postmodern World." *Genders* 10:1–24.

Sargent, Lydia, ed. 1981. *Women and Revolution: A Discussion of the Unhappy Marriage of Marxism and Feminism.* Boston, MA: South End Press.

Schensul, Jean, Iris Nieves, and Maria D. Martinez. 1982. "The Crisis Event in the Puerto Rican Community: Research and Intervention in the Community/Institution Interface." *Urban Anthropology* 11(1):534–568.

Schensul, Stephen L. 1980. "Anthropological Fieldwork and Sociopolitical Change." *Social Problems* 27(3):309–319.

Schechter, Susan. 1982. *Women and Male Violence: The Visions and Struggles of the Battered Women's Movement.* Boston, MA: South End Press.

Schnaiberg, Allan. 1980. *The Environment: From Surplus to Scarcity.* New York, NY: Oxford University Press.

Schneider, Beth. 1986. "Feminist Disclaimers, Stigma, and the Contemporary Women's Movement." Unpublished manuscript, Santa Barbara, California.

Schneider, Beth. 1988. "Political Generations in the Contemporary Women's Movement." Sociological *Inquiry* 58(1):4–21.

Schneider, Beth E., and Nancy E. Stoller, eds. 1995. *Women Resisting AIDS: Feminist Strategies of Empowerment.* Philadelphia, PA: Temple University Press.

Scott, Ellen, and Bindi Shah. 1993. "Future Projects/Future Theorizing in Feminist Field Research Methods: Commentary on Panel Discussion." In *Frontiers.* 13(3):90–103.

Scott, James C. 1985. *Weapons of the Weak: Everyday Forms of Peasant Resistance.* New Haven, CT: Yale University Press.

Scott, James. 1990. *Domination and the Arts of Resistance: Hidden Transcripts.* New Haven, CT: Yale University Press.

Scott, Kisho Y. 1991. *The Habit of Surviving.* New York, NY: Ballantine.

Sedgwick, Eve Kosovsky. 1990. *Epistemology of the Closet.* Berkeley, CA: University of California Press.

Segal, Lynne, and Mary McIntosh. 1993. *Sex Exposed: Sexuality and the Pornography Debate.* New Brunswick, N.J.: Rutgers University Press.

Seitz, Virginia Rinaldo. 1995. *Women, Development, and Communities for Empower-*

*ment in Appalachia.* Albany, NY: State University of New York Press.

Sen, Gita, and Caren Grown. 1987. *Development, Crises, and Alternative Visions: Third World Women's Perspectives.* New York, NY: Monthly Review Press.

Shah, Sonia. 1994. "Presenting the Blue Goddess: Toward a National, Pan-Asian Feminist Agenda." Pp. 147-158 in *The State of Asian America: Activism and Resistance in the 1990s,* edited by Karin Aguilar-San Juan. Boston, MA: South End Press.

Shanley, Kate. 1995. "Thoughts on Indian Feminism." Pp. 416-417 in *Women: Images and Realities, A Multicultural Anthology,* edited by Amy Kesselman et al. Mountain View, CA: Mayfield Publishing.

Sharon, Tanya, Farar Elliott, and Cecile Latham. 1991. "The National Lesbian Conference." *off our backs,* June, 1-4, 18-19.

Shifflett, Crandall. 1991. *Coal Towns: Life, Work, and Culture in Company Towns in Southern Appalachia, 1890-1960.* Knoxville, TN: University of Tennessee Press.

Shor, Ira. 1980. *Critical Teaching and Everyday Life.* Boston, MA: South End Press.

Shor, Ira. 1993. "Education is Politics: Paulo Freire's Critical Pedagogy." Pp. 25-35 in *Paulo Freire: A Critical Encounter,* edited by Peter McLaren and Peter Leonard. London: Routledge.

Siefer, Nancy. 1973. *Absent from the Majority: Working Class Women in America.* New York, NY: American Jewish Committee.

Siefer, Nancy. 1976. *Nobody Speaks for Me: Self-Portraits of American Working Class Women.* New York, NY: Simon and Schuster.

Simon, Rita J., and Margo Corona DeLey. 1984. "The Work Experience of Undocumented Mexican Women Migrants in Los Angeles." *International Migration Review* 18:1212-1229.

Simonds, Wendy. 1996. *Abortion at Work: Ideology and Practice in a Feminist Clinic.* New Brunswick, NJ: Rutgers University Press.

Smart, Carol. 1989. *Feminism and the Power of the Law.* London: Routledge.

Smart, Carol. 1995. *Law, Crime and Sexuality: Essays in Feminism.* London: Sage.

Smeller, Michele M. 1992. "Crossing Over: The Negotiation of Sexual Identity in a Social Movement Community." Unpublished manuscript, Columbus, Ohio.

Smith, Barbara. 1983. *Home Girls: A Black Feminist Anthology.* New York, NY: Kitchen Table; Women of Color Press.

Smith, Dorothy E. 1987a. *The Everyday World as Problematic: A Feminist Sociology.* Boston, MA: Northeastern University Press.

Smith, Dorothy E. 1987b. "Women's Perspective as a Radical Critique of Sociology." Pp. 84-96 in *Feminism and Methodology,* edited by Sandra Harding. Bloomington, IN: Indiana University Press.

Smith, Dorothy E. 1990. *Conceptual Practices of Power.* Boston, MA: Northeastern University Press.

Smith, Dorothy E. 1992. "Sociology from Women's Experience: A Reaffirmation." *Sociological Theory* 10(1):88-98.

Smith, Susan. 1989. "Society, Space and Citizenship: A Human Geography for the New Times?" *Transactions of the Institute of British Geographers* 14: 144–156.

Snitow, Ann, Christine Stansell, and Sharon Thompson, eds. 1983. *Powers of Desire: The Politics of Sexuality.* New York, NY: Monthly Review Press.

Snow, David, and Robert Benford. 1992. "Master frames and cycles of protest." Pp. 133–154 in *Frontiers in Social Movement Theory*, edited by Aldon D. Morris and Carol McClurg Mueller. New Haven, CT: Yale University Press.

Sowell, Thomas. 1981. *Ethnic America: A History.* New York, NY: Basic Books.

Spalter-Roth, Roberta, and Heidi Hartmann. 1996. "Small Happinesses: The Feminist Struggle to Integrate Social Research with Social Activism." Pp. 206–224 in *Feminism and Social Change: Bridging Theory and Practice*, edited by Heidi Gottfried. Urbana and Chicago, IL: University of Illinois Press.

Spalter-Roth, Roberta, Heidi Hartmann, and Linda Andrews. 1992. *Combining Work and Welfare: An Alternative Anti-Poverty Strategy.* Washington, D.C.: Institute for Women's Policy Research.

Spelman, Elizabeth V. 1988. *Inessential Woman: Problems of Exclusion in Feminist Thought.* Boston, MA: Beacon Press.

Spivack, Gayatri Chakravorty. 1987. *In Other Worlds.* New York, NY: Methuen.

Stacey, Judith. 1988. "Can There Be a Feminist Ethnography?" *Women's Studies International Forum* 11(1):21–27.

Staggenborg, Suzanne. 1991. *The Pro-Choice Movement.* New York, NY: Oxford University Press.

Stall, Susan, and Randy Stoecker. 1994. "Community Organizing or Organizing Community? Gender and the Craft of Empowerment." Paper presented at the annual meeting of the American Sociological Association, Los Angeles, California, August.

Stanley, Liz, ed. 1990. *Feminist Praxis: Research, Theory and Epistemology in Feminist Sociology.* New York, NY: Routledge.

Stanley, Liz, and Sue Wise. 1979. "Feminist Research, Feminist Consciousness and Experiences of Sexism." *Women's Studies International Quarterly* 2:359–374.

Stansell, Christine. 1990. "Women, Children and the Uses of the Streets: Class and Gender Conflict in New York City, 1850–1860." Pp. 92–108 in *Unequal Sisters: A Multicultural Reader in U.S. Women's History.* , edited by Vicki Ruiz and Ellen DuBois. New York, NY: Routledge.

Starr, Victoria. 1992. "The Changing Tune of Women's Music." *Advocate* June 2, 68–71.

Stein, Arlene. 1989. "All Dressed Up but No Place to Go? Style Wars and the New Lesbianism." *Out/Look* 1(4):34–42.

Stein, Arlene. 1992. "Sisters and Queers: The Decentering of Lesbian Feminism." *Socialist Review* 22:33–55.

Stein, Arlene, ed. 1993. *Sisters, Sexperts, Queers: Beyond the Lesbian Nation.* New York, NY: Plume.

Stein, George. 1989. "Surge of Violence Breaks Calm at Housing Project." *Los Angeles Times*, 24 May, sec. B, p. 1.

Steinberg, Ronnie J. 1996. "Advocacy Research for Feminist Policy Objectives: Experiences with Comparable Worth." Pp. 225-255 in *Feminism and Social Change: Bridging Theory and Practice*, edited by Heidi Gottfried. Urbana and Chicago, IL: University of Illinois Press.

Steinberg, Ronnie, and Lois Haignere. 1991. "Separate but Equivalent: Equal Pay for Work of Comparable Worth." Pp. 154-170 in *Beyond Methodology: Feminist Scholarship as Lived Research*, edited by Mary Margaret Fonow and Judith A. Cook. Bloomington, IN: Indiana University Press.

Stern, Susan P. 1986. "School Imposed Limits of Black Family 'Participation:' A View from Within and Below." Paper presented at the Annual Meeting of the American Anthropological Association, Philadelphia, December.

Stern, Susan P. 1987a. "Black Parents: Dropouts or Pushouts from School Participation?" Paper presented at the Annual Meeting of the American Anthropological Association, Chicago, November.

Stern, Susan P. 1987b. "Institutional Racial Inequality: Middle-Class Black Parents' Insights from the Everyday Politics of Schooling". Paper presented at the Annual Meeting of the American Sociological Association, Chicago, August.

Stern, Susan P. 1994. "Social Science from Below: Grassroots Knowledge for Science and Emancipation." Ph.D. dissertation, City University of New York.

Stevens, Robin. 1991. "Style vs. Substance at the National Lesbian Conference." *Out/Look* 14:51-53.

Stoecker, Randy. 1995a. "Community Organizing and Community Development in Cedar-Riverside and East Toledo: A Comparative Study." *Journal of Community Practice* 2(3):1-23.

Stoecker, Randy. 1995b. "Community, Movement, Organization: The Problem of Identity Convergence in Collective Action." *The Sociological Quarterly* 36(1):111-130.

Stoecker, Randy, and Edna Bonacich. 1992. "Why Participatory Research?" *The American Sociologist* Winter: 5-14.

Stoecker, Randy, and Mary Schmidbauer. 1991. "Local State Reform and Class Struggle: The Case of Toledo, Ohio." *Critical Sociology* 18(3):99-123.

Stout, Linda. 1996. *Bridging the Class Divide and Other Lesons for Grassroots Organizing*. Boston, MA: Beacon Press.

Sullivan, Gail. 1983. "Ten Years After: Letter from Wounded Knee." *Radical America* 17(1): 75-80.

Susser, Ida. 1982. *Norman Street: Poverty and Politics in an Urban Neighborhood*. New York, NY: Oxford University Press.

Susser, Ida. 1988. "Working-Class Women, Social Protest, and Changing Ideologies." Pp. 257-271 in *Women and the Politics of Empowerment*, edited by Ann Bookman and Sandra Morgen. Philadelphia, PA: Temple University Press.

Suttles, Gerald. 1972. *The Social Construction of Communities.* Chicago, IL: University of Chicago Press.

Suzuki, Bob H. 1989. "Asian Americans as the 'Model Minority': Outdoing Whites? Or Media Hype?" *Change* 21 (6) Nov./Dec.:12–19.

Takaki, Ronald. 1989. *Strangers From a Different Shore: A History of Asian Americans.* Boston, MA: Little Brown and Company.

Tax, Meredith. 1980. *The Rising of the Women: Feminist Solidarity and Class Conflict, 1880–1917.* New York, NY: Monthly Review Press.

Taylor, Dorceta. 1990. "Can the Environmental Movement Attract and Maintain the Support of Minorities." Pp.28–59 in *the Proceedings of the Michigan Conference on Race and the Incidences of Environmental Hazards,* edited by Bunyan Bryant and Paul Mohai.

Taylor, Verta. 1989. "Social Movement Continuity: The Women's Movement in Abeyance." *American Sociological Review* 54 (October): 761–75.

Taylor, Verta, and Nancy E. Whittier. 1992. "Collective Identity in Social Movement Communities: Lesbian Feminist Mobilization." Pp. 104–29 in *Frontiers of Social Movement Theory,* edited by Aldon D. Morris and Carol McClurg Mueller. New Haven, CT: Yale University Press.

Therborn, Goran. 1983. "Why Some Classes Are More Successful Than Others." *New Left Review* 138:37–55.

Thiele, Beverly. 1986. "Vanishing Acts in Social and Political Thought: Tricks of the Trade." Pp. 30–43 in *Feminist Challenges, Social and Political Theory,* edited by Carole Pateman and Elizabeth Gross. Boston, MA: Allen & Unwin.

Thompson, Becky W. 1994. *A Hunger So Wide and So Deep: A Multiracial View of Women's Eating Problems.* Minneapolis: University of Minnesota Press.

Thompson, E.P. 1963. *The Making of the English Working Class.* New York, NY: Pantheon Books.

Thorne, Barrie. 1979. "Political Activist as Participant Observer: Conflicts of Commitment in the Study of the Draft-Resistance Movement of the 1960's." *Symbolic Interaction* 2:73–88.

Tillmon, Johnnie. 1971. "Insights of a Welfare Mother: A Conversation with Johnnie Tillmon." *Journal of Social Issues* Jan–Feb 1971.

Tillmon, Johnnie. 1972. "Welfare is a Woman's Issue," *Ms.*

Tillmon, Johnnie. 1984. Oral History Interview Conducted by Sherna Berger Gluck.

Tillmon, Johnnie. 1991. Oral History Interviews Conducted by Sherna Berger Gluck.

Tilly, Charles. 1978. *From Mobilization to Revolution.* Reading, MA: Addison-Wesley.

Tong, Rosemarie. 1989. *Feminist Thought: A Comprehensive Introduction.* Boulder, CO: Westview.

Trujillo, Carla. 1991. *Chicana Lesbians: The Girls Our Mothers Warned Us About.* Berkeley, CA: Third Woman.

Tulare County Department of Public Social Services. 1991. *Tulare County Depart-*

*ment of Public Social Services: Refugee Services Program Plan.* July 1 1991 Through June 30 1992.

Tulare County Department of Public Social Services. 1992. *Tulare County Department of Public Social Services, Refugee Services Program: Amended Plan Update July 1, 1992 Through September 30, 1993.*

Tulare County Department of Public Social Services. 1993. *Tulare County Department of Public Social Services, Refugee Services Program: Multi-Year Program Plan July 1, 1993 Through September 30, 1995.*

Turner, John F.C. 1977. *Housing by People: Towards Autonomy in Building Environments.* New York, NY: Pantheon Books.

UMWA. 1990. *United Mineworkers Journal.* August–September,7.

U.S. Department of Housing and Urban Development. Undated. *Evaluation of Resident Management in Public Housing.* Research Report of the Office of Policy Development and Research.

Vale, Lawrence. 1995. "Seven Kinds of Success: Assessing Public Housing Comprehensive Redevelopment Efforts in Boston." Pp. 327–340 in *Future Visions of Urban Public Housing,* edited Wolfgang R.E. Preiser, David P. Varady, and Francis P. Russell. Proceedings of An International Forum, Cincinnati, Ohio.

Van Den Bergh, Nan, and Lynn B. Cooper, eds. 1986. *Feminist Visions for Social Work.* Cilver Springs, MD: National Association of Social Workers.

Vance, Carole S. ed. 1984. *Pleasure and Danger: Exploring Female Sexuality.* Boston, MA: Routledge & Kegan Paul.

Vaid, Urvashi. 1991. "Let's Put Our Own House in Order." *Out/Look* 14 (Fall): 55–57.

Vaid, Urvashi. 1995. *Virtual Equality.* New York, NY: Anchor Books.

Viviano, Frank. 1986. "Strangers in the Promised Land." In *Image, The San Francisco. Examiner.* 8/31.

Wagner, David. 1990. *The Quest for a Radical Profession: Social Service Careers and Political Ideology.* Lanham, MD: University Press of America.

Walker, Alice. 1983. *In Search of Our Mothers Gardens: Womanist Prose.* New York, NY: Harcourt Brace Jovanovich.

Walker, Lenore. 1984. *The Battered Woman Syndrome.* New York, NY: Springer Publishing.

Walker, Rebecca. 1992. "Becoming the Third Wave." *Ms.* 2 (January/February):39–41.

Weber, Clare. Forthcoming. "Latino Street Vendors in Los Angeles: Heterogeneous Alliances, Community-Based Activism, and the State." In *Asian and Latino Immigrants in a Restructuring Economy: The Metamorphosis of Los Angeles,* edited by Marta Lopez-Garza and David R. Diaz. Stanford, CA: Stanford University Press.

Wei, William 1993. *The Asian American Movement.* Philadelphia, PA: Temple University.

Weiss, Chris. 1990. "Organizing Women for Local Economic Development." Pp. 61–70 in *Communities in Economic Crisis: Appalachia and the South.* John

Gaventa, Barbara Ellen Smith, and Alex Willingham, eds. Philadelphia, PA: Temple University Press.

Weiss, Penny A., and Marilyn Friedman, eds. 1995. *Feminism & Community*. Philadelphia, PA: Temple University Press.

Weller, Jack E. 1965. *Yesterday's People: Life in Contemporary Appalachia*. Lexington, KY: University of Kentucky Press.

West, Guida. 1981. *The National Welfare Rights Movement: The Social Protest of Poor Women*. New York, NY: Praeger.

West, Guida. 1990. "Conflict and Cooperation among Women in the Welfare Rights Movement." Pp. 149–171 in *Bridges of Power: Women's Multicultural Alliances*, edited by Albrecht and Brewer. Philadelphia, PA: New Society Publishers.

West, Guida and Rhoda Lois Blumberg, eds. 1990. *Women and Social Protest*. New York, NY: Oxford University Press.

White, E. F. 1990. "Africa on My Mind: Gender, Counter Discourses and African-American Nationalism." *Journal of Women's History* 2:73–97.

White, Lucie. 1996. "Searching for the Logic Behind Welfare Reform." *UCLA Women's Law Journal* 6(2):427–442.

Whittier, Nancy E. 1988. "The Construction of a Politicized Collective Identity: Ideology and Symbolism in Contemporary Lesbian Feminist Communities." M.A. thesis, Ohio State University.

Whittier, Nancy E. 1991. "Feminists in the 'Post-Feminist' Age: Collective Identity and the Persistence of the Women's Movement." Ph.D. dissertation, Ohio State University.

Whyte, William Foote, ed. 1991. *Participatory Action Research*. Newbury Park, CA: Sage.

Wilcox, Kathleen A. 1982. "Differential Socialization in the Classroom: Implications for Equal Opportunity." Pp.456–488 in *Doing the Ethnography of Schooling*, edited by G. Spindler. New York, NY: Holt, Rinehart and Winston.

Williams, Brett. 1984. "Why Migrant Women Feed Their Husbands Tamales." Pp. 113–26 in *Ethnic and Regional Foodways in the United States*, edited by Linda Keller Brown and Kay Mussell. Knoxville, TN: University of Tennessee Press.

Williams, Brooke. 1978. "The Retreat to Cultural Feminism." Pp. 65–69 in *Feminist Revolution*, edited by Redstockings of the Women's Liberation Movement. New York, NY: Random House.

Williams, Terry, and William Kornblum. 1994. *The Uptown Kids*. New York, NY: G.P. Putnam's Sons.

Willis, Ellen. 1984. "Radical Feminism and Feminist Radicalism." Pp. 91–118 in *The '60's without Apology*, edited by Sonya Sayres, Anders Stephanson, Stanley Aronowitz, and Fredric Jameson. Minneapolis: University of Minnesota Press.

Wilkey, Cindy. 1991. "The Role of Women in Local Radical Organizations." Unpublished manuscript, Columbus, Ohio.

Williams, Patricia J. 1991. *The Alchemy of Race and Rights*. Cambridge, MA: Harvard University Press.

Witt, Shirley. 1974. "Native Women Today." *Civil Rights Digest* v. 6(2).

Wolf, Diane L., ed. 1996. *Feminist Dilemmas in Fieldwork*. Boulder, CO: Westview.

Wolfe, Leslie, and Tucker, Jennifer. 1995. "Feminism Lives: Building a Multicultural Women's Movement in the United States." Pp. 435–462 in *The Challenge of Local Feminisms: Women's Movements in Global Perspective*, edited by Amrita Basu. Boulder, CO: Westview.

Women of All Red Nations. 1980. "W.A.R.N. Report II." Sioux Fall, South Dakota.

*Womoon Rising*. 1982. Columbus, Ohio, Women's Action Collective Newsletter. September/October and November/December.

Wong, Morrison G. 1986. "Post-1965 Asian Immigrants: Where Do They Come From, Where Are They Now, and Where Are They Going?" *Annals of the American Academy of Political and Social Sciences* 487:150–168.

Wright, Patricia. 1988. *The South Armour Square Strategy Plan*. Report for the Nathalie P. Voorhees Center for Neighborhood and Community Improvement. University of Illinois at Chicago.

Yamada, Mitsuye. 1983. "Asian Pacific American Women and Feminism." Pp. 71–75 in *This Bridge Called My Back: Writing by Radical Women of Color*, edited by Cherríe Moraga and Gloria Anzaldúa, ed. CA: Kitchen Table Press.

Yan-McLaughlin, Virginia. 1990. *Immigration Reconsidered: History, Sociology, and Politics*. New York, NY: Oxford University Press.

Yancey, Dwayne. 1990. "Thunder in the Coalfields." Roanoke, VA: *Roanoke Times and World News*. Sunday, April 29. Special Report.

Yang, Pang. 1993a. "Strengthen Refugee Programs by Making Them Relevant". In *Visalia Times Delta*. 4/13-93, 7A.

Yang, Pang. 1993b. "Feminist Insider Dilemmas: Constructing Ethnic Identity with Chicana Informants." In *Frontiers* 13(3): 53–76.

Yollin, Patricia. 1991. "Painting the Town Lavender." *Image* (San Francisco Examiner), March 10, 18–29.

Young, Iris Marion. 1990. "The Ideal of Community and the Politics of Difference." Pp. 300–323 in *Feminism/ Postmodernism*, edited by Linda J. Nicholson. New York, NY: Routledge.

Young, Kate, ed. 1988. *Women and Economic Development: Local, Regional and National Planning Strategies*. New York, NY: Berg Publishers Limited.

Yngvesson, Barbara. 1993. *Virtuous Citizens, Disruptive Subjects: Order and Complaint in a New England Court*. New York, NY: Routledge.

Yudelman, Sally W. 1987. *Hopeful Openings: A Study of Five Women's Development Organizations in Latin America and the Caribbean*. West Hartford, CT: Kumarian Press.

Zavella, Patricia. 1987. *Women's Work and Chicano Families: Cannery Workers of the Santa Clara Valley*. Ithaca, NY: Cornell University Press.

Zavella, Patricia. 1988. "The Politics of Race and Gender: Organizing Chicana Cannery Workers in Northern California." Pp. 202–224 in *Women and the Politics of Empowerment*, edited by Sandra Morgen and Ann Bookman. Philadelphia, PA: Temple University Press.

Zavella, Patricia. 1993. "Feminist Insider Dilemmas: Constructing Ethnic Identity with Chicana Informants." *Frontiers* 13(3):53–76.

Zeff, Robin Lee. 1989. "Not in My Backyard/Not in Anyone's Back Yard: A Folkloristic Examination of the American Grassroots Movement for Environmental Justice." Ph.D. Dissertation, Indiana University, Indiana.

Zeff, Robin Lee et al., eds. 1989. *Empowering Ourself: Women and Toxics Organizing.* Arlington, VA: Citizens Clearinghouse for Hazardous Wastes, Inc.

Zhang, Ting-Wei, and Patricia Wright. 1992. *The Impact of the Construction of the New Comiskey Park on Local Residents.* Report for the Nathalie P. Voorhees Center for Neighborhood and Community Improvement. University of Illinois at Chicago.

Zhou, Min. 1992. *Chinatown: The Socioeconomic Potential of an Urban Enclave.* Philadelphia, PA: Temple University Press.

Zinn, Maxine Baca, and Bonnie Thornton Dill. 1996. "Theorizing Difference from Multiracial Feminism." *Feminist Studies* 22(2):321–331.

# *Permissions*

Pierrette Hondagneu-Sotelo, "Latina Immigrant Women and Paid Domestic Work: Upgrading the Occupation." Originally published in *Clinical Sociology Review*, vol. 12, 1994, pp. 257–270. Reprinted by permission of the author and the Sociological Practice Association.

Mary Pardo, "Creating Community: Mexican American Women in Eastside Los Angeles." Originally published in *Aztlán*, vol. 20, no. 1/2, 1991, pp. 39–67. Reprinted by permission of the author and Chicano Studies Research Center Publications.

Verta Taylor and Leila J. Rupp, "Women's Culture and Lesbian Feminist Activism: A Reconsideration of Cultural Feminism." Originally published in *Signs*, vol. 19, no. 1, 1993, pp. 32–61. Reprinted by permission of the authors and the University of Chicago Press.

# Contributors

**Sharon Bays** was raised in Fresno and nearby Visalia, where she conducted her doctoral research with Hmong immigrants. Her family's working-class and Greek immigrant history combined with that of her husband's family—dust bowl farming migrants from Oklahoma—have formed in her an enduring interest about and concern for California's agricultural immigrants. During the late 1970s and 1980s she photographed images from California's San Joaquin Valley and created both an exhibit and a calendar appropriately called *From the San Joaquin*. She completed her doctoral work at UCLA in 1994. She teaches Anthropology and Women's Studies at UCLA.

**Maylei Blackwell** is currently obtaining a Ph.D. in the History of Consciousness Program at the University of California, Santa Cruz. The oral history project with members of *las Hijas de Cuauhtémoc* which she began in 1991 will be the topic of a forthcoming essay in *Inscriptions 8*. Her dissertation research examines Latin American popular culture and social movements as well as U.S. women of color historiography and film practices.

**Sharon Cotrell** is a master's candidate in Applied Anthropology at California State University, Long Beach, and is the designated Tribal Researcher for the local Gabrieleno/Tongva Indian tribe. Her master's project will be part of the tribe's application for federal recognition. Her oral history project with contemporary American Indian women community leaders is ongoing. Sharon's more than twenty-five years experience in community organizing includes the struggle for civil rights and women's rights, as well as involvement in the antiwar movement, Students for a Democratic Society, and efforts to expand citizen participation in community decision-making in Long Beach. Sharon has successfully managed six city council elections and two issue campaigns. She is the first female marine dockworker in the United States, a job she has held for twenty-three years. In 1975, she helped found and lead the Teamsters for a Democratic Union, a national rank and file movement to democratize the Teamsters Union.

**Roberta M. Feldman** is an architectural researcher and environmental psychologist in the School of Architecture and Co-Director of the City Design Center at of the University of Illinois at Chicago. Dr. Feldman is an educator and activist who advocates for and supports socially responsible design. Dr. Feldman's work focuses on housing and community planning and design, with an emphasis on underhoused Americans. During the past few years, she has been doing action research and participatory design with women public housing residents.

**Sherna Berger Gluck** coordinates the oral history program at California State University, where she also teaches Women's Studies. Gluck's early book on U.S. suffragists, *From Parlor to Prison* (New York: Vintage, 1976; reprinted: New York: Monthly Review Press, 1985), was one of the first products of women's oral history and is still used widely, especially in women's history. Gluck's research has focused on the development of women's consciousness, on women and work, and on working-class feminism. Her most recent book based on oral history is *Rosie the Riveter Revisited: Women, the War and Social Change* (Boston: G.K. Hall, 1987; and New York: New American Library, 1988). She is currently working on the topic of women's liberation in occupied Palestine.

**Karen S. harper** completed an M.A. in Interdisciplinary Studies (English, Women's Studies, History) at California State University, Long Beach, in 1995 with an oral history focus. She brings a feminist perspective to her research, which includes the Hmong immigrant community in Long Beach and the Asian American Women's Movement in Los Angeles. She developed and directs the women's oral history project "Tell Me Your Story" in Long Beach schools (1988–1997).

**Pierrette Hondagneu-Sotelo** is Assistant Professor of Sociology at the University of Southern California, where she also teaches in the Program for the Study of Women and Men in Society, and in the American Studies and Chicano/Latino Studies Program. She is the author of *Gendered Transitions: Mexican Experiences of Immigration* (University of California Press, 1994). She is currently researching and writing about paid domestic work in Los Angeles, and she works with an activist organization of domestic workers.

**Carolyn Howe** is Associate Professor of Sociology at College of the Holy Cross in Worcester, MA. She has been involved in struggles in the public schools around issues of funding, curriculum, and bilingual education in her community. She is the author of *Political, Ideology and Class Formation: A Study of the Middle Class* (Praeger, 1992).

**Karen Kendrick** is a Ph.D. candidate in Social Relations and the Graduate Feminist Emphasis at the University of California, Irvine. Her research interests include strategies to fight abuse against women, women's diversity and activism, body image and consumer culture, and the social construction of self.

**Celene Krauss** is Associate Professor of Sociology at Kean College of New Jersey and Co-Director of Women's Studies. She has written extensively about women and toxic-waste protests, with a focus on issues of race, ethnicity, and class, and is working on a book on this subject. Her work has appeared in *Sociological Forum*, *Qualitative Sociology*, and other journals and books.

**Nancy A. Naples** is a faculty member in Sociology and Women's Studies at the University of California at Irvine. She has written on low-income women's community-based activism, social policies designed to counter poverty in the United States, and the construction of inequality in a rural context. Her work has appeared in *Gender & Society*, *Rural Sociology*, *Social Problems*, and *Signs* among other journals and books. She is author of *Grassroots Warriors: Activist Mothering, Community Work, and the War on Poverty*.

**Mary Pardo** teaches in the Department of Chicano Studies at California State University, Northridge. Her work appeared in the edited collection *Feminist Organizations: Harvest of the New Women's Movement*. She is the author of *Mexican American Women Activists: Identity and Resistance in Two Los Angeles Communities* forthcoming from Temple University Press..

**Lisa Sun-Hee Park** is a graduate student in Sociology at Northwestern University and a feminist activist-organizer working with the Korean American community in Chicago. Her research and activism focuses on the political economy of Asian American and immigrant families and communities, feminist politics, and domestic violence.

**Leila J. Rupp** teaches women's history and the history of same-sex sexuality at Ohio State University. She is the author of *Mobilizing Women for the War: German and American Propaganda, 1939–1945* (1978) and coauthor, with Verta Taylor, of *Survival in the Doldrums: The American Women's Rights Movement, 1945 to the 1960s* (1987). Her most recent book, *Worlds of Women: International Women's Organizations, 1888–1945*, is forthcoming from Princeton University Press.

**Virginia Rinaldo Seitz** is Director of World WID (Women In Development) Fellows Program, International Studies, University of Florida. She received a Ph.D. in Environmental Design and Planning in 1992 with a specialization in gender and development planning. Dr. Seitz's areas of interest include women and work, global political economy, gender and grassroots collective action, gender analysis in development, qualitative and participatory research methods, sociology of agriculture and natural resource management, feminist theory, and Appalachian Studies. Her book, *Women, Development, and Communities for Empowerment in Appalachia* has been published by SUNY Press.

**Susan Stall** is a teacher, activist, and a sociologist and Women's Studies scholar at Northeastern Illinois University. As a housing activist she has coordinated two conference projects: "Women and Safe Shelter: Creating and Recreating Community" in 1986, and "Women and Public Housing: Hidden Strength, Unclaimed Power" in 1987. As a community consultant, she worked with residents in public housing to form the citywide advocacy organization, Chicago Housing Authority Residents Taking Action (CHARTA). Her research focuses on women's organizing, community-building, and leadership development in both rural and urban settings.

**Susan Parkison Stern** is an independent scholar/researcher/activist. An educator by earlier training and experience, her work has focused primarily on community struggles against racial educational injustice and inequality, especially the contributions that social science research can bring to those real-life struggles at the local level.

**Verta Taylor** teaches Sociology at Ohio State University. She is coauthor, with Leila J. Rupp, of *Survival in the Doldrums: The American Women's Rights Movement, 1945 to the 1960s* (1987), coeditor of *Feminist Frontiers* (now in its fourth edition), and has published numerous articles on women's movements, lesbian feminism, and social movement theory. Her newest book is *Rock-a-by Baby: Feminism, Self-Help, and Postpartum Depression* (Routledge, 1996).

**Judith Wittner** is Associate Professor of Sociology and Anthropology at Loyola University. She helped found the Women's Studies Program at Loyola in 1979, the first such program at a Jesuit university, and directed the program from 1987 to 1993. She has conducted research for and about displaced women factory workers, state wards in the child welfare system, and women's community organizations. Recently she has been working with feminist advocates on a study of Chicago's centralized domestic violence courts.

**Patricia A. Wright** is an urban planner with the Nathalie P. Voorhees Center for Neighborhood and Community Improvement at the University of Illinois at Chicago. She began working with Chicago public housing resident activists in 1988 on an organizing campaign against the construction of a new baseball stadium, and with resident participants she developed a strategic neighborhood plan. Recently, acting as a consultant, she worked with residents to conduct a market feasibility study for a proposed commercial center.

# Index